100 Albums
That Changed Music

100 Albums
That Changed Music

EDITED by SEAN EGAN

ROBINSON
London

Constable & Robinson Ltd
3 The Lanchesters
162 Fulham Palace Road
London W6 9ER
www.constablerobinson.com

This edition published by Robinson,
an imprint of Constable & Robinson Ltd, 2006

A copy of the British Library Cataloguing in
Publication Data is available from the British Library

ISBN-10: 1-84529-495-5
ISBN-13: 978-1-84529-495-3

Printed and bound in China

1 3 5 7 9 10 8 6 4 2

Contents

Introduction

Not another book on the greatest albums ever?!?

Actually, no. There have of course been many, many books and magazine polls examining the best albums released in the history of rock and pop, as adjudged by music critics and/or the general public. Very entertaining many of them have been too, but we are well aware that the world hardly needs another.

100 Albums That Changed Music is somewhat different to those aforementioned tomes. This is not a book about the *best* rock & pop long players but rather the most *important*. The one hundred albums whose details and histories you will find in these pages are ones that have had a crucial influence on the development of what was originally called (and still is by many) rock 'n' roll. Of course, there is very often an overlap between aesthetic greatness and influence: few of a musician's peers (or musos of subsequent generations) are going to take their creative cue from an album they consider execrable. However, while we do not consider any of the albums in these pages to be truly awful, it has to be acknowledged that some of them will never feature in any poll to determine history's finest. For instance, while most critics are prepared to admit finding the exercise in over-the-top melodramatic rock that is Meat Loaf's *Bat Out Of Hell* thoroughly enjoyable, they simultaneously find it so close to laughable as to be reluctant to grant it a place in the annals of the Significant. Similarly, *Frampton Comes Alive!* by Peter Frampton was omnipresent upon its release but is now barely mentioned at all, let alone discussed in terms of epoch-marking. Yet *Bat Out Of Hell* inspired a return to unashamed, if epic-sized, rock 'n' roll and *Frampton Comes Alive!* created the market for the double-live album that ultimately became a multi-million dollar industry (albeit one now blurred by the existence of the compact disc, with its greater space capacity). These and many other albums all played a part in subtly (sometimes dramatically) altering the path of musical development. Sometimes for the better (Big Brother And The Holding Company's *Cheap Thrills* giving would-be female rockers a positive role model) and sometimes with less unequivocally positive results (the dinosaur rock partly ushered in by the extemporizations of Iron Butterfly's *In-A-Gadda-Da-Vida* and Quicksilver Messenger Service's *Happy Trails*). However, good or bad though the consequences of their release or success may have been, all these albums have interesting stories behind them - in many cases somewhat more interesting than the over-familiar tales attending the making of the usual-suspect albums commonly examined in books.

There are some complications engendered by this approach. For instance, Elvis Presley's *Sun Sessions* (in whatever configuration) was considered for inclusion but ultimately rejected. Though the music within it has of course been massively influential - in fact, for some, none of the music in this book would have come into existence without it - The King's Sun single sides were not collected together onto an album (bar the odd track dotted on his post-Sun long players) until 1975. It therefore can't be said that a Presley Sun *album* changed the course of popular music. Instead, you will find his first RCA LP - which did have such an effect - herein.

That notwithstanding, we brazenly admit that a certain amount of cheating has gone into the compiling of this book. While we have done our best to not include compilations – which mop up a series of individual statements rather than function as organic entities the way albums are intended to – some of the artists herein were mainly influential in the medium of the single (or even in some cases 78rpm discs). However, a book that overlooked the profound and long-term influence on their fellow artists - even in some cases on the outlook of the western world - of the likes of The Creation, Woody Guthrie, Bill Haley and his Comets, Muddy Waters or Hank Williams just wouldn't *feel* right, so - to use the politician's favorite get-out-of-jail phrase – we have 'walked the faultline' and found ways to include them. Similarly, we have chosen the album which best sums up the singular talents of Smokey Robinson rather than ignore him simply because Motown did not have the knack of translating their finesse at singles to the album format. Moreover, we've also tried to trace a bigger picture, touching all bases by including at least one album representing the major changes in rock & pop styles, fashions and outlooks down the years (e.g., *Happy Trails* is partly here as a tip of the hat to the mid-'Sixties Haight-Ashbury scene; Joy Division represent post-punk).

We've also cheated by limiting the number of entries each artist is allowed. While the Rolling Stones are represented by three albums, the Beatles four and Bob Dylan no less than five, it is no exaggeration to say that we could have easily included more by those musical titans. Indeed, it could be argued that technically, such was their reach and brilliance, that all eleven proper UK Beatles albums are more influential than any non-Beatles album in this book. However, a book discussing the influence of the work of a handful of superstars plus a few miscellaneous others would be boring. We have opted instead to strike a balance between the earthquakes the major artists caused and the pebble-in-the-pond ripples generated in more arcane parts of the musical universe by the likes of Captain Beefheart and Pere Ubu.

Partly to acknowledge the quasi-arbitrariness of this approach - and partly to squeeze in mentions of great songs not represented because of the nature of these books, even ones more geared toward aesthetic quality than influence - we have interspersed the album overviews with lists of individual songs, including great B-sides, great singles by acts who never made great albums, great songs by artists you usually despise, great songs on bad albums, and so on.

The overall result is, we hope, the book that plugs the gap in the market. We also hope that it is - courtesy of a line-up of notable and sometimes award-winning writers - highly entertaining.

Naturally, it will cause many arguments, but in that instance at least we confess to - and are unapologetic about - a similarity to other albums books. It's part of the fun, isn't it?
- Sean Egan, Editor

ACKNOWLEDGMENTS

The editor would like to gratefully thank the following for their responses to queries during the preparation of this book: Tom Boon of EnoWeb, Roy Carr, George Chkiantz, Rob Jovanovic, Ian McLagan, Vic Coppersmith-Heaven, Ken Scott, John Stax, Malcolm Stewart, Dick Taylor and Pete Townshend.

1. Dust Bowl Ballads
Woody Guthrie

TRACKLISTING
The Great Dust Storm (Dust Storm Disaster)/I Ain't Got No Home/Talking Dust Bowl Blues/Vigilante Man/Dust Can't Kill Me/Pretty Boy Floyd/Dust Pneumonia Blues/Blowin' Down This Old Dusty Road/Tom Joad Part 1/Tom Joad Part 2/Dust Bowl Refugee/(If You Ain't Got The) Do Re Mi/Dust Bowl Blues/Dusty Old Dust (So Long, It's Been Good To Know Yuh)

RELEASED
US: July 1940 UK: 1964

PRODUCED BY
R. P. Weatherald

In his long travels throughout 1930s, '40s and '50s America, folk guitarist and singer Woody Guthrie saw firsthand the hardships of society's most disenfranchised and through his songs, poems, essays and novels positioned himself as their staunch defender. Guthrie once wrote that his aim was to "sing songs that'll prove to you that this is your world no matter how hard it has run you down and rolled over you. I am out to sing songs that will make you take pride in yourself." As a reflection of his passion and commitment to a cause, Guthrie's art could not be separated from his role as social agitator.

If there was an album that encapsulated Guthrie's renegade spirit it was his first commercial recording, the landmark *Dust Bowl Ballads* (originally released across two 78 rpm records). A commercial failure in its time, RCA Victor released no more than 500 to 1,000 copies. *Dust Bowl Ballads* was recorded in one day on April 26 1940 and released in early July of that year. Guthrie himself said he was sure Victor never issued a more radical album. At the time he was right. The whole production has a rough-hewn feel right down to Guthrie's ragged delivery. Accompanying himself on acoustic guitar and harmonica, Guthrie's voice has a flat, droning quality in contrast to the vividness of his lyrical imagery, the overriding theme of which is the 1935-40 Dust Bowl migration which saw redundant farmers moving to big cities to find work.

There are no losers in Guthrie's songs. Instead they possess a pronounced dignity and defiance. In 'Dust Can't Kill Me' the dust storms take everything the protagonist owns, yet he vows "it can't get me". Most of these songs chronicle the hard, bitter experience of hordes of displaced people in search of a better life: 'Dust Bowl Refugees', 'Dusty Old Dust (So Long, It's Been Good To Know Yuh)', 'Talking Dust Bowl Blues' (the latter written as he rode the rails in the mid '30s). Guthrie was a writer with a rebel spirit, condemning people taking up arms to repel the hungry migrants in 'Vigilante Man' and in his famous ballad 'Pretty Boy Floyd' championing the outlaw as Robin Hood-style hero. (The latter, like 'Dust Bowl Blues', was not included in the original 1940 release; both have been added to subsequent releases.) 'Dust Pneumonia Blues' is a stinging riposte to the 1929 Jimmie Rodgers number 'California Blues (Blue Yodel No. 4)' with its imagery of yodeling all the way to California on the road to the good life. In Guthrie's song, yodeling wasn't an option due to the "rattlin' in my lung". In one of his most emotionally devastating ballads, 'I Ain't Got No Home', Guthrie rewrote the Baptist hymn 'This World Is Not My Home', made popular by The Carter Family.

Bound for glory – Woody Guthrie pictured in the 1940s.

Guthrie had come to detest the Carter Family hit for its implication that migrants should passively accept their fate in the hope of a reward in the afterlife. Guthrie's version depicts the desolation of a soul who has utterly lost his place in the world, and his bitterness at the forces that have conspired against him, from the police that hassle him to the bankers who took his home made plain.

If Guthrie's songs were somewhat underappreciated in his time, they would become the catalyst for the folk resurgence of the late '50s and early '60s and the more socially aware folk-rock of the mid-'60s. Guthrie's work gained a new appreciation from and served as a source of inspiration for a new generation who found in the folk idiom a sense of meaning and relevance that made it a cooler, hipper alternative to the prevailing vacuity of rock 'n' roll. By the time his influence was strongly felt Guthrie was undergoing a long physical decline from the neurological disorder Huntington's Chorea, an affliction that would eventually take his life in 1967. Commercial success may have eluded Guthrie but the topical singers who followed him like Joan Baez, Peter Paul And Mary, Ramblin' Jack Elliott, Tom Paxton and Phil Ochs enjoyed a higher profile.

And then of course there was Bob Dylan. When Dylan first heard Guthrie he listened, as he put it in his 2005 autobiography, "as if in a trance". It was an experience that sent him on a journey of self-discovery, helped him find a new form of creative expression and broke him of the habit, he wrote, "of thinking in short song cycles". Gripped too by Guthrie's autobiography *Bound For Glory*, Dylan would become Guthrie's devoted disciple. Copying his look and stance in slavish imitation of his hero, Dylan openly acknowledged his fixation in his 1962 self-titled debut album which contained a tribute to his idol ('Song To Woody') and a stylistic tip of the hat to Guthrie's 'Talking Dust Bowl Blues' ('Talkin' New York'). Scottish singer Donovan has stated that Jack Elliott was Guthrie's first disciple, Dylan his second. As for himself, Donovan has admitted it was Guthrie, not – as widely believed – Dylan, he was imitating on his own early incarnation as folk-style troubadour. Guthrie's style of unflinching honesty echoes in the work of everyone from folk/alternative singer Ani DiFranco to British punk-folk protest singer Billy Bragg. Bragg's stated admiration for the sense of humor Guthrie brought to even his most pointed songs is displayed in his own political-but-entertaining compositions. Longtime Guthrie admirer Bruce Springsteen has appropriated Guthrie's affinity for the hardships of the common man throughout the course of a career that has taken on an increasingly socially conscious bent over the years (i.e., *Nebraska*, *The Ghost Of Tom Joad* and *Devils And Dust*).

For every voice raised in social protest, be it the gentle folk troubadours Peter Paul And Mary or the thrashing sound of Rage Against The Machine, Woody Guthrie led the way, shining the light of truth on all manner of injustice and establishing for all time protest's durability as a musical force. - Tierney Smith

2. Hank Williams Sings Hank Williams

TRACKLISTING
House Without Love (Is Not a Home)/Wedding Bells/Mansion on the Hill/Wealth Won't Save Your Soul/I Saw the Light/Six More Miles/Lost Highway/I've Just Told Mama Goodbye

RELEASED
US: November 1951 UK: October 1952

PRODUCED BY
Fred Rose

Hiram "Hank" Williams died aged 29, in the back seat of a car on his way to a gig, the result of medicating a spine condition he'd had since birth, and a troubled mind he'd had almost as long, with a mixture of quack-prescribed drugs and copious quantities of alcohol. His time on earth had had more than its share of pain, heartache and self-destructive addiction, and his life story provided the template for every live-fast, die-young star who would follow; but it was the body of work he left behind that created the legend. Whether subsequent generations of musicians knew it or not, Hank Williams' music was the well-spring for the confessional song, the Beautiful Loser anthem and the insertion into country of a rebellious and anarchic spirit. In an age when the form of music did not yet exist, he was the first rock 'n' roll star.

Williams grew up in a series of boarding houses in the American south run by his single mother. Everyone had to pay their way during the Depression, and as a young boy he began busking. He learned blues from a black street musician called Rufus "Tee-Tot" Payne, and by the time he first entered a recording studio, Williams had made the other most important connection in his professional life. Fred Rose had founded a music publishing company with Roy Acuff, and after Williams approached him for

Hank Williams (1923–1952).

a publishing deal, the older man took him under his wing. Rose helped Hank add conventional songwriting chops to his innate feel for country and blues. The most important figure in Williams' musical life, Rose not only co-authored some of Hank's finest songs, he produced every label session the singer ever undertook.

Hank Williams Sings was one of only two LPs released during Williams' lifetime. It was made available in the new 10-inch LP format, but also as boxed sets of 78 rpm discs and 45rpm singles. Hank's music was made to be played in the jukeboxes of the roadhouses and honky tonks where he had made his name (sales to jukebox operators reportedly still accounted for more than half of his sales in 1950), and on the radio stations where, as a regular on the live shows *Louisiana Hayride* and *Grand Ole Opry*, he had risen to fame. The liberal use of Hawaiian pedal steel guitar, now a country staple but then a new instrument to the genre, was very deliberately calculated by Rose to ensure the records could be heard clearly over drinkin' and fightin', and would cut through the thickest of static interference to reach those listening to weak AM radio signals in homes, bars and cars.

The eight tracks included on *Hank Williams Sings* were made at six different sessions between 1946 and 1949. In an era where the concept of an album hadn't yet 'taken', Williams and Rose never concerned themselves with making a longer body of work to be played at a single sitting. The record exemplifies the other meaning of the term "album": an assemblage of musical snapshots. As snapshots often do, they offer some insights into their creator's life and work.

The standouts are 'Mansion On The Hill', 'I Saw The Light' and 'Lost Highway'. The latter, like 'Lovesick Blues', the 1949 hit that turned Hank from a hillbilly hero into a genuine pop star, is a song he did not write but which has become irrevocably associated with him by virtue of his stunning performance. A *cri de coeur* from a dejected, exiled loner, 'Lost Highway' was a perfect fit for Hank's troubled soul: the man knew heartache, and few songs have better suited a singer. 'I Saw The Light' was reputedly inspired by numerous early-hours journeys back from distant gigs, where the driver – often Williams' mother – would wake the slumbering band when they were close to home with news that she'd seen the lights of the nearby airport. Turning the phrase into a declaration of faith was a natural move for an artist who, like so many since, struggled throughout his life and work to reconcile the sacred and the profane. 1947's 'Mansion On The Hill' provided an early illustration of the Rose/Williams writing partnership at work. Rose gave Hank the title and the storyline – boy in log cabin sings to girl in grand house who's spurned his love – and Hank went away to craft them into a song.

'Wedding Bells', another cover, is credited to Claude Boone, though it seems to have been written by Arthur Q Smith, an alcoholic Knoxville musician who was in the habit of selling the copyright in his compositions to buy drink. 'I've Just Told Mama Goodbye' was recorded at the same March 1949, session: Hank, his finger on the pulse of rural sentimentality, wanted it released in time for Mother's Day. The tracks became the A and B-sides of a single. 'Six More Miles', recorded at the April 1947 session that yielded both 'I Saw The Light' and Williams' breakthrough hit, the proto-rock 'n' roll 'Move It On Over', was also originally a B-side.

The other two tracks are from opposite ends of Williams' writerly spectrum. 'Wealth Won't Save Your Soul', recorded at his first ever studio session at WSM in Nashville on December 11 1946, is a spiritually-inclined song with a message writ large in the title. It became his second single, released on the New York-based independent label Sterling to little fanfare. 'A House Without Love', although couched as fiction, touches on the very real trials Hank and his domineering first wife, Audrey, were going through in a marriage that seems to have never had any extended spells of pure happiness.

Between his first session in December 1946 to his last, in September 1952, just weeks before his death, Williams's studio work amounted to only 89 tracks. 77 of those songs were self-penned or co-written, a highly unusual degree of self-reliance for the time. Cementing the notion of the singer as being only truly authentic when singing his own songs is perhaps, after everything else, his most remarkable legacy. It might not seem that big, but Williams' canon has been described as perhaps the most significant of any American songwriter, and the title "the Hillbilly Shakespeare", bestowed for his prowess at articulating the hopes, fears, dreams and nightmares of the ordinary American, was certainly one he earned. - Angus Batey

3. Shake, Rattle & Roll
Bill Haley and his Comets

TRACKLISTING
(We're Gonna) Rock Around the Clock/Thirteen Women/Shake, Rattle & Roll/ABC Boogie/Happy Baby/Dim, Dim the Lights (I Want Some Atmosphere)/Birth of the Boogie/Mambo Rock

RELEASED
US: September 1955 UK: Not issued

PRODUCED BY
Milt Gabler

"If I could take, say, a Dixieland tune and drop the first and third beats, and accentuate the second and fourth, and add a beat the listeners could clap to as well as dance, this could be what they were after."

Thus did Bill Haley describe a form of music that would come to be called rock 'n' roll and would take over the world and without which few of the albums in this book would ever have been recorded, even those that are technically not rock albums.

Bill Haley's recording career peaked just on the cusp of the 12-inch album format but it would be unfair to exclude him from this book on that technicality. This 10-inch record contained Haley's four hits to date (of which 'Rock Around The Clock' was not at this point the biggest or most famous) augmented by four other recordings. It was later superseded by a 12-inch album called *Rock Around The Clock* (1956) which added four more tracks. (Three further tracks are available on the current Decca CD issue of the latter, catalogue number B0001705-02, one of which is Haley's second best-known record 'See You Later, Alligator'.)

Bill Haley and the Saddlemen were an essentially Country &

Western band – replete with cowboy outfits – but could see which way the wind was blowing, to such an extent that in 1951 they recorded a cover of the Jackie Brenston single 'Rocket 88': many now consider that Brenston record the first ever recorded example of rock 'n' roll. That the Comets (as they restyled themselves come 1952) covered it of course might mean nothing on its own. However Haley and his colleagues began acquiring a reputation for crossing their natural country instincts with hitching a lift on the R&B train that was going places commercially. That combination of white music (country) and black music (rhythm & blues) is the alchemy that

Bill Haley and his Comets pictured in the 1960s.

produces the music we now call rock 'n' roll. In fact, it would be termed such by DJ Alan Freed, who was a big fan of Haley's early single 'Rock The Joint'. Memories differ as to whether Freed coined the term specifically because of 'Rock The Joint' or the Comets' later teenage-argot appropriating single 'Crazy Man Crazy' – or even a different record by another artist - but it can't be disputed that Haley and his men were playing a form of music that was considered to be rock 'n' roll before Elvis recorded a note, let alone became famous.

The record that made Haley a legend, of course, is '(We're Gonna) Rock Around The Clock'. Written by Max Freedman and James E Myers, it was offered to Haley – a veritable stripling of 25 compared to the sixty-year-old Freedman - but it was turned down on Haley's behalf by his record company and was first recorded by Sunny Dae and his Knights. When Haley moved to the Decca label, 'Rock Around The Clock' was one of the first things he recorded, although it was only the B-side of 1954 single 'Thirteen Women'. 'Clock''s chart-toping feat (both UK and US) didn't come until the following year when it was used on the soundtrack to the teenage delinquency movie *Blackboard Jungle*. The theoretical link between rock and violence was established by that film, although the moral guardians who objected to the new loud, throbbing form of music were too unhip to realize that the title of Haley's song itself meant 24-hour fornication. The record is relatively tame by today's standards but the sparkling guitar solo (by hired hand Danny Cedrone) and the way the sax bludgeons its way in at the end remain impressive by any generation's standards. 'Shake, Rattle & Roll' is highly agreeable, even if Charles Calhoun's original lyric was censored by Haley and even if it sounds more like jump blues (for some, the third, less-known ingredient of rock 'n' roll music) than anything else.

It has to be said that much of the rest of the material here is samey or boring or both, whether it be Haley's own co-writes like 'Two Hound Dogs' or less-than-climatic closer 'Mambo Rock'. The frequent boast in the lyrics Haley sings about how the joint is jumpin' or the beat pumpin' is somewhat undermined by his characterless voice and the Comets' almost gentle instrumentation. However Haley's co-write 'Birth Of The Boogie' has some fine drumming, blueswailing sax work and mellifluous guitar, even if its jungle animals lyric is inane.

Some would dispute the idea of Haley even playing rock 'n' roll let alone inventing or popularizing it. Animals guitarist Hilton Valentine once opined of Haley, "There isn't any touch of rhythm and blues in that – *totally* country-western." Some also are somewhat discomforted by the idea of a rotund opportunistic journeyman like Haley having kick-started the rock industry rather than the alternate, far more romantic, story that it was the lean, mean, broody and in-it-for-love figure of Elvis Presley. However, true though it is that Haley and his music began to look staid as soon as Presley arrived on the scene and that his records now have a patina of age about them – compared to the way that, say, 'Heartbreak Hotel' sounds like it could have been recorded yesterday – Haley's status as rock pioneer and the influence of his important records, all contained herein except for 'See You Later, Alligator', cannot be disputed. - Sean Egan

Rock 'n' Roll is the New Rock 'n' Roll

They were the artists who turned on the world to the first form of popular music that put the emphasis on beat, not melody. Music has changed in the half-century since but has always taken its cue from their rhythm-oriented pioneering. Some of the classics of that **first rock 'n' roll wave**...

1.	**Rocket 88**	Jackie Brenston and his Delta Cats
2.	**Long Tall Sally**	Little Richard
3.	**Whole Lotta Shakin' Goin' On**	Jerry Lee Lewis
4.	**Blueberry Hill**	Fats Domino
5.	**Summertime Blues**	Eddie Cochran
6.	**Be-Bop-A-Lu-La**	Gene Vincent And The Blue Caps
7.	**Bye Bye Love**	The Everly Brothers
8.	**Rebel-'Rouser**	Duane Eddy
9.	**Train Kept A-Rollin'**	The Rock & Roll Trio
10.	**I Put A Spell On You**	Screamin' Jay Hawkins
11.	**La Bamba**	Richie Valens
12.	**Bony Moronie**	Larry Williams
13.	**Somethin' Else**	Eddie Cochran
14.	**Chantilly Lace**	The Big Bopper
15.	**Good Golly Miss Molly**	Little Richard
16.	**I'm Walkin'**	Fats Domino
17.	**Great Balls Of Fire**	Jerry Lee Lewis
18.	**Move It**	Cliff Richard
19.	**Blue Suede Shoes**	Carl Perkins
20.	**Shake, Rattle And Roll**	Big Joe Turner

4. Elvis Presley (UK TITLE: Rock 'n' Roll)
Elvis Presley

TRACKLISTING

US: Blue Suede Shoes/I'm Counting On You/I Got A Woman/One-Sided Love Affair/I Love You Because/Just Because/Tutti Frutti/Trying To Get To You/I'm Gonna Sit Right Down And Cry (Over You)/I'll Never Let You Go (Little Darlin')/Blue Moon/Money Honey

UK: Blue Suede Shoes/I Got A Sweetie (I Got A Woman)/I'm Counting On You/I'm Left, You're Right, She's Gone/That's All Right (Mama)/Money Honey/Mystery Train/I'm Gonna Sit Right Down And Cry (Over You)/One-Sided Love Affair/Lawdy, Miss Clawdy/Shake, Rattle & Roll

RELEASED

US: March 1956 UK: November 1956

PRODUCED BY

Sam Phillips, Bob Ferris, Ernie Oehlrich

Though Bill Haley had hit big with the singles 'Shake, Rattle & Roll' and '(We're Gonna) Rock Around The Clock', Elvis Presley was the first rock 'n' roll artist to make an impression in the album format, then a new medium: this eponymous debut LP was the first rock 'n' roll record to top the American album charts. This is really only fitting, for while Haley may have been the first rock 'n' roll idol, Presley was not merely a fine practitioner of this new genre but the physical embodiment of its sensual, animalistic virtues. The album was a big hit in Britain too, although there it had a different slightly tracklisting and was (somewhat crassly) re-titled *Rock 'N' Roll*.

Five of the songs on the American album originated at Sam Phillips' now legendary Memphis Sun studios, the venue at which over the course of 1954 and 1955 Elvis Aaron Presley is supposed to have invented a new form of music that married the propulsion of the black man's rhythm & blues with inflections of the white man's country & western. Many will dispute this suggestion, which would in turn lead us into that unwinnable battle to determine the first rock 'n' roll record ever recorded, so this is a subject we will bypass. Suffice it to say that in being a main wellspring for literally every album in this book – one of the foundation stones for all of rock music, which on this occasion we are using to describe any music that does not conform to social or musical conventionalism, including reggae, soul and everything else – *Elvis Presley* is without question one of the most influential albums ever made.

Presley released ten single sides for Sun. Elvis purists cite these as his greatest creative achievements. Others, noting that several of them feature no drums, might suggest that they barely resemble rock music as they term is now understood at all. However, it was clear to the mighty RCA label that Phillips had something extraordinary on his hands. Phillips has been subsequently ridiculed for selling Presley's contract to RCA for a mere $35,000 and thereby seeming to contradict his assertion that if he found a white man who could sing like a black man he would make a million dollars. But Phillips used the money to set up the ultra-successful Holiday Inn chain, as well as to try to make a star of another of his charges, Carl Perkins.

Speaking of whom, an utterly blistering version of that artist's composition 'Blue Suede Shoes' kicks off the proceedings here. The song depicts a man who can endure any indignity except his precious footwear being stepped on. It captures perfectly the utterly stupid, but somehow cool, vanity of youth. In any other musical medium before this, such vanity would have been written about simply in order to ridicule it but Perkins' first person narrator is *celebrating* such an attitude, and Presley invests the vocal with complete, if frantic, seriousness. This utterly idiotic sense of priorities – as well as the song's breakneck tempo, which to the old guard just seemed like a blur too fast to follow or enjoy – was exactly what the older generation hated about rock 'n' roll. And didn't Presley and his cohorts know it and exult in it. Side two also starts with a rip-roaring number, 'Tutti Frutti', though this one was already an iconic rock 'n' roll classic through its author Little Richard. Scotty Moore provides an extraordinary little trill on electric guitar every time Presley repeats the title phrase. Also galvanizing is 'Money Honey'.

Elvis with artists Johnny Cash, Carl Perkins and Jerry Lee Lewis at the 'Million Dollar Quartet' jam, Sun Records, 1956.

There's also plenty of balladry. 'Just Because', with its spoken word interlude, and 'Blue Moon' even verge on schmaltz and would have been palatable to people who couldn't stand this new-fangled rock 'n' roll. The latter are both songs recorded when Presley was at Sun but, like the other three Sun songs on the US version of this album, were previously unreleased. Another of the Sun-era recordings here is actually the best of the lot: 'Trying To Get To You', a shuffling pledge of love to an absent partner whose middle-eight allows Presley's voice to soar beautifully to the heavens.

In some senses, the UK edition of the album was a better listen. Not only did it contain more uptempo rock – including a truely fine recording of 'Lawdy Miss Clawdy' - but it featured iconic Sun recordings 'That's All Right (Mama)' and 'Mystery Train' (albeit ludicrously treated with echo). However, it is to both albums' considerable detriment that neither included ''Heartbreak Hotel', that slinky slice of rock *noir* with which Presley had recently announced himself to the public beyond his regional fans.

The record came in a sleeve that itself captured wonderfully the vitality of the new form of music the grooves within contained: a close-up, black & white torso shot of the artist emoting over an acoustic guitar with his name superimposed in giant, day-glo letters down the left and along the bottom. That the music in the grooves still had relevance more than two decades afterwards was proven when The Clash cocked a snook at both punk's year zero policy and their own "No Elvis, Beatles or the Rolling Stones" songline, and used the same design and lettering on the cover of their 1979 album *London Calling*. - Sean Egan

5. Bo Diddley
Bo Diddley

TRACKLISTING
Bo Diddley/I'm a Man/Bring It to Jerome/Before You Accuse Me/Hey! Bo Diddley/Dearest Darling/Hush Your Mouth/Say Bossman/Diddley Daddy/Diddy Wah Diddy/Who Do You Love?/Pretty Thing

RELEASED
US: 1958 UK: 1963

PRODUCED BY
Leonard Chess, Phil Chess

Bo Diddley did not invent rock 'n' roll, but he did invent the 'Bo Diddley beat', which is one of rock's cornerstones. The beat was simple — one long beat followed by three short beats — but it was infectious. The beat was an essential bridge between the regimented structure of the blues and the looser and more danceable sound of early rock 'n' roll. The Diddley beat was revolutionary at the time, and it immediately established Diddley as one of the most innovative composers on the scene. He also didn't use chord changes on many of his songs. This odd structure allowed his songs to stretch on and on without any obvious end, and as such they were great dancer numbers in live performance. The emotional release came not from a change in the tempo, which never varied, but instead from a vocal aside. As a result, Bo Diddley songs don't so much as end they fade away.

There are few records in history as influential as *Bo Diddley*. The rumbling beat is present on every song, but most obvious on the self-titled 'Bo Diddley'. Upon a bedrock of maracas, drums, and a killer guitar riff, Diddley lays down self-referential lyrics. The first two Rolling Stones albums were simply minor variations on this same beat, though the Stones, like many of the other British bands, were quick to admit how much Diddley had inspired them. Diddley's sphere of influence was so large in the 'Sixties that you'd be quicker to list the bands that were *not* inspired by him than the ones who owed him a debt. Without Diddley's beat, what we call rock would have no roll, or at least a different kind of roll.

Ellas Otha Bates McDaniel, better known as Bo Diddley.

Like most albums from the early days of rock, *Bo Diddley* is really a collection of singles - but what singles they are. Diddley's debut single release was 'Bo Diddley' backed with 'I'm A Man', and to call it the greatest debut record of all-time is no exaggeration. Diddley could have halted his career right there and still been inducted into the Hall Of Fame. The rest of the album is packed, however, with other tunes that became immediate classics. 'Hey! Bo Diddley' and 'Diddley Daddy' are two more variations on the Diddley beat, and again the singer uses himself as the main subject of these excellent songs.

Diddley not only sang, and played the guitar riffs that launched a thousand young guitar players, but he also wrote these songs, and that is perhaps his most remarkable achievement. Diddley recorded in an era when most Chicago bluesmen were simply re-crafting traditional songs and perfecting them for live performance. Diddley's music did play homage to his blues forefathers, but with songs like 'Who Do You Love' and 'Diddy Wah Diddy', he also changed the strict blues rhythmic structure and created songs that were danceable. It is worth noting, however, than none of the songs on *Bo Diddley* ever made it into the mainstream American Top-40 pop charts, at least not as recorded by Bo Diddley – later covers of his tunes by The Animals, Manfred Mann, and other white artists did chart. On the R&B charts, Diddley fared better, and 'Bo Diddley' was a number two hit there. Diddley's fame and acclaim was always greater among musicians than the general public.

Diddley was born Ellas Otha Bates McDaniel and raised on a farm in southern Mississippi. When he was five, he moved to Chicago where he was trained in classical violin. Later he learned to play guitar on street corners. He described his guitar style as an attempt to capture the sound of a freight car rolling past at night. His unique technique gained him many admirers among the tight-knit group of musicians who were playing on Chicago's Southside. He submitted his demo of 'I'm a Man' to several record companies but initially found rejection. When Leonard Chess heard the song, though, he immediately signed Diddley to Chess Records, and recut the track. It was recorded on March 2, 1955, which places it near the very beginning of the rock 'n' roll evolutionary chart. It was issued as a single just a few weeks later. It wasn't until a couple of years later that *Bo Diddley*, his first long player, came out.

Diddley was never as popular with white audiences as his Chess label mate Chuck Berry, but he did break many barriers and was the first African-American to appear on *The Ed Sullivan Show*. Sullivan had asked Diddley to sing a Tennessee Ernie Ford song, 'Sixteen Tons', but in a rebellious move Diddley sang 'Bo Diddley' instead. This infuriated Sullivan, who told Diddley he would never be successful and that his career would be over in six months.

By the mid-'Sixties, Diddley had stopped recording new material but his legend only grew when The Beatles and the Rolling Stones cited him as an influence, and when bands like The Animals turned his songs into hits. Jimi Hendrix wanted little more, early in his career, than to be the next Bo Diddley. Buddy Holly owed much to Diddley, as did Bruce Springsteen: they used the Diddley-style beat on 'Not Fade Away' and 'She's the One' respectively. The Who covered Bo Diddley, as did the Doors.

Diddley toured in 1979 with The Clash. In the 'Eighties, the British pop band Bow Wow Wow had a monster smash with 'I Want Candy', the most obvious of all uses of the Bo Diddley beat in recent years. Few artists have influenced so many diverse acts. The Jesus and Mary Chain even released a song titled 'Bo Diddley Is Jesus' - for many of Diddley's disparate and numerous followers, not an exaggeration.
- Charles R. Cross

Leiber & Stoller

Jerry Leiber and Mike Stoller were the first non-performing songwriters of the rock era to become famous in their own right. A mere sampling of the classic records they are responsible for.

1.	**Hound Dog**	Elvis Presley
2.	**Kansas City**	Wilbert Harrison
3.	**Yakety Yak**	The Coasters
4.	**Riot In Cell Block No. 9**	The Robins
5.	**Poison Ivy**	The Coasters
6.	**Baby I Don't Care**	Elvis Presley
7.	**Three Cool Cats**	The Coasters
8.	**King Creole**	Elvis Presley
9.	**Love Potion No. 9**	The Clovers
10.	**DW Washburn**	The Monkees
11.	**Stand By Me**	Ben E. King
12.	**Pearl's A Singer**	Elkie Brooks
13.	**The Girls I Never Kissed**	Frank Sinatra
14.	**Is That All There Is?**	Peggy Lee
15.	**Ruby Baby**	Dion
16.	**Jailhouse Rock**	Elvis Presley
17.	**Bazoom (I Need Your Lovin')**	The Cheers
18.	**Don't**	Elvis Presley
19.	**Bossa Nova Baby**	Tippie And The Clovers
20.	**Love Me**	Elvis Presley

6. Buddy Holly

Buddy Holly

TRACKLISTING

I'm Gonna Love You Too/Peggy Sue/Look At Me/Listen to Me/Valley of Tears/Ready Teddy/Everyday/Mailman, Bring Me No More Blues/Words of Love/(You're So Square) Baby I Don't Care/Rave On/Little Baby

RELEASED

US: March 1958 UK: July 1958

PRODUCED BY

Norman Petty, Buddy Holly

Some will baulk at the inclusion of this album in preference to 1957's *The "Chirping" Crickets* (credited to The Crickets but featuring the exact same personnel as this album) and in truth it's a borderline decision. However, though that former album includes the Holly signature song 'That'll Be The Day', track for track, *Buddy Holly* - the only other album released by Holly during his short life – feels the aesthetic superior, even if of precisely the same degree of historical influence. In any case, the recording of the tracks on this album is intertwined with that of those on its predecessor.

The contents of both albums were massively influential in the development of rock from an immature twangy form of music not hugely different to the formulaic rockabilly into a genre with far broader horizons. Though many artists were influenced by the songs from Holly's albums, the effect of them (which would have been mostly through the singles and B-sides that each are half composed of) on The Beatles alone makes them phenomenally important. The deeper one thinks about it, the more one realizes that The Beatles – at least in the first couple of years of their recording career - were not so much a development of The Crickets but more the English version of them. The Crickets – some of whose records were put out under their frontman's name on a different label so as to accommodate Holly's prolific songwriting without making the public and media feel like the market was being saturated – were the first rock band to not have an individual's name in their title. (The phrase "Buddy Holly and The Crickets" is colloquially commonplace but no record ever featured that credit.) The Crickets were the first major rock band to be self-contained, both in their permanent guitars-bass-drums line-up and in their ability to generate their own material. They were also the first artists to marry the streamlined melody traditions of Tin Pan Alley to the raw rhythmic style that rock 'n' roll had introduced to popular music. All of these things made up a metaphorical ball that The Beatles grabbed and ran with.

Holly's first pair of commercially released singles – 'Blue Days, Black Nights' and 'Modern Don Juan' (both 1956) were okay but did not feature The Crickets and he had no hand in their composition. His 'real' career began in spectacular fashion in May 1957 with The Crickets' 'That'll Be The Day', a piece of perfection from its swaggering, descending guitar intro onwards. 'Words Of Love', released as a Holly single the following month, was the first of the tracks on the *Buddy Holly* album to be released. Like most of the tracks on both, it was recorded at the modest New Mexico studio of Norman Petty, around 100 miles north-west of the Lubbock, Texas hometown of Holly and his colleagues. Petty acted as producer but the presence of his name on the songwriting credits can be dismissed as the product of the era of payola: The Crickets in various combinations wrote all their original songs, with Holly having the main creative input in almost everything.

A languid, almost droning ballad, 'Words Of Love' featured Holly double tracking his own voice, an unusual sound for those days. B-side 'Mailman, Bring Me No More Blues' was in the same relaxed vein, though a cover. Although the 'Oh Boy!'/'Not Fade Away' combination that saw release in October and featured on *The "Chirping" Crickets* was a magnificent single it was no greater a double-whammy than the 'Peggy Sue'/'Everyday' pairing of September '57 that would end up on this album. The titular fiancé of Crickets drummer Jerry Allison to whom this was a midtempo tribute was no doubt thrilled by her instant immortality but other listeners would have been galvanized more by a rhythm track that seemed to simply *thrum* and a guitar break from Holly staggering in both its primitivism and – contrarily – its inventiveness. Flip 'Everyday' was a ballad exquisite in its candidness and uncertainty ("Everyone says go up and ask her") and in its stark instrumentation – a Celeste augmented by little other than a rhythm provided by Allison patting his thighs.

A 1958 publicity shot of Buddy Holly.

Buddy Holly's closer 'I'm Gonna Love You Too' was a single A-side in February '58. (By this time, original Crickets second guitarist Niki Sullivan had left, leaving The Crickets to record further tracks as a trio.) It was pretty good, although not as classy as flip and future *Buddy Holly* companion 'Listen To Me', which saw Holly ratchet up the emotion of another sweet, delicate ballad with a spoken-word part that miraculously sidestepped kitschiness. That very same month saw the Crickets single 'Maybe Baby' b/w 'Tell Me How'. The next single bearing Holly's name came in April. 'Rave On' (a product of a recording session in New York, where the band were playing TV dates, and therefore a rare non-Clovis track) was ostensibly not a Holly original. Written by the team of Sonny West and Bill Tilghman, who had provided The Crickets 'Oh Boy!', it was really such a reinvention of the song as to almost constitute a new composition: who else but Holly could transport listeners to a state of instant excitement with the startling multi-syllable yodel – his familiar hiccupping vocal gimmick taken to the nth degree – at the song's beginning and who else but he and The Crickets could produce such fabulous breakneck instrumentation?

Buddy Holly was bulked out with recordings that seem always destined to have been mere album tracks, mainly cover versions. They were still enjoyable: that a supposedly four-eyed geek like Holly could inject such passion into a song like 'Reddy Teddy' was another example of the way he redefined the assumptions behind rock.

'Rave On' was the last recording found on this album to appear as a single side: possibly because as the *Buddy Holly* album had appeared months before, more singles might appear to be milking it. There again, the prolific Holly was already moving onto other songs and sounds – a vast appetite for the creation of new and different material was yet another quality Holly had in common with his Liverpudlian disciples.
- Sean Egan

7. Chuck Berry is on Top
Chuck Berry

TRACKLISTING
Almost Grown/Carol/Maybellene/Sweet Little Rock & Roller/Anthony Boy/Johnny B. Goode/Little Queenie/Jo Jo Gunne/Roll Over Beethoven/Around And Around/Hey Pedro/Blues For Hawaiians

RELEASED
US: January 1959 UK: 1959

PRODUCED BY
Leonard Chess, Phil Chess

John Lennon once said that if you wanted to come up with another name for rock 'n' roll, "you might call it 'Chuck Berry.'" That kind of endorsement speaks to the hallowed place Berry holds in rock music. With a series of late 'Fifties singles, Berry transformed rock 'n' roll by becoming the first

African-American to infuse pop into the form. He created a body of classic songs that fifty years later stand as manifestoes in the same way the Old Testament is the font from which much of modern religion springs. Without 'Maybellene' or 'Johnny B. Goode', Saturday night wouldn't be the same, and life as we know it might not be as sweet.

Instead of merely using this new medium to write about romance like everyone else, Berry made rock itself one of the subjects of his songs, his lyrics celebrating the music's virtues, often asserting its validity in the face of parental hostility. Berry was thus the first musician to mythologize rock. He was one of the first musicians to write songs to fit a style, concentrating on a few central themes. This was in dramatic contrast to most musicians at the time who simply sought a hit and tried a variety of styles chasing success. Berry, in contrast, rarely varied his musical or lyrical substance, which is one reason so much of his work sounds the same – there isn't all that much difference between 'Sweet Little Sixteen' and 'Maybellene', as anyone who has ever played them on guitar can attest. But in that simplicity there was genius because it allowed Berry to create a body of work that had cohesion: he wrote 'Chuck Berry songs', not 'rock 'n' roll songs,' and in doing so he turned himself into a genre. He forever linked rock and the three themes he exclusively wrote about: lust, angst and rebellion. The only time Berry varied from this formula was 'My Ding-A-Ling', his 1972 novelty hit, which ironically was his only number

Chuck Berry, King of Rock 'n' Roll.

one. Even that song was fuelled by lust but Berry was long past teenager-hood when he was performing it and the creepy sexual nature of the song, considering some of Berry's offstage problems, makes it the one embarrassment in his catalog.

Chuck Berry On Top is Berry's most influential album. Aerosmith's Joe Perry once said of the disc, "It defines rock 'n' roll". The album, like most in the day, is mainly a collection of singles but these are the singles that made rock: 'Johnny B. Goode', rock's ultimate guitar hero anthem; 'Maybellene,' the original cheating girlfriend song; 'Carol', in which Berry beseeches his girl; 'Roll Over Beethoven', which in its title asserts rock as the new king of music; 'Around and Around', with a rhythm guitar part to die for; 'Little Queenie', a stage charmer. There are several others equally iconic. Six songs on the record were top ten hits, a claim that almost no other album that is not a greatest hits compilation can make. And because Berry's work was so stylistically similar, this album almost sounds like a concept record. The two exceptions are the Latin-influenced 'Hey Pedro' and the steel-guitar piece 'Blues for Hawaiians', which serve as filler here, though Chuck Berry's filler is of a higher standard than that served up by most artists.

Some of the credit for the majesty of these songs goes to the stellar band that Chuck played with in this era. Pianist Johnnie Johnson long claimed that he deserved more writing and arranging credit for this material, and he had much to do with keeping Berry's sound rooted in R&B at the same point that it expanded to encompass pop. All of these singles were recorded for Chess Records, and the house band that Berry found in that studio was an all-star dream line-up. Contributing musicians include Bo Diddley on guitar, Willie Dixon on bass, Fred Below on drums, and The Moonglows on backing vocals.

This was Berry's fourth record. His earlier releases were more blues-oriented, as Chuck had yet to perfect his own unique style. It was Muddy Waters who steered Berry to Chess, and Berry's first Chess single was 'Maybellene', which went to number five and made Berry a star. *On Top* came out around the time Berry peaked — he had such a large catalog of hits at that point that he essentially began touring as one of rock's first oldies acts. There are other collections of Berry's hits that are also worth considering, but short of adding 'Nadine,' *On Top* covers Berry's biggest hits and his best work. And if only for the reason that it doesn't include 'My Ding-A-Ling,' Berry's worst musical moment, *On Top* may be preferable to the 'best of' collections hawked on late-night television.

Berry's reputation grew exponentially in the 'Sixties when a number of bands in the British Invasion embraced him. When the Stones and The Beatles covered him, he regained icon status, a new wave of covers of his hits bringing his songs to a new generation. "To me, Chuck Berry always was the epitome of rhythm & blues playing, rock 'n' roll playing", Keith Richards once said. "It was beautiful, effortless, and his timing was perfection. He is rhythm supreme." Richards felt so strongly about his idol that he served as musical director of Taylor Hackford's 1987 film, *Hail, Hail, Rock 'n' Roll*, which chronicles a tribute concert put together to honor Berry. In the movie, Berry berates Richards and proves the adage that he is the bitterest man in rock. Yet that offstage rancor hardly matters when the first chords of 'Maybellene' begin. Almost despite himself, Chuck Berry created a body of work that will long outlive him and that will forever be thought of as the center of rock 'n' roll. - Charles R. Cross

8. Muddy Waters at Newport 1960
Muddy Waters

TRACKLISTING
I Got My Brand On You/(I'm Your) Hoochie Coochie Man/Baby, Please Don't Go/Soon Forgotten/Tiger in Your Tank/I Feel So Good/I've Got My Mojo Working/I've Got My Mojo Working, Part 2/Goodbye Newport Blues

RELEASED
US: 1960 UK: September 1961

PRODUCED BY
No producer listed.

Newport Festivals were responsible for two career-changing appearances within five years in the first half of the 1960s.

The second, most famous one was the occasion in 1965 when Bob Dylan proceeded to bring a rock band with him to the Newport Folk Festival, causing the audience to boo. Some have disputed the idea that the folkies were booing the electric instruments – but the fact that Dylan faced similar crowd reactions when he proceeded to travel the world with a backing band indicates that this was at least partly true. In contrast to the negative reception for Dylan by the Newport crowd, the appearance at the Newport Jazz Festival by Muddy Waters in 1960 revitalized a career for a man who was already in his mid-forties and helped set him up as a major figure for a movement that worshipped at the feet of the blues and R&B he traded in – a movement that was located, strangely, not in Waters' native America but thousands of miles away in Great Britain.

Though after this album Waters would seem to seek to catch a ride on the acoustic folk movement led by Bob Dylan with the album *Folk Singer*, he actually made his name as one of the people who electrified the blues. In the 1930s and 1940s, American rural blacks began flocking to the cities, their destination dependent on the metropolis most readily accessible on their area's railway line. Waters – born McKinley Morganfield – was one of those who landed up in Chicago. Once he relocated there in 1943, he became king of what would become known as the Chicago electric blues sound. In this he was assisted – as were so many blues artists of the era – by songwriter Willie Dixon, whose name can be found in the parentheses beneath the titles of what seems like at least half of all iconic blues and R&B tracks of that vintage.

Three live renditions of Dixon compositions appear here, 'I Got My Brand On You', '(I'm Your) Hoochie Coochie Man' and 'Tiger In Your Tank', all of them dripping with the lascivious innuendo that was Dixon's trademark. Waters and his crack band of James Cotton, Pat Hare and Otis Spann drive them home with stinging relish. Some of this material was undoubtedly rather populist and even vulgar for the tastes of Newport's predominately jazz aficionados but the power of Waters and his men won them over and many reported dancing in the aisles. 'Baby Please Don't Go' is here credited to Waters, although it was first recorded by Big Joe Williams in 1935 – an example of how the overlap between the traditional song handed down over generations and new songs based on traditional structures was so great in the blues that songs ended up being appropriated by others. Waters would also cheekily appropriate the publishing credit for 'I've Got My Mojo Working', actually written by Preston Foster. Perhaps

Muddy Waters at the 1960 Newport Festival.

Waters can be forgiven, for the consensus is that his barnstorming version of that composition on *Live At Newport* is the definitive one. A measure of how well Waters and co were going down is the way the crowd insisted on a repeat of the song. The closing 'Goodbye Newport Blues' was reportedly something ad libbed as the band were preparing to take the stage and then vamped on.

As with several people in the first part of this book, Waters' main influence was far more through singles, EPs and 78s than through albums. Indeed, it should be noted that despite releasing records since 1948, Waters' first album only appeared in 1958 – and that itself was a greatest hits package. A tribute album to mentor Big Bill Broonzy followed in 1959 before the release of *Live At Newport*, Waters' third long player, which was also one of the first live blues records.

Though many of the real blues fanatics possessed a copy of *Live At Newport*, in some senses the influence that this album had was more cultural than musical, especially in Britain. The R&B loving kids in a class-bound country in which rationing had not long ago ended could not afford to buy many albums and tended to consume Muddy Waters product on single and EP. However, though they might not have had easy access to the *Newport* album, Waters' name had a greater cachet to them in this timeframe through it because of the way it embellished his legend. Overnight, Waters' name was hip again. Not only had he galvanized an alien audience on the day but the record of it preserved for posterity – and commercial release – provided both proof of his enduring dynamism, despite him being middle-aged, and a reminder of why he had come to epitomize modern blues.

Three of those impressed impoverished UK blues lovers were living in Chelsea, South West London in 1962/63. Though there is some confusion about whether they decided to name their band the Rollin' (later Rolling) Stones because of Waters' 'Rolling Stone Blues' or because of his 'Mannish Boy' (which contains the line "I'm a rollin' stone"), either way the name is testament to the esteem in which he was held, an esteem for which this album is largely responsible. - Sean Egan

9. King of the Delta Blues Singers
Robert Johnson

TRACKLISTING
Cross Road Blues/Terraplane Blues/Come On In My Kitchen/Walking Blues/Last Fair Deal Gone Down/32-20 Blues/Kindhearted Woman Blues/If I Had Possession Over Judgment Day/Preaching Blues (Up Jumped The Devil)/When You Got A Good Friend/Rambling On My Mind/Stones In My Passway/Traveling Riverside Blues/Milkcow's Calf Blues/Me And The Devil Blues/Hellhound On My Trail

RELEASED
US: 1961 UK: 1966

PRODUCED BY
Don Law

When down the years old bluesmen have reminisced to journalists and documentary makers about the times they spent with guitarist and singer Robert Johnson, it has always been an almost jaw-dropping matter. Not necessarily because their anecdotes have been particularly enthralling but simply because it is astonishing to contemplate the fact of somebody living and talking who has known Johnson. Robert Johnson is a figure so wrapped up in myth that it barely seems conceivable that anybody still on this earth breathed the same air as he.

Robert Johnson was born and died in poverty, achieved no fame as we understand the term in his lifetime and left behind a meager quantity of recordings – all of them one-man affairs – that sold in the mere low thousands. Yet a roll-call of the names that have covered his compositions reveals some of the biggest luminaries in rock history, Canned Heat, Eric Clapton, Cream, Bob Dylan, Fleetwood Mac, Led Zeppelin, Lynyrd Skynyrd, the Rolling Stones, Status Quo and the Steve Miller Band among them. Clapton released an entire album of Johnson covers in 2004, fully 66 years after Johnson's death. The Stones' Keith Richards is such a fan that he possesses a copy of Johnson's death certificate.

Born illegitimately in 1911 in Hazelhurst, Mississippi, Johnson was brought up by his mother. The two frequently moved during his childhood. Johnson worked as a cotton picker while very young. There was a brief period of stability in his life when he married at the age of seventeen but the marriage only lasted just over a year. It ended when Johnson's wife died during childbirth. Johnson's wanderlust returned, one for which there seems to be a deep-seated, if unknown, psychological reason. His lyrics teemed with imagery of a man fleeing his demons, epitomized by the song 'Hellhound On My Trail'. In turn, these fearful lyrics helped perpetuate a myth about Johnson: that he pledged his soul to the devil in order to become a great guitarist. The myth was first propagated by Son House who stated "He sold his soul to play like that" in what sounds like an offhand remark at the way that Johnson had turned from a mediocre player into a man of quite extraordinary technique in an uncannily short space of time.

Johnson's playing remolded the blues in his image. Johnny Shines once observed, "Some of the things that Robert did with the guitar affected the way everybody played. He'd do rundowns and turnbacks. He'd do repeats… In the early '30s, boogie on the guitar was rare, something to be heard. Because of Robert, people learned to complement theirselves." Or as Keith Richards once put it, "When I first heard it, I said to Brian [Jones], 'Who's that?' 'Robert Johnson', he said. 'Yeah, but who's the other guy playing with him?' Because I was hearing two guitars, and it took me a long time to realize he was actually doing it all by himself."

Of course, the legend that Johnson strolled down to the

ROBERT JOHNSON
KING OF THE DELTA BLUES SINGER

COLUM

Original artwork for King of the Delta Blues Singers.

crossroads at Highways 61 and 49 in Clarksdale, Missouri where he met a large black man who took his guitar, tuned it for him and in the act of giving it back to him purchased Johnson's eternal damnation in exchange for superhuman musical abilities is far more attractive and romantic an idea than the suggestion that Johnson gained his skills by diligent practice. But how could the former idea not take hold when not only did Johnson at one point have a cataract in one eye that gave him a sly, sinister appearance but he additionally insisted on writing such numbers as 'Me And The Devil Blues' and 'Cross Road Blues'? Johnson's mythological status was cemented by his premature death in 1938, allegedly poisoned by a jealous love rival.

All of Johnson's recordings were laid down under the aegis of Don Law's American Record Company, who in 1936 took receipt from him of seventeen songs (plus alternate takes) recorded in a three-day period in a hotel room. Johnson recorded a dozen more songs in '37 at the Brunswick Records Building in Dallas, Texas. Most of the recordings contained on this album were originally released as 78rpm discs. They generally did not sell well, except 'Terraplane Blues', because it was named after a car. Many of the songs herein have since sold many millions of units by their inclusion on albums by Johnson disciples. Particularly iconic are 'Traveling Riverside Blues' (Led Zeppelin paraphrased its horny line, "You can squeeze my lemon 'til the juice run down my leg" on 'The Lemon Song'), 'Cross Road Blues', 'Terraplane Blues', 'Rambling On My Mind', 'Me And The Devil Blues' and 'Hellhound On My Trail'.

For an entire generation of future superstars who learnt their craft on the UK R&B scene of the early 'Sixties, *King Of The Delta Blues Singers* was almost a Holy Bible, both a primer on the blues and a guitar technique masterclass. Part of its appeal was its mystique – the only recordings available on album of a legend-draped figure. Eventually his other recordings (some previously unreleased) did surface and appeared on bootleg circa 1968. These additional songs were promptly raided by Johnson's former disciples, many of them now having becoming colossal recordings acts: for example, the Rolling Stones put a version of 'Love In Vain' on their 1969 *Let It Bleed* album long after they had ceased being a blues outfit. Eventually, this new cache of recordings was commercially released as *King Of The Delta Blues Singers Vol. 2* and one can now easily find both caches commercially available in one package.

Originally, this album was housed in a sleeve with a drawing of the artist seen from the back, guitar on lap, singing into a corner. This was because, as befitting someone who had the feel of being more myth than real person, there were no known photographs of Johnson in existence. Two verified ones have emerged since, one of which shows Johnson to be – of course – a dapper man who looks every inch the star. - Sean Egan

Short for Brilliant?

The famous Brill Building was located at 1619 Broadway, New York NY. It and the other music publishers' offices around it such as Aldon Music (1650 Broadway) employed freelance songwriters like Goffin & King, Mann & Weil, Sedaka & Greenfield, Pomus & Shuman and Bacharach & David who were responsible for so many hits in the early 1960s that a generic name was given them: **Brill Building pop**.

1.	**Leader Of The Pack**	The Shangri-Las
2.	**The Loco-Motion**	Little Eva
3.	**The Boy From New York City**	The Ad Libs
4.	**Chapel Of Love**	The Dixie Cups
5.	**Take Good Care Of My Baby**	Bobby Vee
6.	**Will You Love Me Tomorrow?**	The Shirelles
7.	**Oh Carol**	Neil Sedaka
8.	**Blame It On The Bossa Nova**	Eydie Gorme
9.	**He's Sure The Boy I Love**	The Crystals
10.	**On Broadway**	The Drifters
11.	**You've Lost That Lovin' Feelin'**	The Righteous Brothers
12.	**Teenager In Love**	Dion And The Belmonts
13.	**Stupid Cupid**	Connie Francis
14.	**Tell Laura I Love Her**	Ray Peterson
15.	**Twenty Four Hours From Tulsa**	Gene Pitney
16.	**Da Doo Ron Ron**	The Crystals
17.	**I Can Hear Music**	The Ronettes
18.	**Wishin' And Hopin'**	Dusty Springfield
19.	**Only Love Can Break A Heart**	Gene Pitney
20.	**Remember (Walkin' In The Sand)**	The Shangri-Las

10. Show Case

Patsy Cline

TRACKLISTING
I Fall to Pieces/Foolin' Around/The Wayward Wind/South of the Border/
I Love You So Much It Hurts/Seven Lonely Days/Crazy/San Antonio
Rose/True Love/Walkin' After Midnight/A Poor Man's Roses (Or a Rich
Man's Gold)/Have You Ever Been Lonely (Have You Ever Been Blue)

RELEASED
US: September 1961 UK: 1961

PRODUCED BY
Owen Bradley

Patsy Cline's second album is her best, and one of the greatest in the history of country music. If there were justice, every jukebox in the world would come pre-loaded with 'I Fall to Pieces', 'Crazy', 'The Wayward Wind', and 'Walkin' After Midnight'. These songs, and Cline's voice, represent the very definition of what heartache sounds like.

Patsy Cline
(1932 – 1963).

Cline's life story reads like the lyrics to one of her songs. She was born under the name Virginia Patterson Hensley in the hill country of Winchester, Virginia. In 1953, aged 21, she began to work as a rockabilly singer, though success was hard to come by. She divorced Gerald Cline in 1957, but married Charlie Dick that fall and he was the love of her life. Around the time of the second marriage, she scored her breakthrough with 'Walkin' After Midnight', which became a hit after she performed it on *Arthur Godfrey's Talent Scouts*. The song earned her a regular spot on the Grand Ole Opry.

Cline's luck changed for the worse in June 1961 when she was in a head-on car crash. The impact almost killed her, and kept her in the hospital for over a month. She survived, but left the hospital with scars that never went away.

That same year she released *Showcase*, the best of the three albums she released during her lifetime. *Showcase* represented a shift away from the hillbilly holler music Cline had grown up with, and towards a more mature pop vocal sound. Produced by the brilliant Owen Bradley, *Showcase* made Cline's voice the central part of each recording, and her singing is intimate, breathy, and full of emotion.

About half of *Showcase* was recorded before Cline's accident, including her take of the Harlan Howard song 'I Fall to Pieces'. Though 'I Fall to Pieces' had been a number one hit on the country chart, Cline's label pressured her and Bradley to head in more of a pop direction for their next single. They chose Willie Nelson's 'Crazy', a song Dick had heard on a jukebox and thought was appropriate for his wife. Cline had to re-cut the song because at the original recording session – not long after her car accident – she was unable to sing with enough power to hit her notes. The second session, done a few weeks after her accident, provided the proper master. The result was almost beyond definition – was it country or jazz? – but indisputably brilliant. Bradley called the song, "one of the best tracks I ever had anything to do with", and, considering his lengthy discography, tha is high praise. 'Crazy' was released as a single in November 1961, and became Cline's highest charting hit, reaching Number 9. It remains the most famous song she is associated with and epitomizes the way that Cline's small but telling legacy helped redefine country. Glossily recorded and oozing sophistication and class, it – like so much of her *oeuvre* – could never be dismissed as "shit-kicker" music.

Cline had other hits after *Showcase*, including 'Sweet Dreams (Of You)', but her death in a plane crash on March 5 1963 just two years after the release of *Showcase* ended her career prematurely. Though the airplane crash that killed Buddy Holly is the most famous in rock, Cline's accident was the most tragic in country music. Cline was only 30. Her manager Randy Hughes and singers Hankshaw Hawkins and Cowboy Copas also perished. As if Cline's legacy wasn't dark enough, country legend Jack Anglin died in a car crash on the way to Cline's funeral.

The critical assessment of Cline's work, and of *Showcase*, grew after her death, as her songs became staples of jukeboxes and late night radio. Due in part to the material on *Showcase*, Cline became the biggest selling female artist in the history of Decca Records. Her songs have always been popular with filmmakers, particularly when they want to evoke a lonely and desperate mood. Her legacy has also been strengthened by a number of covers of the songs that Cline made famous — k.d. lang was enough of a fan of Cline that she tracked down Owen Bradley and made her own album with him. A 1985 film of Cline's life was made and titled *Sweet Dreams*. It starred Jessica Lange and brought Cline's life story and music to an entirely new generation. A number of greatest hits packages have continued to come out and most generously cull songs from *Showcase*.

Patsy Cline also had a resurrection of sorts when a thirteen-year-old singer named LeAnn Rimes released 'Blue' in 1996 and made the song a top ten country hit. 'Blue' was the song that Cline was set to record next, before her plane crash. Though the song had been subsequently offered to a number of other singers, including Cline's friend Loretta Lynn, no one had wanted to cover a song so closely associated with Cline. Rimes said she tried to emulate Cline. The song would be LeAnn's first hit and one that launched her career. - Charles R. Cross

11. Howlin' Wolf

Howlin' Wolf

TRACKLISTING
Shake For Me/The Red Rooster/You'll Be Mine/Who's Been Talkin'/ Wang-Dang-Doodle/Little Baby/Spoonful/Going Down Slow/Down In the Bottom/Back Door Man/Howlin' For My Baby/Tell Me

RELEASED
US: 1962 UK: Not issued

PRODUCED BY
No producer listed.

When the Rolling Stones – flush with the success of '(I Can't Get No) Satisfaction', which had made them superstars – were guesting on US TV pop program *Shindig* in 1965, they were asked if they had in mind a musical guest they would like to feature. "Howlin' Wolf" came the reply.

The Wolf – real name Chester Burnett – was a massive influence on not just the Stones but just about all of their contemporaries in the early 'Sixties UK blues and R&B boom. Though the couple of pounds price tag attached to this eponymous album – colloquially referred to as "The Rocking Chair Album" because of its cover design – would have meant comparatively few of the principals of that scene owned it, its contents were very familiar to them. Essentially a collection of Wolf's best 'Fifties and 'Sixties singles, where they didn't know them from records they would have known them from the sets of dozens of their musical contemporaries.

Sam Phillips may be best known for discovering Elvis Presley but the Sun label owner alighted on Wolf a decade earlier than The King after hearing him on his own Memphis radio show, in which he not only played but gave farm reports. Eventually, Wolf was able to move away from the farming trade as the Phillips discovery led to two simultaneous R&B-chart hits due to the canny Phillips licensing the Wolf songs he'd recorded to separate labels. Wolf ultimately signed to Chess and relocated to their base in Chicago. One of the first in his region to have used an electric guitar in his music, Wolf there became – along with Muddy Waters – one of the defining artists of the Chicago electric blues sound.

Wolf's name and career are inextricably bound up with Willie Dixon. Dixon was a Chess staff writer and stand-up bassist and the label clearly felt that Wolf would have more success with his songs. Wolf was never happy about this, once publicly lamenting "I can do my own songs better but they won't let me." However, if any blues artists was going to have a writer forced on him, they couldn't do better than Dixon, who had an unusual knack for writing songs that were recognizably in the blues idiom but which stayed clear of generic cliché. Significantly, bar for 'Going Down Slow', every single one of the tracks here is either written by Dixon or by Dixon in collaboration with Wolf. They include some of the most iconic blues tracks of all time, including 'Back Door Man' (covered by the Doors), 'Spoonful' (covered by Cream) and 'The Red Rooster', which – as 'Little Red Rooster' – was turned by the Rolling Stones into surely the most unlikely UK pop chart number one in history. - Sean Egan

12. The Freewheelin' Bob Dylan
Bob Dylan

TRACKLISTING
Blowin' In The Wind/Girl From The North Country/Masters Of War/Down The Highway/Bob Dylan's Blues/A Hard Rain's A-Gonna Fall/Don't Think Twice, It's All Right/Bob Dylan's Dream/Oxford Town/Talkin' World War III Blues/Corrina, Corrina/Honey, Just Allow Me One More Chance/I Shall Be Free

RELEASED
US: May 1963 UK: November 1963

PRODUCED BY
John Hammond

Bob Dylan's eponymous 1962 solo album was an unremarkable collection of covers of folk standards with a couple of his own tentative compositions sprinkled in. The public clearly wondered why they would want to hear new versions of songs as old as the hills sung by what the front cover photo made clear was a puppy-fat laden kid: it sold a paltry 5000 in its first year.

But Dylan did a lot of growing up before the release of his next album. In fact, he did quite a lot of growing up before the release of his first one: it took five months to reach the stores following the two sessions at which he laid it down. The very month after *Bob Dylan*'s release, the artist wrote the song that would set him on the path to becoming a legend: 'Blowin' In The Wind'. It was an instant classic, a contemporary protest anthem that also sounded like a hymn. Its lyric was printed in *Sing Out!* magazine and the song became famous before he did, covered by all and sundry and soon a staple of rallies and demos.

A former teenage sweetheart who met up in the early 1960s with the boy she had known as Bobby Zimmerman later recalled how he had informed her he was now a folkie. She exclaimed that it was "hillbilly garbage". Dylan unblushingly replied, "That's the coming thing. That's how I'm going to make it." Many have continued to harbor suspicions of similar mercenaryism about the way Dylan embraced protest songs in the period leading up to *Freewheelin'*, especially as he almost never attended rallies or espoused particular causes. Those same people, however, could not deny that Dylan was articulating better than any other songwriter the mindset of a generation who were more concerned with what their country could do for them than vice versa.

'Blowin' In The Wind' utilized the melody of a folk song called 'No More Auction Block', just as *Freewheelin'*'s epic 'A Hard Rain's A–Gonna Fall' – a nuclear war horror story – employed the tune of the equally traditional 'Lord Randall'. Dylan's talent at this time was primarily lyrics. He himself later admitted to his early lyrics being "rolled up" in folk melodies. Meanwhile, though he would develop into a genuinely great harmonica player and his voice would mature into a superb instrument within a couple of years, at this juncture his abilities in those areas were enthusiastic and passionate rather than technically impressive.

Though Dylan's subsequent two acoustic albums *The Times They Are A-Changin'* and *Another Side Of Bob Dylan* also made a mark, they were nothing like as influential as *Freewheelin'*, in the case of the former because it – title track aside – was a slightly dull affair and in the case of the latter because it saw Dylan abandon formal protest. *Freewheelin'* however was packed to the gunnels with protest. 'Oxford Town' concisely and quite passionlessly examines the furor caused by the enforced enrollment at the University of Mississippi of its first black student. 'Talkin' World War III Blues' is the comedic version of 'Hard Rain', 'Masters Of War' is an intense, relentless broadside against the arms trade. Even the songs that weren't actually overtly political seemed implicitly so: the frankness about sex and relationships in the likes of 'Don't Think Twice, It's Alright' and 'Honey Just Allow Me One More Chance' were them-selves throwing down a gauntlet to the ludicrously squeaky clean, conflict-less portrayed at the cinema and on radio and television.

Bob Zimmerman with his trusty acoustic guitar.

The Beatles were amongst the artists who were mightily impressed by this album but they were just one of many. Within a couple of years, its influence was to be heard all over the airwaves. It wasn't notable even so much through the cover versions (Peter, Paul and Mary had successive top tens with sweetened-up versions of 'Blowin' In The Wind' and 'Don't Think Twice, It's Alright'; the Four Seasons also had a hit with the latter under a pseudonym.) What was most notable was that an entire generation of musicians seemed to adopt Dylan's sneering, wise-cracking cooland disdain for both authority and romantic conventions. Everywhere, there seemed to be Dylan songs that weren't actually written by Dylan: Sonny & Cher had a Transatlantic number one in late summer '65 with 'I Got You Babe' which in its depiction of love in the face of parental hostility and its elongated, groaning vocal melody lines was instantly recognizable as inspired by Bob. Those groaning inflections also turned up in The Beatles' album track 'You've Got To Hide Your Love Away'. 'Eve Of Destruction' by Barry

McGuire, written by PF Sloan, was a Dylan protest pastiche (though set to a rock backing) so adept that people took it seriously. Buffy Saint-Marie's 'Universal Soldier', covered by Donovan and Glen Campbell, seemed a cross of 'Masters Of War' and 'Blowin' In The Wind'. So unusual were these impolite rock and pop chart records that they required the invention of a new generic name: folk-rock. And though it contained no folk element, even '(I Can't Get No) Satisfaction' by the Rolling Stones could arguably be said to be a song that could not have existed without the permission for expressions of disaffection in popular song granted by Dylan's example.

By then, Dylan had moved on, having written scornfully of believing in "lies that life is black and white" in *Another Side Of Bob Dylan's* 'My Back Pages' and saying of his old self (from which he was actually mere months removed), "I was so much older then, I'm younger than that now". Which either proved that his mind worked a thousand times faster than everyone else's and he had already developed the world weariness and disillusion with political activism that most radicals only acquire in middle age or that he really hadn't been joking about his opportunism to his old sweetheart. Dylan himself said in 1965, "I never wanted to write topical songs. That was my chance I wasn't getting far with the things I was doing." No matter: he had encouraged an entire generation to challenge the eminently questionable values of their elders and made some timeless music into the bargain. – Sean Egan

13. Night Beat

Sam Cooke

TRACKLISTING

Nobody Knows The Trouble I've Seen/Lost And Lookin'/Mean Old World/Please Don't Drive Me Away/I Lost Everything/Get Yourself Another Fool/Little Red Rooster/Laughin' And Clownin'/Trouble Blues/You Gotta Move/Fool's Paradise/Shake, Rattle And Roll

RELEASED

US: September 1963 UK: September 1963

PRODUCED BY

Hugo and Luigi

Night Beat is, quite simply, one of the greatest soul records of all-time. Though Sam Cooke had other pop albums that contained more hits, and gospel records that were better loved by fans of spiritual music,

Night Beat represents the apex of his overall artistic achievement, and that's quite a statement considering that Cooke was one of the best singers popular music ever had.

Recorded in just three sessions over a single weekend in February 1963, *Night Beat* was Cooke's attempt to make a concept record. His idea was to craft an album that captured the songs a singer might sing after closing time, when he is the only person left in the club. It is a downhearted record - these are songs of heartache and loneliness sung by a

man who knew despair all too well. Most of Cooke's hits – songs like 'Chain Gang' and 'You Send Me' – were upbeat on their surface but had a hint of wistfulness. On *Night Beat*, however, even that wistfulness is gone and there is only melancholy. This is Cooke's darkest record, but by daring to show his shadow self, Cooke created a masterpiece of sadness. In some ways the album begs comparisons to some of the best work of Frank Sinatra like *In the Wee Small Hours*. Yet Sinatra was never this vulnerable. One of Cooke's biggest pop hits was 'Another Saturday Night', but *Night Beat* is Sam Cooke at 4 a.m. after that night is over and he's alone.

A publicity shot of Sam Cooke from the early 1960s.

Almost all of Cooke's hits were songs he wrote himself – he was one of the first African-American artists to write, produce, and arrange all his own music. At one point Cooke even owned his own record label. Underneath that self-assured personality was a man who suffered from depression for most of his life, and treated it primarily by acting out his sexual addictions. Cooke kept his secret life out of the headlines for the most part, but he was a tormented man and *Night Beat* is the distillation of that inner conflict. In a way, Cooke's private scandals make his art all the more poignant and the sorrow he sings about on *Night Beat* is believable in a way that most pop singing is not.

For this album Cooke decided to record mostly covers, but while he chose well-known gospel and blues songs, he changed the arrangements. Every song is slowed down, every syllable that Cooke sings is stretched out, and even the drumbeats are muted. Cooke is backed by a stellar group of jazz musicians including guitarist Barney Kessell, drummer Hal Blaine, organist Billy Preston, and pianist Ray Johnson. The piano is the main instrument, working as a counterpoint to Cooke's voice.

The album starts with 'Nobody Knows the Trouble I've Seen', a despairing number which sets the tone, and could have served as an alternative album title. One of Cooke's greatest gifts as a singer was his ability to turn a 'no' or an 'oh' into an entire chorus. He uses that technique here, but even the 'Glory hallelujah' he ends the song with sounds like the cry of a defeated man and not the celebration of the saved. Other song titles explain the rest of the mood: 'Lost and Lookin'', 'Mean Old World', 'I Lost Everything', 'Trouble Blues'. Even on Cooke's cover of Willie Dixon's 'Little Red Rooster', though it is slightly more upbeat due to a killer organ lick from Billy Preston, he sounds more like a defeated rooster than one with swagger.

What makes this material most remarkable is Cooke's voice. It is smooth, sad, resigned, and full of feeling. Many of the songs on *Night Beat* only have six to eight true lines of verse — Cooke repeats the chorus to fill out the rest of the song. This doesn't matter. Ray Charles once said of Cooke, "He hit every note where it was supposed to be. And not only hit the note, but hit the note with feeling." Cooke's greatest gift as a singer is his ability to put emotion into anything he sings, whether it is an "Ooh" or the line "All by yourself", that ends the chorus of 'Mean Old World'. No one in music ever sang an "Ooh" better than Sam Cooke.

Even as he finished *Night Beat,* Cooke himself seemed to doubt the material and whether it was the direction he wanted to present. Two days after finishing the album sessions, he was back in the studio working on another pop single. And though *Night Beat* was acclaimed by critics when it was eventually released, it failed to sell anywhere near the numbers that Cooke's pop hits did. Sam Cooke died just eight months later, shot down in a motel lobby on a night when he was out with a suspected prostitute. The clerk mistook him for a robber. *Night Beat* sounds like a funeral dirge at times, and it makes one wonder whether Cooke had a premonition that his time was short. Though his death remains one of the most tragic in all of music, *Night Beat* is a perfect requiem for a tremendous talent.

Cooke's vocal style influenced everyone from Stevie Wonder to Harry Connick, Jr. His albums have been reissued several times, and remain popular. *Night Beat* itself has had two different releases, and has been remastered. The late critic Robert Palmer wrote the liner notes to the 1995 edition and called it "one of the most accomplished and emotionally devastating examples of American vocal artistry."

With his pop hits, Sam Cooke ruled Saturday night for the better part of a decade. *Night Beat* is the only peek Sam Cooke ever gave us into the early hours of his Sunday morning, but on it he found his greatest voice. - Charles R. Cross

The Wall of Sound

He was the producer who turned pop records into what have been described as "operas for the kids", creating his trademark Wall Of Sound via multiple, simultaneously played instruments. Twenty of the best **Phil Spector productions**.

1.	**Baby I Love You**	The Ronettes
2.	**To Know Him Is To Love Him**	Teddy Bears
3.	**Spanish Harlem**	Ben E KIng
4.	**Uptown**	The Crystals
5.	**Pretty Little Angel Eyes**	Curtis Lee
6.	**He Hit Me (It Felt Like A Kiss)**	The Crystals
7.	**Under The Moon Of Love**	Curtis Lee
8.	**You've Lost That Lovin' Feelin'**	The Righteous Brothers
9.	**He's A Rebel**	The Crystals
10.	**Why Do Lovers Break Each Others Hearts**	Bob B Soxx and the Blue Jeans
11.	**Da Doo Ron Ron**	The Crystals
12.	**Be My Baby**	The Ronettes
13.	**Then He Kissed Me**	The Crystals
14.	**Walking In The Rain**	The Ronettes
15.	**Unchained Melody**	The Righteous Brothers
16.	**River Deep Mountain High**	Ike & Tina Turner
17.	**Frosty The Snowman**	The Ronettes
18.	**Santa Claus Is Coming To Town**	The Crystals
19.	**Imagine**	John Lennon
20.	**Baby I Love You**	The Ramones

14. A Hard Day's Night
The Beatles

TRACKLISTING

US: A Hard Day's Night/Tell Me Why/I'll Cry Instead/I Should Have Known Better (Instrumental)/I'm Happy Just To Dance With You/And I Love Her (Instrumental)/ I Should Have Known Better/If I Fell/And I Love Her/Ringo's Theme - This Boy (Instrumental)/Can't Buy Me Love/A Hard Day's Night (Instrumental)

UK: A Hard Day's Night/I Should Have Know Better/If I Fell/I'm Happy Just to Dance With You/And I Love Her/Tell Me Why/Can't Bye Me Love/Any Time At All/I'll Cry Instead/Things We Said Today/When I Get Home/You Can't Do That/I'll Be Back

RELEASED

US: June 1964 UK: August 1964

PRODUCED BY

George Martin

Every Beatles album was massively influential, including the two (UK) LPs that preceded this, *Please Please Me* and *With the Beatles* (both from 1963). *A Hard Day's Night*, however, was yet more so. No, it didn't quite match the astonishing commercial success of its two predecessors, which had topped the UK chart for about a year running (though *A Hard Day's Night* did quite well, thank you, holding down the #1 spot for 21 weeks). It *was*, however, the first Beatles album containing *only* original material. And while it retained the enormously melodic, ingratiating qualities that had launched Beatlemania in 1963, it also served notice that the group was not content to rest on a formula. Instead, they restlessly expanded their instrumental and lyrical sophistication, even if (at least by their later standards) it was still quite innocent, romantic stuff. Particularly in America, it (and its accompanying movie) served as both a model and an inspiration for young musicians not only to hardily embrace rock 'n' roll as a creative form on par with other styles of popular music, but also to compose and record on their own terms, with a constant eye toward artistic growth and personal expression.

The album's wall-to-wall strength and varied invention were somewhat miraculous considering the hectic circumstances under which it was recorded. For several weeks just after New Year's in 1964, The Beatles were performing in Paris; just after that, they flew to the States for a few weeks to launch Beatlemania on an unprecedented scale; and just after *that*, they were committed to six weeks of filming for their first feature movie. Somehow, they had to fit in both the writing and recording of a record that was not only expected to be a commercial blockbuster, but needed to contain at least half a dozen numbers that could both complement and fit into the *A Hard Day's Night* film. Sessions were squeezed in in Paris, back at Abbey Road studios for a few days just before filming began, and for a couple days at the beginning of June just before they set off on a world tour. Yet for all that, *A Hard Day's Night* doesn't sound at all rushed. It's supremely confident and assured, bursting with an ebullient glow, particularly in the giddy close vocal harmonies that decorate almost every track.

A Hard Day's Night is sometimes said to be an album on which rhythm guitarist and vocalist John Lennon asserted his early creative dominance of the group, and it is true that, by numbers alone, he's the major contributor in the Lennon-McCartney material here. His breadth as both a writer and singer on the album is extraordinary, from the all-out romantic utopianism of the classic title track, the gorgeous bittersweet romantic balladry of 'If I Fell', and the proto-country-rock of 'I'll Cry Instead' to the vicious R&B-influenced 'You Can't Do That', the playful 'I Should Have Known Better', and the tender 'I'll Be Back', which looks forward to folk-rock.

It must be noted, however, that much of his work wouldn't have half the impact it had without bassist and vocalist Paul McCartney's harmonies and finishing touches, whether it be the exhilarating bridge of 'A Hard Day's Night' (where the lead vocal is handed off to Paul with all the finesse of a gold medal-winning Olympic relay team) or the way their voices masterfully weave around each other's on 'I'll Be Back' and 'If I Fell'. And McCartney's own contributions as chief composer, though relatively few in number, are all aces: 'Can't Buy Me Love' (actually released as a single months in advance of the LP, and one of their best upbeat raunchy belters, as well as the background to the key romp-in-the-field scene in the movie), 'And I Love Her' (an exceptionally haunting ballad with a quasi-classical flavor), and 'Things We Said Today' (another proto-folk-rocker, whose reflective tone was proof that Paul could be just as deep and serious as his celebrated partner).

Although lead guitarist George Harrison doesn't have any compositions of his own on the LP (he sings 'I'm Happy Just To Dance With You'), his electric 12-string guitar work (most famously heard in the magnificently reverberant opening chord of 'A Hard Day's Night', which opens both the album and film) broke new ground in rock music. That electric 12-string, as well as the film for which it served as curtain-raiser, would prove especially influential in the United States, where many of the most creative young musicians had abandoned rock 'n' roll for folk music in the early 1960s. *A Hard Day's Night* couldn't help but draw them back in, so good were the songs, so much fun were The Beatles having on screen.

The group's intelligence, rebellion against the status quo (if only implicit at this stage), and independent steering of their creative destiny were obvious, both on vinyl and in the cinema. Unfortunately, the album was diluted for the US market, where it was marketed as a soundtrack LP, including just eight of the thirteen tracks (filled out by Muzak-ish instrumentals crafted by their producer, George Martin). All the material got out in the States eventually, however (the other cuts showing up on the Capitol LPs *Something New* and *Beatles '65*), and in any case, the film was so popular that the seven songs used in the movie had a seismic impact beyond the radio or the turntable.

Most specifically, a young group of Los Angeles folk musicians, though already Beatles fans, were so struck by the movie — which many in

The original cover for *A Hard Day's Night*.

their crowd would see not just once, but over and over — that it gave them special incentive to forge ahead with a rock group of their own, The Byrds. When they rocked up Bob Dylan's 'Mr. Tambourine Man' to kick off folk-rock in 1965, it was an electric 12-string Rickenbacker guitar that Jim (later Roger) McGuinn was playing, specifically inspired by Harrison's use of the instrument in *A Hard Day's Night*. Those electric 12-string riffs would, in turn, became the signature sound of folk-rock. Just a year-and-a-half after *A Hard Day's Night*, a full circle was completed when folk-rock pushed The Beatles themselves into newly personal lyrical territory and multi-dimensional vocal/instrumental textures on their *Rubber Soul* album of late 1965. - Richie Unterberger

15. Highway 61 Revisited
Bob Dylan

TRACKLISTING
Like A Rolling Stone/Tombstone Blues/It Takes a Lot to Laugh, It Takes a Train to Cry/From a Buick 6/Ballad of a Thin Man/Queen Jane Approximately/Highway 61 Revisited/Just Like Tom Thumb's Blues/ Desolation Row

RELEASED
US: August 1965 UK: September 1965

PRODUCED BY
Tom Wilson, Bob Johnston

In 1964, Bob Dylan was only a few months (but a seismic change), away from achieving what he thought was his particular sound.

At the time, there was no reason to think that the protest lyrics and acoustic music with which he had already become a semi-legend was not his real sound. Others who had known him longer were better informed. The young musicians of his hometown of Hibbing, Minnesota with whom he had once played in amateur bands knew that his first love was rock 'n' roll. And, though they would not have been interested in such things, even Dylan's high school teachers would have been able to correct those who thought Dylan a folkie to his roots. After all, when required to state his ambition in his high school yearbook, Dylan had written that it was to "join Little Richard".

There was probably only one thing stopping Dylan from attempting to join Little Richard: he might lose his audience in an attempt to break through to rock's mass market. In the mid-'Sixties, a folkie becoming a rocker would be perceived as an act of betrayal analogous to a defection from the West to the East. Things really were that divided – at least from the folkies' side. The Beatles and The Animals had expressed their admiration for Dylan but the kind of people who formed Dylan's audience looked down their noses at rock and pop as juvenile music of no lyrical substance. Should Dylan fail to become a hit parader, he might be left with egg on his face and no career to go back to.

What folk and rock needed was an artist to break through the barrier that separated the two and invent the previously non-existent: records that married folk's intellectual and socio-political lyrics with music of rock's visceral, populist power. Bob Dylan achieved that dream by recording this, quite possibly the greatest album ever made.

Dylan had released the album *Bringing It All Back Home* in March 1965. The second side was acoustic but the first was choc-ful of gutsy R&B with a full band backing, the result of Dylan having been stunned by The Animals' electric version of his arrangement of standard 'The House Of The Rising Sun'.

It seems symbolic that the week before the release of the single 'Like A Rolling Stone' – the first song from *Highway 61 Revisited* to be heard by the public – saw Dylan booed off the stage at the Newport Folk Festival, allegedly for bringing a rock band with him. That Dylan should care. 'Subterranean Homesick Blues', a rock track from *Home*, had been a top ten hit when released as a single in the UK and a Top Forty US chart entry. In the summer of '65, not only did The Byrds confirm the viability of Dylan covers in the pop marketplace via a Transatlantic number one with his 'Mr. Tambourine Man' but 'Like A Rolling Stone' soared up the singles chart as well. Pace the folkies, there was no crass commercialism or compromise involved: '...Stone' was a gritty,

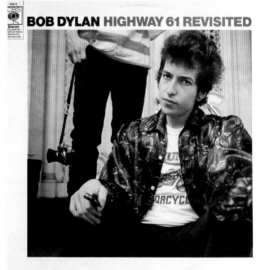

The original cover for Dylan's ground-breaking *Highway 61 Revisited*.

streetwise blast of (melodic) venom of a groundbreaking length of six minutes. At a time when The Beatles were still struggling to find rhymes more sophisticated than moon and June, Dylan had blown apart the assumptions about what constituted hit parade material. Although a tip of the hat should be made in the Stones' direction for the groundbreaking nature of the spite behind their 'Satisfaction' single – released just before 'Like A Rolling Stone' – their contemporaneous album *Out Of Our Heads* was fairly tame stuff.

Highway 61 Revisited triumphantly delivered on the promise of 'Like A Rolling Stone'. The album was recorded in seven sessions, starting May 12 1965 and ending on August 4 of that year. There were nine tracks (including that seismic single), all except one featuring a full band. Apart from ace blues guitarist Mike Bloomfield, the session musicians were nobody special but the beautiful sound paintings they created behind Dylan made his previous one-man records sound like pencil sketches. Dylan himself sang and played harmonica beautifully throughout in a perfect riposte to those who had alleged his skills in those departments were rudimentary. 'It Takes A Lot To Laugh, It Takes A Train To Cry' and 'Queen Jane Approximately' were shimmering, heart tugging concoctions. 'Ballad Of A Thin Man' was a neon-lit spooky denunciation of a 'straight' with a whirlpool of a middle eight. 'Just Like Tom Thumb's Blues' saw Dylan portraying himself as battered by life's complications to the accompaniment of beautiful piano work. 'Desolation Row' was a closing epic that was like a modern-day version of T.S. Eliot's *The Waste Land* set to music, portraying a nightmare zone wherein seemed to be located all of the world's sickos and evil-doers, a vista made all the more disquieting because it becomes apparent that 'Desolation Row' may merely be society in general and its inhabitants a cross section of humanity.

Musical excellence aside, rock and pop had never heard anything like this. All of the songs were well over the three minute pop norm, one of them – 'Desolation Row' – spanning eleven minutes. The songwords were like poetry, shimmering with metaphors, similes and delightful phrases that made normal popular music lyrics sound like nursery rhyme. *Highway 61 Revisited* proved what was possible in a medium that had previously been assumed to have an audience that wanted only depictions of sentiment or adolescent defiance. Its success granted permission for other artists to imitate its adult concerns. The resistance would continue for a while – epitomized by the way Dylan would be booed by the purists at his concerts when he got the band out – but Dylan had succeeded in smashing the division that had kept rock/pop simple and folk unexciting.

Though he was a friend of Dylan, the comments of folk singer Phil Ochs perhaps sum up the slack-jawed wonderment this record caused. Explaining that with each record release by Dylan, he assumed that he couldn't possibly top it, Ochs recalled that when he heard *Highway 61*, "I laughed and said it's so ridiculous. It's impossibly good, it just can't be that good... How can a human mind do this? The writing was so rich I just couldn't believe it." - Sean Egan

The Big Beat

In the wake of The Beatles came a plethora of British bands, none of them as good but many of them with the capacity for at least one thumpin' great record. Twenty classic **'Sixties UK group** chart singles.

1.	**Gimme Some Loving**	Spencer Davis Group
2.	**Sha La La La Lee**	Small Faces
3.	**Ferry Cross The Mersey**	Gerry And The Pacemakers
4.	**You Really Got Me**	The Kinks
5.	**I Can't Let Go**	The Hollies
6.	**I'm Into Something Good**	Herman's Hermits
7.	**Sweets For My Sweet**	The Searchers
8.	**I'm Crying**	The Animals
9.	**Pretty Flamingo**	Manfred Mann
10.	**Hippy Hippy Shake**	The Swinging Blue Jeans
11.	**Tobacco Road**	The Nashville Teens
12.	**Gloria**	Them
13.	**Glad All Over**	The Dave Clark Five
14.	**For Your Love**	The Yardbirds
15.	**Wild Thing**	The Troggs
16.	**The House Of The Rising Sun**	The Animals
17.	**Concrete And Clay**	Unit 4 + 2
18.	**Go Now**	The Moody Blues
19.	**Just One Look**	The Hollies
20.	**Needles And Pins**	The Searchers

16. Going to a Go-Go

Smokey Robinson and The Miracles

TRACKLISTING

The Tracks Of My Tears/Going To A Go-Go/Ooo Baby Baby/My Girl Has Gone/In Case You Need Love/Choosey Beggar/Since You Won My Heart/From Head To Toe/All That's Good/My Baby Changes Like The Weather/Let Me Have Some/A Fork In The Road

RELEASED

US: November 1965 UK: February 1966

PRODUCED BY

William 'Smokey' Robinson

Bob Dylan once called Smokey Robinson America's greatest living poet. He may have said it in that half-joking and labored-enigmatic way that he employed to wind up interviewers, but ironically he may just have been right. Sure, he wasn't going to be appreciated in the same academic circles as Delmore Schwarz, but Robinson had the knack of speaking in a language that the girl employed as a waitress in a coffee shop or the guy who worked double shifts at the local auto assembly plant could understand. He was the poet laureate of love and romance. Handily, he was able to deliver his fine lyrics with a tenor voice as smooth as velvet.

His lyrics are witty, smart and profound: he is a storyteller, never afraid to confess his hurt in the first person. His voice is cool and reasonable unlike the aching, obsessed Temptations singer Levi Stubbs or passionate and hurting Marvin Gaye. Yet the laid-back and affable delivery is a front for the pain that permeates his songs. There's a whiff of the elegance of Nat King Cole in both his writing and his performance, albeit updated for the hipper '60s generation. Between 1959 and 1972, he wrote a string of hits, both for the Miracles and for other Tamla Motown acts – Mary Wells, The Temptations, The Four Tops and Marvin Gaye – and was one of the figures instrumental in shaping American pop music.

It was Robinson who suggested to fellow Detroit songwriter Berry Gordy that he set up his own label. This he did. The Miracles were one of the first acts signed to Tamla Motown. They also gave the label its first number one with 'Shop Around' (1960). Robinson was appointed Vice Chairman of the label and remained in that position as long as Gordy ran it.

Motown was not, initially, a great albums label. It was like a factory that just churned out hit singles, by artists that while not exactly manufactured were certainly groomed for success in a 'charm school' run by the label. The Motown Sound was the optimistic soundtrack of integration: Motown was a black-owned business that competed on seemingly equal terms with the white music establishment. Much has been made of Gordy

William ('Smokey') Robinson with the early 1960s' Miracles: Claudette Rogers Robinson, Ronald White, Pete Moore, and Bobby Rogers.

taking his inspiration from the Ford car factory production line as the model for Motown. Yet while the hits may have been mass produced, each song was lovingly hand finished. 'Going To A Go-Go' is a sleek Rolls Royce Silver Shadow in a marketplace of Model Ts.

Prior to Marvin Gaye's 1971 masterpiece *What's Going On*, a typical Motown album fulfilled the Phil Spector definition of "two hit singles and eight pieces of shit." Albums like The Four Tops' *Soul Spin*, The Vandellas' *Natural Resources*, and The Supremes' *Cream Of The Crop* were rather hokey cash-ins on the success of their hit singles padded out with some dismal filler. *Going To A Go-Go* bucks that trend by having a much lower shit-to-hit ratio. In fact the first side is almost like a Miracles Greatest Hits: the album contains all of their 1965 singles and their B-sides. It was the first release to give star billing to Smokey Robinson – previous releases had come out under the name "The Miracles" – and he wrote or co-wrote all but one of the 12 cuts. Despite the upbeat title track, a stomping partying dance craze song, many of the tracks are sad, filled with an aching yearning typified by the languid updated doo wop of 'Ooo Baby Baby'. It also contains some of Robinson's best, though least-known, songs like 'My Girl Has Gone' and the incredible 'A Fork in the Road', songs that could have been hits in their own right. Oddly, although it is probably the song most associated with Smokey Robinson and The Miracles, the opener 'Tracks Of My Tears' never actually made the Top 10 when it was released in 1965. It did well in the R&B charts but only went to Number 16 on the *Billboard* pop charts. Like many similar sophisticated '60s songs, its reputation grew years after it had dropped out of the Top 40.

This was the high water mark of Motown: after 1965 as America was torn apart by racial violence, anger about the war in Vietnam and a new spirit of militancy and black consciousness arose, the classy pop that Smokey Robinson produced started to seem a little old fashioned, like a strand of the '50s that had somehow lasted beyond its natural lifespan. Compared with Sly And The Family Stone, or even with the more raucous southern soul being released on Stax, Motown was starting to acquire a whiff of 'Uncle Tom'. The departure of the label's other main songwriters, the team of Holland-Dozier-Holland, in 1967 didn't help matters. Yet at its peak Motown was turning out a hit single a week and the label's slogan The Sound Of Young America was justified.

The *Going To A Go-Go* album was recorded relatively quickly while Robinson was in the midst of a writing and producing flurry that saw him create a string of hits for Marvin Gaye and The Temptations. It's a testament to everyone concerned – Robinson, The Miracles, the Motown house band The Funk Brothers – that they were able to maintain high quality under such arduous conditions. Few could have done it.

Even fewer displayed Robinson's elegant turn of phrase and knack for a dazzling couplet. Dylan may not have been serious but Robinson was a poet and he knew it. He proved to other songwriters that they could also put stylish and complicated words and phrases into songs even if they were aiming for the charts. - Tommy Udo

17. Aftermath
The Rolling Stones

TRACKLISTING
US:Paint It Black/ Stupid Girl/Lady Jane/Under My Thumb/Doncha Bother Me/Think/Flight 505/High And Dry/It's Not Easy/I Am Waiting/Goin' Home

UK:Mother's Little Helper/Stupid Girl/Lady Jane/Under My Thumb/ Doncha Bother Me/Goin' Home/Flight 505/High And Dry/Out of Time/ It's Not Easy/I Am Waiting/Take It Or Leave It/Think/What To Do

RELEASED
US: July 1966 UK: April 1966

PRODUCED BY
Andrew Loog Oldham

"The Rolling Stones are more than just a group – they are a way of life", asserted their manager, Andrew Loog Oldham, on the back cover of their debut LP. But as Greil Marcus contended in his 1979 anthology *Stranded*, it wasn't until *Aftermath* was released two years later that "the 'way of life'... Oldham had promised the Stones would carry forth fell into place." For while the Stones had started writing their own singles (and classic ones) a year earlier, *Aftermath* was their first album to feature entirely original material – indeed, their first LP in which compositions by vocalist Mick Jagger and guitarist Keith Richards even comprised the majority of the set.

Their arch-rivals, the Beatles, had long outdistanced them in this respect, putting their first all-original album together back in mid-1964 with *A Hard Day's Night*. At the same time, the Fabs and Bob Dylan were raising the bar for pop lyrics to previously unimagined heights. *Aftermath* was the Rolling Stones' bid to be taken as seriously as the rest of '60s rock's Big Three.

On most counts, *Aftermath* was a raging success in that regard. To again drag out the Beatles-Dylan comparisons, Jagger and Richard were never going to be the equal of John Lennon and Paul McCartney as melodicists; nor were they going to touch Dylan as wordsmiths. Yet, at the same time, they possessed an earthier raunch than the Beatles and a far keener grasp of pop hooks than Dylan. Most importantly, their attitude was both poles apart from either of those artists, and one that set them aside from any stars in their field. There was a realistic cynicism that nicely countered the far more upbeat, optimistic Beatles, and a sexual frankness that was far more

The original cover
for *Aftermath*.

magnetic than Dylan's surrealistic ruminations. Hand-in-hand with that
sexual frankness, perhaps, was a rebellious (although not political) tone.

　　In purely musical terms, *Aftermath* established the Rolling Stones
as masters of combining the blues and soul they loved with pop appeal,
putting the whole brew into a contemporary context relevant to their own
lives. The blues-pop fusion sensibilities of the Stones have been overlooked,
with many critics preferring to emphasize the group's roots in African-

American music. But the Stones had already proved they could respectfully translate black soul and blues for a young white audience; now they were meeting the new challenge of using tunes and song structures without obvious precedents in R&B. None of the album's standouts - 'Mother's Little Helper', 'Lady Jane', 'Out of Time', and 'Under My Thumb' - follow anything like blues progressions, adding liberal pop, jazz, and folk elements to the proceedings. In this respect, multi-instrumentalist Brian Jones deserves a great deal of credit for expanding the group's range of sonic colors, contributing such exotic sounds as sitar, marimbas and dulcimer.

Aftermath's biggest (though not necessarily great) contribution to the pop lexicon, however, was its no-holds-barred depiction of lust. No white performers had sung, at such length anyway, about sexual games with such unapologetic straightforwardness, or such unapologetic snideness. Here resides the track, more than any other, that has generated accusations that the Stones are misogynists, 'Under My Thumb' (grounded as it is by a dynamite riff that could have made it a huge hit single). The blunter and less impressive 'Stupid Girl' will not win any awards for political correctness either, while 'Out Of Time' - another cut that could have been a huge hit single, as Chris Farlowe's much inferior, poppier UK chart-topping cover demonstrated - is the most eloquent girlfriend-as-doormat kiss-off ever devised. Other, more minor cuts – 'Think', 'Doncha Bother Me', 'Take It or Leave It' - are similar exercises in the art of putdown, viewing women as rather unnecessary, replaceable pains in the ass. All of this solidified the group's image as anti-heroes, determined to be their own men even if it meant adding insult to injury.

Yet it would be a mistake to dismiss Aftermath as a one-dimensional album. Mick Jagger showed a surprisingly courtly side in the Elizabethan folk ballad 'Lady Jane' (a minor US hit single), and the group took on subjects beyond bruised romance on 'Mother's Little Helper' (a Top Ten US hit), which examined themes (pill-popping dependency, fear of aging) virtually no one was dealing with in pop songs in early 1966. Their underrated zeal for pure shit-kicking country music came to the fore in 'High and Dry'. The underrated 'I Am Waiting', as well as 'Take It Or Leave It' (covered for a small UK hit by The Searchers), showed a similarly overlooked penchant for brooding, reflective folk-rock. And 'Flight 505', though unremarkable musically, was a story-song with nothing to do, oddly enough, with sex, drugs, or rock 'n' roll.

There are flaws to Aftermath, the biggest being its inconsistency. It's far more uneven than the mid-'60s LPs by the Beatles and Dylan, with some melodically drab, drearily world-weary tunes ('Doncha Bother Me', 'What to Do'). Too, while the eleven-minute blues jam 'Goin' Home' was lauded for its barrier-breaking (for a rock recording) length, the fact is that it's not much of a song. That particular track's influence, too, could have been more negative than constructive, encouraging less talented bands to put their own overlong jams on record.

Entirely recorded in Hollywood, *Aftermath*, like so many British Invasion albums, was butchered for release in the US. 'What to Do', 'Take It Or Leave It', and (most unforgivably) 'Out of Time' were removed, though the latter two did appear the following year on the *Flowers* compilation; the admittedly brilliant #1 raga-rock single 'Paint It Black', was added as the leadoff track. Still, its influence in the US was considerable, particularly on countless American garage bands who emulated its sneer, albeit in a far more adolescent fashion. Its greater influence would be as a model for white groups of all kinds to sing what they felt, even if the subjects were unpleasant or the way the message was delivered might reflect unflatteringly on the performers or the song's characters. It wasn't the most admirable way of life, but after *Aftermath*, for many rock 'n' roll musicians and fans, it was *the* way of life. - Richie Unterberger

18. Blonde on Blonde
Bob Dylan

TRACKLISTING
Rainy Day Women #12 & 35/Pledging My Time/Visions Of Johanna/One Of Us Must Know (Sooner Or Later)/I Want You/Stuck Inside Of Mobile With The Memphis Blues Again/Leopard-Skin Pill-Box Hat/Just Like A Woman/Most Likely You Go Your Way And I'll Go Mine/Temporary Like Achilles/Absolutely Sweet Marie/4th Time Around/Obviously 5 Believers/Sad Eyed Lady Of The Lowlands

RELEASED
US: May 1966 UK: August 1966

PRODUCED BY
Bob Johnston

In the early '70s Bob Dylan said to his biographer Anthony Scaduto of *Highway 61 Revisited*, "I'm not gonna be able to make a record better than that one. *Highway 61* is just too good." While not unaware of *Highway 61 Revisited*'s brilliance, many people beg to differ with Dylan, citing this album as his *mesiterwerk*. It was the third Dylan album released in the space of fourteen months that was destined to be considered a classic, a quite staggering statistic. But then in 1965/66, Dylan was on a roll unequalled in popular music history.

Dylan however was not a hero in all quarters. The people who had followed Dylan before 'Like A Rolling Stone' were so outraged by his conversion to electric music/pop that they were not going to be mollified by classic records. However anti-The Man 'Like A Rolling Stone' might seem, that Dylan was clearly not interested in denouncing the likes of the persecution of James Meredith or the killing of Hattie Carroll anymore was unforgivable. The combination of that and his adoption of the trappings of supposed adolescent trash music – its clothing fashions and its instrumentation – were just too much. When Dylan went on a world tour in 1966, the – often pedestrian - acoustic set with which he opened each gig was received well but when he then returned from the wings with a full group (The Hawks) and played the audience some of the greatest music ever heard on a concert stage, he was consistently booed to the rafters.

This wasn't the only pressure on Dylan at the time. When *Blonde On Blonde* appeared, it featured a cover picture in which Dylan would have seemed frazzled even if the shot were not out of focus. His manager Albert Grossman was treating Dylan in a way that was playing havoc with Dylan's well-being, working him beyond the limits of his constitution and acting as Dylan's drug supplier so as to artificially ensure his ability to maintain his inhuman workload and the revenue stream of which he had 25 per cent.

The original cover for *Blonde on Blonde*.

All of this formed the bizarrely mixed backdrop against which Dylan began working on the follow-up to *Highway 61*. In contrast to the way that Dylan had turned around that album in less than a week, creating *Blonde On Blonde* was a more difficult process. Recorded in between concert dates from October '65 to March '66, it got off to a rather stuttering start. Dylan did the logical thing of taking his road band into the studio but their sessions at Columbia Studios in New York yielded only 'One Of Us Must Know' and 'Can You Please Crawl Out Your Window'. Though the former did make the album and the latter (an ersatz 'Like A Rolling Stone') was released as a stand-alone single, Dylan was distraught by the lack of results. He then made an astonishing decision, one prompted by a comment a year or so previously by his producer Bob Johnston: he relocated the recording sessions to Nashville. This was astonishing because Nashville was a town then just as synonymous with musical and sociological conservatism as rock and pop were bywords for all things radical. However, it worked: all of the rest of the album was assembled from four days of Nashville sessions in February '66 and three more in March.

The good ol' boys of Music Row Studios, Tennessee – joined by keyboardist Al Kooper and Hawks guitarist Robbie Robertson – might have been bemused by the presence of the epitome of East Coast cool in their midst but this didn't stop them behaving with absolute professionalism as Dylan set them the challenge of playing along to songs the like of which neither they nor anybody else had ever heard. Also new to them was Dylan's singular method of recording. For instance, they were given scant instructions about a song called 'Sad Eyed Lady Of The Lowlands' and kept building up to a climax – then kept having to do it again when it transpired the song lasted more than eleven minutes. However, with other songs, the band knew them by heart before Dylan got to the studio, courtesy of Kooper, to whom Dylan played the songs in his hotel room.

'I Want You' and 'Just Like A Woman' dress subversive lyrics up in pretty pop structures. 'Pledging My Time' and 'Temporary Like Achilles' are black comedy blues numbers. 'Leopard Skin Pill-box Hat' is slapstick comedy blues. '4th Time Around' is also comedic, though in a mellow way. It's title probably refers to the fact that after Dylan gave John Lennon a demo version, a similar sounding song called 'Norwegian Wood' turned up on the next Beatles LP, *Rubber Soul*. 'Most Likely You Go Your Way And I'll Go Mine' and 'Obviously 5 Believers' are rip-roaring rock 'n' roll tracks. 'Visions Of Johanna' is an utterly beautiful depiction of a man distraught by the end of a love affair which never outstays its welcome despite its running time of 7:27. Some dispute the same can be said of 'Sad Eyed Lady Of The Lowlands' but the vulnerability and tenderness of this paean to Dylan's new wife Sara cannot be denied.

Dylan chose to climax the album with the latter number and to make it the only track on the last vinyl side – which was the first fourth vinyl side in rock history. *Blonde On Blonde* was the first double album, beating The Mothers Of Invention's *Freak Out* to the stores by two months.

Blonde On Blonde (no-one knows the meaning of the album title, but check the initials) completed the electric trio of albums begun with *Bringing It All Back Home* quite splendidly. Its influence is probably indistinguishable from that of those previous two records: they are all of a piece, each breathtaking in how intellectually and spiritually far ahead they were of everything else in music.

Though Dylan might consider *Highway 61* the better record, he does think that the type of music heard on *Blonde On Blonde* is his true sound. "The closest I ever got the sound I hear in my mind was on *Blonde*

On Blonde," he has said. "It's that thin, wild mercury sound. Its metallic and bright gold, with whatever that conjures up. That's my particular sound."
- Sean Egan

19. Pet Sounds
The Beach Boys

TRACKLISTING
Wouldn't It Be Nice/You Still Believe in Me/That's Not Me/Don't Talk (Put Your Head on My Shoulder)/I'm Waiting for the Day/Let's Go Away For Awhile/Sloop John B/God Only Knows/I Know There's An Answer/Here Today/I Just Wasn't Made for These Times/Pet Sounds/Caroline No
RELEASED
US: May 1966 UK: May 1966

PRODUCED BY
Brian Wilson

There has been surprisingly little written about the ramifications of the fact that the story of the entity known as the Beach Boys his been divided into several different phases.

Up to and including their third album *Surfer Girl* (1963), they were a band as people understand that term. From thereon through the original, unreleased *Smile* (circa 1967) they increasingly constituted merely bassist/melody writer/producer Brian Wilson and whichever session musicians he hired on the day – or, looking at it another way, they mutated into a mere vocal group, leaving the instruments and the lyrics to Wilson and *his* collaborators. From *Wild Honey* (1967) onwards, the band members who toured under the Beach Boys banner started playing on their record releases again. However, this wasn't the Beach Boys as in the pre-*Surfer Girl* era, for Wilson was no longer the creative fulcrum, his mental instability relegating him to being an equal member or, at times, a largely absent ghost. It's difficult to think of a major rock act that has gone through so many fundamental changes to its character, to such an extent that one wonders whether one can even claim a thread throughout the incarnations – unless those distinctive harmonies suffice.

In a sense, therefore, it makes one wonder whether one should examine *Pet Sounds* – the album intended as Wilson's response to The Beatles' *Rubber Soul*, which he was mesmerized by – as a part of the Beach Boys' development or as the beginning of Brian Wilson's stuttering solo career in which he was using "The Beach Boys" as a brand name. (Closer 'Caroline No' was actually released as a Wilson solo single.) Either way, the record had a massive effect. It was one of four giant albums

of its year of release: *Aftermath* by the Rolling Stones, *Revolver* by The Beatles and Dylan's *Blonde On Blonde* being the other three. Yet while the sales of those other three albums were in the region of what you would expect of product by such luminaries, *Pet Sounds'* sales were a relative damp-squib.

Not only that, but the group did not

The Brian Wilson-era Beach Boys, feeding the animals on the Pet Sounds cover.

even get much in the way of artistic kudos. At the time, they simply did not enjoy the sort of respect those other three artists did. When the Beach Boys pulled out of the 1967 Monterey festival and Jimi Hendrix made the caustic comment from the stage that "This ain't no surf music", people knew what he meant. With their neat hair, candy stripe suits, pristine harmonies and the conventional sentiments of songs like 'Wouldn't It Be Nice', the Beach Boys hardly seemed in step with the headband-sporting, bead-draped, authority-flouting ethics of the Love Generation. The fact that this album's 'God Only Knows' was the first pop single to feature the word "God" cut no ice with them. Wilson, though, had the last laugh: not only does *Pet Sounds* now frequently top polls to discover the greatest album ever recorded but its commercial viability has endured where other Beach Boys product has not: in 1997 It was the subject of a four-CD box-set release that included mono, true stereo, instrumental and vocal versions of the album, a deluxe treatment no other Beach Boys album is ever likely to be granted.

Not that the record was un-appreciated by Wilson's contemporaries at the time. Paul McCartney was stunned by it, recognizing that its lush vocals, mordant lyrics and symphonic textures raised the bar for popular music that little bit higher. Beatles producer George Martin has gone as far as to say that *Sgt Pepper…* would not have been made without the influence of *Pet Sounds*. Rolling Stones manager Andrew Loog Oldham took out music paper ads in the UK urging the public to buy it.

Pet Sounds marked the point where Wilson largely dispensed with the lyric writing services of Beach Boys vocalist Mike Love. Though the latter had helped seal the band's success with his finely observed vignettes of Californian teen life, Wilson specifically wanted his new collaborator to put out of his mind anything he associated with the Beach Boys precisely because he wanted to effect a departure form the band's previous sounds. His choice of collaborator was somewhat bizarre. Tony Asher was an advertising jingle writer with no experience of writing songs whom Wilson had met briefly in a recording studio. To his credit, Asher rose to the occasion marvelously, providing lyrics to some of the most well-loved – and most karaoke'd - Beach Boys songs ever. Amongst these are the opener 'Wouldn't It Be Nice', a creation whose jolly ambience disguises an aching lyric in which the narrator wishes that he and his lover did not have to part each night, and 'God Only Knows', less musically chirpy but a similarly exquisite, devotional love song.

The album certainly does sound unlike any previous Beach Boys record. The songs are awash in strings, keyboards, theramin and instruments so arcane that most had no idea they existed. Even the harmonies sound grander than normal, more like a celestial choir than a vocal group. (This may be something to do with a fact that has only recently emerged, namely that most of the vocals were performed by Wilson alone, re-doing parts without his colleagues' knowledge.) At times, the harmonies threaten to swamp the proceedings in a syrupy glop, but when the album is good it is stunning.

Because so many of the songs revolved around vulnerability, insecurity and alienation, some *Pet Sounds* fans have half-heartedly tried to portray the album as a concept piece. It's clearly not but it is undeniable that the sophisticated issues dealt with in tracks like 'You Still Believe In Me' and the quasi-disturbed 'I Just Wasn't Made For These Times' were not the stuff of which most pop was made in 1966. The jarring note on the album is provided by 'Sloop John B', a West Indies folk song released as a single the previous March. Though the idea that Wilson was forced to include it by the record company has been shown to be myth, its non-Wilson derivation, simplistic melody and lyrical irrelevance made it a throwback in the context of *Pet Sounds*. Whether Wilson appreciated it or not, 'Sloop John B' served the function of showing how laughable songs that had been considered acceptable began to seem as a consequence of the pioneering of Brian Wilson on this album. - Sean Egan

Don't Forget the Motor City!

(Tamla) **Motown** were the Sound Of Young America they claimed to be – but only in the singles charts. A list of great 45s by the record label that, up until What's Going On at least, just never seemed to care about albums.

1.	**Stop! In The Name Of Love**	The Supremes
2.	**Please Mr. Postman**	The Marvelettes
3.	**I Can't Help Myself (Sugar Pie Honey Bunch)**	The Four Tops
4.	**Heat Wave**	Martha And The Vandellas
5.	**Since I Lost My Baby**	The Temptations
6.	**ABC**	The Jackson 5
7.	**Money**	Barrett Strong
8.	**It's The Same Old Song**	The Four Tops
9.	**You've Really Got A Hold On Me**	The Miracles
10.	**This Old Heart Of Mine**	The Isley Brothers
11.	**Standing In The Shadows Of Love**	The Four Tops
12.	**Reach Out I'll Be There**	Four Tops
13.	**I Second That Emotion**	Smokey Robinson And The Miracles
14.	**First I Look At The Purse**	The Contours
15.	**Uptight (Everything's Alright)**	Stevie Wonder
16.	**(I'm A) Roadrunner**	Jr. Walker & The All Stars
17.	**Every Little Bit Hurts**	Brenda Holloway
18.	**I Heard It Through The Grapevine**	Marvin Gaye
19.	**War**	Edwin Starr
20.	**Where Did Our Love Go**	The Supremes

20. Freak Out!

The Mothers of Invention

TRACKLISTING

Hungry Freaks, Daddy/I Ain't Got No Heart/Who Are the Brain Police?/Go Cry on Somebody Else's Shoulder/Motherly Love/How Could I Be Such a Fool/Wowie Zowie/You Didn't Try to Call Me/Any Way the Wind Blows/I'm Not Satisfied/You're Probably Wondering Why I'm Here/Trouble Every Day/Help, I'm a Rock/It Can't Happen Here/The Return of the Son of Monster Magnet

RELEASED

US: June 1966 UK: March 1967

PRODUCED BY

Tom Wilson

There's some debate as to whether *Freak Out!* was the first double LP, as Bob Dylan's *Blonde on Blonde* came out around the same time; which was first depends on which reported release dates you believe. What no one denies, however, is that the absurdist satirical rock on *Freak Out!* had no real antecedents, with the marginal exceptions of the early recordings by The Fugs. Whereas the leaders of The Fugs were near-amateurs in the musical sophistication department, however (which was part of their very appeal), the Mothers were if anything so sophisticated that at times they seemed too highbrow for the rock-pop scene. Mothers frontman and guitarist Frank Zappa made liberal use of ideas from leading figures of the classical avant-garde, particularly Edgar Varese; it was also obvious that he was conversant with orchestral composition and aspects of cutting-edge contemporary jazz. The Mothers, too, were not the average Sunset Strip aspiring rock band in their late teens and early twenties, but relatively hardened veterans of the bar band circuit with serious journeyman R&B/doo wop chops. No one had really thought of mixing all this stuff together before, and no one, really, could have done it as well as Zappa.

Zappa's own view of rock 'n' roll, and its audience, seemed to waver between affection and contempt. That strange duality would both inspire some of his best work, and plague his attempts to find a wide audience throughout his entire career. Make no mistake, however: Zappa was, particularly at the outset of the Mothers' recording career, a *funny* guy. That much was evident from the relatively 'normal', song-oriented, first disc of this set. Never before (again, with the exception of the less musical Fugs) had anyone sung rock 'n' roll with such a sharply honed sense of social satire.

Never before, too, had this been done with compositions that simultaneously paid homage to and skewered rock 'n' roll musical idioms. A few of the tracks on disc one – 'How Could I Be Such a Fool', 'You Didn't Try To Call Me', 'Any Way The Wind Blows', 'Go Cry On Somebody Else's Shoulder' - could have been doo wop rock tunes if played straight. The Mothers *didn't* play them straight, however. They were sung and performed with out-and-out tongue-in-cheek sarcasm, as if devised expressly to piss off some typical exploitative indie label chief who'd ordered them to come up with formulaic teen mini-tragedies. But now, instead of getting fired by said indie label chief, the group was getting blessings from a major label (Verve, part of MGM) to sell these deconstructions to the public, even if Zappa would claim that producer Tom Wilson didn't really know what he was in for when he added the Mothers to Verve's roster, thinking they were "a rhythm & blues band."

The song-oriented disc of *Freak Out!*, however, contains much more than mere pastiches. There's paranoia ('Who Are the Brain Police?'), lust ('Motherly Love'), deliberately vacuous bubblegum ('Wowie Zowie'), a vicious anti-romantic screed ('I Ain't Go No Heart'), a jaded portrait of the self-styled 'freaks' populating Sunset Strip ('Hungry Freaks, Daddy'), surrealistic existentialism ('You're Probably Wondering Why I'm Here'), and a sourpuss pisstake of adolescent frustration in general ('I'm Not Satisfied'). All of it's sung with the knowing sarcasm common to the youth on the street, but which had yet to make its way into popular song. It could have made for a silly, or worse, grating listen. The thing is, though, that most of the tunes - as much as the late Zappa might roll over in his grave at the praise - are actually damned catchy, almost in spite of themselves. It's hard to combine comedy and rock; almost no one's been successful at it, other than Zappa and a precious few others. Disc one of *Freak Out!*, however, succeeds because it's not just funny (if sometimes mean-spiritedly so), but also pretty enjoyable musically on its own terms. Even all those thrown-in quotes from horror movie soundtracks and sardonically scatted doo wop phrases serve as loving punctuation marks, not distractions.

Disc two of *Freak Out!* is more challenging and notorious, almost as if Zappa planned to lull the listener into a happily comic (if adventurous) frame of mind with the first set. 'Trouble Every Day', the song that first brought the Mothers to the attention of Tom Wilson, is a straight six-minute doom-laden blues, but one that again evokes paranoia (this particular tune inspired by the then-recent Watts Riots in Los Angeles). The eight-minute 'Help I'm a Rock' gets much stranger, however, though its bad acid trip soundtrack elements and self-conscious references to freaking out have dated it, as much of a favorite as it was to college kids turning on for the first time in their dormitories. The grating sound collage hinted at with 'Help! I'm a Rock' was mild, though, compared to the all-out assaultive musique concrete of the side-long 'The Return Of The Son of Monster Magnet'. As a sort of *avant-garde* disaster film soundtrack, it's undeniably bold and experimental; as a piece of music, it makes for tough, unpleasant listening, though that might have been the point.

Freak Out!'s influence was not so much in inspiring similar albums, as few could hope to emulate its idiosyncrasy. Its effect was more to inspire similarly risk-taking, precedent-shattering ventures in all of rock music, whether in presenting deliberately experimental, inaccessible work, or putting together double-LPs of such length in the first place. Certainly

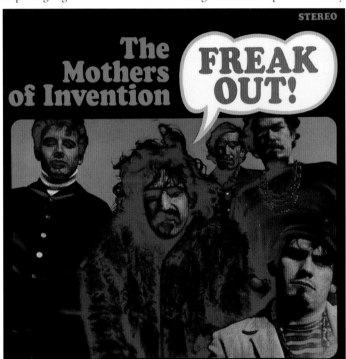

The original *Freak Out!* artwork.

Captain Beefheart went to even more extreme lengths in his late-'60s Zappa-produced double album *Trout Mask Replica*, which used some similar *avant-garde* concepts within rock music, though with a very individual style. Lou Reed went to even more extreme lengths than 'The Return Of The Son of Monster Magnet' with his legendarily unlistenable mid-'70s double album of electronic noise, *Metal Machine Music*. And the legions of alternative rock bands from the past decade or two who've made sarcastic, smutty satire a linchpin of their worldview owe a considerable, if distant, debt to the early work of the Mothers of Invention. In that sense,

the Mothers might have been more at home in a later era than their own - though, as so often is the case, their work as originators of the form stands head and shoulders over what their descendants have produced.
- Richie Unterberger

21. Fifth Dimension
The Byrds

TRACKLISTING
5-D (Fifth Dimension)/Wild Mountain Thyme/Mr. Spaceman/I See You/ What's Happening?!?!/I Come And Stand At Every Door/Eight Miles High/Hey Joe (Where You Gonna Go)/Captain Soul/John Riley/2-4-2 Fox Trot (The Lear Jet Song)

RELEASED
US: July 1966 UK: September 1966

PRODUCED BY
Allen Stanton

Few albums are at once as exhilarating and frustrating as *Fifth Dimension*. Its most magical moments soar as high as the magic carpet on which the artists are pictured on the cover. Its lesser tracks are not just filler in comparison, but wouldn't have even made for interesting outtakes, the band making major missteps as both stylists and performers. Yet even at the worst of times, The Byrds were always eclectic experimentalists, determined to meld the best of the folk traditions in which they were grounded with the most futuristic sounds of tomorrow and there are few more eclectic albums by a major 1960s rock group than *Fifth Dimension*.

Fifth Dimension's key track, 'Eight Miles High', alone carried more innovation than most entire albums. This was the recording, more than any other, responsible for introducing Indian influences and jazz improvisation into rock music, combining the sitar ragas of Ravi Shankar and the free flights of John Coltrane with a wholly electric rock energy. On top of this were the foreboding (yet angelically harmonized) lyrics, at once suggestive of both figurative flights to the cosmos and quite literal LSD trips. Byrds singer-guitarist Roger McGuinn, who wrote the song with fellow original Byrds guitarists Gene Clark and David Crosby, always insisted that the composition was not inspired by drugs, instead being a quite literal tale of their mixed impressions (and reception) during their first trip to the UK on a 1965 tour. That wasn't the way many listeners heard it, however. Unfortunately, that wasn't the way some key radio programmers heard it either, and it stalled at #14 in the US in early 1966 after airplay had been banned or curtailed in some major markets.

'Eight Miles High' was actually released four months before *Fifth Dimension* hit the shops. In the meantime, The Byrds, always a volatile group despite the harmonious, even-keeled tone of their records, had undergone some troubling changes. Gene Clark had left the group, and although he didn't have the public profile of McGuinn and Crosby, he *had* been responsible for writing most of their original material. There were fears that the rest of the Byrds wouldn't come close to picking up the slack. The alternative might have been continuing to rework songs by the likes of Bob Dylan and Pete Seeger, as they'd done for their big hits 'Mr. Tambourine Man' and 'Turn! Turn! Turn!' respectively. As innovative as those folk-rock classics were when they first appeared, sticking to such electrified interpretations would have led to an artistic dead end. Too, the group ended their association with their original producer, Terry Melcher, who'd lent vital assistance to their first two albums.

Remarkably, however, The Byrds not only continued as a quartet (not even bothering to replace Clark), but with *Fifth Dimension*, McGuinn in particular proved up to the task of crafting some striking original material for the group (with some help from Crosby) that staked out new directions that the original quintet had never explored. Melcher was replaced by Allen Stanton, and if Stanton was more a caretaker than a collaborator, he at least had the good sense not to interfere with what were, for 1966, some pretty far-out ideas. At the forefront in that respect is the LP's title track, which put McGuinn's fascination with science fiction into lyrics that made a trip (again, one sometimes construed as drug-inspired) into outer space sound like nothing less than a portal into an entirely different, blissful state of consciousness.

Yet at its heart, '5-D (Fifth Dimension)' is much like the wayfarer folk ballads with which he and Crosby had cut their teeth on the early-'60s folk circuit, now stripped of corniness and dragged not only into the twentieth century, but somewhere beyond that. 'Mr. Spaceman' (which, like '5-D (Fifth Dimension)', was a minor hit single) might have even done the title track one better, as its jaunty narrative of space exploration is married to a bluegrass-like tune and beat that anticipates country-rock by a good two years or so. 'I See You' doesn't even reference folk or country forms, its succession of mystical images connected by the group's trademark ghostly harmonies and McGuinn's peerless jagged jazz-raga-rock 12-string guitar rips.

When *Fifth Dimension* stumbles, however, it falls on its face. 'Captain Soul' is a lame Booker T. & the MGs-type soul-blues jam; 'What's Happening?!?!' unveils Crosby's weakness for stoned, almost instantly dated hippyisms; 'Hey Joe', surprisingly, is one of the least memorable versions of that oft-covered '60s standard (Crosby again being at fault, with his mediocre vocal); and '2-4-2 Fox Trot (The Lear Jet Song)' is ambitious space-age experimentation without the content of 'Fifth Dimension', 'Eight Miles High', or 'Mr. Spaceman'.

Yet even as they threatened to vaporize into the next galaxy, the Byrds reinforced their credentials as the best folk-rock interpreters

The mid-1960s Byrds – Gene Clark, David Crosby, Roger McGuinn, Michael Clarke, Chris Hillman

with updates of traditionally-structured folk songs that were both tasteful and adventurous. 'Wild Mountain Thyme' and 'John Riley' are gorgeously harmonized electrified traditional tunes with subdued string arrangements that manage to enhance the drama rather than pour on the syrup. 'I Come And Stand at Every Door' is brilliant from every angle, taking a Seeger translation of an obscure poem, putting it to a melody of a familiar folk ballad ('Great Selchie Of Shule Skerry'), and turning the whole thing into a scary-yet-dignified caution against nuclear holocaust.

Fifth Dimension's commercial impact was relatively modest, The Byrds already fading in popularity even as their musical brilliance continued unabated. Yet its combination of American roots music and '60s rock 'n' roll with then-exotic elements of Indian music and jazz improvisation - as well as its sly references to outer space, inner consciousness, and drugs - had a far-reaching effect that can't be overstated. Innumerable late-'60s psychedelic albums would follow a similar model, in terms of both the specific elements they incorporated and a dedication to risk-taking eclecticism. Alas, that often led to self-indulgent excess. What the Byrds understood - and what so many who followed didn't - was that psychedelic invention was best served by a combination of the best of old and new, rather than all-out kamikaze missions into the heart of the sun.
- Richie Unterberger

22. Revolver

The Beatles

TRACKLISTING

US: Taxman/Eleanor Rigby/Love You To/Here, There And Everywhere/
Yellow Submarine/She Said, She Said/Good Day Sunshine/For No
One/I Want To Tell You/Got To Get You Into My Life/Tomorrow
Never Knows

UK: Taxman/Eleanor Rigby/I'm Only Sleeping/Love You To/Here, There
And Everywhere/Yellow Submarine/She Said She Said/Good Day
Sunshine/And Your Bird Can Sing/For No One/Doctor Robert/I Want To
Tell You/Got To Get You Into My Life/Tomorrow Never Knows

RELEASED

US: August 1966 UK: August 1966

PRODUCED BY

George Martin

Something was going on on *Rubber Soul*, The Beatles' sixth (going by UK
configurations) album, released in December 1965. The cover was weird for
a start: the Fab Four's handsome faces distorted in a way that must have
seemed horrendous to the teenyboppers amongst their audience. The music
was mainly acoustic. Who were they trying to be? That Dylan chappie from
America? And what did that title mean – it had nothing to do with the
songs on the album, as far as anyone could make out. Additionally, there was
a line in 'Norwegian Wood' that raised a few eyebrows: "And then she said
it's time for bed."

      Utterly unremarkable though those things might seem from
today's perspective, they created a *frisson* of mild shock for those who
perceived The Beatles as charming and sexless as choir boys (i.e. everyone
except their wives/girlfriends, groupies and their inner circle). The Beatles
were growing up. *Rubber Soul* though was musically fairly tentative in its
explorations of new territory – there wasn't anything on it that would cause
much more than a crinkled nose amongst those who bought their records
because they and their music were so *nice*. *Revolver*, however, was a different
kettle of fish. Everything about it sounded sophisticated. There was a
burnished tone to every track, a sparkling, almost precision-tooled slickness
(contributed to by the almost complete absence of acoustic instruments).
Though the distinctive three-part Beatles harmonies were still present, they
now sounded aloof where before they had been giddy. There were also

outside instrumentalists, hitherto rare on Beatles product. The album's songs weren't just sophisticated. Some were weird and some were shot through with a cynicism one would not previously have imagined of the happy, smiling mop tops, a couple of tracks on *Rubber Soul* excepted.

The feeling of polish and layering was the consequence of the band having a previously unimaginable luxury in the studio: time. 1966 was their first full year as recording artists in which they did not release two albums. In contrast to the last-minute scramble that saw them having to come up with two songs overnight to fill out *Rubber Soul* in time for the Christmas market, they spent two months in the studio recording *Revolver* and both sides of the 'Paperback Writer' single that came out two months before. Almost as if to illustrate a point, the first thing they worked on was a song without precedent in The Beatles' catalogue: 'Tomorrow Never Knows'. More a sound collage than a song, it features a hypnotic, colossal drum track, tapes tweaked to sound like seagulls, a droning ambience and a vocal from John that sees him intoning parts of hippie bible *The Tibetan Book Of The Dead* from what sounds like the top of a canyon. The fans who had bought 'She Loves You' had grown up – but *that* much? Much the same could be said of Harrison's 'Love You To', a philosophical treatise with a background of pounding tablas and groaning sitars.

The album (or the UK version thereof; this was the last Beatles album with differences in tracklistings either side of the Atlantic) starts with a triumvirate of devastating brilliance, collectively displaying the breathtaking breadth of The Beatles' abilities and each a showcase for an individual Beatle's writing gifts. George's 'Taxman' is glorious hard rock and a track that could hardly be said to be pandering to their audience's daily concerns, being a rich man's lament notable for the un-Beatle-like scathing nature of its comments about prime ministers Ted Heath and Harold Wilson. Paul's 'Eleanor Rigby' is a dissection of the desolation of loneliness, credit for much of the icy beauty of which must go to George Martin, who devised the swooping string arrangement. The lovely 'I'm Only Sleeping' (John) is a suitably puffy-eyed paean to the glories of turning the pillow over to the cool side.

While the Lennon/McCartney songwriting axis was clearly going from strength to strength, this was the album where Harrison and Starr really came into their own as instrumentalists. As well as his flowering composing abilities, Harrison shows great development in his guitar work, which is gleaming, streamlined and fluid throughout – especially on hard rockers 'And Your Bird Can Sing' and 'She Said, She Said' – and a stark contrast to the way his lip-bitten contributions made songs sag in the middle on the first two Beatles LPs. Starr, meanwhile, is stunning on 'Tomorrow Never Knows' (and thunderously magnificent on 'Rain', flipside of 'Paperback Writer').

Up until perhaps the early 'Eighties, the prevailing wisdom was that each Beatles album up to and including *Sgt. Pepper..* was an incremental advance. Today, the consensus is that *Revolver* is actually the superior record, its concise songs making it a sort of pop version of the more discursive *Pepper.* Some Beatles fans, though, don't actually like *Revolver.* It has a cold tone unusual for The Beatles, who if they were anything were an act whose music pulsated with warmth and humanity. The horn chart in Stax-pastiche/ tribute 'Got To Get You Into My Life', for instance, is breathtaking but ultimately the song feels empty. 'Here, There and Everywhere' is undoubtedly pretty but again the overall impression is

The Beatles at Plymouth Hoe, 12 September 1967.

of mere surface polish and little emotional substance. Only the children's singalong 'Yellow Submarine' (sung by Ringo) and the happy-and-I-know-it 'Good Day Sunshine' exhibit the familiar Beatles mateyness, although the exquisite 'For No One' can also tug heartstrings.

In term of its influence, it is not an insult to say that *Revolver* mainly inspired people by default. Though containing its own innovations, on *Revolver* The Beatles were mainly following in the footsteps of Dylan's broadening of rock's lyrical possibilities and The Byrds' and the Stones' expanding of its musical horizons. But in taking the ideas and innovations of others to a mass market that Dylan, The Byrds and even the Stones could not, they introduced those new ideas to a whole swathe of a generation of kids and budding musicians that would have otherwise remained untouched by them. The Beatles were music's gods: what they did today, the rock world did tomorrow. But they were gods for a reason: sheer glorious craftsmanship, the type of which is to be discerned in so many places here. - Sean Egan

Do Ya Like Good Music?

Just after it had evolved out of rhythm & blues and just before it mutated into funk, black music often featured plenty of brass, sometimes lots of stomping but always a shedload of passion. A selection, from the era when sweet **soul music** was dominant and beyond.

1.	**Sweet Soul Music**	Arthur Conley
2.	**Twistin' The Night Away**	Sam Cooke
3.	**Green Onions**	Booker T & The MGs
4.	**Reet Petite**	Jackie Wilson
5.	**Papa's Got A Brand New Bag**	James Brown
6.	**Sittin' On The Dock Of The Bay**	Otis Redding
7.	**When A Man Loves A Woman**	Percy Sledge
8.	**What'd I Say**	Ray Charles
9.	**In The Midnight Hour**	Wilson Pickett
10.	**Hold Back The Night**	The Trammps
11.	**Midnight Train To Georgia**	Gladys Knight And The Pips
12.	**Walk On By**	Dionne Warwick
13.	**Knock On Wood**	Eddie Floyd
14.	**Tired Of Being Alone**	Al Green
15.	**When Will I See You Again**	The Three Degrees
16.	**It's A Man's Man's Man's World**	James Brown
17.	**Cry To Me**	Solomon Burke
18.	**Theme From Shaft**	Isaac Hayes
19.	**I've Been Loving You Too Long**	Otis Redding
20.	**Soul Man**	Sam And Dave

23. Parsley, Sage, Rosemary and Thyme
Simon & Garfunkel

TRACKLISTING
Scarborough Fair-Canticle/Patterns/Cloudy/Homeward Bound/The Big Bright Green Pleasure Machine/The 59th Street Bridge Song (Feelin' Groovy)/The Dangling Conversation/Flowers Never Bend with the Rainfall/A Simple Desultory Philippic (Or How I Was Robert McNamara'd into Submission)/For Emily, Wherever I May Find Her/A Poem on the Underground Wall/7 O'Clock News-Silent Night

RELEASED
US: September 1966 UK: October 1966

PRODUCED BY
Bob Johnston

"I never considered that the Rolling Stones were at the same level. I always was well aware of the fact that S&G was a much bigger phenomenon in general."

At first, this quote from Paul Simon, in response to the information that every Simon & Garfunkel album had sold more copies than any Stones album except *Sticky Fingers*, seems preposterous. The Rolling Stones were the swaggering epitome of the rebellious spirit of the 1960s and their music the very quintessence of the aesthetics of rock. Simon & Garfunkel were a couple of well-mannered, uncharismatic preppies whose music was seen as the soft option for those who wanted to embrace protest but turned up their noses at both raw music and civil disobedience. They were whitebread radicals not far removed from Peter, Paul and Mary.

In actual fact, Simon & Garfunkel arguably did more to change society than Jagger & co could ever claim. Yes, one can make the point that sales are no barometer of anything in particular but one can also make the point that in order to be populist, one has to be popular. Simon & Garfunkel's (relative) tameness was what made them palatable to a middle America that could barely tolerate the presence of the records of the Stones or The Doors in their households. And it wasn't just teens and twentysomethings who bought Simon & Garfunkel records: parents were also partial to their pretty harmonies and sumptuous melodies. Because of this, the values and beliefs of Simon & Garfunkel's generation were exposed to a far more conservative audience than had ever previously listened to post-Elvis pop and the pair's very niceness helped convince that audience that their values were not something to be scared of.

This was the third album recorded together by singer Art Garfunkel and guitarist/songwriter/singer Paul Simon, but in a sense their first 'real' one. 1964 debut release *Wednesday Morning, 3am* was a hesitant affair, half comprised of covers. Simon blossomed as a songwriter in the year-and-a-quarter between that and the 1966 follow-up *Sounds Of Silence* and he filled an entire solo album, *The Paul Simon Songbook* (1965), with originals. That aforesaid second Simon & Garfunkel long player contained a lot of songs from *Songbook* and was recorded in something of a rush following the pair having been unexpectedly given a smash record by producer Tom Wilson, who had added electric instrumentation to their original acoustic version of 'The Sound Of Silence'. Finally, with the album currently under discussion, the pair were able to relax. In fact, the three months they took to record this album was a veritable marathon for the period – although the rather speedier scheduling process of the day and the perceived hunger of the market ensured it appeared in the same calendar year as *Sounds Of Silence*. Though the subsequent *Bookends* and *Bridge Over Troubled Water* were even more considered, and possibly more accomplished, artistic statements, the apex of the influence of S&G was this record, which sounded young and vigorous in contrast to a certain world weariness that seemed to set in prematurely on its successors.

The album opens and closes with songs so old as to be susceptible to the old trick of claiming them as the artist's with no fear of legal comeback, 'Scarborough Fair' and 'Silent Night'. The former is intertwined with a Simon original called 'Canticle'. The latter sees a hymn of tranquility counterpointed by a solemn-voiced newsreader intoning the day's reports of death and destruction. The political message of the latter is trite, even meaningless, and is exactly the kind of thing that made many people despise Simon & Garfunkel. As is 'The Dangling Conversation', a tortured dissection of a fading love affair with the irredeemably bourgeois line, "You read your Emily Dickinson, and I my Robert Frost". While this might make hardcore rockers guffaw, many of them will have been reduced to apoplexy by 'A Simple Desultory Philippic (Or How I Was Robert McNamara'd Into Submission)', a send-up of Bob Dylan's singular writing style that was a bloody cheek coming from somebody whose idea of protest was this album's anti-materialist 'The Big Bright Green Pleasure Machine'. The latter was utterly toytown in comparison to Dylan protest like, say, 'The Lonesome Death Of Hattie Carroll'.

However, at their very worst, all the tracks mentioned so far are supremely listenable, helped in no small measure by the aural candyfloss that are the pair's harmonies. In any case, one can forgive the duo just about anything for the album's highlights. Hit single 'Homeward Bound' is an aching autobiographical lament about a touring solo singer who finds the applause of the audience no compensation for his loneliness.

'Cloudy' is a dreamy, onomatopoeic ditty about feeling lighter than air. 'A Poem On The Underground Wall' is a story of a graffiti artist so urgent as to leaveone too breathless to follow through one's suspicions of pretentiousness. 'For Emily, Whenever I May Find Her' is simply a touching love song of an unadorned, non ironic tenderness that Dylan at that stage would probably not have been capable of. Nor would he have been capable of the sheer giddy happiness conveyed in – and induced by – 'The 59th Street Bridge Song (Feelin' Groovy)'. His loss. The song is glorious, a typically gorgeous Simon melody decorated by fluid acoustic guitar figures and topped off with some more duo harmonizing in the celebratory chorus.

As well as their sociological importance discussed above, Simon & Garfunkel were musically as important as Dylan in the folk-rock genre that tore down the wall between the intellectual-but-dull folk genre and the exciting-but-simple medium of rock/pop. Though the whole movement

Paul Simon and Art Garfunkel, pictured on the 1966 album artwork.

81

was indisputably started by Dylan, it should be remembered that Dylan by this point had abandoned ordinary language for messages wrapped up in highly poetic but sometimes impenetrable metaphor. In remaining ultra accessible in both their music and lyrics, Simon & Garfunkel were ultimately just as responsible for the intellectualization of pop by dint of their very popularity. Perhaps sales sometimes are a barometer of something.

- Sean Egan

24. '66–'67

The Creation

TRACKLISTING
Making Time/Life Is Just Beginning/If I Stay Too Long/Through My Eyes/Hey Joe/Painter Man/Cool Jerk/How Does It Feel To Feel (UK version)/Try And Stop Me/I Am The Walker/Can I Join Your Band/Tom Tom

RELEASED
US: Not issued UK: July 1973

PRODUCED BY
Shel Talmy

As mentioned in the introduction to this book, a certain amount of cheating has gone on in the selection of albums featured herein. This is probably the most blatant example of such, for – excepting a continental European release *We Are Paintermen* – The Creation never actually issued an album during their original lifespan of 1966 to 1968. However, their influence on other musicians and music industry figures both of their own and subsequent generations, has – considering their lack of sales – been little short of amazing and demands their inclusion.

This compilation album was barely noticed upon its release, it being probably a sentimental gesture on the part of Charisma label head – and ex-Creation manager – Tony Stratton-Smith, but it does round up most of the recordings that made their reputation.

The original line-up of The Creation was comprised of Kenny Pickett on vocals, Eddie Phillips on guitar, Bob Garner on bass and Jack Jones on drums, all except Northerner Garner originating from London and its outskirts. They were taken under the wing of legendary producer Shel Talmy not long after his acrimonious split with The Who. Their debut single was 'Making Time'. It summed up their ability to straddle pop and the *avant-garde*: a catchy rebel's anthem, it featured utterly brutal instrumentation and electric guitar played with a violin bow, an innovation of Phillips that would become their sonic and visual trademark. The record only just climbed into the UK top fifty.

The group followed up that remarkable debut with art scene failure's anthem 'Painter Man'. This one was even more uncompromising in its use of the violin bow on Phillips' Gibson 335 but at the same time was actually more melodic than its predecessor. The contrast between the clipped, infectious chorus and snarling, buzzsaw instrumental break (broken catguts a go-go) was sublime. Flipside 'Biff Bang Pow' was a turbo-charged anthem for the Adam West *Batman*-literate. 'Painter Man' achieved a respectable UK chart placing of 36 but The Creation were not to build on that momentum, there being a – then huge – gap of eight months before their next record. By then Pickett had left and been replaced on vocals by Garner, with Kim Gardner coming in to cover bass duties. Remarkably, the result was an improvement.

At one point, The Creation's third single was going to be 'Can I Join Your Band', a track actually recorded during Pickett's tenure but really Phillips's showcase: he wrote both melody and lyric and performed vocals. It was a magnificent piece of work containing a picaresque lyric of gritty verisimilitude and alternately jaunty and barnstorming instrumentation (complete with double-time finale). If issued as a single it would have been the climax of one of the most impressive debut trio of singles in rock history. Instead it appeared only as a Belgian EP cut and to the band's bewilderment – their power over such things being non-existent – either Talmy or their record company decided to issue in the UK and US instead 'If I Stay Too Long', a fine, atmospheric ballad but a record that achieved a difficult feat in managing to make The Creation sound conventional. A better option would have been the proud, chest-out 'Tom Tom', chosen as the follow-up single in West Germany, which country gave The Creation their only real taste of being pop stars.

As would all their subsequent releases, 'If I Stay Too Long' failed to chart. At least on their next single they returned to their radical strengths. 'How Does It Feel To Feel' was an inferno of a record, the surrealism of Phillips' gargantuan guitar perfectly complemented by a glittering Garner lyric featuring lines like "How does it feel to slide down a sunbeam, bursting clouds on your way". By now, however, The Creation's moment had clearly passed. There was one last throw of the dice with 'Life Is Just Beginning', a beautiful meld of rock and classical but by the time it was released the creative fulcrum Phillips – weary of continual failure and experiencing problems in his marriage – had left, Garner following soon after. There were more singles from a new Creation which featured the return of Pickett but though quite enjoyable they lacked the cutting edge imparted by Phillips and were not included on this album. (Neither was a stunning version of 'How Does It Feel To Feel' released in America only which saw Phillips up the ante with the violin bow to create what was surely The Creation's masterpiece.) By April '68, The Creation in any format had ceased to exist and not long after that Phillips had turned to driving a bus for a living. He must have been kicking himself at having turned down the previous year an invite from admirer Pete Townshend to join either The Who or a new post-Who band (Townshend is not sure which but has verified the story).

But The Creation lived on in metaphysical ways. Led Zeppelin's Jimmy Page pinched the bowed electric guitar trick from Phillips and made it famous. '70s Disco sensation Boney M had an international hit with a cover of 'Painter Man'. The Sex Pistols performed 'Through My Eyes' live. The Jam issued a song called 'Private Hell', the name of a never completed Creation composition. Alan McGee was such a fan that he named his record label – a phenomenon of the '90s – after the band. (McGee's fanhood was also manifested in his later financing a pretty good 1996 studio reunion album by the original line-up.) Ride covered 'How Does It Feel To Feel', kyboshing a planned version by Oasis. The band's music now turns up in films ('Making Time' appeared in *Rushmore*) and on television ('Biff Bang Pow' has featured on a British television commercial).

Just as everybody who saw the Sex Pistols live seemed to form a band, so a disproportionate number of the very few people who ever heard a Creation record seemed never to forget it. - Sean Egan

25. The Doors
The Doors

TRACKLISTING
Break On Through (To The Other Side)/Soul Kitchen/The Crystal Ship/Twentieth Century Fox/Alabama Song (Whisky Bar)/Light My Fire/Back Door Man/I Looked At You/End Of The Night/Take It As It Comes/The End

RELEASED
US: January 1967 UK: March 1967

PRODUCED BY
Paul Rothchild

While most bands take a while to ramp up to their peak, The Doors started *at* their peak.

The Doors is a solid contender for the best debut album in rock history. They'd match its heights throughout the rest of their short career, but they'd never match its consistency. Too, its groundbreaking fusion of rock, blues, jazz, classical, poetry, and drug-laced lyricism would never again sound as startling. In part, that's because The Doors didn't evolve as substantially as many other top bands did. In part, however, it's because they had a hard time matching the standard that their inaugural release set.

In addition, *The Doors* was one of the first albums to start out as an underground phenomenon of sorts, and then spread over a period of months – by word of mouth, by the band's electrifying live performances, and finally, by snowballing airplay for the 'Light My Fire' single – into a massive hit record, reaching #2 in the US charts. The keys to its appeal are no secret. Jim Morrison's rich, resonant vocals might be the most renowned element, projecting both sexual intrigue and metaphysical mystery – which, in turn, were found in spades in the group's lyrics. But the contributions of the rest of the band can't be overstated. Ray Manzarek's organ took the haunting funereal grace of The Zombies to a new level; Robbie Krieger, who along with Morrison wrote a good deal of the material (it was Krieger who was largely responsible for 'Light My Fire'), played fluid but piercing jazz-blues guitar licks; and John Densmore, also taking many cues from jazz, played with far more varied imagination and drive than the average rock drummer. Plus, for all their adventurousness, The Doors' songs were very hummable and catchy, though retaining a sense of daring exploration that placed them squarely in the forefront of Californian psychedelia. (Unfortunately, neither the album nor 'Light My Fire' were hits in the UK, though eventually both were accorded respect as familiar classic rock recordings.)

Assessing the *influence* of *The Doors* is a tougher matter than explaining its popularity. The group's blend of tributaries was so idiosyncratic and identifiable that it was difficult to credibly imitate. It wasn't that hard, for instance, to sound *like* The Byrds (though sounding as *good* as The Byrds was an entirely different matter); it was almost impossible, however, to even sound *like* the Doors, let alone sound nearly as good. The album's significance, inasmuch as it impacted the larger rock scene, could be down to some factors beyond the style of the music.

First, the overwhelming majority of mid-'60s artists who had started taking rock music as a serious art form and a vehicle for sophisticated, poetic lyrics came from folk backgrounds (e.g., Bob Dylan, The Byrds). The Doors, however, were neither folk-rockers nor ex-folkies, even if Krieger was conversant with acoustic country blues styles such as bottleneck guitar, and Morrison an admirer of Dylan. Yet they were just as determined to insert poetry and art into the pop song. *The Doors* served notice to those not schooled in coffeehouse folk bohemia that such lyrical ambitions were now open season for anyone. It also served notice to the folk-rockers that they no longer had this field to themselves.

Second, even though 'Light My Fire' was a #1 single, The Doors were from their outset a very album-oriented act. 'Light My Fire' hadn't even been intended as a single release; the first 45 issued off the LP was 'Break On Through (To The Other Side)', which was only a hit in their local Los Angeles stomping grounds. It was only after 'Light My Fire'

The Doors, on the cover of their eponymous 1967 debut album.

started to get an avalanche of requests from their audience that it was pulled off the album as a single (and even then, its length was shortened by half, courtesy of deft editing to remove most of the instrumental break, to ensure AM radio airplay). Virtually all rock artists were in the game, from a commercial viewpoint at least, to get hit singles (and pop stardom) first, and hit albums (and critical respect) second. The Doors were among the first to approach this from the opposite direction. If they had hit singles, fine. But album-length artistic statements came first, and *The Doors* and Jefferson Airplane's *Surrealistic Pillow* were among the first to build followings through the still-young outlets of FM radio airplay and the psychedelic counterculture.

Speaking of which, *The Doors* was certainly an album on which many of the songs, particularly those whose lyrics were principally authored by Morrison, were strongly informed by actual acid trips. Morrison's LSD consumption in the mid-1960s is legendary, but as destructive as it might have been in some respects, it was certainly productive insofar as yielding some striking lyrical imagery. The enchanting 'The Crystal Ship' is a highlight in that respect. But his ability to draw from serious literature, drama, and philosophy - still a novelty when this album was recorded in Hollywood in late 1966 - must be noted and appreciated as well. The propulsive 'Break On Through (To The Other Side)' was a manifesto of sorts for his obsessions with transcending barriers into new realms of consciousness; 'End of the Night' took its title from a Louis Ferdinand-Celine novel; and the eleven-minute 'The End' was a shocking-for-its-time reenactment of Oedipal myth.

Although the excesses (and substance abuses) of Morrison's personal life are now renowned, what's remarkable is how focused he and the band are throughout this record.

Some feel that the more pretentious aspects of *The Doors* had a lamentable influence upon rock, inciting less talented blowhards to pontificate with far less skill. Yet its key role in introducing literary poetic sensibilities into rock was more worthy than not, and had an influence beyond psychedelia that extended to rock-poets of future generations. Certainly Patti Smith's fusions of dramatic poetry and hard-nosed rock 'n' roll owed a visible debt to the pioneering work of Morrison and The Doors, as did, more distantly, a whole school of new wave goth bands. And innumerable artists have borrowed liberally from the theatricality that the Doors introduced into rock on record and on stage, albeit usually in a far more lunkheaded way, from Alice Cooper to Marilyn Manson.
- Richie Unterberger

26. More of The Monkees

The Monkees

TRACKLISTING

She/When Love Comes Knockin' (At Your Door)/Mary, Mary/Hold On
Girl/Your Auntie Grizelda/(I'm Not Your) Steppin' Stone/Look Out (Here
Comes Tomorrow)/The Kind Of Girl I Could Love/The Day We Fall In
Love/Sometime In The Morning/Laugh/I'm A Believer

RELEASED

US: January 1967 UK: April 1967

PRODUCED BY

Tommy Boyce & Bobby Hart, Neil Sedaka & Carol Bayer, Michael
Nesmith, Jeff Barry, Jack Keller, Gerry Goffin & Carole King

Monkee Mike Nesmith once described this as the worst album ever made.
But then he and his colleagues were furious that it had been released
without their permission, that they had not been given the amount of
musical contribution to it they were promised and that The Monkees were
being denounced as frauds.

The Monkees were created as an American answer to
The Beatles – or, more specifically, a TV equivalent of the Fab Four
madcap-antics in their movie *A Hard Day's Night*. Although they released
records in a commercial double whammy, The Monkees' personnel was
hired primarily for their acting skills. Their first two albums contained a
couple of tracks which featured their own playing and writing but were
predominately comprised of recordings to which their only input was
vocals. Yet there were no outside musicians credited on the sleeves and in
an era where authenticity and credibility were everything, they found
themselves widely ridiculed, something which not even the fact that
they were top of both the ratings and the charts could act as consolation for.
This was particularly vexing to both Nesmith and Peter Tork, both able
instrumentalists and the former a gifted songwriter. (They would shortly
win the right to play on their records if they wished.)

More Of The Monkees, The Monkees' second album, is – contrary
to Nesmith's embittered assessment – pop bliss and testament to the
benefits of what became known as bubblegum music but which at the time
had no name because The Monkees were pioneering it: when the
powers-that-be behind a record decide that the demographic at which a
record is aimed isn't going to agonize or even care about who played on it,
they are then free to employ the top session musicians in the business on

songs provided by the industry's best freelance writers – to delirious effect.

Whereas the first Monkees album had been mainly supervised by songwriters Tommy Boyce and Bobby Hart (composers of their '(Theme From) The Monkees' signature number), their second long-playing effort featured a disparate array of producers and writers, something which Don Kirshner – president of record label Colgems – interminably made a virtue of in the sleevenotes. Boyce & Hart numbers did, however, open and close the original vinyl side one: 'She' was a stop-start piece of melodrama whose denunciatory lyric was impressively rendered by Micky Dolenz in his inimitable breathy style; he was equally impressive on '(I'm Not Your) Steppin' Stone', another denunciatory track (this time in the first person), a blistering put-down that was also done by Paul Revere and the Raiders but which has become indelibly associated with The Monkees.

The non-Boyce & Hart compositions were generally just as good. 'When Loves Comes Knockin' (At Your Door)' saw Davy Jones – diminutive heart-throb with a Beatles mop top – render a classy Neil Sedaka/Carole Bayer mid-tempo anthem with appropriate tenderness. Jones is just as good on the Neil Diamond song 'Look Out (Here Comes Tomorrow)' – even sort-of-daringly singing in his Manchester accent – but he really excels himself on 'The Day We Fall In Love', written by Sandy Linzer and Denny Randell. A spoken-word pledge of romantic devotion to an epic orchestral backing, it could easily have come across as preposterous but, by dint of his absolute sincerity, he makes it miraculously moving. Tork's vocal showcase 'Your Auntie Grizelda' could equally have backfired, not least because the classically trained pianist with the sad face couldn't really sing. However, this Keller & Hilderbrand-written comedy number in which a young man finds his ardor toward his girlfriend thwarted by the glacial disapproval of the titular auntie is genuinely quirky and funny – especially its raspberry solo. Nesmith gets a couple of tracks to prove his composing mettle and does so triumphantly: 'The Kind of Girl I Could Love' is a fine trip down Country Road while 'Mary, Mary', a sinewy mid-paced R&B number, is simply one of the best tracks here.

The icing on the cake is that the album closes with probably the archetypal Monkees hit of all time, 'I'm A Believer'. Neil Diamond's second contribution to the record, this instantly singalongable and euphoric track sees Dolenz doing his sighing thing for all he's worth. It went to number one in both the UK and US.

More Of The Monkees was the apotheosis of the bubblegum idea and its effects incalculable. Along with its parent TV, it show opened up popular music to a whole new audience (kids who had previously been thought too young to be interested) and to a new breed of music maker: people totally unconcerned with art, only with sales. Though this latter approach might nauseate some, as detailed above it can, as a by-product,

The fictional Monkees, played by the real band in a scene from the TV show *The Monkees*.

actually lead to great art. The year following the album's release Kasenetz and Katz would take the bubblegum cue and put out singles by the Ohio Express ('Chewy Chewy') and the 1910 Fruitgum Co ('Simon Says'), records whose musicians bore no relation to official band line-ups and which were deliberately pitched to kids who didn't care whether or not it was cool to like them. This thread has been present in popular music ever since, from The Archies (a project which took brazenness about artificiality to its logical extreme by marketing a cartoon group) and the Banana Splits through the Bay City Rollers on to much disco and later acts such as the Spice Girls.

A generation or two removed, this album is still in print, something that would have been unthinkable at the time, and testament to the fact that ultimately most are now concerned not with issues of authenticity but with the ultimate bottom line: listenability. - Sean Egan

27. I Never Loved a Man the Way I Love You
Aretha Franklin

TRACKLISTING
Respect/Drown in My Own Tears/I Never Loved a Man (The Way I Love You)/Soul Serenade/Don't Let Me Lose This Dream/Baby, Baby, Baby/Dr. Feelgood (Love Is a Serious Business)/Good Times/Do Right Woman—Do Right Man/Save Me/A Change Is Gonna Come

RELEASED
US: March 1967 UK: April 1967

PRODUCED BY
Jerry Wexler

Aretha Franklin really didn't find her artistic feet until signing to Atlantic and being allowed, and/or encouraged, to really let her gospel-fired soul loose. Almost right away, it resulted in two classic hit singles, 'I Never Loved a Man (The Way I Love You)' and 'Respect', both of them included in her first Atlantic LP, 1967's *I Never Loved a Man The Way I Love You*.

The singles, and this album, were groundbreaking on a number of fronts, even aside from their considerable artistic merits and their vast importance to Franklin's own career. There had been 'crossover' hits by black artists that appealed to both African-American and white audiences since rock began. But this was a crossover on a huge scale, experiencing simply vast (and roughly equal) popularity in both soul and pop charts, and in both black and white neighborhoods (and both ghetto and middle-class). In an era when it was uncommon for a soul LP to be consistently good-to-excellent throughout and a big success on the pop charts, *I Never Loved a Man The Way I Love You* was both, soaring to #2 in *Billboard*. The material itself, as well as most particularly the way Franklin delivered it, might have been only subtly sociopolitical, but both blacks and women – then, even more than now, disenfranchised in so many ways by mainstream society – found it (and 'Respect' especially) enormously empowering. All this, hearteningly, was achieved by an artist specifically prodded to be artistically uncompromising and sing from the gut, rather than to, as is so often the case in the music business, make the hit parade by softening or entirely avoiding those very qualities.

Though she had hitherto produced the occasional first-rate soul track (particularly with 'Lee Cross' and 'Soulville'), until her move to Atlantic Records, Franklin was generally saddled with ill-advised pop-oriented arrangementsand material. And whether she was pressured to smooth out her rough edges, or simply not properly directed or encouraged, she seemed reluctant to draw from the most personal, grittiest recesses of her physical voice and emotional soul.

Fortunately, Atlantic executive Jerry Wexler was astute enough to realize that, given the proper handling and musical backing, Aretha was capable of far more than she was delivering at Columbia. Signing her to Atlantic when her Columbia contract expired, his intention was to record her with top-flight Southern musicians to draw out her most soulful qualities. Wexler would in fact use this strategy with underachieving musicians on a number of occasionsin the ensuing years with white female singers (including Dusty Springfield, Lulu, Cher, and Ronee Blakley), and then, famously, with Bob Dylan during that singer's born-again period. His first idea was to record Franklin at the studios of Stax Records (which

Aretha Franklin, pictured on the cover of *I Never Loved a Man the Way I Love You.*

Atlantic was distributing at the time), but when that didn't work out, he arranged to take her to Muscle Shoals, producing the session himself.

That didn't quite work out either, though it did yield a Top Ten single (her first), 'I Never Loved a Man (The Way I Love You)'. The exact circumstances remain a bit murky, but Franklin's husband of the time got into a fight with a member of the all-white band, and the Franklins left Muscle Shoals the next day, even though the B-side (the quite excellent-in-its-own-right slow-burner 'Do Right Woman – Do Right Man') wasn't yet finished. Arguably, Wexler's decision to record Franklin with southern soul musicians was a key impetus to unlocking the soul she'd been harboring all along. As it happened, however, most of the album – all of it, in fact, except the title track and part of its B-side – would be recorded not in the South, but in New York, albeit with the participation of several of the Muscle Shoals players who'd been on the original session.

The singles were, as was the case with most LPs of the time, the standouts. The funky ballad 'I Never Loved a Man (The Way I Love You)' might have been the initial pick for a single, and an R&B chart-topper in addition to making the Top Ten. But it was her reinvention of Otis Redding's 'Respect' – remade from the inside out, and now not so much a plea as a demand – that really made her a superstar, getting all the way to #1 in the pop chart. Aretha wasn't involved in writing any of those 45 sides, but the album allowed her to present some of her own material, which stretched out into a rather poppier direction on 'Don't Let Me Lose This Dream' (co-written with her then-husband Ted White), which sounded a little like a more down-home Dionne Warwick. On the other hand, 'Dr. Feelgood (Love Is a Serious Business)' went all the way back to her gospel roots, as well as – like most of the LP – showcasing her bluesy piano playing, which was her most underrated asset. 'Save Me' was gospel-soul at its most galvanizing, and, like 'Do Right Woman – Do Right Man,' really could have been a chart hit in its own right. While the covers that filled out the album (Sam Cooke's 'Good Times', Ray Charles' 'Drown In My Own Tears', and Cooke again for 'A Change Is Gonna Come') weren't as remarkable, they also testified to Franklin's freedom to delve into juicier material than had found its way onto her Columbia discs.

While many hit singles and albums would follow for Franklin, none carried the impact of this debut. Let's leave the last word to Peter Guralnick's recollection of the event in his book *Sweet Soul Music*. Remembering the day *I Never Loved A Man* came out in Boston, he recalled going over to a local record store: "The little speaker over the door that was beamed to the sidewalk trade was filled with Aretha. People were dancing on the frosty street.. and lining up at the counter to get a purchase on that magic sound as the record kept playing over and over.." - Richie Unterberger

Cosmic

The late 'Sixties were the years when the possibilities afforded by the advancing recording studio technology and the desire to replicate the experience achieved by the ingestion of LSD converged, although some artists were buzzing on only pints of bitter as they did their **psychedelic** thing. Whatever the stimulus, some weird and wonderful records were the result.

1. **Pictures Of Matchstick Men** — Status Quo
2. **Crimson And Clover** — Tommy James And The Shondells
3. **King Midas In Reverse** — The Hollies
4. **See Emily Play** — Pink Floyd
5. **My White Bicycle** — Tomorrow
6. **Walking Through My Dreams** — The Pretty Things
7. **2000 Light Years From Home** — The Rolling Stones
8. **Hole In My Shoe** — Traffic
9. **White Rabbit** — Jefferson Airplane
10. **Green Tambourine** — The Lemon Pipers
11. **Children Of The Sun** — The Misunderstood
12. **My Friend Jack** — The Smoke
13. **Tapioca Tundra** — The Monkees
14. **Incense And Peppermints** — Strawberry Alarm Clock
15. **A Whiter Shade Of Pale** — Procul Harum
16. **Arnold Layne** — Pink Floyd
17. **Magic Carpet Ride** — Steppenwolf
18. **Ride My Seesaw** — The Moody Blues
19. **On A Carousel** — The Hollies
20. **Over Under Sideways Down** — The Yardbirds

28. Happy Trails

Quicksilver Messenger Service

TRACKLISTING
Who Do You Love, Pt. 1/When Do You Love/Where Do You Love/How
Do You Love/Which Do You Love/Who Do You Love, Pt. 2/Mona/
Maiden of the Cancer Moon/Calvary/Happy Trails

RELEASED
US: March 1969 UK: March 1969

PRODUCED BY
No producer credited

No major 1960s San Francisco rock band is as frustrating to critically evaluate as Quicksilver Messenger Service. On the one hand, in certain respects they were among the finest instrumentalists the Bay Area psychedelic scene produced. On the other, they had severe

Quicksilver
Messenger Service.

limitations as both singers and song writers. And while legend would have it that they could be a breathtaking group on stage, they had problems translating that magic to the cold, unforgiving format of a vinyl LP. Although *Happy Trails* was unquestionably their most popular album, and one of the most popular and influential among the entire San Francisco psychedelic genre, it suffered from major flaws that in some ways epitomized the more self-indulgent excesses of the style.

Quicksilver Messenger Service's eponymous debut LP (1968) was a decent record, but it was more oriented toward sturdy, rather modest folk-rock than the wilder, longer improvisations for which they were known in a live setting. Whether it was a conscious decision to set the record straight or not, the follow-up album, *Happy Trails,* focused very much on those long, live improvisations. To begin with, most of it was actually recorded live, in both the Fillmore West and Fillmore East. Even the sole track that wasn't done before an audience, 'Calvary', was cut live in the studio. Plus the tracks were, with a couple exceptions, *very* long. The cover of Bo Diddley's 'Who Do You Love', occupying all of side one, took no less than 25 minutes, most likely setting a record for the longest song that had been placed onto a rock album to that point. (And that track was actually edited together from longer performances!) Bo Diddley's 'Mona', leading off side two, was 'only' seven minutes. At that point, the album could have been titled *Quicksilver Messenger Service Does Bo Diddley*, but the band trailed off into a couple of instrumentals penned by guitarist Gary Duncan – one of which, 'Calvary', marched on for 13 minutes – before adding the unnecessary brief tag of 'Happy Trails' itself.

In its favor, *Happy Trails* did contain some sterling guitar work, particularly from John Cipollina. The problem was that the material was stretched out beyond all justification, leading to many extended bits where there was nothing to hold on to save the virtuosity of the players. Long, long rock songs *could* be innovative and thrilling on those occasions when the improvisation was set within solid melodic ideas and tightly executed alternation of contrasting passages, Paul Butterfield's 13-minute 'East West' and fellow Bay Area band Country Joe & the Fish's 'Section 43' being outstanding examples. 'Who Do You Love', however, was bending and distending a rock/R&B classic out of shape just for the sake of making it go on as long as it could. It was packaged in such a way as to modify its outrageous conceit, ostensibly (and pretentiously) divided into six differently-titled sections, some of them highlighting – *a la* countless jazz improvisations - the instrumental work of individual members.

But psychedelic rock, as much as it was influenced by the likes of John Coltrane and Ravi Shankar, isn't the same thing as free jazz or Indian raga. With rare exceptions, rock doesn't lend itself well to side-long jams, and 'Who Do You Love' takes too many liberties to be effective or all that interesting. However, it's true that it did fit in well with the Haight-Ashbury-spawned psychedelic scene inasmuch as it reflected that community's (and the Fillmore concert audience's) inclination to turn on to lengthy soundtracks for their acid trips, as reflected in other improvisations done (both on record and live) at the time by Jefferson Airplane, the Grateful Dead, the aforementioned Country Joe & the Fish, Big Brother & the Holding Company, Santana, and the Steve Miller Band. While 'Mona' is much shorter than 'Who Do You Love', it reflects another flaw afflicting many San Francisco bands (including all of the top ones): a weakness for long psychedelic covers of classic blues/R&B tunes that they couldn't sing nearly as well or soulfully as the original artists, compensating by pounding the songs into submission with extemporization.

The two Duncan instrumentals point to a weakness afflicting Quicksilver in particular: a shortage of strong original material, with both pieces drifting haphazardly, 'Calvary' meandering beyond all reason despite some flashes of arresting dramatic Spanish-tinged riffs. Although as noted most other San Francisco bands were prone to similar indulgences, they kept them in far greater check and compensated in other ways: the Airplane, for instance, weighted much of their repertoire toward strong concise folk-rock-flavored originals with exceptional vocal harmonies, while Big Brother had Janis Joplin's superlative commanding, bluesy singing and stage presence.

Happy Trails was, however, embraced by significant numbers of listeners who wouldn't agree with those criticisms. It made the Top Thirty, and picked up plenty of airplay on emerging FM rock stations, where the long songs fit in well with the underground format those outlets pioneered. In a larger and arguably less constructive sense, it helped popularize the notion of long, long jams on rock LPs (though these had been around, in some fashion, since 1966, with 'East West' and the Rolling Stones' 'Goin' Home'). Some groups would take the guitar-oriented improvisational approach to even greater lengths – the Allman Brothers' early-'70s albums had a similar concentration of long live numbers with extended instrumental passages, as well as a multi-guitar attack for which Quicksilver could have served as a partial model. (The Allmans' 'Mountain Jam', in fact, went 'Who Do You Love' one better, clocking in at an astounding 33 minutes.) Many bands less skilled as either Quicksilver or the Allmans would, alas, pick up the cue to put their own marathon blues-rock jams on record, many of them so awful as to make Quicksilver sound like masters of tasteful economy in comparison.

For all the influence *Happy Trails* might have had, – and as far-out and futuristic as it might have seemed upon its release in 1969 – the irony is that it now sounds not only dated, but in some ways very much a relic of its age. - Richie Unterberger

29. The Velvet Underground and Nico
The Velvet Underground and Nico

TRACKLISTING
Sunday Morning/I'm Waiting for The Man/Femme Fatale/Venus in Furs/Run Run Run/All Tomorrow's Parties/Heroin/There She Goes Again/I'll Be Your Mirror/The Black Angel's Death Song/European Son

RELEASED
US: March 1967 UK: October 1967

PRODUCED BY
Andy Warhol, Tom Wilson

It's hard to believe from our twenty-first century vantage point, when it's roundly acknowledged as one of the best and most influential rock albums ever, but when it was first released in 1967, The Velvet Underground And Nico was not only a commercial failure, peaking at a mere #171 in the charts, it also made relatively scant impact on critics and connoisseurs of the rock underground.

Part of the problem, perhaps, was that there really weren't many places to get an uncompromising album of this sort played on the radio, particularly as hip FM rock stations were just getting off the ground. The larger problem, however, was that much of the world just wasn't ready for rock music that unflinchingly reflected the darker sides of sex, drugs, and urban life, at a time when uplifting psychedelic music was reaching the peak of its vogue. Despite being produced and managed by one of the most popular visual artists of the twentieth century, Andy Warhol (who also designed its famous peelable banana cover), the group languished in obscurity.

All that's changed now, of course. As Brian Eno has famously said, "Only a few thousand people bought that record, but all of them formed a band of their own." That opinion is actually rather extreme but it is true that the album, though hardly a seller on the order of Abbey Road, was appreciated more zealously by those who heard it than almost any other. It's also true that some of those zealots formed proto-punk-new wave bands (such as Eno's Roxy Music), and subsequently actual punk and new wave bands, whose debts to the Velvet Underground were quite explicit. Although The Velvet Underground And Nico can't possibly sound as daring these days as it did upon its initial release, it sounds plenty radical enough. They weren't the first to write about sex and drugs in rock 'n' roll; fellow New York band The Fugs had preceded them, and there were coy, veiled references aplenty in the mid-'60s work of major artists like Bob Dylan, The Beatles, and the Rolling Stones. The Velvet Underground's biggest break-

The Velvet Underground – Mo Tucker, Sterling Morrison, Lou Reed and John Cale – with Nico.

through, however, was in writing about such taboo subjects in a direct fashion. There aren't just code words for marijuana or getting stoned in The Velvet Underground And Nico; there are play-by-play narratives of shooting smack ('Heroin', natch) and traveling to Harlem to score ('I'm Waiting For The Man'). There aren't just intimations of sadistic and masochistic sex; it's spelled out, albeit with a literary sensibility, in 'Venus in Furs' (with more violence hinted at, if only briefly in passing, in 'There She Goes Again'). If decadence isn't as explicitly delineated in 'All Tomorrow's Parties', that song masterfully evokes all-consuming modern ennui and gloom – unfashionable subjects in 1966 (when the album was recorded), and still not a ticket to mainstream success today.

The Velvet Underground and Nico, it should be stressed, was just as radical musically as it was lyrically. John Cale, with more roots in the *avant-garde* classical world than the pop-rock one, adds droning textures with his viola and piano that lodge themselves inside our craniums. Lou Reed and Sterling Morrison play guitar with a hypnotic, at times strangled grunge effect; Maureen Tucker's drumming is almost tribal in its primitivism; and Nico's occasional vocals put a gothic, glacial veneer on some of the stronger tunes. The sensationalistic drug'n'sex songs, especially 'Heroin', 'I'm Waiting For The Man', and 'Venus In Furs', are the ones that continue to attract the most attention. But it's important to emphasize that they're not wholly characteristic of the band, who offered far more varied and accessible material than is customarily acknowledged. Principal songwriter Lou Reed proves himself capable of surprisingly melodic, romantic sensitivity on 'Sunday Morning' and 'I'll Be Your Mirror', even if another pretty tune, 'Femme Fatale', has seductive undertones of unfulfilled lust and demonic temptation. 'Run Run Run' and 'There She Goes Again' grind along with arresting, fairly conventional guitar riffs. For those who like the Velvets at their most radical, 'The Black Angel's Death Song' is like a literary witch dance, while 'European Son' takes an all-out plunge into *avant-garde* noise rock. Tying it all together are the sing-speak vocals of Reed (who executes lead vocal on all the material save the three Nico-fronted tracks), which project a direct, street-tough honesty unmatched by any other rock performer.

For such a classic album, The Velvet Underground & Nico was certainly plagued by its share of logistical problems. Much of it was recorded almost a year before its release, which was delayed interminably. (An early acetate version with some different takes and mixes, including a version of 'Heroin' in which Reed actually utters the word 'shit,' was recently discovered and bootlegged.) When it finally came out, the album was temporarily pulled from distribution when the artwork had to be altered after an *habitué* of Andy Warhol's factory, Eric Emerson, expressed unhappiness over its use of his picture on the back cover. The record itself was difficult to find for years after the Velvet Underground broke up.

But The Velvet Underground And Nico - often known colloquially as "the banana album", just as The Beatles is usually known as "the white album" - did have an almost immediate influence. David Bowie was a big Velvets fan from the late '60s, even reviewing the two-CD 'deluxe edition' 35 years later in MOJO. Mick Jagger admitted that the droning sound of 'Stray Cat Blues', from the Rolling Stones' Beggars Banquet, was lifted from 'Heroin'. Jonathan Richman was a huge Velvets fan, and Patti Smith was not only a fan, but covered some of their songs in concert. And as Billy Altman noted in the first edition of The Rolling Stone Record Guide, "the band's uncompromising, committed playing is arguably the source of most punk/new wave music." Bands overground and underground continue to pay homage to the album today, in their now-standard lyrical examinations of depravity and the use of droning textures and tightly wound, basic song structures - though rarely with the finesse of Lou Reed and his cohorts. - Richie Unterberger

30. Tim Hardin 2
Tim Hardin

TRACKLISTING

If I Were a Carpenter/Red Balloon/Black Sheep Boy/Lady Came from Baltimore/Baby Close Its Eyes/You Upset the Grace of Living When You Lie/Speak Like a Child/See Where You Are and Get Out/It's Hard to Believe in Love for Long/Tribute to Hank Williams

RELEASED

US: May 1967 UK: September 1967

PRODUCED BY

Charles Koppelman, Don Rubin

There are some artists whose influence on music is hard to define. Yet though they may have broken down no particular barriers or been responsible for identifiable innovation, their impact is undeniable. Tim Hardin is such an artist.

Hardin himself never had anything approaching a big hit but in the mid-'Sixties he released a brace of folk-blues albums which were plundered by recording artists, several of them massively more successful in terms of sales than he. His sensibility – one which was more folky and more poetic than most songwriters - therefore seeped out into the wider world and subtly altered the DNA of popular music. Some have also attributed a significant Hardin influence to Van Morrison (especially *Astral Weeks*) and Nick Drake.

The almost elusive nature of Hardin's influence is exacerbated for some by the fact that those who covered Hardin's material tended to use his songs as launching pads rather than moulds, teasing out fuller melodies from his raw material. Some are actually disappointed when they hear *Tim Hardin* and *Tim Hardin 2*, surprised at the sparse arrangements of songs they are more familiar with ornate versions of. To such individuals, these recordings sound like demo tapes. Others find the likes of Bobby Darin's and Rod Stewart's versions over-wrought, preferring the original intimate simplicity.

As with *The "Chirping" Crickets* and *Buddy Holly*, *Tim Hardin* and *2* are a pair of albums recorded so closely together, of such similar timbre and of such similarity of influence that it's difficult to select one over the other for a book like this. However, *2* has been chosen because it more fully expressed Hardin's personal style – the first album featured a number of generic blues cuts, included against Hardin's wishes. We should pause to admire, though, the first album's worshipful 'Misty Roses', which was covered by – amongst others – Colin Blunstone, the 5th Dimension, the Four Freshmen and Sonny & Cher, and the wracked, beautiful 'Reason To Believe', a version of which Rod Stewart included on his multi-million selling *Every Picture Tells A Story* album (1971).

Tim Hardin, pictured at the Woodstock Festival in 1969.

On *Tim Hardin 2*, the artist was allowed to follow his head and was vindicated by the fact that much of its contents were the subject of lucrative covers. The breadth of Hardin's fan base amongst recording artists was quite amazing. 'If I Were A Carpenter' alone, this album's remarkable opener, was covered by artists as varied as the Small Faces, Bobby Darin, the Four Tops, Leif Garrett, Bert Jansch, Robert Plant and Dolly Parton. It was Darin – a leftover from the pre-Beatles pompadoured era – who incongruously had the first hit single of this densely-worded but sweet rumination on alternate-universe possibilities. Perhaps even more incongruously – and only two years later – black soul vocal group the Four Tops took it into both the US and UK charts again. Two years after that, country merchants Johnny Cash & June Carter had a joint US top forty hit with it. Darin, incidentally, was something of a champion of Hardin's music and recorded several of his songs, with his version of 'If I Were A Carpenter' and 'Red Balloon' actually released before their author's. In a supreme irony, the only entry Hardin ever had in the US single chart was 'Simple Song Of Freedom' – written by Darin.

The pretty 'Red Balloon' deliberately sounds like a love song but is actually a tribute to heroin, which at one point was sold by dealers in balloons. Hardin had a recurring problem with smack which eventually claimed his life at the age of 39. The Small Faces recorded a version first released on their posthumous *The Autumn Stone* album that seemed to take it at face value but was beautiful nonetheless. (The song 'The Autumn Stone' itself, recorded in the same period, was rather Hardin-esque.) 'Lady Came From Baltimore' is typical of the confessional nature of Hardin's work, name-checking his wife Susan Moore in an admission of falling in love with a woman he had intended to swindle. Scott Walker recorded a version, as (strangely) did Joan Baez. 'Black Sheep Boy' would also seem to be autobiographical. A high school drop-out who joined the marines, Hardin pointedly started his set with the song when he played his hometown of Eugene, Oregon in the 1970s. However, it should be pointed out that the song – like just about all his compositions – contains no real trace of bitterness, only sorrow, something that stood in contrast to his sometimes grumpy interviews.

Hardin was a very serious artist. There is no jollity to be found here or pretty much anywhere else in his *oeuvre*. Nonetheless, he provides a chirpy vaudeville flavor to the homily-like 'See Where You Are And Get Out', a track that at just over a minute is frustratingly short. In additional mitigation, in an era where genuine vulnerability amongst male performers' compositions was thin on the ground, he apparently thought nothing of writing a heart-on-sleeve song like 'Baby Close Its Eyes', in which he rejoices in the sight of his infant son laying in his cot.

An interesting footnote is provided by the fact that, like Bob Dylan, Hardin lived in Woodstock in the late 'Sixties. Some believe that he was an influence on Dylan's sparse 1968 comeback album *John Wesley Harding*. If Dylan disguised the influence by adding a 'g' to the name of the titular Wild West outlaw (of whom Hardin was then rumored to be a direct descendant), it is perfectly in keeping with the discreet nature of Hardin's influence on music. - Sean Egan

31. Are You Experienced
The Jimi Hendrix Experience

TRACKLISTING

US: Purple Haze/Manic Depression/Hey Joe/Love Or Confusion/May This Be Love/I Don't Live Today/The Wind Cries Mary/Fire/Third Stone From The Sun/Foxey Lady/Are You Experienced

UK: Foxy Lady/Manic Depression/Red House/Can You See Me/Love or Confusion/I Don't Live Today/May This Be Love/Fire/3rd Stone from the Sun/Remember/Are You Experienced

[Note: 'Foxy Lady' and '3rd Stone From The Sun' spelt differently on US and UK releases.]

RELEASED

US: September 1967 UK: May 1967

PRODUCED BY

Chas Chandler

The two most remarkable albums of 1967 appeared (in Britain) within three weeks of each other: The Beatles' *Sgt. Pepper's Lonely Hearts Club* Band and this album. Yet whereas *Pepper* was the result of the most intensive and protracted sessions for any album in history thus far, *Are You Experienced* achieved arguably even greater aural novelty and barrier-smashing with unarguably far fewer resources and recording hours.

At one point during the recording of this album, the manager of a recording studio refused to release the broke Experience's tapes until they had settled his bill. That the Experience triumphantly transcended petty travails like this to produce a dazzling album that provided the perfect lyrical and musical adventurism for the New Age supposedly heralded by the Summer Of Love is testament to their professionalism and to their leader's genius.

Jimi Hendrix was discovered in New York in autumn 1966 by ex-Animals bassist Chas Chandler, who promptly became his manager. Such was Chandler's wonderment at Hendrix's blurred-fingered fretwork skills that he had been blinded to the fact that at the point he signed him, Hendrix had no real songs under his belt, unless the generic blues 'Red House' counts. A cover of 'Hey Joe' bridged the gap temporarily and became the Jimi Hendrix Experience's debut and a UK hit. Though nobody thinks anything of it now, it is little short of miraculous that when Hendrix did start, on Chandler's insistence, to concentrate on writing it transpired that he had a composing gift almost on the same level as his guitar skills. The brutally self-assertive 'Stone Free' was his first attempt. Two months later he had come up with the immortal hard rock psychedelic anthem 'Purple Haze'. The latter, like 'Hey Joe' and the succeeding single, the tender 'The Wind Cries Mary', wasn't included on the album he recorded at the time – as was the norm in Britain – but were much-loved fixtures of the American version of *Are You Experienced*.

The recording of the album was a bitty process in which a couple of hours recording work would be snatched at a studio before a dash was made to a less-than-salubrious live venue in order to generate sufficient money to keep the wolf from the door. De Lane Lea, CBS, Pye and

The original cover for
Are You Experienced.

Olympic were the London studios in which the band pieced together the record, starting in mid-December '66 (discounting the first, singles sessions) and finishing in the second week of April '67. Despite his inexperience, Chandler acted as producer, and judging by Hendrix's subsequent career, almost certainly provided the crucial boundaries necessary to hem Hendrix's cosmic visions and outlandish sound ideas into something sufficiently concise and quickly assimilable as to have hit parade potential. Hendrix's colleagues were sterling: Mitch Mitchell was a musician whose flailing, hyperactive drum work was the perfect ingredient for a trio with large gaps in the aural soundscape to fill. Noel Redding, as an ex-guitarist, had a similarly conveniently wide span of sound.

Although Hendrix's talents were clearly bigger than the limitations of any recording studio, of all the recording venues he used in this period, he was most comfortable at Olympic, not least because of the assistance of engineer Eddie Kramer and tape op George Chkiantz, who were able to translate the wild sonic ideas that Hendrix had into reality.

On its release, by which time Hendrix's three singles had made him a star in Britain, *Are You Experienced* transpired to be a musical smorgasbord, encapsulating several different genres. There was soul, in the shape of the love-lorn 'Remember'. There was blues in the form of 'Red House', whose generic nature was transformed by Hendrix's brilliant quick-time, ear-splitting fretwork. There is straight-ahead rock (the menacing 'Can You See Me'). With its lengthy drum passages, 'Fire' most closely resembles jazz of any musical form, albeit a somewhat incendiary form of it. But many of the musical genres heard on the album had no name yet – this record genuinely contained music the like of which the human eardrum had never previously heard: 'Manic Depression', a thunderous heavy metal waltz; 'Love Or Confusion', a song composed of a mosaic of overlapping and interlocking guitar runs and washes of feedback while Hendrix intones a bewildered lyric seemingly from atop a mountain; the distortion-drenched ode to the plight of the native American 'I Don't Live Today'; '3rd Stone From The Sun', which starts out like a space age version of a Shadows instrumental before exploding into the sonic equivalent of an acid trip, achieved with backward guitar, feedback and guitar work designed for the most surreal effect imaginable. Similar effects attend the closing title track, a heavily pe cussive recruitment speech to the uninitiated that feels like the aural equivalent of a view through a kaleidoscope.

Are You Experienced is remarkable not just for the extent of its influence but the breadth of it. Mainstream rock artists saw it as another incremental step in the mission to prove that pop was a sophisticated art form: how could this kind of barrier-smashing work be dismissed as teenybopper fare? The psychedelia merchants were given clearance to go even more way out. '3rd Stone From The Sun' was a keystone for progressive rock in its length and refusal to adhere to expected musical conventions. Those involved in intellectual musical styles like jazz and the *avant-garde* realized that they could engage with rock with a clear conscience. Meanwhile, the brutal riffs and anthemic qualities of the likes of 'Foxy Lady' and 'I Don't Live Today' were adopted as their currency by generations of hard rockers and heavy metallers. Truly an album that was all things to all men. - Sean Egan

Hit Man

Tony Macaulay won the Ivor Novello songwriter of the year award in both 1969 and 1978, bookending a decade in which he wrote or co-wrote some of the more memorable chart hits either side of the Atlantic.

1.	**Build Me Up Buttercup**	The Foundations
2.	**Love Grows (Where My Rosemary Goes)**	Edison Lighthouse
3.	**Don't Give Up On Us Baby**	David Soul
4.	**Smile A Little Smile For Me**	The Flying Machine
5.	**Sorry Suzanne**	The Hollies
6.	**Something Here In My Heart**	The Paper Dolls
7.	**Baby Make It Soon**	Marmalade
8.	**Baby, Now That I've Found You**	The Foundations
9.	**You're A Star**	Carl Wayne
10.	**Let The Heartaches Begin**	Long John Baldry
11.	**Kissin' In The Back Row Of The Movies**	The Drifters
12.	**Gasoline Alley Bred**	The Hollies
13.	**Blame It On The Pony Express**	Johnny Johnson And The Bandwagon
14.	**My Marie**	Englebert Humperdink
15.	**If I Get Home On Christmas Day**	Elvis Presley
16.	**You Won't Find Another Fool Like Me**	The New Seekers
17.	**You're More Than A Number In My Little Red Book**	The Drifters
18.	**Play Me Like You Play Your Guitar**	Duane Eddy
19.	**I Can Take Or Leave Your Loving**	Herman's Hermits
20.	**Silver Lady**	David Soul

32. Sgt Pepper's Lonley Hearts Club Band
The Beatles

TRACKLISTING

Sgt. Pepper's Lonely Hearts Club Band/With A Little Help From My Friends/Lucy In The Sky With Diamonds/Getting Better/Fixing A Hole/She's Leaving Home/Being For The Benefit of Mr. Kite!/Within You Without You/When I'm Sixty-Four/Lovely Rita/Good Morning Good Morning/Sgt. Pepper's Lonely Hearts Club Band (Reprise)/A Day In The Life

RELEASED

US: June 1967 UK: June 1967

PRODUCED BY

George Martin

Upon its release, *Sgt Pepper* was hailed as "a decisive moment in the history of western civilization". Not by some gushing pop paper pundit but London *Times* newspaper critic Kenneth Tynan.

Those people who weren't around upon the release of The Beatles' eighth (UK) album who sit down to listen to the record now will be puzzled, even contemptuous, of such apparent hyperbole (especially if they listen to the watery stereo mix that is the only version available on CD). However, at the time such was the richness, inventiveness, colorfulness and exoticness of *Pepper* and such was its omnipresence that even years later such remarks do not seem too much like overkill to those who witnessed its unveiling first-hand. Although they would remain popular after this album – always perceived as being on a plateau above all other artists, artistically and commercially - its release was the crescendo of the world's love affair with The Beatles.

Revolver was the first Beatles album on which the Fab Four began to seem like something a little more than consummate pop craftsmen. Wonderful though their music had been hitherto, and despite their minor pieces of innovation in terms of such things as descending middle-eights and modest studio experimentation, it was only with the likes of that album's 'Tomorrow Never Knows' that they began to profoundly question and explore the boundaries of modern popular music. In this sense, they lagged behind contemporaries like Bob Dylan and The Byrds (the latter had recorded a version of jazz-rock number 'Eight Miles High' as early as December 1965, though the song was unreleased until March '66). However, on *Sgt Pepper* The Beatles made up for their previous relative conservatism with a vengeance. Rock and pop had never been so kaleidoscopic, dazzling and sophisticated.

This was partly because no rock artist had ever had the breathing space The Beatles had at this point. Having completed their final tour in August 1966, they now had nothing else to do, at least collectively, but to record. The four months and cumulative 700 hours that they took to complete *Pepper* is nothing by today's standards but then it was unprecedented. So much so that it alarmed their record company. The assumption was that fans would lose interest if new product was not available every three months. Hence Parlophone insisting on the Beatles delivering a stop-gap single: 'Penny Lane'/'Strawberry Fields Forever', whose commercial release in February 1967 dismayed producer George Martin, who realized that this prohibited – as was then the tradition – the songs appearing on the subsequent album, which he felt weakened it. Hence also the sniffy article in the *News Of The World* newspaper in the months preceding *Pepper*'s release, which lambasted the band for their recent reclusiveness and rumors of their musical self-indulgence.

Pepper was essentially McCartney's idea. What if The Beatles weren't The Beatles but a completely new band and therefore able to do whatever they wanted musically because nobody had any prior expectations of them? They would need a new name. McCartney came up with the sobriquet "Sgt. Pepper's Lonely Hearts Club Band" after being inspired by the unwieldy and frequently official-sounding titles of bands in San Francisco's contemporaneous psychedelic scene (e.g. Quicksilver Messenger Service, Big Brother And The Holding Company, Jefferson Airplane). The antediluvian militaristic clothing fashions to be seen on the streets of London at the time may have also been an influence. Of course, everybody would know it was actually The Beatles so there would be no point trying to hide it – but if the music is anything to go by, psychologically it did the track. This record was the aural equivalent of the way that The Beatles at this juncture suddenly sprouted moustaches and adorned themselves in flower power finery: *Pepper* was still the Beatles but not as we had known them.

In fact, it is surprising in many ways that *Pepper* does sound like a Beatles album, rather than a McCartney solo project. Lennon contributes only four songs, one of which has a McCartney middle eight, and George Harrison – according to McCartney – barely turned up for sessions. But The Beatles' imprimatur is present and correct: those unique, glorious three-part harmonies that had soundtracked so many people's journeys from adolescence to adulthood the past five years.

The album is nominally a performance by the titular showband but only the segue between the opening anthem and 'With A Little Help From My Friends' and the reprise of the anthem really conform to the concept. Though a showband might at a stretch be able to produce jaunty numbers like 'When I'm Sixty-Four' and 'Lovely Rita', are we really to

believe they could replicate the shimmering, fish-eyed-lens soundscape of 'Lucy In The Sky With Diamonds', the orchestral sweep of coming-of-age kitchen sink drama 'She's Leaving Home', the carnival ambience of showbill-brought-to-life 'Being For The Benefit of Mr. Kite!', the sitar drenched philosophical musing 'Within You, Without You' or the growling

Peter Blake's cover artwork for *Sergeant Pepper's Lonely Hearts Club Band.*

hard rock of 'Good Morning, Good Morning'? And where does 'A Day In The Life' fit into all this, a haunting epic that comes *after* the Sgt. Pepper reprise and across which Lennon's chanted backing vocals and Starr's thunderous tom-toms drift quite eerily? The answer of course is that it doesn't matter: such is the brilliance of what we are hearing that nobody really cares that the conceit is sustained only by smoke and mirrors.

Pepper was not just exotic musically. Everything about the album felt weird and wonderful, from the fact that Englishness was a flavor running through it to the fact that that there were no pauses between the tracks, to its title – utterly bizarre until people got used to it – to the sumptuousness of it as an artefact: its cover simply bursting with color, its back cover sporting song lyrics reminiscent of the libretto provided for people attending an opera, its unusual gatefold sleeve, its unashamedly silly cardboard cut-out inserts of things like the sergeant's moustache and (now long forgotten by most) the record's original psychedelically colored inner sleeve. This very sumptuousness was influential in itself: albums were often henceforth things into whose design great thought went.

The underlying thread in this book is how the release of great and innovative music has inspired rock artists to make great and innovative music of their own. Though *Pepper* caused this process more than perhaps any album ever (and inspired a parody from the Mothers Of Invention called *We're Only In It For The Money*), it also saw the sad flipside of this virtuous circle. The Beach Boys' leader Brian Wilson instead of being inspired to make great music the way that he had by *Rubber Soul*, this time didn't come up with a masterpiece like *Pet Sounds* but gave up the ghost and returned to his room, never to be the same talent again. Though his psychological condition at the time seems to be rather complicated – he had several other worries including conflicts with his Beach Boys colleagues, paranoia and mental problems caused by LSD – the forbidding magnificence of *Pepper* played its part in his *Smile* would-be *opus* failing to see the light of day for nearly forty years.

Although nobody suggests that *Pepper's* brilliance was a completely illusory product of a heady time, the album has fallen down the esteem scale in recent years, both as a piece of art and as part of the Beatles *oeuvre*. Certainly, it possesses an emotional hole that almost no other Beatles album does: love songs are very thin on the ground. Nor does it have that punchiness that the no-frills *Revolver* boasts.

However, as an influential album its status can't be disputed. *Sgt. Pepper's Lonely Hearts Club Band* redrew all popular music boundaries forever. - Sean Egan

Heavy Metal Thunder

Doesn't matter how old you are, if the combination of adolescent snarl, thumping rhythm and – most importantly – galvanizing guitar riff is right, you just want to punch your fist in the air and party 'til you puke. Twenty great **hard rock and heavy metal anthems**.

1.	**You Ain't Seen Nothin' Yet**	Bachman-Turner Overdrive
2.	**Pour Some Sugar On Me**	Def Leppard
3.	**All Right Now**	Free
4.	**Can't Get Enough**	Bad Company
5.	**School's Out**	Alice Cooper
6.	**Paranoid**	Black Sabbath
7.	**Don't Fear The Reaper**	Blue Oyster Cult
8.	**I Surrender**	Rainbow
9.	**Ace Of Spades**	Motorhead
10.	**The Boys Are Back In Town**	Thin Lizzy
11.	**Born To Be Wild**	Steppenwolf
12.	**We're An American Band**	Grand Funk
13.	**Stone Hearted Mama**	The Pretty Things
14.	**Rock And Roll All Nite**	Kiss
15.	**Breaking The Law**	Judas Priest
16.	**Gimme All Your Lovin'**	ZZ Top
17.	**You Give Love A Bad Name**	Bon Jovi
18.	**I Love Rock 'N' Roll**	Joan Jett And The Blackhearts
19.	**Saturday Night's Alright For Fighting**	Elton John
20.	**Smoke On The Water**	Deep Purple

33. Something Else By The Kinks
The Kinks

TRACKLISTING
David Watts/Death Of A Clown/Two Sisters/No Return/Harry Rag/Tin
Soldier Man/Situation Vacant/Love Me Till The Sun Shines/Lazy Old
Sun/Afternoon Tea/Funny Face/End of the Season/Waterloo Sunset

RELEASED
UK: September 1967 US: January 1968

PRODUCED BY
Shel Talmy, Ray Davies

American boogie band Grand Funk Railroad once had a heated argument
with British boogie band Humble Pie about whether American or British
rock 'n' roll was intrinsically superior.

    The impetus behind the Pie's argument – aside from patriotism
– was presumably that as rock 'n' roll had been rescued from its early 'Sixties
nadir (and possibly death) by The Beatles and the other bands in the British
Invasion that took over the US charts in 1964-onwards, and as so many
British artists had been amongst the major talents in rock history, it had
effectively become a British medium. Grand Funk, meanwhile, must have
been simply bewildered how a medium that sprang out of America,
and whose King will always be for some Elvis Presley, could possibly be
considered anything other than intrinsically American.

    One thing can't be disputed however which is that even the best
UK bands seemed to feel a certain inferiority complex about what they
were doing. Every UK rock singer sang in an American drawl. Everyone
agreed that to sing rock in the inflections of the English region from which
one hailed would sound ridiculous. Similarly, all artists tended as a rule to
write songs set in American locales and using American terminology: many
were the English boys who sang of cruising down the 'highway' with
their 'baby' in song but would not dare speak in such a manner in real life,
knowing they would be ridiculed for their phoniness if they did. Somehow
British landscape and customs – gray weather, terraced slums, the ingestion
of endless cups of tea and a rather stoical and polite national character – did
not seem the stuff of which an earthy, uptempo medium like rock
was made.

    The Kinks were one of the few British artists to dispute this
outlook. Though The Beatles had flirted with overt Englishness ('Taxman',
'Penny Lane', etc.), during the 'Sixties and early 'Seventies only the songs

of Kinks rhythm guitarist/singer Ray Davies insisted on the legitimacy of the pointedly English rock/pop song over a long period. In doing this, Davies legitimized writing about one's own background in rock. He therefore paved the way for the UK punk movement, whose bands decided that to sing in anything other than their own accents would be a betrayal of principles. Although composing vignettes of life on the dole and hating the monarchy was hardly compatible with mid-Atlanticisms, it

The Kinks – Ray Davies, Dave Davies, Peter Quaife and Mick Avory.

is difficult to see the punks having the courage to act on this realization without the precedent that Davies had set.

Ironically, the very ultra-Englishness of The Kinks came about – or was at least maintained – because of a ban on the group visiting America that operated between 1965 and 1969 following a dispute with a promoter. Davies has gone on record as saying he thinks this inability to tour the States caused him to focus on his home country in his writing. The Kinks' loss of the American market was rock music's gain. Ultimately, in an example of either irony or karma, it was the very Englishness of The Kinks that would make them the recipients of an affection that turned them into a viable commodity in the States from the late 'Seventies-onwards.

The start of Davies' drift toward parochial subject matter can be traced back to February 1966 and the release of the single 'Dedicated Follower Of Fashion', a pisstake (to use an English expression for mockery) of the type of Carnaby Street dandy then making the headlines. That street of fashion shops is only mentioned tangentially in the lyric ("Carnabetian army") but Regent Street is namechecked. As is Leicester Square – and only the British would knew that it was spelt this way, not "Lester".

Davies' determination to be English went hand in hand with his increasing penchant for depicting proletarian tableaux: he was being true to his roots on both counts. These English working class tableaux were by definition grimmer than American equivalents: white trash though Presley and Eddie Cochran and their values may have been, their poverty was nothing compared to a class-bound country where rationing was still a living memory and where tailfins were the stuff of legend, not an everyday sighting.

Something Else was the long-playing crystallization of this self-conscious Englishness, right down to the liner notes, which talk of everybody in "Daviesland" wearing bowler hats and carrying cricket bats. It was recorded in environs familiar to the band: Pye Studios, owned by their record label. Though engineer Alan MacKenzie and tape operator Alan O' Duffy were also familiar fixtures, the recording of this album marked the departure of producer and mentor Shel Talmy, with Davies talking over his role. The album was recorded at a relatively relaxed pace, with the band slotting in gigs in between sessions, but that still didn't stop Davies giving the album a title that implied it was being treated like mere treadmill product. It was no such thing but, in fact, a masterpiece.

Though there is a slickness and polish about *Something Else* not hitherto evident on Kinks long players, there is still something about it that is very modest-sounding considering its release date: 1967 was the year of psychedelic weirdness, manifested in hallucinogenic lyrics and speaker-panning sonic experimentation. In contrast, *Something Else* sounded sober-headed and utterly down-to-earth (though not earth-bound).

Something Else is simply suffused with Englishness. It's not just the mention of the Queen in 'David Watts' for instance but the fact that the backing chant is that uniquely British attention-demander, "Oi!" The track 'Harry Rag' takes its name from cockney rhyming slang for 'fag' – which itself is English for cigarette and has a very different meaning outside UK shores. All this reaches its apotheosis on 'Afternoon Tea', which frankly seems determined to live up to foreign clichés of English behavior rather than accurately describe it. However, Davies redeems himself for this – and the fact that the album tails off in quality on side two – with the closing 'Waterloo Sunset', his beautiful, dappled description of the sight of the titular London bridge as people scurry home over it at dusk. - Sean Egan

34. Forever Changes

Love

TRACKLISTING
Alone Again Or/A House Is Not a Motel/Andmoreagain/The Daily Planet/Old Man/The Red Telephone/Maybe the People Would Be the Times or Between Clark and Hilldale/Live and Let Live/The Good Humor Man He Sees Everything Like This/Bummer in the Summer/You Set the Scene

RELEASED
US: November 1967 UK: February 1968

PRODUCED BY
Arthur Lee, Bruce Botnick

Arguably the most popular rock 'cult' album of all time – if that's not a contradiction in terms – *Forever Changes* actually had relatively little artistic influence, and even less commercial impact, when it came out in late 1967. Although the group had experienced some modest chart success with earlier albums and singles (and were actual stars in their native Southern California), *Forever Changes* made a mere #154 in the US charts. It did somewhat better in Britain, where Love became one of the first US rock bands to develop a wide underground following, and where *Forever Changes* managed to reach #24. Yet, for all its folk-rock-psychedelic brilliance, *Forever Changes* was not a much-discussed item among the mainstream rock audience, perhaps in part because the Love lineup that had recorded the LP broke up soon after its release.

If there's one aspect in which *Forever Changes* turned out to be influential, however, it was that it was one of the very first rock albums whose impact grew and grew after its release, instead of leveling off or receding into history. Like another low-selling record from the era discussed in this volume, The Velvet Underground And Nico, it continued to show up on rock critics' all-time best-of lists decades after its release. In that way, it was a testament to how rock music of great artistic worth, no matter how relatively ignored it was in its own era, would eventually find its audience – something that few popular culture pundits would have thought possible in 1967, when rock was largely considered a disposable commodity. Not that it's much consolation to the actual members of Love, several of whom died prematurely or struggled mightily without reaping the material rewards of fame, principal Love singer-songwriter Arthur Lee being foremost among them.

　　Part of *Forever Changes*' failure to find a wide audience upon its

The original cover artwork for *Forever Changes*.

initial release could be due to its subtle, low-key tone (and, more mundanely, to the band's legendary refusal to tour significantly beyond its Southern Californian base). On their first, self-titled album from 1966, Love had demonstrated a capacity for sullen, if still sometimes derivative, folk-rock; on *Da Capo*, the group had absorbed jazz, flamenco, and proto-punk elements to leap into a more enchantingly psychedelic realm (even if the side-long jam 'Revelation' was a disappointment). *Forever Changes* didn't, as so many bands were doing in 1967, take things yet more outrageous steps further with more far-out experiments. Instead, it scaled back to a folkier, more acoustic-driven sound, embellished by - in a move that was actually more adventurous than many of the hard rock psychedelicisms of other groups of the period - light orchestration, often with a definite Latin tinge.

As pretty as the songs were, however, there was often a hard edge to the music, via some off-the-wall brittle electric rock guitar solos and the hurt pout of Arthur Lee's vocals. As icing on the cake, there were the enigmatic lyrics. Like Bob Dylan's, these were often meaningless on the surface, yet with intricate wordplay and phrasing that both provoked thought and rewarded repeated listening. But Lee, unlike Dylan, had a gentle touch that was more seductive than cynical, often delivered here with a psychedelic Johnny Mathis croon of sorts.

Some latter-day critics, egged on in parts by comments from Lee himself, have emphasized the darker side of his vision, as though *Forever Changes* is one man's diary of Los Angeles entering the apocalypse as he watches it burn from the Hollywood Hills. While there is certainly some dark ambiguity in the album, to focus on those aspects is to deny the quite attractive, downright pretty textures and vibes of most of the music. If these are bitter ruminations, never in the history of rock have they been as candy-coated. 'Andmoreagain' and 'The Good Humor Man He Sees Everything Like This' in particular are lovely, psychedelically blissful ballads, as fragrant as a hot summer day's breeze. Even Lee's tougher and moodier tracks, such as 'A House Is Not a Motel' and 'Live And Let Live' (with its memorable opening line "The snot has caked against my pants"), are dusted with beautifully strummed acoustic folky guitars, letting us know there's humanity as well as bitterness in his world vision.

One of the most impressive traits of *Forever Changes* is its maintenance of a consistent tone, and consistently strong songs, without sounding repetitious or monotonous. It helped to have a couple of songs by Bryan MacLean to vary the pace, including the record's most popular number, 'Alone Again Or', whose flamenco guitars and mariachi horns acted as emollients to a song that defined bittersweet romanticism as much as any ever written. Many if not most albums of the time threw on a long track almost as if to try and prove that it could be done, but the LP-closing 'You Set the Scene', which clocks in at nearly seven minutes, is one of the rare such multi-part suites that maintains focus and economy throughout.

As previously mentioned, there are few albums that sound like *Forever Changes* but the album's greatest significance is not inconsiderable: it has stood as a sign of encouragement to all bands making music out of step with current sales trends. For it's the ultimate example of a record that might not find its listenership right away, but eventually comes to be appreciated as a timeless masterwork – a reward perhaps more important than fame or money. – Richie Unterberger

35. Truth
Jeff Beck

TRACKLISTING
Shapes of Things/Let Me Love You/Morning Dew/You Shook Me/Ol' Man River/Greensleeves/Rock My Plimsoul/Beck's Bolero/Blues Deluxe /I Ain't Superstitious

RELEASED
US: August 1968 UK: July 1968

PRODUCED BY
Mickie Most

In an alternate universe, the Jeff Beck Group (the artists behind this album, although it was credited to just Beck himself) remained intact and produced a string of classic albums appropriate to their stellar cast. This means that the solo career of Rod Stewart never happened, preventing the creation of classic albums like *Every Picture Tells A Story*, that The Faces never existed and that the Rolling Stones had to find someone other than Ron Wood to replace Mick Taylor following the latter's departure from that band. On the plus side, the titular guitar hero whom many think the greatest British guitarist of all time would have not sunk into the bewildering obscurity in which he now resides. The Jeff Beck Group, meanwhile, would have got the credit for inventing heavy metal.

Some would dispute that Led Zeppelin should even be described as heavy metal let alone be given the credit, as they often are, for inventing that notable genre. It would also be difficult to discount claims made for the Jimi Hendrix Experience's 'Purple Haze' as the first recorded example of metal. However those who do consider Zeppelin to be practitioners of the genre and credit them with the creation of it are arguably off-beam, for Zeppelin had a template – that template being to a large extent this band and this album.

This is not particularly surprising if one traces back the roots of the two bands for, of course, they bisect two years prior to the release of *Truth* with The Yardbirds. For one brief and potentially glorious period, Jeff Beck and Jimmy Page – who, along with Eric Clapton, made up the holy trinity of UK '60s virtuoso guitarists – were in The Yardbirds together. Some observers have spoken of a twin guitar attack onstage that was breathtaking and one of the only two tracks this line-up recorded was indeed superb – the alternately mysterious and fiery 'Happenings Ten Years Time Ago' – but by November 1966 it was all over amid talk of hatred between Page and Beck and even rumors of violence. Beck left and Page took over The Yardbirds. Page, though, still had his eye on his former friend and colleague.

Beck recruited the services of the then little-known Rod Stewart, a young man with an extraordinarily aged voice. Drumming was provided by Mickey Waller, an eccentric but powerful sticksman. Ron Wood, another future superstar, was more naturally a guitarist but served ably on bass. After a ludicrous start for this fine band – Stewart was not allowed to sing on their first couple of singles by producer Mickie Most, one of which was the nice but hardly representative pop hit 'Hi Ho Silver

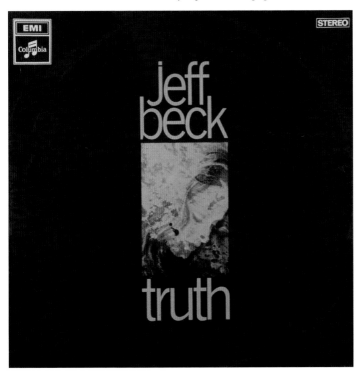

One of the greatest British '60s guitarists: Jeff Beck's *Truth*.

Lining' – they were finally allowed their head on their debut LP, presumably because hitmaker Most wasn't interested in albums. Nor B-sides. There's a fine one on this record, 'Beck's Bolero', the flip of 'Hi Ho Silver Lining', an instrumental featuring the amazing line-up of Beck and Page plus John Paul

Jones on bass and Keith Moon on drums. There are disagreements over whether its recording predated Beck leaving The Yardbirds, but an apparent unanimity that this supergroup was going to be a permanent one if Moon left The Who, as he was then contemplating.

Beck has said that after the release of *Truth*, Page was hanging around the band in America, paying close attention to their sound. He has also said that he was reduced to tears of rage when he heard the demo of 'You Shook Me' by a new band Page had put together called Led Zeppelin that would feature on the latter's eponymous debut album of early 1969. The track wasn't written by Beck – it being one of two numbers on *Truth* composed by one-man blues Brill Building Willie Dixon – but Zeppelin's version bore a notable similarity to the Jeff Beck Group's growling, swaggering rendition here.

Certainly, much of the recipe for which Zeppelin would become famous – gargantuan blues, the overlaying of virtuosity on traditional structures, alternately anguished and sighing delivery – is present on *Truth*. The Jeff Beck Group shared another similarity with Zeppelin, namely the way their utter, almost agonized belief in their material was often in danger of spilling over into absurdity.

As well as reviving, 'Beck's Bolero', Beck chose to revisit The Yardbirds' groundbreaking slice of weirdness 'Shapes Of Things', in a slowed-down re-recording which is nice enough but helped emphasize a lack of a songwriting base within the group. Even the Beck/Stewart collaborations 'Let Me Love You', 'Rock My Plimsoul' and 'Blues Deluxe' are essentially generic blues numbers, albeit dramatically rescued from mediocrity by some stunning bulldozing guitar work, wonderfully gravelly singing or, in the case of the live recording 'Blues Deluxe', some magnificent piano work by Nicky Hopkins, a mellifluous musician whose work would in time grace the records of all of the big three in UK rock, The Beatles, the Stones and The Who. Hopkins also lent his vast skills to the moody, wah-wah inflected 'Morning Dew'.

There are a couple of tracks here of a type which one could not really imagine on a Zeppelin LP. Partly this is because they are such hoary old chestnuts: 'Greensleeves', of such vintage that it was supposedly written by King Henry VIII, and 'Ol' Man River', which even then must have had a certain ring of minstrel-show parody to it. Nonetheless, the former is pretty and the latter is turned into something dark and profound-sounding via a slow, serious arrangement. The album climaxes with Willie Dixon's 'I Ain't Superstitious', in which Beck goes into wah-wah overload and Waller thrashes his kit in sympathy.

Nicky Hopkins would become a full member of the Jeff Beck Group in October 1968 (interestingly, having allegedly turned down Led Zeppelin's overtures), thus completing possibly the greatest – on paper –

band line-up of all time. However, this incarnation of the Jeff Beck Group didn't last long enough to record an album, Tony Newman taking over drums for follow-up *Beck-Ola*. Soon after that, Stewart and Wood were gone, unable to put up with Beck's notorious temperament any longer. Jimmy Page and co were there, ready to exploit the audience the Jeff Beck Group had helped create for a type of music that would shortly become a multi-million-dollar industry. - Sean Egan

36. Cheap Thrills
Big Brother And The Holding Company

TRACKLISTING
Combination Of The Two/I Need A Man To Love/Summertime/Piece of My Heart/Turtle Blues/Oh, Sweet Mary/Ball And Chain

RELEASED
US: July 1968 UK: September 1968

PRODUCED BY
John Simon

Cheap Thrills was the major label debut of singer Janis Joplin and few artists have had such an impressive coming out.

Joplin had originally made her mark at the Monterey Pop Festival in June 1967 with a set that many consider one of the seminal moments of the 'Sixties. Her performance at the festival attracted the attention of Columbia Records, and the next spring she and her band, Big Brother and the Holding Company, recorded *Cheap Thrills*.

Big Brother had already released a self-titled debut album on tiny independent label Mainstream Records, but that record, despite Joplin's intense vocals on 'Down On Me', was a sub-par effort plagued by cheap production values. For *Cheap Thrills*, Columbia paired Joplin with producer John Simon and put her in a top-notch recording studio, and the effort paid off. While Big Brother demonstrate themselves to be a competent acid-rock band, *Cheap Thrills* is Janis's album and was her vehicle to stardom. Eventually, Joplin left Big Brother and the band put out other albums without her; all were decidedly inferior.

Cheap Thrills is a landmark record. Though there were only seven songs on the original LP, each of the tracks showcased a different element of Joplin's remarkable voice. On 'I Need a Man to Love', she's a tough mama begging for affection, without showing one hint of vulnerability.

On 'Summertime', she takes the Gershwin classic and simmers it down to a plaintive Spanish-inflected moaner. On 'Oh, Sweet Mary', she shows her gospel side and belts it out like a hippie Aretha Franklin. On 'Turtle Blues', she sounds exactly like blueswoman Bessie Smith, her greatest influence. The range of vocal ability that Joplin displays on this diverse material is nothing short of astounding.

But as impressive as Joplin's range is, it is the amount of feeling she puts into her singing that makes *Cheap Thrills* a work of genius. On both 'Piece of My Heart' and 'Ball and Chain', Joplin delivers performances that are so potent they have no antecedents: They represent a new kind of standard for rock vocals. 'Ball and Chain' is the more traditional of the two songs, but what Joplin does with it is anything but expected. The song had been a minor hit for Big Mama Thornton, and had become a popular standard for blues singers during the previous decade. Joplin never sang anything as a straightforward blues, however, and rather than simply sing this song, she moans it. Her vocal asides, her 'la las', and her guttural screams on 'Ball and Chain' are more than just remarkable - they represent the kind of extraordinary performance that comes along in popular music maybe once a decade. Joplin stretches out 'Ball And Chain' for nine-and-a-half minutes on *Cheap Thrills* and even that seems too short. Her performance is an absolute *tour de force*. What is perhaps even more incredible is that the version on *Cheap Thrills*, while well-recorded, still pales compared to live recordings of Joplin singing this song.

The anthemic but tortured 'Piece of My Heart' was the more personal masterpiece from *Cheap Thrills*, and became Joplin's first Top 40 hit. The song went as high as Number 12 on the US pop charts, and it became one of the signature songs on FM and underground stations. Though on *Cheap Thrills* the song is only four-and-a-half minutes, in concert 'Piece of My Heart' could go stretch twice as long. Every one of Joplin's big hits were about unrequited love but none were as devastating as 'Piece of My Heart'. As Joplin's own life descended into drugs and alcoholism, the song became even more bittersweet, and began to sound like an epitaph.

Cheap Thrills also benefits from album art by Robert Crumb, whose underground cartooning style was just taking off in the late 'Sixties. Crumb's 16-panel cover cartoon, complete with a decidedly politically incorrect 'mammy' figure, is one of the classic pieces of 'Sixties pop art. Though *Cheap Thrills* would have been a brilliant record in a brown paper bag, Crumb's art adds to the package and gives Joplin's blues covers some context if only because the 'freak' art modernizes the themes of the songs. The fact that Joplin's name does not appear in the title of the original LP, except in one of Crumb's cartoons, forever confused buyers searching for the big Janis Joplin album. Able musicians though the Holding company were, the true star was Joplin.

As big a hit as *Cheap Thrills* was at the time, it has seen its influence grow rather than fade over time. *Cheap Thrills* marked Janis Joplin's emergence as the first iconic female star in rock 'n' roll. As Chrissie Hynde recently noted of Joplin, "She was great because it was all heart. Watching her perform was like watching a boxing match. She might come out of it all bloody, but you knew she'd be standing tall at the end. Janis had a rock heart." Hynde and countless other female musicians cite Joplin as a role model, and her success was proof that a woman could succeed in an art form that had been primarily male-dominated. Yet Joplin also influenced many men by illustrating that a performer who sings with emotional depth can find an audience. Without Joplin, and *Cheap Thrills*, it is hard to imagine a place in rock for artists from Melissa Etheridge to the Black Crowes.

Though *Cheap Thrills* represents Joplin's best album, there have been numerous collections since her death that pair this material with her other hits. Look for one that also includes her later hit 'Me And Bobby McGee'. As an icon, Joplin's status continues to grow as her life story is portrayed in numerous books and films. There have been many contenders for the title of the best female singer in rock 'n' roll – no-one has yet to come close to matching Janis Joplin. - Charles R. Cross

Janis Joplin (third from right in band) singing with Big Brother and the Holding Company, 1967.

Oh You Pretty Things!

There was always confusion over whether early '70s **UK glam rock** was a look or a musical style, and in any case the term has become conflated in the public mind with early 1970s British pop. Overall, much of the music in the singles charts of the era was very silly - but undeniably glorious.

1.	**Blockbuster**	Sweet
2.	**I Love You Love Me Love**	Gary Glitter
3.	**Devil Gate Drive**	Suzi Quatro
4.	**Cum On Feel The Noize**	Slade
5.	**Tiger Feet**	Mud
6.	**Metal Guru**	T. Rex
7.	**My Coo-Ca-Choo**	Alvin Stardust
8.	**Fancy Pants**	Kenny
9.	**See My Baby Jive**	Wizzard
10.	**Children Of The Revolution**	T. Rex
11.	**Coz I Luv You**	Slade
12.	**Let's Get Together Again**	The Glitter Band
13.	**The Bump**	Kenny
14.	**Make Me Smile (Come Up And See Me)**	Steve Harley And Cockney Rebel
15.	**School's Out**	Alice Cooper
16.	**Virginia Plain**	Roxy Music
17.	**New York Groove**	Hello
18.	**Sugar Baby Love**	The Rubettes
19.	**Rock And Roll Part 2**	Gary Glitter
20.	**Ballroom Blitz**	Sweet

37. Iron Butterfly
In-A-Gadda-Da-Vida

TRACKLISTING
Most Anything You Want/Flowers And Beads/My Mirage/Termination
/Are You Happy/ In-A-Gadda-Da-Vida

RELEASED
US: July 1968 UK: September 1968

PRODUCED BY
Jim Hilton

In a parallel universe somewhere, Neil Young joined Iron Butterfly as their guitarist and sang the lead vocals on their epic 17-minute signature song 'In-A-Gadda-Da-Vida'.

It actually could have happened... Shortly before the release of the Butterfly's 1968 debut *Heavy*, the San Diego band split, leaving organist Doug Ingle and drummer Ron Bushy to find replacements quickly. The label wasn't going to release the album if there wasn't a group to promote it. As well as Neil Young, other rumored candidates were Jeff Beck and Steppenwolf guitarist Michael Monarch. In the end they settled for the brilliant former child prodigy Eric Brann and bassist Lee Dorman.

Arguments about who started heavy metal and when have raged for years. 1968 was the year of Blue Cheer's *Vincebus Eruptum*, Vanilla Fudge's *Renaissance* and Jeff Beck's *Truth*, while the debut Led Zeppelin album appeared in January 1969, all suitable and deserving candidates for the title of first-ever metal album. Iron Butterfly were at best a marginal influence on later early metal bands like Deep Purple, Uriah Heep and Black Sabbath but there is a case for saying that Iron Butterfly influenced the choice of name for this new and more brutal manifestation of electric blues rock. Calling their debut *Heavy* was a pretty clear statement of intent. In the liner notes for *In-A-Gadda-Da-Vida* they define their name thus: "Iron - symbolic of something heavy as in sound, Butterfly - light, appealing and versatile...an object that can be used freely in the imagination..." It was a pattern that Led Zeppelin also followed when adopting their name.

To say that the Butterfly's second LP *In-A-Gadda-Da-Vida* is a great album is to massively overstate the case. It's a fairly standard post-garage rock album, typical of those churned out by former surf and R&B combos trying to jump onto the psychedelic bandwagon. Heavily driven by Ingle's keyboards and Brann's occasionally inspired guitar work, songs like the surprising swipe at the hippie culture 'Flowers And Beads' are, at best, the sort of novelty psyche-garage fare that turns up on those *Pebbles*-style compilations that mine the seemingly inexhaustible seam of mid-'60s acid rock. No, *In-A-Gadda-Da-Vida* is important solely because of the title track. It is one of rock's most memorable riffs, and like all such great riffs, so simple that any moron can play it within ten minutes of picking up a guitar for the first time. The song's structure is similar to Dave Brubeck's jazz hit of 12 years before, 'Take Five': the main – and memorable – body of the song followed by a looser jam leading into an extended drum solo before a return to the original tune.

Iron Butterfly's second album was recorded and released very quickly in the wake of their debut. According to a later interview with producer Jim Hilton, the song 'In-A-Gadda-Da-Vida' was recorded in a single take with only a few overdubs added later. You can hear this: it is littered with bum notes, mistakes, mumbling – Ron Bushy's inadvertently hilarious "1-2-3-4…huh!" towards the last section of the song, completely out of time with the music – and missed beats. In today's more antiseptic musical climate, it wouldn't even be acceptable as a demo.

There are countless rumors and counter rumors about the track's name: some have suggested that it was originally called 'In The Garden Of Eden', but that Bushy was either tripping or drunk when they rehearsed the song and so slurred and mangled the words. In the liner notes to *The Best Of Iron Butterfly*, Ron Bushy claims that he heard the track on headphones and simply couldn't hear Bushy when he asked him what the title was.

The real innovation was that it was one of the first ever rock songs to feature an extended drum solo and as such opened the way for many more of the same – Zeppelin's 'Moby Dick', Deep Purple's 'The Mule' – which was to be the bane of many a gig-goer's life in the '70s. How hearts would sink when the drummer started working his way around the kit while the rest of the band walked offstage.

Long, extended tracks weren't unusual in 1968: Love had devoted the whole of side two of *Da Capo* to the single track 'Revelations' and the Grateful Dead had put two extended complex jams on side two of *Anthem For The Sun* and, live, they had been known to drag 'Dark Star' out for almost an hour. What was different about 'In-A-Gadda-Da-Vida' was that when Iron Butterfly released an edited version of the song as a single, which became a massive national hit, the FM stations started playing the full 17-minute version. (A similar thing had happened to The Doors with 'Light My Fire'.) For better or worse, the popularity of *In-A-Gadda-Da-Vida* helped to prepare the way for progressive rock in that it got a much wider public used to the idea of a piece of music that didn't follow the conventional structure of the pop song and might meander on for anything up to half an hour.

Iron Butterfly themselves were never able to repeat its success. The follow-up album *Ball* sold well thanks to the momentum generated by *In-A-Gadda-Da-Vida*, but it sounded like a second-rate Doors album. Erik Brann left in 1970 and the band's next album *Metamorphosis* was appalling. Though the band reformed in the mid-'70s and actually continue to tour today, they will always be the ultimate one-hit-wonders. But what a truly massive and influential one-hit 'In-A-Gadda-Da-Vida' – both album and single – were. - Tommy Udo

38. Music From Big Pink
The Band

TRACKLISTING
Tears Of Rage/To Kingdom Come/In A Station/Caledonia Mission/The Weight/We Can Talk/Long Black Veil/Chest Fever/Lonesome Suzie/This Wheel's On Fire/I Shall Be Released

RELEASED
US: July 1968 UK: August 1968

PRODUCED BY
John Simon

In a musical climate that was rapidly giving way to the noisier, amped up sounds of psychedelia and harder rock, The Band were truly an anachronism. Their rejection of current trends and embracement of a solidly roots-oriented approach set them distinctly apart from the pack. *Music From Big Pink* stills stands as one of the most singular debuts in rock history.

In an era of rebellion against the existing social mores and the generational divide, The Band conveyed a sense of tradition, family and roots. Consider the photos that illustrated *Music From Big Pink*'s gatefold sleeve: The Band surrounded by four generations of family members, and in one shot the group looking like mysterious rural folk from another century. Going against the grain was, said guitarist Robbie Robertson, a deliberate act of rebellion against the prevailing cultural norms: "It was an instinct to separate ourselves from the pack." As backing band for Toronto-based rockabilly wildman Ronnie Hawkins, The Band, then known as The Hawks, specialized in raging R&B style rock. From there they backed Dylan on his tumultuous 1965-1966 electric tour where they faced hordes of booing folk purists. Their alliance with Dylan continued off the road

when mutual manager Albert Grossman invited The Band to join Dylan for informal sessions that would find the group exploring a wide spectrum of uniquely American roots music. Writing and recording in a rented house dubbed Big Pink in West Saugerties near Woodstock, they came up with a batch of largely original songs with a traditional feel, resulting in a legendary bootleg later officially released as *The Basement Tapes*.

It was Grossman who secured The Band their recording contract with Capitol. *Music From Big Pink* was a logical

Bob Dylan's cover painting for *Music From Big Pink*.

extension of *The Basement Tapes* sessions, a hard to categorize amalgam of gospel, rock, country and folk influences that resulted in a sound firmly rooted in a rural past yet felt like a work of startling originality. Who before or since has ever sounded anything like them? Consider the musical landscape just six months earlier, which saw the release of multi-colored extravaganzas like the Beach Boys' *Pet Sounds*, Cream's *Disraeli Gears*, The Jimi Hendrix Experience's *Are You Experienced* and The Beatles' *Sgt. Pepper's Lonely Hearts Club Band* and you get the sense of just how strange The Band must have sounded then.

Each member of The Band – guitarist Robbie Robertson, keyboardist Garth Hudson, pianist Richard Manuel, bassist Rick Danko and drummer Levon Helm - was a musician of consummate skill. The influence of Bob Dylan (who was responsible for the rather simplistic color painting on the LP's cover) coming off the heels of *The Basement Tapes* sessions could be felt on the freewheeling atmosphere at play here. Conjuring up an authentic rustic Southern sensibility (never mind that all of them were Canadians save Helms), their musical versatility matched only by their lyrical intelligence, *Music From Big Pink* is a work of impressive maturity and depth from a band that stood proudly apart. Even their shared camaraderie seemed shrouded in mystique. Their music felt ragged, with both the instrumentation and the singers' vocals in a state of constant flux.

Robertson once commented that it was his choice to begin the album with a slow song to let people know they were in for an unconventional listening experience. That song, the powerful 'Tears Of Rage', sung by Richard Manuel who possessed one of rock's most hauntingly mournful voices, conveys the distress of a father contending with a wayward child. Manuel sings it with heartbreaking anguish, placing it in terms of sheer emotional impact miles above Dylan's far more detached version on *The Basement Tapes*. Manuel brings an equal sense of deep soul conviction to Dylan's prison lament 'I Shall Be Released', sung in a fragile falsetto. The album contains one of The Band's most famous tracks, Robertson's 'The Weight' (featured in the classic counterculture movie *Easy Rider*) whose hapless narrator stumbles into one unfortunate situation after another after agreeing to do a favor for a friend. An air of mournfulness permeates the smoldering allegorical Danko/Dylan number 'This Wheel's On Fire' and The Band's cover of 'Long Black Veil', on which Danko gives voice to a man convicted and executed for a murder he didn't commit rather than use his alibi and admit to being in the arms of his best friend's wife. Musically The Band's attention to detail is unparalleled. Hudson's organ riff that opens the cryptic 'Chest Fever' borrows its melody from Bach's 'Toccata And Fugue in D Minor'.

After Eric Clapton heard *Music From Big Pink*, being in Cream didn't seem quite so desirable anymore. Determined to change course musically, he formed Blind Faith and embarked on a series of solo albums with rootsier leanings. Clapton wasn't alone. Noting the album's impact, Clapton has stated it "had a shocking effect on more people than you could ever realize." George Harrison credits The Band as an influence on his early '70s work, most notably *All Things Must Pass* (Phil Spector's production job notwithstanding), while The Band's influence can be felt over much of Elton John's 1970s work, most notably 1971's rustic *Tumbleweed Connection*. It's there in The Grateful Dead's lauded return to a roots approach on 1970's *Workingman's Dead* and *American Beauty*, Van Morrison's *Moondance* and the alt-country sound of Uncle Tupelo, The Jayhawks and Wilco. The rustic feel of The Rolling Stones' 1968 masterpiece *Beggars Banquet* was heavily influenced by The Band and stands as the earliest manifestation of the Stones' country/roots leanings that would continue to be heard on subsequent recordings like *Sticky Fingers* and *Exile On Main Street* (even if the original bathroom graffiti cover art of *Beggars Banquet* took some digs at both Dylan and The Band, renaming this album "Music From Big Brown").

Released to widespread critical acclaim, *Music From Big Pink* still stands as a testament to pop's capacity for transcendent, meaningful, cerebral songcraft. - Tierney Smith

39. The Basement Tapes
Bob Dylan And The Band

TRACKLISTING
Odds And Ends/Orange Juice Blues (Blues For Breakfast)/Million Dollar Bash/Yazoo Street Scandal/Goin' To Acapulco/Katie's Been Gone/Lo And Behold!/Bessie Smith/Clothes Line Saga/Apple Suckling Tree/Please, Mrs. Henry/Tears Of Rage/Too Much Of Nothing/Yea! Heavy And A Bottle Of Bread/Ain't No More Cane/Crash On The Levee (Down In The Flood)/Ruben Remus/Tiny Montgomery/You Ain't Goin' Nowhere/Don't Ya Tell Henry/Nothing Was Delivered/Open The Door, Homer/Long Distance Operator/This Wheel's On Fire

RELEASED
US: June 1975 UK: July 1975

PRODUCED BY
Bob Dylan, The Band

The Basement Tapes is the title of an official album, whose release dates and tracklisting are detailed above. However, long before that commercial issue, "The Basement Tapes" was a colloquial title given to a cache of Bob Dylan and The Band recordings that, though only available through illicit means, possessed such singularity and power that they had a huge influence on music.

Though Dylan's collaboration with The Band stands as one of his greatest recordings, it was never intended for official release. Instead it began its commercial life as the first bootleg of the rock era, the popularity of which eventually led to its official Columbia release in June 1975. Originally, it made its way out into the world in 1967 as a 14-song music publisher's acetate for artists who might want to cover new Dylan songs – a plentiful breed in those days. This was only a fraction of the songs that were recorded. If these songs weren't intended for public consumption, that didn't stop some enterprising California record plant workers from taking the initiative by pressing their own vinyl copies, a move that would essentially kick start the lucrative bootleg business. Seven of those 14 songs appeared in 1968 on *The Great White Wonder*. (The latter illegal album also featured some miscellaneous unreleased Dylan recordings, some from as far back as 1961.) The official release – supervised by The Band's Robbie Robertson – did not include some key Basement Tape songs, added a few tracks that weren't from these sessions, as well as some overdubs, and gave disproportionate prominence to the non-Dylan songs.

The Great White Wonder had an unprepossessing blank white cover and label. Inside though was real treasure, even though it was cut live on a home tape recorder. The magic made in the basement of a rented house in upstate New York (famously named Big Pink) in the spring of 1967 has become the stuff of legend. In the aftermath of his '66 motorcycle accident, Dylan had joined up with his live band The Hawks (soon to be re-christened The Band) who had backed him on his legendary '65-'66 electric tour. Dylan was at a creative peak having released *Blonde On Blonde* the year before but was re-evaluating his life and determined to make a change. At the time recording began in the spring of 1967, psychedelic rock was exploding on the scene. Dylan and The Band would take a radical turn away from the prevailing multi-colored, special effects-employing musical climate to embrace a defiantly unvarnished, musty, rustic sound. They were musicians playing for the fun of it, their informal freewheeling sessions characterized by a creative spontaneity and mutual camaraderie. Dylan traded lead vocals with Band members Richard Manuel, Rick Danko and drummer Levon Helm and there is rousing harmony all around. Said Dylan looking back in 1967, "That's really the way to do a recording. In a peaceful, relaxed setting in somebody's basement with the windows open and a dog lying on the floor."

Accordionist/keyboardist Garth Hudson recalls them performing up to 15 songs a day and if nothing else Dylan and The Band proved how keenly inspiration can strike when allowed to flow unhindered. With no commercial pressures or considerations, they recorded 105 songs in all, only a tiny portion of which appeared on the official *Basement Tapes* release. That an expanded version has still not seen official release is one of the great music mysteries of our time.

The mood of these songs often spoke louder than their actual meanings, which were more often than not negotiable, given that some of these lyrics were made up on the spot. The traditional chain gang song 'Ain't No More Cane' established the mood and feel of a bygone era, of music rooted in a ghostly arcane past. Listen as Dylan talks his way though 'Clothes Line Saga' in the mundane across-the-fence conversation of rural "plain folk". Elsewhere there is bawdy humor ('Odds And Ends', 'Please Mrs. Henry'), irreverent weirdness ('Lo And Behold', 'Yea! Heavy And A Bottle

Of Bread'), wistful remembrances ('Bessie Smith', 'Goin' To Acapulco') and the emotionally ravaging 'Tears Of Rage'.

The songs then made their way into the hands of record collectors and fellow musicians. Dylan's music publisher's circulation of

the songs with the aim of generating cover versions certainly worked. By November 1967 folk trio Peter Paul And Mary had charted with their version of 'Too Much Of Nothing'. Manfred Mann scored a hit with a buoyant cover of 'The Mighty Quinn' (one of the curious omissions from the official *Basement Tapes* release). The Byrds, always skilled interpreters of the Dylan *oeuvre*, covered 'You Ain't Going Nowhere' and 'Nothing Was Delivered' on their landmark 1968 country-rock album *Sweetheart Of The Rodeo* while The Band themselves recorded new versions of 'Tears Of Rage' and 'I Shall Be Released' on their 1968 debut *Music From Big Pink*.

These recordings had a profound and unintended effect on the rock industry. The popularity of *The Great White Wonder* led to the UK bootleg release of a live Jimi Hendrix performance at the Royal Albert Hall. That the new bootleg industry was not going to go away was quickly apprehended by rock acts. The Rolling Stones issued the in-concert album *Get Yer Ya-Ya's Out* after a 1970 bootleg *LIVEr Than You'll Ever Be* took off. Dylan stayed ahead of the bootleggers by releasing a live album of his 1974 tour – *Before The Flood* – before they could issue one of their own. Many subsequent official retrospective releases of rock's biggest artists exploited the interest generated by illicit collections of their work by containing tracks that were first leaked out in bootleg form, including The Beatles' *Anthology* series and Bruce Springsteen's *Tracks*, not to mention Dylan's own *Biograph*.

The *Basement Tapes* were naturally also influential on a purely musical level. If Dylan and The Band sounded out of time on *The Basement Tapes* it may have been because they were ahead of their time. Before long, the Stones had put out the largely 'back porch' album *Beggar's Banquet*. The Beatles embraced a similar back-to-basics ethic with the 'Get Back' sessions, designed to capture a rock band unadorned by effects and overdubs, even if it did end up in the botched *Let It Be* album. Both Eric Clapton and George Harrison have acknowledged The Band's influence on their late '60s and early '70s sound. Clapton has admitted he wanted to join The Band when Cream broke up. The visionary nature of the album is clearly evident many years later, its rustic feel predating similar efforts by The Byrds on *Sweetheart Of The Rodeo* and by The Flying Burrito Brothers, which led in turn to the commercially successful wave of southern California country-rock of The Eagles, Poco and Pure Prairie League and on to today's Americana artists and roots rockers. Dylan himself followed his sessions at Big Pink with the austere sound of *John Wesley Harding*.

The Band would go on to expand the sound to brilliant effect on *Music From Big Pink*, but the music they and Dylan made together at the height of their creative powers with its fresh spin on the American folk tradition remains a classic document of roots rock authenticity. - Tierney Smith

40. Wheels Of Fire

Cream

TRACKLISTING
White Room/Sitting On Top Of The World/Passing The Time/As You Said/Pressed Rat And Warthog/Politician/Those Were The Days/Born Under A Bad Sign/Deserted Cities Of The Heart/Crossroads/Spoonful/ Traintime/Toad

RELEASED
US: July 1968 UK: August 1968

PRODUCED BY
Felix Pappalardi

By the summer of 1968, Cream had decided to split. They still, however, managed to issue two further albums, one – this set – a double.

But then how could they not take this opportunity to squeeze the last dregs from the barrel despite barely being able to sit in the same room together? Since their inception in 1966, they had become one of the biggest attractions in the world. They had also helped transform perceptions about what was possible or permissible in rock music, helping usher in the age of extemporization and virtuosity.

In many ways, Cream ploughed the same furrow as the Jimi Hendrix Experience, with whose formation date, line-up and style there was an almost eerie synchronicity. However, though the Experience played in the same trio format and though Mitch Mitchell was a superb drummer, it was Hendrix who was the star of that vehicle and the instrumental showboating was almost exclusively his preserve. In Cream, it was nigh on inconceivable that it should be any other way than that all three members should get their lengthy turn in the spotlight: the very name of the band was a boast about the reputations that guitarist Eric Clapton, bassist Jack Bruce and drummer Ginger Baker enjoyed in their home country when they decided to pool their considerable talents.

Some people think the influence of Cream on popular music was a detrimental one. Their argument goes that through their pioneering work in making concise instrumental breaks seem like teenybopper stuff, they made acceptable a whole genre of musical masturbation that blighted 'Seventies rock. Some even talk of Cream blighting their own work with such proclivities. Certainly, many cite the version of 'Toad' on the live section of this album as a track that represents everything that was abominable about the musical fashions that Cream unleashed. It had started life as a track on their 1966 debut album *Fresh Cream*. Essentially a drum solo, it had actually helped lift what was a surprisingly lackluster long playing entrée. However, by the time of *Wheels Of Fire*, 'Toad' had been transformed from a nifty five-minute showcase of Baker's extraordinary skills into a bloated monstrosity that lasted a mind-numbing quarter of an hour. One influence this album had is therefore a paradoxical one: it could be argued that without Cream we wouldn't be able to thank them for many of the classic records of the punk era, punk being the movement that sprang up as a response to the self-indulgence to which Cream unlocked the doors.

However, sight should not be lost of the fact that extemporization and virtuosity made people – including a media that was still rather sniffy about it ten years after its inception – realize that rock was a serious art form, not a soundtrack for a phase that teenagers went through. Nor of the fact that Cream made some fine music, of which this album boasts several examples.

Following that rather dull album debut, Cream really began to live up to their promise with *Disraeli Gears*, released at the end of 1967. Although not quite as colorful as its dazzling psychedelic sleeve implied, it saw them dispensing with the blues covers that had made up such a big part of their first album and finding their own sound: a colossal yet restrained blues-inflected rock.

Despite its quality, however, Cream were reduced on *Disraeli Gears* to including a couple of tracks written by producer Felix Pappalardi and his wife. It was also not the 'real' sound of the band: a dichotomy frequently existed between Cream's bluesy, lengthy live workouts and their chart-oriented studio recordings. *Wheels Of Fire* was an album intended to some extent to address this contradiction. Divided down the middle between studio and live recordings, it presented to the world both

sides of the band. It is therefore the quintessential Cream product. (Originally, UK listeners could opt to buy the double album or the live and studio sections separately.)

Apart from a couple of oldies, all the studio tracks were self-generated, although bizarrely most of the material had been written at the same time as the *Disraeli Gears* songs. Bruce continued his curious reliance on outside lyricist Pete Brown, while Baker collaborated on this record with jazz pianist Mike Taylor. Clapton, though, contributed nothing: his legend at this juncture rested entirely on his guitar playing. As he has since admitted, "At that stage I was good for about a song a year". ('Anyone For Tennis', a Clapton co-write that is to be found on some CD versions of the album, was a May 1968 single not originally part of the album.)

The studio tracks were recorded over the space of just under a year, some in London's IBC Studios, some in Atlantic Studios in New York. However, the lengthy recording process that implies is not the case: sessions were squeezed in between extensive live commitments. The live material was claimed to be from Fillmore dates – probably for the *cachet* – but in fact three of the four live tracks originated from gigs at San Francisco's Winterland.

The studio tracks are a mixed bunch. Baker's 'Pressed Rat And Warthog' is a completely insubstantial piece of spoken word whimsy. However, Brown's and Bruce's 'White Room' and 'Politician' were scorching, powerful and instantly iconic Cream recordings.

Wheels Of Fire went platinum but by this time the band's audience had more faith in Cream than Eric Clapton who literally fainted after reading a review of the group in *Rolling Stone* that described him as the "master of the blues cliché". It was this that made a devastated Clapton decide he wanted to quit the group. The title of the record was a clue to the simpler direction in which Clapton now wanted to go: it was a tribute to 'This Wheel's On Fire', one of the highlights of Dylan's rustic "Basement Tapes" and of the Band's *Music From Big Pink*. - Sean Egan

41. Sweetheart Of The Rodeo
The Byrds

TRACKLISTING
You Ain't Going Nowhere/I Am a Pilgrim/The Christian Life/You Don't Miss Your Water/You're Still on My Mind/Pretty Boy Floyd/Hickory Wind/One Hundred Years From Now/Blue Canadian Rockies/Life in Prison/Nothing Was Delivered

RELEASED
US: August 1968 UK: September 1968

PRODUCED BY
Gary Usher

For many record buyers in the 'Sixties, the gleaming, streamlined sound of The Byrds' Jim (aka Roger) McGuinn's 12-string Rickenbacker guitar was the sound of the future. To the same people, the mewling sound of the pedal steel guitar, beloved of country musicians, was the sound of the past. Past in more ways than one. Country was the music of the 'redneck', whose conservative values were despised by the liberals and radicals who tended to make up rock's audience. When, therefore, The Byrds released a country album in the form of *Sweetheart Of The Rodeo*, their fans were utterly shocked. Their shock was not eased by the religiosity of a couple of its tracks, 'I Am A Pilgrim' and 'The Christian Life'.

On *Sweetheart* much of the lead vocal duties were supposed to have been handled by guitarist Gram Parsons, who had recently joined up with long-serving Byrds McGuinn and Chris Hillman and newer recruit Kevin Kelley. Parsons had previously tried to fuse country and rock in the little known International Submarine Band and was originally recruited to The Byrds as a keyboardist – and on a "hired hand" basis according to Hillman – but within weeks had become the *de facto* leader. Hillman insists The Byrds had spoken of making a country album already. Some tracks on previous Byrds albums had certainly featured country strains. However, Parsons – a Southern man with a deep knowledge of the music – knew the territory better than they. "We're going to let him do his thing," McGuinn said of Parsons to *Rolling Stone* at the time. This plan was to some extent stymied by Parsons' former label, which claimed he was still under contract. The Byrds' label, Columbia, quickly ensured that Parsons' lead vocals on 'The Christian Life' and 'You Don't Miss Your Water' were replaced by McGuinn's. A Parsons song, 'Lazy Days' also fell victim to the legal dispute.

Studying the history of The Byrds throws up a surprising fact. Though he was The Byrds' mainstay and though his quavery vocals and Rickenbacker were signature sounds – ensuring he *is* The Byrds in the eyes of many – Jim/Roger McGuinn was rarely the main songwriting talent of any of their many line-ups. Just as Gene Clark and then Chris Hillman and David Crosby had been significant creative compositional forces pre-*Sweetheart*, so on this album Parsons provides the original songs. Not that there are many of them. The dearth of new material here was a self-sustained injury, strengthening the suspicion of those hostile to the country excursion that it was an act of desperation by a fading band. Ironically – or perhaps significantly – Parsons' songs are the most enjoyable performances. 'One Hundred Years From Now', the only genuinely uptempo track on the album, is steeped in the epic self-pity of country music, portraying a protagonist who has been dumped and is being dissed by his ex's family but ridiculously wonders whether the passage of a century will redeem his reputation. Meanwhile, 'Hickory Wind' is a pine for the distant locales of a rustic childhood that is utterly beautiful, even if the melody does owe something to country standard 'Satisfied Mind' (previously covered by both The Byrds and the International Submarine Band.)

Despite their own considerable in-house songwriting abilities, the employment of the songs of Bob Dylan ran like a thread through The Byrds' career and *Sweetheart* is no exception. The album opens and closes with 'You Ain't Going Nowhere' and 'Nothing Was Delivered', two Dylan songs that most people hadn't yet heard, being part of the legendary so-called "Basement Tapes" that had recently begun circulating in illegal copies. The first was an interesting jaunty countrified take. However, the overly mordant nature of the latter ensured that it was not going to be salvaged by any arrangement whatsoever and the track is really notable only for the fact that its bass line is one of the few examples of a rock sound present on this album.

If truth be told *Sweetheart Of The Rodeo* is not significant on an aesthetic level. There's no real zip or grit and rather too much moroseness, something exacerbated by the overuse of pedal steel. Hillman has himself admitted, "*Sweetheart* was a great idea but it was real sophomore in its attempt at country music. It's good, but it was a beginning. It wasn't something we were very well versed in."

Though it has been described as such, it's also not actually a country-rock album but rather a country album played by rock musicians. This made many country fans wonder why on earth they would want to

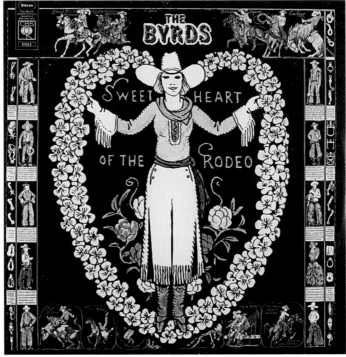

listen to rock musicians sing country when they could hear established country stars do it better. They had a point. The Byrds brought nothing new to the table. Even the use of Dylan songs wasn't that significant. These were more recent, elliptical Dylan numbers, not the kind of protest song that would have shaken up the reactionary values of the country market and, wonderful though Dylan's words always were at that time, country music itself has never suffered from an absence of good lyrics. However, *Sweetheart..* isimportantbecause of the barriers it broke down and the crossover of markets it helped open up. By doing the unthinkable in going country, The Byrds ensured that rock and pop musicians were now free to acknowledge their country tastes and inspirations and act on their hankerings to play it if they wished. Within a year, Bob Dylan, the perceived king of the counter culture, had made a country album, *Nashville Skyline*. Gram Parsons, who left the Byrds before *Sweetheart..* was even released, went on to record genuine country rock with the Flying Burrito Brothers and on his acclaimed solo albums before his premature death. Amongstother real country-rock acts were the highly successful Poco. Meanwhile *Their Greatest Hits* by The Eagles, the ultimate country rock band, is reputed by some sources to be the biggest selling album of all time. - Sean Egan

138

Dancefloor Decadence

From sexualized and subversive roots, through to the giddy excess of its commercial peak, these are the **classics of disco**. Get your dancing boots on...

1.	**Salsoul Hustle**	Salsoul Orchestra
2.	**Love's Theme**	Love Unlimited Orchestra
3.	**Love In C Minor**	Cerrone
4.	**Lady Marmalade**	Labelle
5.	**You Make Me Feel (Mighty Real)**	Sylvester
6.	**We Are Family**	Sister Sledge
7.	**Le Freak**	Chic
8.	**Young Hearts, Run Free**	Candi Staton
9.	**Ring My Bell**	Anita Ward
10.	**I Feel Love**	Donna Summer
11.	**Boogie Wonderland**	Earth Wind And Fire
12.	**Don't Leave Me This Way**	Thelma Houston
13.	**Going Back To My Roots**	Lamont Dozier
14.	**Relight My Fire**	Dan Hartman
15.	**Do What You Wanna Do**	T-Connection
16.	**Cherchez La Femme/Se Si Bon**	Dr Buzzard's Original Savannah Band
17.	**Tragedy**	The Bee Gees
18.	**So Many Men, So Little Time**	Miquel Brown
19.	**Don't Stop 'Til You Get Enough**	Michael Jackson
20.	**Celebration**	Kool And The Gang

42. The Beatles
The Beatles

TRACKLISTING

Back in the U.S.S.R./Dear Prudence/Glass Onion/Ob-La-Di, Ob-La-Da/Wild Honey Pie/The Continuing Story of Bungalow Bill/While My Guitar Gently Weeps/Happiness Is a Warm Gun/Martha My Dear/I'm So Tired/Blackbird/Piggies/Rocky Raccoon/Don't Pass Me By/Why Don't We Do It in the Road?/I Will/Julia/Birthday/Yer Blues/Mother Nature's Son/Everybody's Got Something to Hide Except Me and My Monkey/Sexy Sadie/Helter Skelter/Long Long Long/Revolution 1/Honey Pie/Savoy Truffle/Cry Baby Cry/Revolution 9/Good Night

RELEASED

US: November 1968 UK: November 1968

PRODUCED BY

George Martin

The Beatles' artistic progression between 1963 and 1967 had been so phenomenal that just one thing could be certain as the world awaited their 1968 album release: that it would be a surprise. On that count, the double-LP *The Beatles*, colloquially referred to almost from the day of its release as "The White Album" in reference to the hue of its cover, delivered mightily. The surprise was not, however, so much in the progression of the music as in its regression to more basic rock 'n' roll and folk textures.

By the end of 1967, such was the speed of the group's technological innovations in the studio, and their increased removal from rock roots, that some might have been expecting dives into yet further reaches of the cosmos, along the lines of what bands like Pink Floyd were doing in the late 1960s. But the group's previous 1968 singles ('Lady Madonna' and 'Hey Jude'/'Revolution') had already foretold a return to an earthier approach, although in many respects (particularly the lyrics), the band remained as adventurous as ever.

Another surprise was the extraordinary diversity, and fragmentation, of styles The White Album traversed in the course of its thirty songs. The Beatles had always been eclectic – indeed, that was one of their defining traits – but now, for the first time, they almost seemed like several bands operating at once. The White Album has folk ballads, blues-rock, vaudeville, soul-rock, country & western, tumultuous noise rock, '50s style rock 'n' rollers, lush orchestrated gush, mini-suites, love songs, social commentary, surrealism, lewdness, a hardcore avant-garde eight-minute noise collage, and even some faint echoes of their *Sgt. Pepper*-era psychedelic whimsy. Numerous tracks feature just three, two or even one of the Beatles, rather than the whole group; some are wholly acoustic, others are garnished with multi-layered production and exotic instrumentation.

Producer George Martin was so concerned that there was too much material, in fact, that he wanted to trim it down to one disc. The Beatles vetoed the notion, a wise move as the very sprawl of The White Album is one of its greatest strengths.

The naiveté that had informed The Beatles' early work (and had been much of its charm), and even much of their psychedelic exploration, had largely vanished. They were in their late twenties now, finding increasingly distinct and separate identities as songwriters, and unconcerned with living up to any aspects of their early mop top image. Indeed, at times it seems like they are deliberately tearing down any vestiges of the clean-cut attributes they'd somehow been assigned in Beatlemania. This especially

John Lennon, George Harrison and Paul McCartney listening to the Maharishi, the inspiration for Lennon's 'Sexy Sadie'.

applies to John Lennon. In the songs that are primarily or wholly his own work, he unveils an appetite for biting observation, whether by ambivalently both throwing his lot in with revolutionaries and cautioning against revolutionary violence ('Revolution 1'); self-referentially making fun of listeners who scanned Beatles songs for hidden clues and answers ('Glass Onion'); simultaneously skewering the British blues boom and declaring himself suicidal, to the point of even hating rock 'n' roll ('Yer Blues'); and taking jabs at characters who'd gotten his goat during the group's recent, aborted trip to study with the Maharishi in India ('Sexy Sadie', 'The Continuing Story Of Bungalow Bill'). However, though the abrasive side of John's work draws the most attention, he could be just as romantic a softie as Paul McCartney, as 'Julia', 'Dear Prudence', 'Cry Baby Cry', and 'Good Night' demonstrate. Of course, 'Good Night' is preceded by the record's most extreme (and unpopular) track, the heavily Yoko Ono-influenced soundtrack-to-apocalypse 'Revolution 9', which wholly undercuts any sentimentality 'Good Night' itself might have carried.

Paul McCartney isn't nearly as personal in his songwriting as Lennon, and his White Album contributions have sometimes been characterized (and, occasionally, castigated) as pastiches of various popular music forms. Still, as pastiche craftsmen goes, he's unsurpassed, and the lyrics do often have an irreverence wholly beyond the originators he's emulating. That quality's never better than in the opening 'Back in the U.S.S.R.', where Chuck Berry meets the Beach Boys in the former Soviet Union. 'Rocky Raccoon' is right out of a Western movie saloon gunfight; 'Ob-La-Di, Ob-La-Da' appropriates reggae, with sly hints of transvestism; and 'Honey Pie' is Paul as Fred Astaire. For all his bent toward lightweight fare, however, he could be surprisingly ballsy, literally so with 'Why Don't We Do It In The Road?', which wholly undercut his image as the cute Beatle; his 'Helter Skelter', likewise, is about the most aggressive, ominous rocker the group ever cut. The influence of Donovan (who'd been with the Beatles in India, where he taught John how to play finger-style folk guitar picking), meanwhile, is felt on the acoustic ballads 'Blackbird', 'I Will', and 'Mother Nature's Son'. In combination with Lennon's 'Julia' and 'Dear Prudence', that makes The White Album one of the Beatles' most folk-influenced LPs.

George Harrison was writing more than ever by the time of The White Album, and he was granted four songs here, all of them decent-to-excellent (with 'While My Guitar Gently Weeps' being the most acclaimed). As for The White Album's effect on the world at large, it's sometimes lumped in with such 1968 records as Bob Dylan's *John Wesley Harding*, the Rolling Stones' *Beggars Banquet*, The Byrds' *Sweetheart Of The Rodeo*, and The Band's *Music From Big Pink* as heralding a back-to-basics movement in the aftermath of psychedelia. Indeed, much of the White Album has a 'live' sounding feel, as well as an acoustic one, attributable in parts to the composition of many of the songs in India, where only acoustic guitars were available. Yet that back-to-basics label is true only up to a point. The White Album used just as much multi-layered production as the group's 1966-67 recordings, and at times used some technologically advanced (by 1968 standards) trickery, such as the Mellotron on 'Bungalow Bill' and the tape loops of 'Revolution 9'. The record might indeed have encouraged others to refocus on more song-oriented, organically developed material. Its true legacy, however, was to extend unspoken permission to all rock artists to do whatever they wanted with the LP format, without feeling obligated to stick to a certain style or image. - Richie Unterberger

43. S. F. Sorrow
The Pretty Things

TRACKLISTING
S.F. Sorrow Is Born/Bracelets of Fingers/She Says Good Morning/Private Sorrow/Balloon Burning/Death/Baron Saturday/The Journey/I See You/Well of Destiny/Trust/Old Man Song/Loneliest Person

RELEASED
US: Late 1969 UK: December 1968

PRODUCED BY
Norman Smith

It has long been assumed that the album-long narrative format of *S.F. Sorrow* by the Pretty Things, though commercially unsuccessful, inspired The Who's mega-successful rock opera *Tommy*. Pretty Things vocalist Phil May has recalled The Who's Pete Townshend being stunned by an acetate of *S.F. Sorrow* that was played at a Who party but this second-hand information doesn't necessarily prove his assumption that it provided an impetus or encouragement for *Tommy*, which of course would make it very influential indeed. Speaking exclusively for this book, Townshend himself says of *Sorrow*, "I believe I only listened to it after *Tommy* was released. I maybe once felt that rock opera had been my 'idea', and that maybe Viv Prince [Pretty Things drummer] who had deputised for Keith [Moon, Who drummer] when he had to have some surgery had learned about my plan and spoken to his band about it. I'm not saying I thought they stole my idea. I believe rock opera or songs linked to tell a story were already indicated in *Sgt Pepper* and *Pet Sounds*."

In fact there were more than indications before that, even if they were either fragmentary or non-influential. Some have suggested that the

little known Bacharach & David-penned music for the TV drama *On The Flip Side* (1966) could legitimately be called the first rock opera. It might well be the first example of the phenomenon, but as it barely registered on the public radar it can't really be said to count, culturally. Others have posited the 1967 Keith West single 'Excerpt From A Teenage Opera', but this record – though it resembled a mini-opera in the way it lurched between different melodies, flavours and tempos – did not result

in the promised album-length song cycle. The Small Faces' superb 1968 album *Ogden's Nut Gone Flake* featured a narrative spread over the course of different compositions but that narrative occupied only one side of the vinyl. And while Nirvana's *The Story of Simon Simopath* (1967) and Five Day Week Straw People's eponymous 1968 LP loosely told a story across two sides of 12-inch vinyl, they seemed to create no ripple in the pool in which they were dropped. Plus, Townshend himself had written a couple of 'mini-operas' on The Who's second and third albums.

All of which only serves to muddy the waters about who took their cue from whom. Perhaps its best to simply take the position that the idea of rock being used to tell a story was something in the ether in the late-'Sixties and that *S.F. Sorrow* was a project that did more than most to popularise it.

For his part, Pretties guitarist Dick Taylor recalls band bassist Wally Allen being under the erroneous impression that The Beatles' *Sergeant Pepper* was a narrative album. When he found that it wasn't, he suggested the Pretty Things make one. However he also recalls Phil May having wanted to record a themed album for some time already and even suggests John Coltrane's themed but vocals-less 1964 album *A Love Supreme* was an influence.

When work began on *S.F. Sorrow*, the storyline didn't yet exist.

"We wrote three songs before it solidified," Taylor has recalled. Though the first two tracks on the finished album were the first recorded, the rest of it wasn't written or recorded chronologically. The narrative of *S.F. Sorrow* is opaque but from subsequent band interviews we know that the album essentially tells a straightforward story of the life of the titular English Northerner, through birth ('S.F. Sorrow Is Born'), discovery of masturbation ('Bracelets of Fingers'), first love (the joyous 'She Says Good Morning'), the loss of Sorrow's girlfriend in the 1937 Hindenberg Zeppelin explosion over New Jersey (the almost unbearably exciting 'This Balloon Burning'), seeking solace through acid adventures alongside a sinister figure (the doomy 'Baron Saturday') and old age (the utterly resigned 'Loneliest Person').

The Pretty Things had the luxury of unlimited time in the studio and the privilege of working with producer Norman Smith, one of the then fairly rare breed of producers who could cope with, and indeed would positively encourage, their innovations. However, technology was still fairly limited and only the ambition and enthusiasm of youth prevented the band throwing their hands up in the air as they had to deal with the trauma of the likes of getting down on their hands and knees to find a quarter-inch sliver of tape containing the last note of a guitar solo and the inadequacies of four-track recording (to this day, May insists that only the mono version should be listened to, as so many 'bounce-downs' were done as to lose the option of real, as opposed to mock, stereo).

Though the band had been pleased by the indulgence EMI had shown while they were making the record, they were utterly dismayed at the attitude the label took to promoting it. Aware that neither EMI nor any other company had ever been presented with anything quite like this by their artists, the band arranged a special presentation for the company complete with the playing in full of the record, a light show and Norman Smith providing linking narrative between the tracks. May has recalled the reaction from the 'suits' as bewilderment. The hoped-for special marketing campaign the band felt was necessary for such a unique product was not forthcoming: EMI dumped the album onto the market as merely the new Pretty Things LP, thus losing the column inches the novelty of the record would have guaranteed had its singular nature been brought to the media's and public's attention. Things however were far worse on the other side of the Atlantic, where the group signed to Motown progressive subsidiary Rare Earth. So much did Rare Earth dilly-dally that *S.F. Sorrow* actually appeared on the market in the States after The Who's *Tommy*. The Pretty Things found themselves accused of jumping on the rock opera bandwagon The Who had supposedly started with the May 1969 release of that saga of a deaf, dumb and blind boy. - Sean Egan

44. Led Zeppelin

Led Zeppelin

TRACKLISTING
Good Times Bad Times/Babe I'm Gonna Leave You/You Shook Me/
Dazed and Confused/Your Time is Gonna Come/Black Mountain
Side/Communication Breakdown/I Can't Quit You Baby/How Many
More Times

RELEASED
US: January 1969 UK: March 1969

PRODUCED BY
Jimmy Page

The band were partly named, jokingly, as a variation on the quip, "You'll go
over like a lead balloon", but their success was anything but a joke. Led
Zeppelin became one of the biggest and most influential bands in rock
history in the matter of just a few months. Though other Zeppelin
albums have sold more, and few can argue with the longevity of the
later 'Stairway To Heaven', it was the sound Led Zeppelin exhibited on
their self-titled debut that changed the shape of rock 'n' roll.

There were several elements of Zeppelin's style that were
revolutionary, but none was greater than the alchemy with which they
mixed blues licks into weighty rock songs. They achieved this by speeding
the songs up, adding lengthy guitar and drum solos, and letting singer
Robert Plant improvise yelps and shouts as part of the vocals. There were
many other bands in Britain at the time who were inspired by American
blues, but none injected the blues into a sound that was as heavy, loud, and
raucous as Zeppelin's. Some of this credit goes to producer/guitarist Jimmy
Page, who was the mastermind behind this amalgamation. Still, one cannot
underestimate the singular role played by drummer John Bonham, who was
able to out-power all-comers. Bonham was the best drummer rock ever
had, and considering the importance of rhythm to rock music, this was an
advantage that no other band could match and an under-recognized part ofr
Zeppelin's success.

One can see the achievement of *Led Zeppelin* by comparing the
version of 'You Shook Me' on this album with the one done by the Jeff
Beck Group on *Truth*. Beck's version predated the Zeppelin session, and he
later accused Page of stealing his idea but while Beck's version has a more
authentic blues feel, and more traditional instrumentation the Zeppelin
cover is superior because they take the song to a new energetic level,

driven by the drums and bass. Zeppelin turn 'You Shook Me' into something that is far more than an homage to the blues – it becomes a battle between Plant and Page, and a battle between Bonham and bassist John Paul Jones. This kind of wild interplay would rarely show up in a traditional blues song, where the guitar player wouldn't dare outshine the vocalist, and where all musicians would attempt to keep the same beat. Yet it is this internal tension, and the interplay between the four musicians, that gives Zeppelin's 'You Shook Me' a resonance that goes beyond any other covers of the song, even the Willie Dixon original.

Though Page was ringmaster of Led Zeppelin, the group also succeeded because they were an egalitarian band, with all four members contributing equally. Some might argue the merits of the Who's John Entwistle versus Zeppelin's John Paul Jones but few could suggest that any rock rhythm section could best the driving power that Bonham and Jones create on 'Communication Breakdown', the first underground hit to break out from *Led Zeppelin*. The other

Zeppelin 'greatest hit' here is 'Dazed And Confused', which is often cited as one of the first salvos of a genre that would later come to be known as 'Heavy Metal'. Heavy Metal is a pigeonhole Zeppelin are often put into but that classification is not exactly accurate: they were always heavier than they were metallic, and they would have preferred to be shelved in the blues-rock section. While 'Dazed and Confused' and 'Communication Breakdown' were the songs that received the most airplay from this record - though neither could truly

George Hardie's Zeppelin cover design for Led Zeppelin's debut album.

be a considered a hit single – it was 'You Shook Me', 'Your Time is Gonna Come', and 'Babe I'm Gonna Leave You' that made Zeppelin's first album shine. Here is the great strength of *Led Zeppelin*: The album shows many diverse influences, including folk and eastern music, along with the more obvious blues inspirations. Ironically, during the interviews the band gave on their first tour, they talked about California folk rock being one of their greatest loves. Much of the Zeppelin magic was their ability to mix all these disparate elements into song structures that were based on folk songs, but had exotic textures. This delicate seasoning was unfortunately lost on their future imitators who imagined the key to sounding like Zeppelin was simply louder guitars and more bombast.

Led Zeppelin was an album that also changed the way the music industry operated. The success of this record launched a shift in power away from record companies and producers and towards bands and their managers. Without any promotion and without the benefit of any radio play on commercial Top 40 stations, *Led Zeppelin* stormed up the charts and became a Top Ten hit album, and that made many in the industry rethink the way rock was marketed. For future albums, Zeppelin were given unheard of control over the recording and marketing of their music. They became the first post-Beatles superstar band to emerge in rock, and groups that formed after them modeled their organizations on the Zeppelin machine. Their manager, Peter Grant, became one of the most powerful men in showbusiness, and made Led Zeppelin the most successful and best-paid live act of their era.

Unfortunately, as Zeppelin's commercial impact grew, the band became so large that their shadow overwhelmed their musicianship. Despite some great later-era albums, they became known in the press for their off-stage sexual antics, with the most famous incident being the 'mud shark' brouhaha that occurred at a Seattle waterfront hotel and was later chronicled in a Frank Zappa song. And though Page was truly one of the flashiest guitar players in rock, many later wannabe's forgot that what made Zeppelin great was the texture and subtly to their music, and not the showy solos. The eastern, folk, and blues influences that are so apparent on *Led Zeppelin* were quickly tossed aside by future metal bands, and even, some might argue, by Zeppelin themselves as the band became stadium headliners. *Led Zeppelin* is Led Zeppelin before they became *Led* Zeppelin, and this album is the purest distillation of the band before italics took over their every move. - Charles R. Cross

45. Crosby, Stills & Nash
Crosby, Stills & Nash

TRACKLISTING
Suite: Judy Blue Eyes/Marrakesh Express/Guinnevere/You Don't Have to Cry/Pre-Road Downs/Wooden Ships/Lady Of The Island/Helplessly Hoping/Long Time Gone/49 Bye-Byes

RELEASED
US: May 1969 UK: June 1969

PRODUCED BY
Bill Halverson

Crosby, Stills & Nash were the voice of the Woodstock generation, the epitome of the increasingly hairy youth of late 'Sixties/early 'Seventies America who were united against the Vietnam War and social injustice and in favor of recreational drugs and whose spiritual peak was the aforementioned festival of August 1969. Crosby, Stills & Nash performed there and their song 'Long Time Gone' was played over the opening titles of the movie of the event. To cap it all, they recorded the famous version of the song 'Woodstock', written by (non-attendee) Joni Mitchell to celebrate the happening.

For one brief moment, they were perfectly in tune with the *zeitgeist*, even to the extent of their confessional, acoustic songs heralding the shift from political activism into the more reflective tones of the 1970s, although thankfully without the self-obsession that began to characterize a period eventually dubbed the Me-Decade. That confessional style was one of the most successful genres of the first half of the 'Seventies.

Crosby, Stills' & Nash were one of the first supergroups. However, they weren't initially that super: though all came from successful bands, none was the most celebrated or prominent of their previous ensembles, The Byrds, Buffalo Springfield and The Hollies respectively. They also weren't actually a group as such. David Crosby, Stephen Stills and Graham Nash were all guitarists and vocalists so they would always need to augment their line-up with a drummer. However, neither of these things bothered the public much and the success of this, their first album, and the iconic status they achieved soon after meant that the trio eclipsed the achievements of their previous bands - that is, if one discounts the Byrds', Hollies' and Buffalo Springfield's hit singles. Many did, as by this point singles were becoming an irrelevance to rock acts, yet another sign of the growing maturity of the rock audience that Crosby, Still & Nash were both reflecting and capitalizing on.

The amazing transcendent blend of the trio's collective voices revealed itself in an informal singing session one day at the home of Cass Elliot of the Mamas And The Papas. It made them consider working together. Though both The Hollies and The Byrds had been famous for their three-part harmonies, the singing mode of CS&N sounded more like The Byrds' elegant vocal style than the more widescreen and often over-polished Hollies trilling. In fact, several tracks on this album sound almost eerily like outtakes from Byrds albums *Fifth Dimension* and *Younger Than Yesterday*.

Crosby, Stills & Nash opens with a couple of point-stating tracks. As if to emphasize their radicalism, they daringly begin the album with a seven-and-a-half-minute epic, Stills's 'Suite: Judy Blue Eyes', a wandering, earnest number which makes the listener feel like he has walked in on the middle of a lovers' heart-to-heart. One of the two songs Stills contributed about partner Judy Collins to the album (the other, 'You Don't Have To Cry', is the one on which the trio were harmonizing at Elliot's house that fateful day), it might have inspired guffaws amongst some for the way it agonizes over a romance but that was partly because the rock audience hitherto was generally used to somewhat more juvenile analyses of the interaction between men and women. This sort of sophistication about relationships would be a feature of CS&N albums. Meanwhile, the following track, 'Marrakesh Express' sees Graham Nash making a point to The Hollies. Nash felt that his old mates weren't taking the track seriously

when he presented it to them and, though some of them dispute this, it was his frustration at this kind of reception to his newer material that made Nash want to leave the fold. The song was sort of political because it had a vaguely eastern air: in that day and age, suggesting that there were enviable cultures and lifestyles beyond the orbit of western consumerist societies felt like a political act, even if the song is ultimately more a travelogue than anything else.

The most overtly political song on the record comes from David Crosby. The man who

David Crosby, Stephen Stills and Graham Nash on the cover of their eponymous debut.

denounced from the stage at Monterey the cover-up, as he saw it, over the Kennedy assassination wrote two songs on the night of JFK's murder, one almost sublime, one fairly ridiculous. 'Almost Cut My Hair' was the latter (held over to this album's follow-up), the other was 'Long Time Gone'. Seeming to allude to Sam Cooke's 'A Change Is Gonna Come' in the song's title refrain, Crosby advises listeners not to try to get themselves elected, adding, "If you do, you had better cut your hair".

The album's pace is relentlessly stately, aside from 'Marrakesh Express', which retains some of The Hollies' chirpiness (and should really have been the opener). Some might find this calm air, the tasteful and never gritty instrumentation and the washes of harmonizing soporific − there is no difference, for instance, in the timbre of 'Long Time Gone' and any of the love songs - but there is no doubting that it was to the public's taste and that furthermore that it was the 'hip' public that was buying this material. It should also be noted that the prettiness of the harmonies disguised at least one shortcoming, namely Crosby's typically meandering melodies and lazy, sometimes non-existent, rhyming schemes.

This would actually be the last CS&N album for eight years, the band mutating into Crosby, Stills, Nash & Young for the following year's *Déjà Vu*. Because of the additional bite and high quality songs that Neil Young brought to the table, many are under the impression that Stills' former Buffalo Springfield colleague was doing CS&N a favor by signing up. In fact, Young admitted at the time that in joining he was partly motivated by money. It should not be forgotten: Crosby, Stills & Nash – mostly because of this album – were huge. - Sean Egan

46. Tommy
The Who

TRACKLISTING
Overture/It's a Boy/1921/Amazing Journey/Sparks/Eyesight To The Blind (The Hawker)/Christmas/Cousin Kevin/The Acid Queen/Underture/Do You Think It's Alright?/Fiddle About/Pinball Wizard/There's A Doctor/Go to the Mirror!/Tommy Can You Hear Me?/Smash The Mirror/Sensation/Miracle Cure/Sally Simpson/I'm Free/Welcome/Tommy's Holiday Camp/We're Not Gonna Take It

RELEASED
US: May 1969 UK: May 1969

PRODUCED BY
Kit Lambert

As discussed previously, *Tommy* was not the first rock opera. However, *Tommy* was the first rock opera to gain a broad worldwide audience. In fact, it remains the most famous rock opera, by a considerable margin. It was, also, the album that broke The Who as superstars in the United States, where the band (despite a few hits) had been a rather cultish pursuit, and not the consistent chart act they'd been in the UK since 1965.

While this two-album set was greeted by much of the media as a startling innovation upon its original release, Who guitarist and principal songwriter Pete Townshend had actually been toying increasingly seriously with operatic, classical-influenced concepts for some time. Recording *Tommy*, the band's guiding considerations were not purely artistic. Performing as The Who was an expensive proposition, what with their constant equipment smashing/abuse and various other excesses. They needed a blockbuster not only to get out of debt, but to even stay together. *Tommy* producer (and Who co-manager) Kit Lambert was vital to helping Townshend and the band shape the *Tommy* concept and see it through to completion.

Tommy was an instant success in both the US and the UK, aided by the release, slightly in advance of the album, of its most obviously commercial track ('Pinball Wizard') as a single. Even so, its storyline to some degree remains obscure to many of its listeners, with the most disturbing elements sailing right over many of their heads. For *Tommy* is not just the story of a "deaf, dumb and blind boy" who is miraculously cured. It's also the story of parental physical, emotional, and even sexual abuse; the inner shell into which victims withdraw as protection; and, with perhaps even more disturbing implications for the rock audience, the blind faith followers are wont to invest in their leaders (and the bitter disillusionment that follows when those leaders don't say what the audience wants to hear). Keeping the ostensible story going, too, required a few expository 'link' tracks that couldn't hope to be as musically impressive as the more fully thought-out, proper songs.

What listeners likely responded to most - certainly more than the fractured plot - was the operatic feel conveyed not by the lyrics so much as the constant echoing and referencing of musical motifs throughout the record, many of them memorable and deftly placed. The underrated, vastly dramatic ten-minute instrumental 'Underture' contains several of these, and it's there where The Who really get closest to an effective rock-classical fusion. Plus, for all its pretensions, the record contains an astonishing number of the effective power-rock riffs that the group had been so crucial to popularizing in rock as a whole – 'Amazing Journey', 'The Acid Queen', 'Pinball Wizard', 'I'm Free', and 'We're Not Gonna Take It' are full of 'em.

Other songs (particularly another underrated track, 'Sensation') have a delicacy and philosophical grace, and the band's overlooked skill at devising fine high vocal harmonies does much to put the message across. And, for all the undercurrents of abuse and torment in *Tommy*, there's much redemption and optimism to be found in how its protagonist finds some inner peace and strength amidst (and possibly as a result of) his trials. Townshend removes any question of cynical exploitation/contempt for his own audience with the closing 'See Me Feel Me/Listening to You,' in which he makes it clear that Tommy - perhaps a stand-in for Townshend himself - is at least as enlightened by his audience as the audience is enlightened by his leadership.

For The Who, *Tommy*'s significance was to vault them into the inner sanctum of rock superstardom. For all the wealth and fame it brought them, however, The Who eventually got tired of *Tommy*, or at least, as they said in various wordings, an audience who thought the band were named Tommy and the album was called *The Who*. If they'd really wanted to sweep it under the rug, however, they probably wouldn't have gotten involved in the far gaucher film and stage adaptations of the record, which have done their part to keep the *Tommy* torch burning.

In the wider world, *Tommy*'s influence was to confer some cultural legitimacy on rock 'n' roll as a whole, albeit from quarters that often didn't really understand or appreciate rock music itself. Within the rock

Keith Moon and Roger Daltrey rocking out in Copenhagen, 1970.

community, it legitimized the full-length album-opera (or at least album-story) approach, and further legitimized the vague 'concept album' format that had been in some vogue at least since *Sgt. Pepper*. Numerous actual rock operas or pseudo-operas did follow, though none with the same combination of artistic and commercial success of *Tommy*, ranging from the blockbuster (Jethro Tull's *Thick As a Brick,* Pink Floyd's *The Wall*) to cult favorites (The Kinks' *Arthur,* which followed *Tommy* by just a few months so may have been in development simultaneously with *Tommy*; Frank Zappa's *Joe's Garage;* Parliament's *Funkentelechy vs. the Placebo Syndrome*) to the obscure (*666* by Aphrodite's Child, featuring a young Vangelis, and the Bonzo Dog Doo Dah Band's *Keynsham*). Andrew Lloyd Webber and Tim Rice co-opted the concept for the theater, and while it was critically lambasted, their *Jesus Christ Superstar was* a rock opera, and a huge-selling one. Other classic rock albums, such as David Bowie's *Ziggy Stardust*, were more concept works than operas, but took advantage of the vaguely-defined-epic format to both anchor the music and sell records.

Every rock opera or concept album since the late 1960s, in fact, owes something to *Tommy*. For all its influence on other artists, however, the most worthwhile rock opera to follow *Tommy* was the one concocted by The Who themselves, 1973's *Quadrophenia*. - Richie Unterberger

47. Stand!

Sly And The Family Stone

TRACKLISTING
Stand!/Don't Call Me Nigger, Whitey/I Want To Take You Higher/Somebody's Watching You/Sing A Simple Song/Everyday People/Sex Machine/You Can Make It If You Try

RELEASED
US: May 1969 UK: July 1969

PRODUCED BY
Sly Stone

Before the darkness descended, Sly Stone was all about the light.

Sylvester "Sly Stone" Stewart had it within his reach to be perhaps the biggest, certainly the most important pop star of his – or maybe even any – era; but, at the height of his powers, he slipped into a drug-fuelled hell from which his temperamental muse was only sporadically to reappear.

Stewart was a visionary in ways other than to do with writing and performing. His impatience with the boundaries set up to keep musical genres apart led him to conceptualise a band that combined black, white, male, female, pop, funk, soul, rock, jazz and all points in between. By the time he formed Sly And The Family Stone in San Francisco in 1967, he had studied music composition and theory at college, produced records for Bay Area garage bands, DJ-ed on two radio stations and had his own group. But the Family Stone were different.

The band signed to Epic after one locally-released single, but *A Whole New Thing* (1967), a dazzlingly psychedelic debut album made within months of the band's formation, proved too difficult a sell. To rein in its excesses might seem like admitting defeat, as if several exciting avenues had been closed off rather than explored, but Sly was not going to be a martyr to his creative ambition. Within months, the second LP, *Dance To The Music*, had achieved a balance that retained most of the Family Stone's disparate dynamic but hitched it to strong, accessible, immediate pop, epitomised by quirky and innovative but joyous songs like 'I Ain't Got Nobody (For Real)' and the title track. 'Dance To The Music' became their first top 10 hit.

Life, released with barely a pause for breath after Dance…, showed how quickly and effectively Sly and the band were honing their craft. Then, late in 1968, they released the single 'Everyday People'. This infectious and

Sly and the Family Stone.

warm song gave them their first Number One, and sat at the heart of Stand!, their fourth album, which arrived the following year. Although many critics claim to prefer its follow-up and corollary – 1971's darker, slower, absorbing There's A Riot Goin' On, which a paranoid Sly made largely on his own – Stand! is the apotheosis of what the group were all about, before fame quenched their leader's joie de vivre and he began his attempt to self-medicate his demons away.

Stand! is only eight songs long, and one of those – the sleazy jam 'Sex Machine' – takes up a third of its 40-odd minutes' running time. Yet there are more ideas here than most bands manage to generate in an entire career, and the sheer effervescent beauty of the songs is beyond question. It is a record redolent of its times, but never stuck in them, an album that exhorts its listeners to believe that there are things worth fighting for, and that there is both power and joy to be had in recognising that fact.

The title track is an invocation to recognise and remain loyal to the truth, its superb coda reputedly made by Sly on his own after playing an acetate of the song in a Bay Area club and realising it needed another element. 'Don't Call Me Nigger…' puts the racial politics the band's multi-hued line-up exemplified into stark focus, with the opening lines of 'Everyday People' – "Sometimes I'm right, but I can be wrong", followed by a statement that his own beliefs were to be found in his songs – proving similarly strident yet non-didactic, to-the-point yet general and wide-ranging. 'Sing A Simple Song' is more than just a call for clarity – it's one of the finest pieces of funk ever recorded. Greg Errico's steel-hard drumming and Gerry Martini's sax during the break would prove irresistible to dozens of hip hop producers who sampled them years later, showing just how ahead of its time the record's sound was. 'You Can Make It If You Try' closes the album with a glorious, euphoric song of empowerment. Perhaps significantly, this was what the band were playing at the Newport Folk Festival when 20,000 ticketless fans broke down the fence to get in.

Following *Stand!*'s release, the band played at 3am on the second day of Woodstock, and were generally reckoned to have stolen the show. Their blend of politics, pop and panache combined with the *Zeitgeist* to produce a synchronicity of time, place and purpose that was almost unprecedented. But then came the fear. Sly moved to LA, started hanging out with some unsavoury characters, and blitzed his mind on cocaine. Increasingly introverted, he hid from his celebrity, and seemed frozen, as if afraid of exercising the power over his ever-growing audience that was his to wield. ...*Riot*... was his eventual response, a brilliant but desperately bleak record, very much the sound of the morning after the heady, anything-is-possible party that *Stand!* had represented.

Everyone from Prince (who can count the Family Stone's revolutionary bass player, Larry Graham, as a member of his band) to Public Enemy, OutKast to Rocket From The Crypt has picked up Sly Stone's mantle, but it is the Sly of *Stand!* they usually reference. This album proved that commercial success with political music wasn't the preserve of white musicians (although James Brown had also pioneered in that field). It also proved that political music need not be didactic protest but could be life-affirming. Meanwhile, the very way Stewart ignored musical boundaries in his sonic melting pot and skin color in his choice of personnel made it very difficult for people to category-ghettoise him or any other African-American artist ever again.

Contrary to most expectations, he's still out there somewhere, surfacing very occasionally for shambolic, surreal public appearances. In 2006, sporting a blond Mohican and huge black sunglasses, he confounded many naysayers by turning up for a reunion with his former bandmates at the Grammy Awards, their first time playing together in more than 30 years. With them, he performed most of 'I Want To Take You Higher' But as quickly as he had arrived, he vanished, back into the cloak of anonymity he has used as refuge and comfort blanket for three decades. Truly, we will never see his like again. - Angus Batey

One-Two-Free-*Four*!

Most of them were gone as quickly as their emergence in a hail of f-words and saliva but many of them left at least one **classic punk single** in their wake. Twenty to pogo to.

1.	**Complete Control**	The Clash
2.	**Gary Gilmore's Eyes**	The Adverts
3.	**In The City**	The Jam
4.	**Orgasm Addict**	The Buzzcocks
5.	**Ain't Bin To No Music School**	The Nosebleeds
6.	**12XU**	Wire
7.	**Peaches**	The Stranglers
8.	**Oh Bondage, Up Yours!**	X-ray Spex
9.	**Don't Dictate**	Penetration
10.	**Angels With Dirty Faces**	Sham 69
11.	**Cranked Up Really High**	Slaughter And The Dogs
12.	**Holiday In Cambodia**	The Dead Kennedys
13.	**Blank Generation**	Richard Hell And The Voidoids
14.	**She's So Modern**	The Boomtown Rats
15.	**Alternative Ulster**	Stiff Little Fingers
16.	**Teenage Kicks**	The Undertones
17.	**Fascist Dictator**	The Cortinas
18.	**The Dictators**	Search & Destroy
19.	**Dead Boys**	Sonic Reducer
20.	**Babylon's Burning**	The Ruts

48. Five Leaves Left
Nick Drake

TRACKLISTING

Time Has Told Me/River Man/Three Hours/Way To Blue/Day Is Done/Cello Song/The Thoughts Of Mary Jane/Man In A Shed/Fruit Tree/Saturday Sun

RELEASED

US: September 1969 US UK: September 1969

PRODUCED BY

Joe Boyd

Before his 1974 death at 26 from an overdose of anti-depressant medication, British singer-songwriter Nick Drake toiled in Van Gogh-like obscurity, releasing three exquisite folk style albums that were embraced by the critics and his fellow musicians but were commercial failures, none exceeding 5,000 copies sold. The success that eluded Drake in life would be transformed into a growing cult after his passing.

In retrospect, however, it's easy to see why Drake went unrecognized in his lifetime. He was easy to overlook. Quiet, introspective and pathologically shy (during recording sessions he was said to have played to the wall to avoid people's gaze), Drake suffered from severe clinical depression, an affliction that at times made it difficult for him to even speak. He rarely performed in concert and when he did the experience proved to be so awkward and uncomfortable he eventually quit live work altogether. Adding to all that, Drake rarely gave interviews and his songs were not particularly radio-friendly. In fact, he often sounded for all the world like a man out of time. Robert Kirby, who arranged Drake's striking 1969 debut *Five Leaves Left* called him "a lost romantic" who was born in the wrong century and was better suited to the 17th century Elizabe than court. Drake's failure to connect with the public is especially poignant considering that his music was his one true means of communicating with people.

A college dropout who would perform at local clubs and coffeehouses, Drake was discovered by bassist Ashley Hutchings of British folk rockers Fairport Convention who heard him perform at a live show in Cambridge. Hutchings in turn recommended Drake to the band's producer Joe Boyd, which led to a three-album contract with Island Records. The album that would launch his posthumous cult following (which took its name from the warning on a packet of cigarette papers) has the feel of a classic British folk album. The original concept of bringing in a fifteen-piece ensemble was jettisoned by Drake in favor of old Cambridge pal Robert Kirby as arranger of a smaller chamber string ensemble.

Free of any trace of anger and cynicism, Drake comes across as a fragile, sensitive soul. He delivers his songs in a whispery voice reminiscent of Donovan, the lack of strong emotion giving these songs a feel of mournful disconnect. Kirby called Drake the "most all-round perfect artist I've ever worked with". Boyd viewed him as being "outside all trends and all movements". (As an interesting aside, Elton John, hired by Boyd to do a session with Linda Thompson, recorded four songs from *Five Leaves Left* on a demo in 1968 which was subsequently circulated as a bootleg before Drake released his own versions.)

Drake's debut found him backed by a small group of musicians including bassist Danny Thompson and pianist Paul Harris. Featuring Drake's fancy finger picking guitar technique and use of open tunings, *Five Leaves Left* is a gentle, poetic work of sweeping melancholy with lovely baroque touches and lyrics of brooding eloquence. The album's somber opener 'Time Has Told Me' is enlivened by Richard Thompson's twangy guitar fills, 'The Thoughts Of Mary Jane' is pure whimsy, 'Way To Blue' elegant pop classicism. All these songs convey the weight of Drake's sorrows. It's there in the creeping dread of 'Day Is Done', the mournful 'Cello Song' in which he consigns himself to a "cruel world where I belong"; the jazzy 'Man In A Shed', a plea for solace and salvation ("Please stop my world from raining through my head"). But the album's most chilling moment is the ornate, eerily prophetic 'Fruit Tree', a song about fame and recognition achieved only after one's passing: "Don't you worry, they'll stand and stare when you're gone."

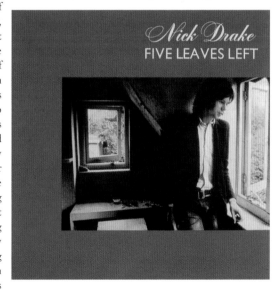

The original cover for *Five Leaves Left*.

Drake's mother once commented that her son felt like a failure because he hadn't reached people through his music. If Drake was in the end demoralized by his lack of support, Boyd for one believed in him. When he sold his Witchseason label to Island in the early '70s it was with the stipulation that Drake's back catalog never be deleted. Though Drake's passing barely rated a mention in the music press, in death his reputation steadily grew. British pop group The Dream Academy dedicated their 1985 hit 'Life In A Northern Town' to Drake. Artists as disparate as Norah Jones, R.E.M. (listen to 'Perfect Circle' from their 1983 debut *Murmur*), Lucinda Williams, Duncan Sheik, Ryan Adams, Blur's Graham Coxon and The Cure's Robert Smith have all acknowledged Drake as an influence. The Black Crowe's guitarist Rich Robinson credited Drake with inspiring his own use of open tunings. One can even hear Drake's influence in the elegance of Paul Weller's more pastoral solo work and in the folk-styled singer-songwriters of the so-called "New Weird America" (i.e., Devendra Banhart, Joanna Newsom, Six Organs Of Admittance). Drake went on to make just two more albums, 1970's jazzier, more uptempo *Bryter Layter* and 1972's stripped-down, harrowingly bleak *Pink Moon*, whose title track won him new converts when it was featured in a 2000 US Volkswagen commercial. 2004 saw a BBC Radio 2 documentary, *Lost Boy: In Search Of Nick Drake*, presented by actor Brad Pitt (clearly Drake's appeal is more far-reaching than we know).

Drake was found dead by his mother at his parents' home two years after he recorded *Pink Moon* (the coroner ruled the death a suicide, though that may be open to dispute), leaving behind a legacy in the form of three somber, soul baring artistic statements, the first instalment of which was this haunting template, one that has over time inspired countless introspective dreamers armed with a song, a guitar and a desire to indulge their deepest feelings of melancholy. - Tierney Smith

49. Trout Mask Replica
Captain Beefheart And The Magic Band

TRACKLISTING
Frownland/The Dust Blows Forward 'N The Dust Blows Back/Dachau Blues/Ella Guru/Hair Pie: Bake 1/Moonlight On Vermont/Pachuco Cadaver/Bill's Corpse/Sweet Sweet Bulbs/Neon Meate Dream Of A Octafish/China Pig/My Human Gets Me Blues/Dali's Car/Hair Pie: Bake 2/Pena/Well/When Big Joan Sets Up / Fallin' Ditch/ Sugar 'N Spikes/Ant Man Bee/Orange Claw Hammer/Wild Life/She's Too Much For My Mirror/Hobo Chang Ba/The Blimp (Mousetrapreplica)/Steal Softly Thru Snow/Old Fart At Play/Veteran's Day Poppy

RELEASED
US: November 1969 UK: November 1969

Unlistenable, insane, and incoherent? Or a work of genius and possibly the greatest album ever recorded? Whichever view you take, *Trout Mask Replica* is an astonishing album.

Captain Beefheart's career had started closer to the mainstream, with the Magic Band's rhythm & blues complemented by his haunting, harsh voice on early recordings. But *Trout Mask Replica* was a complete leap in the dark, made at a time when people still believed that rock music could achieve extraordinary things. It may not be strictly true that Beefheart locked the band in a house for three months to learn the album, or that several of them had never played instruments before (as he claimed on occasion). But the music created on this album is a long, long way from most pop and rock of the period. A recognisable blues element remains (especially in simpler songs such as 'China Pig'), but it is overlaid with elements of a wild, free jazz and experimental rock. This is combined with Captain Beefheart's assonant and bizarrely poetic lyrics, frightening and hilarious nonsense spoken in a bewildering variety of voices, and the appalling caterwauling of Beefheart's beloved saxophones. The interlocking rhythms of the band appear completely random at times, yet they clearly have some logical foundation. But Beefheart's vocals are often sung as though he is in another timezone or even an alternative universe. (He was in fact, producer Zappa has attested, often in a different room to the band, refusing to wear his headphones, thus performing semi-detached from the backing music.)

Beefheart was notoriously difficult to work with. After the exhausting rehearsal period at the band's rented house in Entrada Drive, Woodland Hills, LA, Zappa tried to record the entire album on mobile recording equipment there. But Beefheart thought Zappa was being tight-fisted and insisted on relocating to a studio, although once there the band proceeded to mimic the conditions of the house, even muffling the cymbals with cardboard as they had been doing to keep the noise down. The final album is a mixture of recordings from the two locations.

In between tracks, the voices of Beefheart and the band provide a surreal commentary. A typical song introduction declaims, "A squid eating dough in a polyethylene bag is fast 'n' bulbous, got me?" The lyrics range from the Dadaist weirdness of 'Neon Meate Dream Of A Octofish' and 'The Blimp', through the American gothic of 'Moonlight On Vermont' and the disturbing 'Dachau Blues', to an almost Whitmanesque earthiness on tracks like 'Ant Man Bee' or 'The Dust Blows Forward 'N The Dust Blows Back'. The surrealism is compounded by the fish mask cover, with the band pictured in weird costumes, portraying the personas they adopt on the

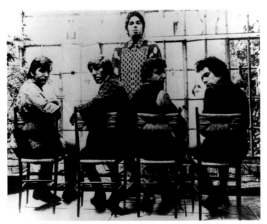

record (Zoot Horn Rollo, The Mascara Snake, *et al*).

The only way to listen to *Trout Mask Replica* is obsessively and repetitively, because the first time you hear it, it makes no sense at all. You might laugh at the outbursts of nonsense, or scratch your head as you try to make sense of the chaos. But if you are intrigued enough to listen to it again and again and again, then finally, somewhere between the twentieth and thirtieth consecutive listening, it will start to sound perfectly sensible. At which stage most other rock albums ever recorded will sound pale and vacuous in comparison.

There were several other notable Captain Beefheart albums, from the follow-up *Lick My Decals Off, Baby* to his swansong *Ice Cream For Crow* in 1982 (after which he quit the music business, returning to live and paint in his Mojave desert home). But *Trout Mask Replica* is still the defining album in his career, perhaps because it is the sound of an artist and band astounding even themselves with the sound they are making.

Beefheart is impossible to imitate. But listen to *Trout Mask Replica* and you hear an artist who is refusing to accept any musical boundaries, who is refusing to be categorised by any genre, and who believes that all kinds of poetry, madness, and peculiarity have their place in rock music. The music disobeys every rule of songwriting. The rhythms are complex and different parts are often played in different time signatures. The Magic Band fully realise Beefheart's dream of sounding like a band who have completely unlearned all the normal rules and are having to recreate music from scratch. The songwriting underpins the extraordinary performances. Some songs are touching, emotional and raw, while others are meandering, weird and opaque, but throughout the album there is a sense that the normal boundaries of music have been torn down.

In the end, this is the real legacy of Captain Beefheart. You can hear direct echoes of his music in artists as disparate as Public Image Ltd and Tortoise, James White and The Blacks and Radiohead (*Kid A* in particular pays homage to Beefheart). But you can also hear reminders of his work anytime you hear an act who are prepared to unlearn normal ways of recording music, and risk producing something that will be dismissed as unlistenable: from Pere Ubu to practitioners of noise music. Or any time an artist is prepared to work with weird and disturbing subjects or styles – from Devo and The Residents to The Chemical Brothers, The Fall, or even Tom Waits.

You can love or hate *Trout Mask Replica*. But once you've heard it, it is an impossible album to ignore. - Hugh Barker

50. Let It Bleed
The Rolling Stones

TRACKLISTING
Gimme Shelter/Love in Vain/Country Honk/Live With Me/Let It Bleed/Midnight Rambler/You Got the Silver/Monkey Man/You Can't Always Get What You Want

RELEASED
US: November 1969 UK: December 1969

PRODUCED BY
Jimmy Miller

With *Let It Bleed*, the Rolling Stones redefined their sound. In so doing, they effectively redefined rock.

The recording of the album spanned November 1968 to November 1969. This non-calendar year was notable for it being one of the most traumatic and seismic passages in the band's history. Though perhaps not quite as bad as the *annus horibilis* of 1967 in which three of the Stones were imprisoned, albeit all briefly, as the establishment of their country made what seemed a concerted effort to punish them for representing the anti-authoritarian spirit of the age, the *Let It Bleed* sessions encompassed the following: Mick Jagger traumatizing Keith Richards by embarking on an affair with Richards' partner Anita Pallenberg, Jagger's partner Marianne Faithfull suffering a miscarriage – after having been denounced for conceiving while unwed by the Archbishop of Canterbury, the hassles of drug busts, embittered exchanges with their manager Allen Klein, the mental deterioration of their founder member Brian Jones and his ultimate dismissal from the group, the shock of Jones' subsequent death by drowning and a suicide attempt by Faithfull, who had been increasingly distressing Jagger with her hard drug use. Amazingly, out of all this trauma, they wrested a superb album, even if the lyrics did seem to betray a certain degree of emotional anguish.

At the end of May 1969, the Stones were joined by guitarist Mick Taylor, whose contributions to 'Live With Me' and 'Honky Tonk

Women' secured him a status as permanent replacement for the increasingly disinterested Brian Jones. 'Honky Tonk Women', a single that presaged *Bleed* by five months, didn't actually appear on the album – a rustic alternate version called 'Country Honk' (which Taylor also played on) featured in its stead – but in its swaggering ambience it summed up the new Stones in just over three minutes. A similar swaggering ambience attends this album's title track, 'Live With Me', and 'Monkey Man', the lyrics of all of which play up to the straight media's debauched image of the group ("I got nasty habits"; "We all need someone we can cream on"; "I hope we're not too messianic, or a trifle too satanic"). 'Midnight Rambler' is a lengthy, slinky, atmospheric track depicting a figure not unadjacent to the Boston Strangler but which could also embody the very bogeyman-like threat that the older generation seemed to imagine the Stones constituted to their values. Elsewhere, though, the band refuted clichéd perceptions regarding the children of the cultural revolution by exhibiting tenderness and vulnerability. 'You Got The Silver' finds Richards seeming to tell Pallenberg of his love for her and the endless capacity for forgiveness she inspires in him, doing so to a pretty acoustic backdrop, albeit one that jumps into anguished double-time toward the end. 'Love In Vain' is a countrified rendition of a then newly discovered love-lorn Robert Johnson song. It features mandolin from multi-instrumentalist Ry Cooder. Though he was present for a while, this was Cooder's only contribution to the record before his departure amidst allegations about the Stones, and Richards in particular, stealing his licks and ideas.

The biggest artistic achievements of the album are its magnificent bookends, 'Gimme Shelter' and 'You Can't Always Get What You Want', epic state-of-the-union addresses by Richards and Jagger respectively. In the latter, Jagger depicts a man shattered by matters both sociological (there is an allusion to the anti-Vietnam rally he attended in London in 1968) and personal (Faithfull has suggested that the talk of a woman meeting her "connection" was the singer's tortured response to her descent into heroin). The song starts out slow with some beautiful mournful brass from American sessioner Al Kooper, then roars into a quasi-samba. The incongruously innocent trilling of the London Bach Choir is dotted at various places throughout the song's 7:28 playing time. 'Gimme Shelter' also seems to address the turmoil of its composer. Though Richards never mentions Jagger or Pallenberg by name, what else is one to make of lines like "Storm is threatening my very life today" other than that their author has been mortally wounded by the betrayal of both his best friend and his lady? The lyric would be remarkable enough but the music that accompanies it turns the whole exercise into what must surely be the greatest recording of the Stones' career, with burning guitar lines, gigantic blasts of harmonica, pummeling piano, pounding drums and Merry Clayton's banshee supporting vocal parts creating a soundscape of utter perfection.

However, the legacy of *Let It Bleed* comes as much from the matter of the Stones finding their sound as it does from its artistic excellence. Though the Stones had made good and influential LPs hitherto, there was really no common thread to them except aesthetic quality: like The Beatles, they spent the 'Sixties recording albums that each sounded different to their predecessor. *Let It Bleed* was really the first Stones album to feature what we now consider the archetypal Stones sound, one that not only they but whole generations of musicians have stuck to ever since.

With the Beatles gone, it was the Stones who were left to be the figureheads for rock and the champions of the values of its followers into the 'Seventies. Thanks in huge part to *Let It Bleed*, they more than lived up to that role. For whereas The Beatles' quartet format and sunny optimism was the model that other musicians aspired to in the 'Sixties, during the 'Seventies and beyond it is the music and morals found on this record to which young bands looked for inspiration. A five-man band – complete with instrument-less, gyrating singer – singing swaggering songs of studied rebelliousness and/or obnoxiousness is now – *reductio ad absurdum* of rock though it may be – the image most instantly associate with the term "rock group". *Let It Bleed* is quite simply rock music *per se*. - Sean Egan

51. Fun House
The Stooges

TRACKLISTING
Down On The Street/Loose/TV Eye/Dirt/1970/Fun House/LA Blues

RELEASED
US: August 1970 UK: December 1970

PRODUCED BY
Don Gallucci

According to punk singer and poet Henry Rollins, it is the greatest album ever recorded. "*Fun House* is thirty-some minutes of loose and dangerous music played by bad men and should be heard once at least," he wrote on *Amazon.com* in his choice of favorite music. Wrote Jack White of The White Stripes in the liner notes to the Rhino 2005 double-disc edition, "I remember screaming in my head, 'This is Detroit!' And that's what *Fun House* is to me, the very definition of Detroit rock 'n' roll, and by proxy, the definitive rock album of America. The record's passion, attitude, power, emotion and destruction are incalculable." Perry Farrell of Jane's Addiction always used to play it before going onstage. "It's pretty hard to go out in a bad mood when you've just heard *Fun House*," he explained.

 Iconic album and revered piece of music it may be now but for about 10 years after it was released in 1970, nobody outside of a tiny clique much cared about The Stooges and sales of *Fun House* were pitiful. Even after the upheaval of punk, The Stooges album of choice tended to be *Raw Power*, a comparatively straightforward record in comparison with the screaming intensity of this, their second album.

 The Psychedelic Stooges were, according to frontman Iggy Pop, "low brow guys" who spent the first year of their collective existence thinking up their name. A typical Stooges live show consisted of two minutes of song followed by some wild free-form improvisations. The Stooges were signed to Elektra records in 1968 by Danny Fields, who also signed the MC5, worked with The Doors and Love and eventually managed The Ramones. Elektra was the pre-eminent American label, capturing the spirit of the times with innovative releases by artists as diverse as The Doors

The original cover for *Funhouse*.

and Judy Collins. Yet for all the success they had had marketing teen rebellion, they didn't really have much of a clue as to what they should do with The Stooges. Initially they tried to sell them – unsuccessfully - as a teen pop act. Their debut *The Stooges* – no longer psychedelic – was produced by John Cale, recently departed from The Velvet Underground. It was recorded in a hurry – 'Real Cool Time', 'Not Right', and 'Little Doll' were apparently written in one night to pad out the album – but remains a classic. *Fun House* was recorded in Los Angeles and was produced by Don Galluci, former keyboard player with The Kingsmen, the Oregon garage combo who'd scored a major hit in 1964 with their cover of 'Louie Louie'. He wanted to try and capture the live sound of the band as much as was possible and so they started recording almost as a live set, playing the songs on the album in the sequence that they appear.

The first order of business was to rip the studio apart: the carpets were taken up, the walls were moved. Then they just mic'ed up all the amps – Iggy sang into a hand-held mic standing in front of the band – and played. What you hear is what you get: there are no overdubs, no studio wizardry, no frills. According to guitar Stooge Ron Asheton, apart from adding a bit of rhythm guitar on a few tracks, what was released was pretty much what they played. It was recorded in sessions that lasted in total just under eight hours. It was very much against the grain of the way that records were made at that time. It had more in common with the way jazz musicians worked: they would book time in the studio, jam, listen back to the bits they thought worked and then release them.

The Stooges originally intended that 'Loose' would be the opening track, but the label preferred the slightly more downbeat 'Down On The Street'. Iggy drafted in sax player Steve MacKay, ex- of Detroit *avant-garde* noise band Carnal Kitchen, literally 48 hours before they started recording. MacKay brought an intense hard jazz quality to hard rock songs like '1970', as well as an almost John Coltrane-like free-form horn to the title track. 'LA Blues' was actually the most insane part of this wig-out excerpted and turned into a separate piece, an idea credited to Galluci. MacKay later said that he was on acid while they recorded the original 17- minute long track, which was initially called 'Freak'.

The album was reviewed favorably but sold badly: the world wasn't quite ready for hard rock delivered with this urgency and intensity. The then prevailing sound was a more laid back stoner-country rock vibe. Not long after its release the band started to disintegrate, due mainly to everyone's involvement in hard drugs. Elektra dropped them from its roster and for most of the mid-'70s, the album was actually deleted. Yet Iggy always had influential champions, among them David Bowie and journalists Nick Kent and Lester Bangs, who kept the flame burning even when it seemed that Iggy had reached the end of the line. The Damned covered '1970' (as 'I Feel Alright') on their first album *Damned Damned Damned* which, for a new generation, was their first taste of Iggy. And although its influence on punk is undeniable, the impact of *Fun House* goes much wider: early hardcore bands like Black Flag, Husker Du and The Minutemen, John Zorn's maniac jazz, the more extreme variants of heavy metal, and Primal

Scream all openly give thanks for this insane 30-odd minutes of freakish primitive distorted rock that still sounds like it was composed by cavemen from Mars. - Tommy Udo

52. Black Sabbath

Black Sabbath

TRACKLISTING
UK:Black Sabbath/The Wizard/Behind The Wall Of Sleep/Nib/Evil Woman/Sleeping Village/Warning

US:Black Sabbath/The Wizard/Behind The Wall Of Sleep/Nib/Wicked World/Sleeping Village/Warning

RELEASED
US: June 1970 UK: February 1970

PRODUCED BY
Roger Bain

Dong...dong...*donggggggg*!
      Are there any greater sounds in the entire history of popular music than the opening clanging chords, profound bass and church bell stabs that kick off Black Sabbath's debut album? As an introduction, a statement of intent, it has to be up there with the opening of Beethoven's Fifth and the theme from *The Flintstones*.
      1970 was a heavy year: the hippie dippy dream had begun to go sour at Altamont the previous December, the war in Vietnam continued to rage, and there was a new mood of paranoia in the air. Sabbath articulated that perfectly. Sabbath spoke to a generation of kids who were too young to give a shit about Bob Dylan or Eastern mysticism or sticking flowers into the barrels of guns. They caught the more pessimistic mood of a generation who really expected to be fried in a nuclear war before they got a whole lot older.
      Black Sabbath was recorded in three days for £600. By their own admission, the band had no idea what they were doing: everything about the album is a sort of happy accident. They were booked into the studio by their then manager Jim Simpson who also secured them a deal with a new and very hip progressive label called Vertigo. Sabbath were apparently very unhappy at the amount of money that they were offered, but went along with the deal because they felt that getting a record out would help them

to get paid more for gigs. The production on the album by Roger Bain was rough; he was to work on the follow up – and commercial breakthrough album – *Paranoid* and its successor *Master Of Reality*, but he was comparatively new to studio production and was appointed by the label rather than being the band's own choice.

The seven songs on the album are fairly representative of the live set that they were playing at that time, though they already had songs like 'Paranoid' written for the second album, which was recorded only a few

The 'occult' artwork for *Black Sabbath*.

months later. They recorded *Black Sabbath* more or less as a live album; apart from a few overdubs and effects like the rainstorm at the beginning of the opening title track, it was pure unadulterated no frills Sabbath.

The album was preceded by the single 'Evil Woman', a cover song originally written and recorded by an American band called Crow, and very untypical of Sabbath's later sound. 'Evil Woman' is a fairly standard R&B riff, an uptempo, soul-influenced song that sounds as though it was tailored for the disco scene of the day. It bombed.

The album fared better, entering the UK album charts where it stayed for 42 weeks, peaking at number eight. The band were also big in Germany, regulars on the rock TV show *Beat Club*. When the album was released in the US in June it quickly accumulated a sort of cult status, mostly through word-of-mouth.

From the start Sabbath faced a press that was at best indifferent and at worst hostile: the term "heavy metal kids" was applied to their fans as an insult, though interestingly they were never actually dubbed "heavy metal" until the very late '70s, "heavy rock" being the preferred – and even the pejorative – term for their music. Sabbath were caricatured as "rock 'n' roll from the building site", a sneer at their unsophisticated origins, or "downer music", referring to the supposed penchant of their fans for cocktails of tranquilizers and cheap wine. Sabbath did it all the hard way, building up a following through hard labor, playing gigs for as little as £70 wherever they could set up.

There are actually no devil-worship songs on the album: the song 'Black Sabbath' is a horror story about demonic possession; 'The Wizard' is about somebody using magical powers for good; 'Evil Woman' is a fairly standard blues theme about a lowdown-cheatin' no-good gal; 'NIB', rumored to stand for 'Nativity In Black' was actually a nickname for bassist "Geezer" Butler (his beard looked like the nib of a pen, according to Sabbath vocalist Ozzy Osbourne); 'Behind The Wall Of Sleep', despite borrowing a title from pulp horror writer HP Lovecraft is just about dreaming and waking up. But decisions made by the record company – the album cover which the band did not see until the record was released with the inverted cross in the gatefold; the publicity department's rumor-mongering about their occult involvement in an attempt to generate press interest – as well as their name tapped them into a growing occult underground, particularly in the US. Their first US visit was supposedly cancelled because of the ongoing Manson Family trial. Alex Sanders, the UK's self-styled King Of The Witches, attended several Sabbath gigs and tried to get them to attend his covens supposedly on the strength of the cover. "I have no idea to this day who the girl on the cover was", says guitarist Tony Iommi. The picture – credited to Marcus Keef, the in-house designer at Vertigo Records – was actually taken at Mapledurham Watermill on the River Thames and supposedly featured an actress hired for the shoot who later met the band long after the album had been released. The washed out colors of the image suggested a witch or a ghost and further reinforced the supposed links to the occult.

Black Sabbath is far from a perfect album – 'Evil Woman' and their cover of Aynsley Dunbar's 'The Warning' are fairly ropey – and the jury is still out as to whether *Master Of Reality* or *Volume 4* is *the* all time classic Sabbath album. But the song 'Black Sabbath' itself doesn't sound dated in the way that, say, most of *Led Zeppelin III* sounds like a period piece. And

the impact of *Black Sabbath* resonates to this day. It helped to spawn a sort of heavy rock arms race, where bands tried to outdo each other for sheer weightiness. Although debate rages as to whether or not this was the first proper heavy metal album – Led Zeppelin, Steppenwolf, Blue Cheer and other bands mentioned in this book had all beaten the Sabs by a couple of years – it did nail down the formula – down-tuned guitars, alleged Satanism, thundering volume – that would eventually become a global business.
- Tommy Udo

53. Back In The USA
MC5

TRACKLISTING
Tutti Frutti/Tonight/Teenage Lust/Let Me Try/Looking At You/High School/Call Me Animal/The American Ruse/Shakin' Street/The Human Being Lawnmower/Back In The USA

RELEASED
US: January 1970 UK: November 1970

PRODUCED BY
Jon Landau

The title was a reference to the cover of the flag waving song by Chuck Berry that closed the album but it was meant sarcastically. *Back In The USA* is an album brimming over with condemnations of the American Dream, its mindset forged in the white heat of the radical late 'Sixties.

On their previous, debut, album, the MC5 had failed to translate the strength of their feelings at racial, social and economic injustice in their homeland into music of corresponding power. Issuing a live recording as their entrée, partly because it had never been done before, they wound up with a sonic porridge. Or at least that's how famous gonzo music journalist Lester Bangs perceived *Kick Out The Jams*, as well as many others. Some however consider it to be a classic record. The very type of people who love that album are inclined to despise *Back In The USA*, considering it a cleaned up, toned-down evisceration of both the MC5's music and their revolutionary stance.

The Clash knew where they stood on the issue, however. When Mick Jones met MC5 guitarist Wayne Kramer in the late 'Seventies, the Englishman informed the American that *Back In The USA* had been a big influence on his band. Certainly, there are great similarities between the debut eponymous Clash album and this one: both contain short and brutal but melodic and anthemic songs that address social issues. Though *Back In The USA* didn't create much work for chart compilers at the time and the controversy surrounding its supposedly emasculated nature effectively destroyed the band's street cred, its long term influence was enormous: not only did it set a template for The Clash, but the great music that latter group created provided a *modus operandi* for many great groups who succeeded *them*.

The "MC" in MC5 stood not for "Master of Ceremonies" but for "Motor City", a reference to Detroit, of which they were natives. The band began in 1964 and by the following year had settled on their definitive line-up of Kramer, guitarist Fred 'Sonic' Smith, vocalist Rob Tyner, bassist Michael Davis and drummer Dennis Thompson. They were taken under the wing of John Sinclair, the head of the notional White Panther Party who further radicalized these blue collar kids. Again, the parallels with The Clash are striking. The White Panther Party sought to make an ideological alliance with the black rights organization the Black Panthers in a similar way to The Clash writing 'White Riot' a decade later to demonstrate their support for a Caucasian equivalent of ethnic civil disobedience. Sinclair meanwhile served a similar role for the MC5 to the one that died-in-the-wool left-winger Bernard Rhodes did for The Clash, encouraging the tone of their songs and coming out with sensational radical sloganeering in their publicity. However, the climate of the 'Sixties dictated that Sinclair was perceived by the authorities as a dangerous individual in a way that Rhodes wasn't. Whereas by The Clash's era, a lot of the old guard were no longer in power through retirement or death, they still held sway in 1969, when Sinclair was sent to prison for up to ten years for possessing two joints.

Sinclair's imprisonment was something of a blow to the MC5, who were still upset over the poor reception to *Kick Out The Jams*. Another blow came when their record label Elektra broke ties with them over an incident in which the band took out an advertisement in an underground newspaper reading "Fuck Hudson's" in retaliation for that local record store refusing to stock their debut because of its bad language. The ad caused Hudson's to boycott all Elektra product. However, the MC5 still had enough of a reputation as a kick-ass rock 'n' roll outfit – and a commercial proposition – for their contract to be picked up by Atlantic at the prompting of rock critic and fan Jon Landau.

Despite his inexperience, Landau was given the role of producer for the 5's first studio album. Landau wasn't happy with the quality of *Kick Out The Jams* and wanted to help create something that would make those who had never seen the band onstage understand why they had attracted critical raves before they'd secured a recording contract.

The MC5 in performance.

The band would be properly produced, and the song lengths their live audience were familiar with – The MC5 took their cue from the likes of jazzers John Coltrane and Sun Ra as much as any rock band – would be reined back in favor of concise, punchy statements. It was a move with which the band were happy to go along. Kramer later said, "I wanted to make a note-perfect record. I... wanted to answer the criticism that we used excessive volume to hide the fact we couldn't play." Landau himself said he would have liked to re-record some of the tracks from the debut but that this was not legally possible.

Disciplined and sharp though the new music might have been, it still also sounded dirty and primeval. Meanwhile, there was no compromise with the market when it came to lyrics, unless their declining to repeat the "motherfuckers" epithet that caused so much trouble on the first album counted. Though only a minority of the tracks are political, there is no mistaking on which side the band stand after listening to 'The American Ruse' – which demolishes the very myths that the title track perpetuates – and the anti-nuclear weapon 'Human Being Lawnmower'. With its half-dozen or so distinct musical parts, the latter was musically almost like a rock opera, only in triple time. 'Let Me Try' is a tender ballad which The Rolling Stones' 'I Got The Blues' from the following year seems to owe a debt to. 'Shakin' Street' is a bitter-sweet vignette of blue collar kids' lives with a partly acoustic backdrop. The majority of the tracks, though, are high velocity melodic rock. Particularly noteworthy are 'Looking At You' – a re-recording of their second single - and the disaffected high school kid' anthem 'Tonight', both of which are heart-stoppingly exciting. - Sean Egan

When the Spitting Had to Stop...

Much of the music that was created by musicians who absorbed and adapted the punk ethic is still highly influential. Arguably more interesting than most punk itself, twenty **post-punk classics**.

1.	**Atmosphere**	Joy Division
2.	**The Light Pours Out Of Me**	Magazine
3.	**Outdoor Miner**	Wire
4.	**At Home He's A Tourist**	Gang Of Four
5.	**Don't Fall**	The Chameleons
6.	**Candyskin**	The Fire Engines
7.	**Falling & Laughing**	Orange Juice
8.	**Headache – For Michelle**	The Au Pairs
9.	**Independence Day**	The Comsat Angels
10.	**Party Fears Two**	The Associates
11.	**Lake Of Fire**	The Meat Puppets
12.	**Hip Priest**	The Fall
13.	**I Will Dare**	The Replacements
14.	**This Is Not A Love Song**	Public Image Limited
15.	**Pretty In Pink**	The Psychedelic Furs
16.	**The Sweetest Girl**	Scritti Politti
17.	**Mutiny In Heaven**	The Birthday Party
18.	**Makes No Sense At All**	Husker Du
19.	**Sally Maclennane**	The Pogues
20.	**Kiss Off**	Violent Femmes

54. Live At Leeds
The Who

TRACKLISTING
Young Man Blues/Substitute/Summertime Blues/Shakin' All Over/My
Generation/Magic Bus

RELEASED
US: May 1970 UK: May 1970

PRODUCED BY
Kit Lambert

Though *Tommy* had catapulted The Who to superstardom and financial
security after years of struggling to keep their heads above water, there was
a slight problem with it. It wasn't, as Pete Townshend would later lament,
the "real Who".

Though naturally proud of the fact that he had come up with an
album that had captured the public imagination, he was also uncomfortably
conscious of the fact that it in no way sounded like the incendiary rock 'n'
roll band The Who had always been. This may have been compounded by
the fact that, that for many people, *Tommy* was the first Who music they had
heard. He may also have been brooding over the fact that, for many of their
fans, The Who had never managed to capture their stage power on record.

The live project that the band began thinking of in 1969 was
partly designed to rectify the problem of this disparity. Additionally, with
Townshend's next concept work *Lifehouse* nowhere near ready, a live album
would serve as a good stop-gap. Accordingly, the group recorded dozens of
gigs in America in the last year of the 1960s. However, when they got back
to the UK, Townshend decided he couldn't face listening to the eighty
hours of tape. Instead, the band decided to record two UK gigs in 1970 and
release the best from those. The US tapes were ordered to be burnt to
thwart bootleggers. This ability to extravagantly write-off live recordings
that had consumed considerable effort and expense was a far cry from the
incident during the recording of the mini-opera 'A Quick One, While He's
Away' in which the band had had to resort to sardonically intoning "Cello
cello cello" over a part they felt had needed that instrument but which
manager Kit Lambert decided they couldn't afford to hire.

The mobile recording unit of London's Pye studio was
employed to record gigs at Hull City Hall and Leeds University. The Hull
tapes malfunctioned so in the end only the recording made at Leeds on
Valentine's Day 1970 could be used. Or some of it. In 1969, the optimum

running time of a vinyl album was forty minutes. Squeezing any more material onto a single LP resulted in a deterioration in sound quality. As the double set had yet to become the *de rigueur* format for the live album, this meant that The Who had to brutally trim down the material they had performed on the day, which constituted 33 songs, including all of the *Tommy* album. Moreover, those 33 songs included a performance of the 'A Quick One, While He's Away' (8:39), a version of 'Magic Bus' approaching eight minutes and a quarter-hour 'My Generation' (although admittedly one that mixed in bits of other songs). Just six songs, therefore, were selected from the two-hour performance.

With a capacity of 74 minutes per disk, CD technology has now transformed running times available to rock artists. A 1995 CD reissue of *Live At Leeds* featured all of the non-*Tommy* recordings of that day except 'Amazing Journey'/'Sparks'. The subsequent 2001 'Deluxe Remaster' was a double CD, thus enabling the group to include everything to which those lucky enough to be in Leeds University that day bore witness. However, the version of the album discussed here is the original, as that is the one that influenced other musicians.

The 'brown paper bag' cover design for *Live At Leeds*.

The main influence of *Live At Leeds* would seem to have been on the heavy metal kids. *Live At Leeds* was the definitive power chord album, proving Pete Townshend one of the most adroit guitarists in the world. That the wall of sound he creates – crashing soon-to-be archetypal metal 5th chords alternating with his unique (for electric guitar) flamenco-style work – is the work of just one guitarist is breathtaking enough but that he was producing it while performing his characteristic leaps and arm swings is awe-inspiring. Just listen to his playing on the cover of adolescents' anthem 'Young Man Blues' by Mose Allison (who became a wealthy man from the decision of the band to include the song herein). The instrumental break is frequently the weakest part of a three-piece band's stage performance due to the necessity for the guitarist to abandon rhythm work to perform a solo, thus leaving a rather glaring hole. Townshend gets round this problem by playing like he is two men, tearing up and down his fretboard in a stunning display of blurred-fingered virtuosity. As well as proving the validity of bulldozing rock crunch, this album also confirmed that the live album could be a commercial proposition and an artistic statement in and of itself, thus helping create a parallel industry to the studio album.

Though the compact disc age has provided a welcome expansion of the possibilities in album length, the demise of the 12-inch vinyl disc has robbed us of the sort of sumptuous package *Live At Leeds* originally constituted. Within its plain beige sleeve, stamped with the title to mockingly imitate the bootleg production values then prevailing, was a goodie bag of Who-nalia, including facsimiles of record company rejection letter, Woodstock contract, notice of court proceedings, gig cancellation letter, etc.

It would be absurd to suggest that listening to *Live At Leeds* is the exact equivalent of catching their stage act in the flesh. Nothing aural can approximate the site of Townshend pounding out chords while leaping and windmilling his right arm, nor Daltrey's barrel-chested stage presence and microphone twirling nor John Entwistle sustaining some of the most imaginative bass runs in the world while looking like he was thinking about his lunch or Keith Moon's facial gurning while pounding around his giant–sized kit.

Nonetheless, *Live At Leeds*, truncated or full-blown, remains the definitive live album. – Sean Egan

55. Tapestry
Carole King

TRACKLISTING
I Feel the Earth Move/So Far Away/It's Too Late/Home Again/Beautiful/ Way Over Yonder/You've Got a Friend/Where You Lead/Will You Love Me Tomorrow?/Smackwater Jack/Tapestry/(You Make Me Feel Like) A Natural Woman

RELEASED
US: November 1970 UK: November 1970

PRODUCED BY
Lou Adler

Carole King can claim a quite remarkable feat: she helped define two distinct eras in music history.

The first was the age of the Brill Building, the New York pop production line of the early-to-mid 1960s. The second was the singer-song-writer era of the early 'Seventies, of which she was the monarch by dint of this album, her second solo effort.

For a while in the 'Sixties, Gerry Goffin and Carole King virtually owned the singles charts in tandem with another husband-and-wife writing team, Barry Mann and Cynthia Weil. King was the melody writer and Goffin the lyricist in a collaborative process that yielded iconic hits like 'Crying In The Rain', 'Don't Bring Me Down', 'I'm Into Something Good', 'The Loco-Motion', 'One Fine Day', 'Pleasant Valley Sunday', 'Take Good Care Of My Baby', 'Up On The Roof' and '(You Make Me Feel Like) A Natural Woman' for everybody from British Invasion bands to soul divas.

Though King and Goffin actually maintained a civil enough relationship following their separation in the late 'Sixties to continue writing together, eventually the inevitable happened and they went their separate ways. King released an album as part of a now-forgotten trio called The City before embarking on her solo career proper. Or perhaps resuming it: she had had a hit in 1962 with 'It Might As Well Rain Until September'. However the peppiness of that song or any of her other Brill Building work would not inform her new material. Instead, a slightly world-weary but meditative spirit – appropriate for a grown woman with children who had gone though a divorce – prevailed. Such a tone chimed perfectly with the maturing rock audience,

Carole King photographed for *Tapestry* by Jim McCrary at her home in Wonderland Avenue, Laurel Canyon, 1971.

who had done all their shouting and screaming in the 'Sixties and were now turning their attention to domestic, not political, matters. That sprit was summed up perfectly by this album's 'It's Too Late' a wistful dissection of a break-up that was utterly adult in its refusal to apportion blame. Some might question King's decision to revisit here compositions of hers whose definitive rendition had already surely been achieved ('Natural Woman') but it can't be denied that the album struck a chord: at one point it was the biggest-selling album of all time.

Amazingly, King has never really been able to capitalize on the success of *Tapestry*, something that can't be anything like completely explained by the semi-seclusion she went into following its release, her natural shyness leading her to decline even cover story interviews. Few people have heard of King's album *Music*, even though it was released in the same year as, and subsequent to, *Tapestry*. Though she has released several decent albums in the intervening years, for the majority of the vast number of people who bought it, *Tapestry* remains the only Carole King album in their collection. Even so, via its remarkable success, she showed that rock could be contemplative, not callow, and encouraged women who had always imagined popular music was somehow the preserve of men to pick up a guitar and begin aiming for stardom. – Sean Egan

56. Sticky Fingers
The Rolling Stones

TRACKLISTING
Brown Sugar/Sway/Wild Horses/Can't You Hear Me Knocking/You Gotta Move/Bitch/I Got The Blues/Sister Morphine/Dead Flowers/ Moonlight Mile

RELEASED
US: April 1971 UK: April 1971

PRODUCED BY
Jimmy Miller

1970 was the first year since their debut long player in 1964 that the Rolling Stones did not issue a studio album.

Some at the time assumed that this was a symptom of a recognition by the band that it would soon be embarrassing to continue. Mick Jagger himself had expressed concern about how long the whole enterprise could go on to journalist Stanley Booth on their 1969 US tour.

But why should a band stop when they are making great art, great money and have an audience that is growing to sizes bigger than ever? Jagger's misgivings about people continuing to be rock stars as they approached that dread age of 30 would seem to have dissipated completely by the time *Sticky Fingers* appeared, possibly something to do with the fact that his two movie performances had been flops. 1971 saw the Stones making a comeback with renewed energy and ambition. Not only was *Sticky Fingers* their first album for whose recording new member Mick Taylor was present from the start (although one track predated his employment), it was also the first on their own eponymous label.

That renewal of energies notwithstanding, *Sticky Fingers* wasn't so much about artistic innovation as consolidation. The album saw the band refine the archetypal Stones sound they had invented on *Let It Bleed* to a fine T. All the same ingredients as before were here but now the final element was put in place: the riffs. Keith Richards had always, of course, had a knack for a good guitar lick – witness that of the instantly unforgettable '(I Can't Get No) Satisfaction' – but they had never before been integral to the band's sound. Those curt and somehow frayed guitar riffs that are now perceived as the Stones' sonic imprimatur started here. The album also saw the Stones' sound narrowed in to what the band presumably considered to be its essence. The studied decadence and unpretentious rock 'n' roll pushed aside more grand musical vistas. They would never again record anything with quite as much menace as 'Gimme Shelter' or as great a sweep as 'You Can't Always Get What You Want'.

But there again, those *Let It Bleed* tracks didn't inspire as many people to pick up a guitar and join bands as this album's glorious, swaggering, riff-bearers. 'Brown Sugar' – released in April 1971 as the Stones' first single for almost two years – is a rousing yet somehow dog-tired anthem to, er, the erotic delights of slave owning. Its dubious message is compensated for by one of Richards' most simple but effective licks, a rousing "Yeah yeah yeah – whoo!" refrain, a sleazy sax solo and exotic, musky percussion. 'Can't You Hear Me Knocking' is a seven-minute album centerpiece which though it doesn't have the feeling of the grand statement and universal relevance that 'Gimme Shelter' and 'You Can't Always Get What You Want' possessed does have a gait as arrogant as a rooster's, quite possibly the greatest and most frayed Richards' riff ever and a reach that sees a typically-Stonesey first third give way to an almost jazzy instrumental second act. 'Bitch' transposes its riff from guitar to a galvanizing horn section.

Let It Bleed had already put the nail in place but *Sticky Fingers* hammered it home, completing the definition of what a modern rock band should sound like. The sound and attitude here – essentially anthems for the stylish social outlaw – were used as a template by The Faces, the New York Dolls, latter-day Mott The Hoople, Aerosmith, the Black Crowes and a thousand and one bands you never heard of. It was also used, albeit modified for the prevailing, less decadent mores, by The Clash and The Sex Pistols.

Many of the countless bands inspired by this music made the mistake of perceiving the Stones' template as that of an almost exclusively full-tilt rock outfit and purveyors of one-dimensional hymns to the rebel. They thereby ignored the band's facility for differing moods and lyrical nuance. In fact, though considered a quintessential Rolling Stones album, the majority of the tracks on *Sticky Fingers* are not uptempo. 'Sway', 'Wild Horses', 'I Got The Blues' and 'Moonlight Mile' are tender and quite affecting ballads that undercut the assumption some might draw from other material here that the artists are macho bullies. The lyric to country number 'Dead Flowers' is a bit more scathing, but even here one can't deny the vulnerability of the train-wreck of a narrator.

Sticky Fingers was influential for a couple of other reasons, neither of them necessarily positive. The first was the drug references. Though allusion to stimulants had been fairly common in pop since the mid-'Sixties, they had always been discreet, partly to avoid the kind of hassle the Stones themselves had been put through by the law in Britain in 1967. The references here, though, are both frequent and blatant. At least half of the songs contain references to cocaine, heroin or morphine. While this may be considered a defiant statement of people not prepared to be dictated to about their recreational activities by spurious authority, it can also be seen as utterly irresponsible. Joe Strummer once opined, "The Stones are responsible for killing people by saying drugs are cool".

Sticky Fingers was also influential in proving that bands could stay away for the previously unimaginable length of time of two years and still be as popular as ever upon their return. (It's true that Dylan had recently done a similar thing but that was for very exceptional reasons.) The very goodwill engendered by their past triumphs not only made this possible but also made it acceptable for bands of the Stones' stature to not release stand-alone singles. 'Honky Tonk Women' was the last of that breed. From now on, all Stones singles would be, like 'Brown Sugar', a promotional device for an album. The age of the rock aristocracy had arrived. - Sean Egan

57. What's Going On
Marvin Gaye

TRACKLISTING
What's Going On/What's Happening Brother/Flyin' High (In The Friendly Sky)/Save The Children/God Is Love/Mercy Mercy Me (The Ecology)/Right On/Wholy Holy/Inner City Blues (Make Me Wanna Holler)

RELEASED
US: May 1971 UK: October 1971

PRODUCED BY
Marvin Gaye

Writing in 2000, for a sleeve note to an expanded edition of this album, Marvin Gaye's Motown peer, Smokey Robinson – a man who knew a thing or two about writing, singing and producing great soul music – opined that *What's Going On* was the greatest album of all time. "Marvin had the talent to use what was flowing through him", he wrote. " 'Smoke', Marvin used to say to me, 'God is writing this album. God is working through me'."

Yet when he started work on it in the early part of 1971, Gaye's path through life did not seem so much divinely ordained as Godforsaken. Uncle Sam was after him for a vast sum in back taxes. His duet partner, Tammi Terrell, collapsed through the effects of a brain tumor no-one had known she had while on stage with Gaye in 1967. (She died in 1970.) His marriage, to Motown boss Berry Gordy's sister, Anna, was fractious and unfulfilling. (The terms of their 1978 divorce stipulated that she receive royalties from his next album: he responded with the lacerating *Here, My Dear*, the greatest break-up album of them all – an entire double LP of songs cynically laying bare the reasons for the disintegration of their relationship.)

A gifted musician with both a fondness and considerable aptitude for jazz, Gaye possessed an incredible voice, and after arriving in Detroit and finding his way to Gordy's Motown, he was groomed as a black Sinatra. He certainly deserved mention in the same breath as Ol' Blue Eyes for his superlative interpretative abilities. But despite the hits he proceeded to rack up at Motown, Marvin wanted more, wanted to make music that didn't just entertain and enrapture, but that spoke to the soul of his listeners. In 1968, his brooding single 'I Heard It Through The Grapevine' became Motown's biggest hit to date. Gaye couldn't get any bigger, but he knew he could get *better*.

Early in 1970, Four Tops singer Obie Benson brought a song to Gaye that he thought his friend might want to record. The song was 'What's Going On', a slow-burning, simmering, angry yet deeply restrained look at a world gone mad: Gaye knew this was just the track to kick off the flow of new music he yearned to make. Making some amendments to the lyrics, he recorded it in the Motown studio with the label's legendary house band, the Funk Brothers, just days after Terrell's death. Embracing accident and chance, Gaye subtly tweaked the Motown work ethic, allowing unforeseen, unbidden magic to find its way onto tape: the song's opening sax solo, instantly recognizable today, was the result of the player warming up. Delighted with a record that at last said what he needed to say, Gaye submitted it to Motown for release as his next single.

But Gordy and the Motown top brass – geared toward non-controversial pop anthems – feared it would bomb and ruin Gaye's career: they refused to release it. Tired of being pushed around, and supremely confident in the song, Gaye dug in his heels. He refused to make any more music until Motown put it out. It took almost a year, but in January 1971, Gordy relented, and lost the argument all ends up: the song became a huge hit, and Gaye now had all the ammunition he needed to insist on going ahead with the album he was burning to make.

Conceived as a view of a decaying America from the point of view of a returning Vietnam veteran, *What's Going On* was inspired by Gaye's feelings about the experiences his brother Frankie had on returning to the US after three years' combat duty in south-east Asia. The ten-day recording was far from straightforward, Gaye's songs being barely finished ahead of the studio dates, and his musical vision requiring the secondment of players from the Detroit Symphony Orchestra. Arranger David Van DePitte turned phrases and ideas the singer had from hummed and sung notions into beautifully scored, fully realized pieces of music; the Funk Brothers, allowed at last to stretch out and test themselves with music that encompassed the jazz they all grew up on as well as the soul and pop they could make in their sleep, turned in their finest work. Still Gaye wasn't happy: while making a film in Los Angeles, he had the tapes couriered to him, and re-mixed them until he was. The album was released in May to rapturous acclaim.

Strung together as an unbroken sequence of interwoven songs, *What's Going On* suffers badly if picked apart. That said, pretty much every track could have been a single, and most of them are so indelibly inked on our collective subconscious that even a newcomer listening to the record for the first time will feel that, on some level, they know it already. The title track blends Gaye's worldview with an uncompromising look at his own life, though quite how much he was giving away when pleading to his dad that "There's no need to escalate", did not become clear until the following decade, when Gaye Snr shot his son dead.

What's Going On is not just a remarkable, beautiful, passionate record: it represents one of those rare watershed moments where a work of art both catches the pulse of the times, and in doing so changes those times.

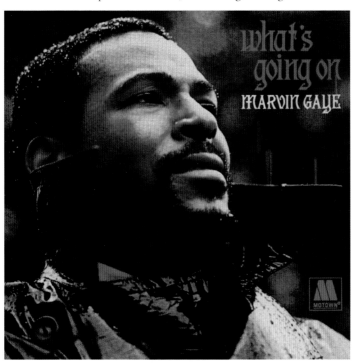

Marvin Gaye, on the original cover for *What's Going On.*

It continues to inspire and influence any musician who wishes to connect their work with the wider world and go beyond pop's essential simplicity of frothy boy-meets-girl concerns. The very fact that the record still retains every ounce of its relevance today has less to do with the Iraq war replacing Vietnam and the continued erosion of healthcare, education and social services in the industrialized West than it does with Gaye's gift for outlining these concerns in terms that were at once all-encompassing and universal, yet deeply, elementally personal. He dared to push popular music beyond its proscribed boundaries, and proved that it had the capacity to provoke, to cajole, to rally, and even to heal. - Angus Batey

58. Blue

Joni Mitchell

TRACKLISTING
All I Want/My Old Man/Little Green/Carey/Blue/California/This Flight
Tonight/River/A Case Of You/The Last Time I Saw Richard

RELEASED
US: July 1971 UK: July 1971

PRODUCED BY
No producer listed

Joni Mitchell was already an artist of considerable popularity and influence
when her fourth album, *Blue*, was released in mid-1971. True, *Blue* did
better commercially than her previous LPs (making #15 in the US and #3
in the UK), but not enormously so. There would, too, be bigger sellers for
her in the mid-1970s, particularly *Court And Spark* (though, interestingly,
Blue remains her highest-charting record in the UK). Yet *Blue* is the Mitchell
album most likely to get five-star ratings, and to show up on critical all-time
best-of lists. Somehow, it's the Mitchell album that most combines critical
and mass popularity, though it's not so much a huge artistic leap forward as
a refinement of territory she'd already mapped to a large degree.

At the outset of her career, Mitchell was often categorized as a
'folk' artist. Though retaining a folk feel in her singing and almost wholly
acoustic instrumentation, in truth her music had less to do with the folk
tradition than with helping to pioneer a new popular style, the singer-songwriter movement. She progressively moved further away from folk stylings
into personal, oft-romantic lyrics that would be dubbed, not always
positively, as part of the 'confessional' wing of the singer-songwriter
spectrum. Though her arrangements often continued to rely on unadorned,
or barely adorned, acoustic guitar and piano, she did introduce more
instrumental textures. More notably, her vocal range – which, on her debut
album, was still very much in the high, pristine upper-register school so
popular among female '60s folkies, though attractively so – both widened and
moved further away from folky phrasing, and closer to jazz-inflected rhythms.

With *Blue*, the move away from folk roots was, if not wholly
decisive, even more pronounced. The singing had a jazz-like sense of glide
and irregular meter, at times jamming in more thoughts and syllables per
measure than almost anyone else working in popular music. It was also
instantly identifiable as *Mitchell's* style, fairly impossible to credibly imitate
(though a few did try). The words were, if not more confessional, certainly

more conversational, as if we were hearing some actual thoughts bouncing around her head, albeit more artfully constructed and distilled than a verbatim transcription of inner thoughts could ever be. The instrumentation, while not going into all-out electric rock, was more varied than ever for Mitchell, using fellow in-crowd superstar Stephen Stills (who plays bass and guitar on 'Crazy'), just-ex-boyfriend James Taylor (who plays guitar on three tracks), Sneaky Pete (who adds pedal steel to two songs), and top L.A. session drummer Russ Kunkel (who plays, softly, on three cuts). Mitchell herself alternated adroitly between guitar, piano, and dulcimer.

Joni Mitchell, pictured on the cover for *Blue*.

Blue is sometimes portrayed as a dark, disturbing album – an impression reinforced by the famous cover shot of Mitchell all but submerged in blue shadow. But while some romantic disillusionment and disappointment is explored in songs like 'A Case of You' and (most famously) 'The Last Time I Saw Richard' (often speculated to be about her ex-husband Chuck Mitchell), it really isn't that dark a record at all. If it had been, it probably wouldn't have been as successful as it was. More important to note, however, is that the melodies and vocal delivery are for the most part quite sunny and upbeat, even ebullient at times. Mitchell does not seem as much embittered by her emotional roller coasters as emboldened, and in the most uplifting, catchiest songs ('All I Want' and 'California'), downright optimistic.

Part of her triumph on the album might be in wrapping such complex, ambiguous feelings in such an appealing package. The downside is that the intensely personal nature of the songs sometimes crossed the line from the confessional to the self-absorbed. Mitchell had a lightness of touch and a certain playful wit that steered it clear of smugness, but that self-involvement was present nonetheless. It wasn't long before that aspect of her work was quite viciously – yet quite humorously and accurately, it must be said – parodied by *National Lampoon Radio Hour* in 'You Put Me Through Hell.'

Blue was released at a time when the singer-songwriter movement was approaching its peak, both in influence and sales. It wouldn't be quite right to say it marked the beginning of Mitchell's own wide influence within popular music. Women singer-songwriters in particular had been inspired to craft more personal (and, yes, confessional) folk-rock statements by Mitchell's work since the late 1960s. In this respect, her influence can be quite audibly heard in the recordings of more numerous (and more obscure) female singer-songwriters of the era than has generally been acknowledged, ranging from some quite good modest-selling or cult figures (Mary McCaslin, Linda Perhacs) to some that neither sold records nor attracted even much belated cult recognition (Mary Catherine Lunsford, Nancy Michaels, Alisha Sufit of Magic Carpet in the UK, and all the way over in Norway, Nina Johansen of Oriental Sunshine). If one of Mitchell's specific influences was to encourage women singer-songwriters to write in a personal, confessional style from a female viewpoint, it was most effectively channeled – both artistically and commercially – by artists who were not as strongly rooted in folk and folk-rock, such as Carole King and Carly Simon.

Summarizing Mitchell's impact in terms of women alone is doing her a disservice, however. She was popular with listeners and musicians of both sexes – Bob Dylan, when asked about his 1975 composition 'Tangled Up In Blue', indicated that part of its impetus was this album – and *Blue*, though it actually lacks some of the crystalline purity that made her earlier albums, especially *Songs to a Seagull*, more enjoyable works in some respects, was at the forefront of a singer-songwriter boom that also included not just King and Simon, but also James Taylor, Neil Young, and (a bit later) Jackson Browne. Among such peers, her early-'70s work holds its own on any terms – in fact, her records from that time have proved more durable than albums by any of those figures except Young.
- Richie Unterberger

Bleep!

Electronic music worked its way from arthouse to mainstream pop success in the late 'Seventies and early 'Eighties with **electro-pop greats** like these...

1.	**The Model**	Kraftwerk
2.	**Cars**	Gary Numan
3.	**Say Hello, Wave Goodbye**	Soft Cell
4.	**Just Can't Get Enough**	Depeche Mode
5.	**(Keep Feeling) Fascination**	Human League
6.	**Hyperactive**	Thomas Dolby
7.	**Only You**	Yazoo
8.	**What Have I Done To Deserve This?**	Pet Shop Boys
9.	**Enola Gay**	Orchestral Manouevres In The Dark
10.	**Vienna**	Ultravox
11.	**Sometimes**	Erasure
12.	**Love Is A Stranger**	The Eurythmics
13.	**Small Town Boy**	Bronski Beat
14.	**Mad World**	Tears For Fears
15.	**The Safety Dance**	Men Without Hats
16.	**The Perfect Kiss**	New Order
17.	**Together In Electric Dreams**	Giorgio Moroder and Philip Oakey
18.	**Ghosts**	Japan
19.	**Chariots Of Fire**	Vangelis
20.	**Temptation**	Heaven 17

59. Electric Warrior

T.Rex

TRACKLISTING

Mambo Sun/Cosmic Dancer/Jeepster/Monolith/Lean Woman Blues/Get It On [U.S. title: Bang a Gong (Get It On)]/ Planet Queen/Girl/The Motivator/Life's a Gas/Rip Off

RELEASED

US: October 1971 UK: September 1971

PRODUCED BY

Tony Visconti

One would imagine that it takes quite a lot to impress an ex-Beatle when it comes to fan mania. However, Ringo Starr himself (the member of the Fab Four, lest we forget, who received the most fan mail) is on record as being staggered by the 'T. Rextasy' inspired by Marc Bolan in the early 'Seventies.

Bolan to some extent was the first pop phenomenon to come along since the advent of The Beatles. That is less impressive than it might sound: during the 'Sixties, bands had increasingly begun to cast themselves not as pop stars but rock artistes. The former term became a pejorative to musicians who wanted their music to be taken seriously instead of culturally ghettoized as teenagers' fare in the way that rock 'n' roll had been in the early days. Bolan – by the sheer audacity of his approach but also partly through the quality of his records – made being an unashamed pop idol acceptable again. He also kicked off a whole movement: glam rock.

Like many artists of the late 'Fifties/early 'Sixties era to which his pop idol persona was a throwback, Bolan wasn't very good at making albums. His *métier* was the three-minute airplay anthem. A slew of classic examples of that genre were generated by him between 1970-1973. The one unequivocally classic long player to which his name is attached is this one. Ironically, it came about through a single.

Up until late 1970, Bolan had been one half of a hippy, folkie duo that featured him on vocals and acoustic guitar and, first Steve Peregrine Took, then Mickey Finn on hand percussion. The duo traded under the name Tyrannosaurus Rex. Bolan's early manager Simon Napier-Bell has reported that Bolan only resorted to the duo format after being devastated when a band he had hired and performed with without rehearsal were booed off the stage in 1967 and he decided that the format in which he had seen Ravi Shankar perform would prevent similar future humiliations. Four albums followed that garnered Bolan a cult audience by dint of his Tolkein-esque lyrics, which were then considered 'alternative', partly because they chimed with the prevailing fashion for all things mystical, which itself was a byword for anti-conventional. What changed Bolan's mind so dramatically was the release in late 1970 of the single 'Ride A White Swan', the culmination of him gradually introducing electric elements into the duo's sound. It was fitting that it was the first release under the truncated sobriquet T. Rex, for this was a complete departure. The fey vocals and fairytale lyrics were still present but now they were borne along by spiky electric guitar, bass and discreet strings (although no drums). It soared to a UK number two spot and Bolan's Greek-god-in-miniature image was soon adorning the bedroom walls of teenage girls nationwide. Strangely neither 'Swan' nor its success was reflected on Bolan's next album, simply called *T. Rex*, which reverted to the acoustic format. However, the permanent change to a full band-line-up – Bolan and Finn augmented by drummer Bill Legend and bassist Steve Currie – was inevitable. Tony Visconti, the man who had procured Bolan his record contract and been his long-term producer, later said, "We kind of realized that we had worn out that duo formula."

Marc Bolan, pictured in 1973.

Though 'Swan' had seemed a logical extension of Bolan's established sound, many were shocked at its successor 'Hot Love', a pop-blues hybrid with riffs, phrases and chants so generic as to be almost ridiculous. DJ John Peel, Bolan's old friend and champion, declined to play it. However, it was undeniably catchy and became Bolan's first UK number one. Its consolidation of his chart success also ensured that *Electric Warrior* was recorded on the fly, Bolan and company squeezing in sessions at studios in London, New York and Los Angeles between gigs and media commitments. This piecemeal process was not apparent in the music, which sounded all of a piece and – despite both the hectic schedule and the switch to electric instrumentation – possessed a strange tranquility.

'Cosmic Dancer' was probably the most tranquil of all the tracks, its elegance heightened by Bolan's insistence on using – unusual in rock – English pronunciation ("Is it strange to daahnce so young?"). It also featured the science fiction imagery that was a theme of the album (and in fact of Bolan's career from hereon). 'Jeepster' was as unashamedly simplistic a pop number as 'Hot Love' had been and achieved similar chart success. Yet ironically, on 'Lean Woman Blues' Bolan avoids the clichés of 12-bar blues, imparting a fresh feeling to an old format. The blissful, melodic 'Life's A Gas' was inexplicably overlooked for single consideration. However the choice of singles from the album can't really be faulted: as well as 'Jeepster', incitement to party 'Get It On' appeared as a 45rpm. As well as predictably topping the UK chart, the latter became Bolan's only American hit (albeit renamed 'Bang A Gong'). Like several tracks on the album, it was graced by the surreally high backing vocals of Flo and Eddie.

In some senses, the impact of *Electric Warrior* was as much sartorial as musical. Its success confirmed Bolan's status as founder and king of glam rock, his penchant for glittered cheeks, feather boas and other forms of adornment normally associated with the fairer sex inspiring an avalanche of artists to do the same, most of whom had little in common musically with him. Nonetheless, the impact he had on British (though not American) music was a huge one. It's difficult to imagine his old mate David Bowie devising the character of that other cosmic dancer, Ziggy Stardust, without the example of Bolan's interstellar imagery. He was also the first idol of a generation that would, upon reaching maturity, become punks. In fact, it was both touching and amusing to witness the way that the UK punks of the late 'Seventies exempted their boyhood hero from their otherwise blanket dismissal of previous generations of rock artists: a starstruck Damned supported him on tour; meanwhile, Mark Perry, editor of hardline punk bible *Sniffin' Glue*, nominated *Electric Warrior* as one of the greatest ten albums of all time in a poll, atop of which he placed the first Clash album.
- Sean Egan

60. Brian Jones Presents The Pan Pipes Of Joujouka

The Master Musicians Of Joujouka

TRACKLISTING
55/War Song-Standing + One Half/Take Me With You My Darling, Take Me With You/Your Eyes Are Like a Cup of Tea/I Am Calling Out/Your Eyes Are Like a Cup of Tea (Reprise with Flute)

RELEASED
US: Not issued UK: October 1971

PRODUCED BY
No producer listed

Though he does not play a note on it, this album was borne of the eclectic musical genius of Brian Jones.

The Rolling Stones guitarist and founder member was famously able to literally pick up any instrument from sitar to marimbas to recorder and learn to play within a day. For George Chkiantz, the engineer who recorded this album, it was Jones' very eclecticism and symbiotic musicality that led the Stone to be interested in the sounds created by the musicians of the Moroccan village tribe called the Jajouka (the spelling has varied with successive releases of this album). "Why wouldn't he be?" he reasons. Indeed, it would seem that Jones – for many intimates, a very often unpleasant and self-centered personality – took an approach of absolute humility in the preparation of this album. For a start, he was prepared to abandon his considerable material comforts and endure the privations of a village with no electricity, running water or sewerage located a full day's journey from 'civilization' in order to record it. While domiciled in Jajouka, Jones – so used to being the center of the universe – was considerate and respectful of the tribe and its traditions.

Those traditions were mind-bogglingly ancient. The Jajouka musical event that Jones had originally wanted to capture was the festival of Bou Jeloud, which runs for a full week. It can supposedly be traced right back to the Rites of Pan from Roman times although customized for the Moslem faith. However, the recording was done at the wrong time of the year for this and instead Jones and his crew obtained from the musicians of the village a sort of 'greatest hits', or as Jones put it in his liner notes, "A specially chosen representation of the type of music which is played and chanted during the festival".

The party that arrived in Jajouka in early 1969, consisted of Jones, his girlfriend Suki Potter, Chkiantz and Brion Gysin, the painter who had first alerted Jones to the existence of the Jajouka. Chkiantz brought with him a UHER 4200 reel-to-reel tape recorder, some spare batteries, two Dynamic Mics, assorted bits of wire and some Gaffa tape. Track separation and close miking wasn't an issue: this was a true field recording in which optimum and most representative results are achieved – even today - by holding the mics up in the air.

A couple, of years previously Chkiantz had been shocked by the volume of The Jimi Hendrix Experience when recording them in a British studio. However, if he had assumed that things couldn't get any louder than that celebrated power trio, he was disproved by the musicians of the Jajouka, a collective of various ages who made money by playing events at surrounding villages and towns. Though somewhat more than a trio – the musicians numbered around 20 to 30 – there was of course no electrical amplification of their instruments, which were drums, flutes and raitas. Chkiantz had to turn the 'gain' on the tape recorder right down and tap the volume controls so that they were just minutely off the zero setting in order to record anything that did not distort. However, no amount of ingenuity could produce a clear recording of a wailing female singer because of the massive tambourine-like instrument she banged before her face. Nor fillet out the sounds of dogs barking and babies crying that can be discerned at some points.

The recording spanned two days, off and on. Though Jones could almost certainly have picked up and mastered any of the instruments present, he mainly kept a respectful distance, sitting quietly behind Chkiantz as the latter recorded, although he did dance and clap during night sessions. The musicians of course had no idea of western concepts like musical climaxes: they simply played until Chkiantz indicated to the musician who was also acting as a conductor that his tape was running out, at which point the conductor would give a signal to his colleagues and the musicians would come to a comically abrupt halt. The 'tidy' endings the musicians promised to think up never materialized.

Jones was pleased by what had been captured but once back in Britain his original plan to use the results for an exotic backdrop to a Rolling Stones track were quickly abandoned, not least because Chkiantz prevailed upon him that to overdub the likes of electric guitar on their more-or-less authentic snapshot of the Jajouka's sound would be a "travesty". Chkiantz: "[He] agreed if and only if we could do something with the material to make it, in his judgment, sufficiently attention grabbing to retain the interest of a Western audience. So then the idea of evoking our journey and impressions evolved."

Some compromise was needed. Though the piece heard on the original side two of the album – titled 'Your Eyes Are Like A Cup Of Tea (Reprise With Flute)' on the CD reissue; there were no track titles on the initial release – stood on its own and needed just a touch of reverb on the last few notes to give it a clean ending, the rest of the material had to be cut down from the approximately six hours of recording to something that could fit on a platter with a maximum playing time of 40-50 minutes.

Though Jones knew that this music would not be a massive bestseller, the assumption by some – noting that it wasn't released until two years after Jones' July 1969 death and even then only on the Rolling Stones' own label – that only sentimentality caused its issue is wrong: at least one record label was interested in the project while Jones was still around.

Joujouka was influential by example. It was World Music before the term was invented. Admittedly, the term is almost meaningless, being a way of hiving off all non-western popular music into a category, no matter the style or the country of origin. But in 1960s Britain and America, curry was looked on with suspicion, let alone exotic music. By attaching his superstar name and endorsement to the music of the Jajouka musicians, Jones was helping create a willingness to listen to and consequently an audience for music which conformed to almost none of the traditions of Western pop. Today, World Music constitutes a significant and ever growing market. - Sean Egan

61. The Concert For Bangla Desh
Various Artists

TRACKLISTING
Ravi Shankar: Bangla Dhun/George Harrison: Wah-Wah/George Harrison: My Sweet Lord/George Harrison: Awaiting On You All/Billy Preston: That's the Way God Planned It/Ringo Starr: It Don't Come Easy/George Harrison and Leon Russell: Beware of Darkness/George Harrison: While My Guitar Gently Weeps/Medley: Leon Russell: Jumpin' Jack Flash-Leon Russell & Don Preston: Young Blood/George Harrison: Here Comes the Sun/Bob Dylan: A Hard Rain's A-Gonna Fall/Bob Dylan: It Takes A Lot To Laugh, It Takes A Train To Cry/Bob Dylan: Blowin' In The Wind/Bob Dylan: Mr. Tambourine Man/Bob Dylan: Just Like a Woman/George Harrison: Something/George Harrison: Bangla Desh

RELEASED
US: December 1971 UK: January 1972

PRODUCED BY
Phil Spector, George Harrison

"If you only buy one album in 1972, for God's sake make it this one."

So said Richard Williams in UK pop weekly *Melody Maker* in January 1972. He was speaking of the live document of the two concerts at New York's Madison Square Gardens on August 1 1971, an event which saw some of the biggest stars in rock congregate to play free of charge to raise money for and to highlight the plight of Bengali refugees who, already made homeless in that country's civil war, were now enduring the devastation caused by severe floods. Mass starvation was likely.

The concert was the brainchild of George Harrison, an ex-Beatle for only a few months when the idea occurred to him and, lest it be forgotten, at the time arguably the most successful former quarter of the Fabs: 'My Sweet Lord' had made number one and his *All Things Must Pass* album, though bloated, had delivered the sort of high quality slick rock Beatles fans had been puzzled to find missing on the first post-Beatles John and Paul albums. Still only 28, Harrison finally seemed to be coming into his own. Though that artistic promise was not really subsequently fulfilled, through the Bangla Desh project he would forever afterwards possess a gravitas and respect for making rock do something that even its

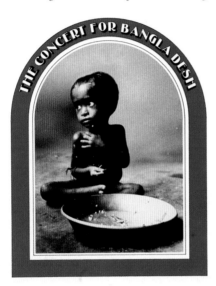

most enthusiastic adherents had not previously imagined it capable of: save people's lives. *The Concert For Bangla Desh* album was not influential because of any music it contained but it started a very agreeable tradition that thrives in music to this day: the benefit concert. It is the example provided by his idea that led to many, many other similar events, including what is possibly the most famous concert of all time, 1985's Live Aid, organized by fellow musician Bob Geldof.

Harrison was first alerted to the plight of the Bengalis by his friend, Indian sitar player Ravi Shankar. "It was the only way George knew how to help," Harrison's widow Olivia explained in 2005. She also pointed out that Harrison was not at all sure that the event would come off: "The music community had never made that sort of endeavor before." Though the idea of performing free was not exactly patentable – after all, people had been belting out tunes into microphones at political rallies and suchlike for donkey's years – this venture was to be on an unprecedented scale. It may even be the case that in order to come off as successfully as it did, Harrison was literally the only man for the job. Easy to laugh it may be at the contrast between Harrison's ideals and his personality – never can somebody so enlightened have been so grumpy – but the fact is that as the Beatle who was actually the closest to fellow superstars Bob Dylan and Eric Clapton, only he may have been in the position to engineer the twin coups he did by persuading both to take the stage.

Though most who took the stage were living legends, the music

The original box design for *The Concert For Bangla Desh.*

they performed was really of little import, if well played. Ravi Shankar opened proceedings with Indian music that would have been of scant interest to most attendees. Harrison, Starr, Clapton, Billy Preston and Bob Dylan generally performed their signature songs.

However, the emotional resonance for those at the event of the appearance of Bob Dylan was huge. Dylan was then a recluse by showbusiness standards, declining to tour and turning out albums whose domestic concerns indicated a stepping away from his 'alternative', implicitly anti-conventional image. The tidal wave of affection that greeted his surprise appearance is clearly audible on the record. The crowd weren't just happy to see Dylan because he hadn't toured since 1966: many of them must have thought that the decision to play this particular gig meant that they might be getting the 'protest' era Dylan back again. Less audible but just as real on the evening was the hope invested by the audience in the spectacle of two Beatles at the same concert: this was 1971, only a few months after the Beatles had done the unthinkable and dissolved their unprecedentedly successful partnership, and people still believed the bond could be unbroken. (Harrison did ask McCartney and Lennon too. The former, still bitter over the dissolution, refused while Lennon failed to take the stage after a row with wife Yoko over Harrison's reluctance to have her on the bill.)

The recording of the concert – a triple vinyl release housed in a sumptuous box with a picture of a starving child on the cover, a piece of emotional blackmail Bob Geldof would have been proud of – was intended to be released a matter of weeks after it had taken place. However, because of disputes with the record company over distribution fees, it didn't reach the stores until Christmas of '71. Critic Robert Christgau sarcastically said, "If you mail your check to the United Nations Children's Fund for Relief to Refugee Children of Bangla Desh you can avoid the middleman." Christgau and those who imagine that rock stars were always bound to have done work for good causes should bear in mind the fact that at the Isle of Wight festival in 1970, a concert-goer who managed to get backstage and proceeded to try to obtain donations from the rock elite gathered there for a fund to free some fellow gig-goers who had been busted was shocked by the contemptuous attitude he encountered from his heroes, finding only an amiable Jim Morrison prepared to dig into his pocket. By 1971, the musicians who had become famous in the 'Sixties were already living in grand seclusion, their mansions and their wealth distancing them from their fans. Though nobody was going to go live in a ghetto because of Harrison – least of all George himself – he made sure with this work that rock stars would never be so separated from real life again.

For the record, the Concert for Bangla Desh and merchandising related to it including this album raised an estimated $15m. - Sean Egan

62. Tago Mago

Can

TRACKLISTING

Paperhouse/Mushroom/Oh Yeah/Halleluhwah/Aumgn/Peking O/Bring Me Coffee Or Tea

RELEASED

US: Not issued UK: February 1972

PRODUCED BY

Can

In retrospect, Can stand out from the cluster of early 'Seventies German bands that were loosely labelled as Krautrock. This grouping, which also included Neu, Amon Duul, Faust and Tangerine Dream, produced music that varied from the wildly inventive to the bizarrely self-indulgent. But there was something special, even magical, about Can. Beyond the use of mystical words, beyond the references to shamanistic practise and Aleister Crowley, Can were artists of intense musical creativity and hypnotic fascination.

Most of their albums stand the test of time well, but their third album *Tago Mago* is their most complete statement. Founder members Holger Czukay (bass), David Johnson (flute), jazz drummer Jaki Liebezeit and guitar player Michael Karoli originally formed the band in the Cologne apartment of classical conductor and piano player Irmin Schmidt in 1968, although Johnson left within a year. Malcolm Mooney, an American artist, was the singer on the early records, but had personal problems and returned to the USA. For *Tago Mago,* he was replaced by Japanese vocalist Damo Suzuki, who the band discovered busking in the street.

Can's music was almost entirely improvised. Liebezeit's powerful, fluid drumming was the driving force of most songs, and rather than shifting between rhythm playing and soloing, each of the other members of the band tended to develop repetitive riffs that gradually mutated and transformed throughout the song. The result was something quite different to the complex song formations of progressive rock or of contemporaries such as Pink Floyd. Instead, Can's music was simple and direct, but ever-changing. One early song, 'You Doo Right', could almost have been a three minute pop classic, except that in their hands it elongated to a twenty minute jam, constantly evolving, breaking down and realigning.

Mooney's vocals were plaintive and (mostly) comprehensible, but now they were replaced by the more esoteric tones of Suzuki. He rarely did anything so simple as 'singing', preferring to mumble, shriek, howl or croon at oblique tangents to the music, becoming in the process another improvisational instrument in the mix rather than a purveyor of lyrics. In addition to this, Holger Czukay was becoming ever more fascinated by experiments with the technology available in the studio and the songs on the album were complemented by backwards vocals, tape loops and sound effects. This could have been an unholy mix, but underpinned by the driving rhythms of Liebezeit, it instead produced

Sleeve artwork for *Tago Mago*.

a record that is trancelike and compelling.

Tago Mago was originally a double vinyl album consisting of only seven songs, two of which ('Halleluhwah' and 'Aumgn') lasted for an entire side. The first side ('Paperhouse', 'Mushroom', 'Oh Yeah') shows the band at their most accessible, with listenable songs that immediately hook the attention in spite of (or because of) Suzuki's rambling lyrical performance. 'Hallehluhwah' is one of the best tracks Can ever recorded. A pattering, dancey drum beat propels a twisting bassline. The shifting riffs of Karoli and Schmidt and the looping vocals of Suzuki give the song a jazzy, joyous feeling which feels like a precursor of later dance genres such as trip-hop, baggy and trance. The second disc is a darker affair – 'Aumgn' reflects the band's fascination with experimental soundtracks. With its moans and discordant shrieks, it could almost be the backing music of a demonic horror film. 'Peking O' ploughs the same territory, before the final track takes us into gentler realms.

Can's immediate influence was slight, although Kraftwerk's early music owed them a debt in several respects, not least in the way they allowed a song to leisurely build and mutate. But Can developed a fervent underground following and their influence grew steadily and manifested itself in extraordinarily diverse ways over subsequent decades. The stubborn singularity of their music was an influence on some of the key players of punk and post-punk, including John Lydon (especially in his Public Image Ltd recordings), Pete Shelley of the Buzzcocks (who has been quoted as saying "I never would have played guitar if not for Marc Bolan and Michael Karoli of Can"), and Mark E. Smith of the Fall, who registered his fandom with a song called "I Am Damo Suzuki".

In the early 'Nineties, a clear Can influence showed up in the music of acts such as The Stone Roses (especially 'Fool's Gold') and The Happy Mondays, as well as in more experimental dance acts such as Tricky. As much as anything, the dynamics and song structures of Can were an influence on modern dance music. As traditional verse-chorus shapes were superseded by the elongated, repetitive tracks of dance, with recurring but mutating elements, the layered improvisations of Can came to seem increasingly ahead of their time. In the more experimental fringes of rock, bands as disparate as Sonic Youth, the Birthday Party and the Butthole Surfers show traces of the weird attack of Can, while experimental outfits like Stereolab and Tortoise learned from their looping improvisational approach. And finally, from *Kid A* onwards, it has been clear that Radiohead have been influenced by them – they even covered a Can song ('The Thief') live on the *Kid A* tour.

The variety of bands that Can influenced is tribute to their versatility and ingenuity. If you're not already initiated, *Tago Mago* is the perfect place to start. - Hugh Barker

63. The Rise And Fall Of Ziggy Stardust And The Spiders From Mars
David Bowie

TRACKLISTING
Five Years/Soul Love/Moonage Daydream/Starman/It Ain't Easy/Lady
Stardust/Star/Hang On To Yourself/Ziggy Stardust/Suffragette City/Rock
'N' Roll Suicide

RELEASED
US: September 1972/UK: June 1972

PRODUCED BY
Ken Scott, David Bowie

In 1971, David Bowie had an impatient record company barking at
his heels.

He had in mind a grand concept album to elevate him back to
the star status he had briefly tasted in 1969 with his UK chart topper 'Space
Oddity'. With his concept not ready, he delivered RCA *Hunky Dory* – a
stop-gap that happens to be one of the greatest albums ever made. The
concept album was *Ziggy Stardust*, released seven months after *Hunky Dory*.
The concept turned out not to be so grand: Bowie paid more attention to
the visuals and the manufacture of headline-generating quotes than he did
a coherent story. However, the Ziggy phenomenon as a whole took rock
into areas that it had never gone before, presenting both a fictional persona
intertwined in many ways with his creator and a brazenness about artifice.
It also created the first openly bi-sexual mainstream pop star.

Ziggy Stardust possibly illustrates that commercial and critical
success are as dependent on context as quality. Many consider *Hunky Dory*
to be the superior album. However, a merely superb record promoted by a
man who at the time looked like a hippie was not going to capture
the imagination of the kids the way that a carrot-topped interplanetary
gender-bender did. In any case, whatever the shortcomings of the concept,
and though it was as skeletal and earthy as *Hunky Dory* had been ornate,
Ziggy was a brilliant collection.

The main inspiration for Ziggy Stardust, the character, was
Vince Taylor, a British 'Fifties rocker chiefly artistically notable for
'Brand New Cadillac', a cover of which features on another album
in this book, *London Calling*. Like Peter Green, Syd Barrett, Brian
Wilson and (possibly) Brian Jones, Taylor was one of that sad breed of

musician whose talent and mental well-being were decimated by the ingestion of LSD, a drug that is considered to be detrimental to those who are already psychologically fragile. Less well-known and less successful than them, Taylor had no financial safety net on which to fall back when he began alarming his friends and colleagues with the manifestations of his illness, which in his case included declaring himself to be Christ reincarnated. Needless to say, whatever vestige of a career he had was destroyed.

Bowie's concept was only loosely based on Taylor, for his hero hailed from outer space. Mr. Stardust's rock 'n' roll superstardom occurs after the planet earth that he had decided to take up residence on is hit with the shock news that it is going to be non-existent within half a decade. From there, the story seems to entail Stardust letting his pre-apocalyptical stardom go to his alien head, resulting in his colleagues in his band the Spiders From Mars conspiring against him to ensure his downfall, which demise sees the titular hero reduced to a shambling wreck by the album's close. One says "seems to" because the narrative is not only difficult to follow but it isn't even maintained. As the album co-producer Ken Scott has said, "Nothing was ever discussed during the recording about it being a concept album and when you consider one of the tracks was taken from the *Hunky Dory* batch of recordings and used on the album and then we had to go in at a later date to do 'Starman'.. It was kind of pieced together."

Because 'Starman' was belatedly recorded at the insistence of a record company who saw no single material on *Ziggy*, Scott considers there to be a mere four songs on the album that adhere to the Ziggy Stardust concept: 'Lady Stardust', 'Hang Onto Yourself', 'Ziggy Stardust' and 'Star'. However, other songs present that can plausibly be added to this concept are 'Five Years', 'Moonage Daydream', 'Starman' and 'Rock 'N' Roll Suicide', even if the sum is non-linear and more like a series of dissociated vignettes of the same subject. The vagueness of Bowie's concept could possibly be due to a certain lack of solemnity in his approach. Witness the way he says to an incongruously smiling character in 'Five Years' – a track about the impending apocalypse that starts the album - "Don't think you knew you were in this song". His rock opera may have been fragmentary but this involving of the listener in his artifice - post-modernism – brought a new dimension to the genre. This very modern ambience was enhanced by the moon landing allusions and then-fashionable phraseology like "Lay the real thing on me" and "Jiving us that we were voodoo", which of course have now dated the album slightly.

Despite the aforementioned long gestation period and the fact that its tracks were laid down from November 1971 to February 1972, *Ziggy Stardust* was recorded in a quite astonishing approximate six cumulative days. Bowie utilized the rhythm section of bassist Trevor Bolder and Mick 'Woody' Woodmansey. Ostensibly not names to conjure with – they are not really well-known outside the fact of being Bowie's band members for the *Ziggy* period – they were responsible for the album's impressive bottom end. Guitar duties were splendidly handled by Mick Ronson (with additional work by Bowie, who also contributed saxophone). 'Ronno' also supplied some keyboard work that is amazingly proficient for somebody who did not consider piano to be his main instrument. There is almost no ornamentation on top of these basic instruments, making for an album that, like The Who's quite spartan *Tommy*, seemed to defy the grandness inherent in the phrase Concept Album. Nonetheless, there was some fine music indeed present. 'Starman', the instantly catchy and somehow unearthly hit single, is the obvious stand-out but similar aesthetic excellence informs the absurdly moving 'Five Years', the thoughtful 'Soul Love', the rockers' anthem 'Star' and the rip-roaring (if incomprehensible) 'Suffragette City'. 'Ziggy Stardust' basically distils the whole Ziggy story into a three minute song with a superbly colloquial lyric and some sublime fretwork that justifies the kiss-off line about the character, "Boy, could he play guitar". - Sean Egan

Fuck Art!

From early US hip-hop and house through to the UK acid house, rave and big beat scene, these are a few **influential and classic '80s and '90s dance tracks**.

1.	**White Lines (Don't Do It)**	Grandmaster Flash and Melle Mel
2.	**Blue Monday**	New Order
3.	**Pump Up The Volume**	M/A/R/R/S
4.	**Rok Da House**	The Beatmasters with The Cookie Crew
5.	**Ill House You**	The Jungle Brothers
6.	**It's House**	Chip E
7.	**Jack Your Body**	Steve "Silk" Hurley
8.	**Voodoo Ray**	A Guy Called Gerald
9.	**You've Got The Love**	Source, Featuring Candi Staton
10.	**Set Me Free**	N-Trance
11.	**What Time Is Love?**	The KLF
12.	**Block Rockin Beats**	Chemical Brothers
13.	**Theme From S'Express**	S'Express
14.	**Back To Life (However Do You Want Me)**	Soul II Soul, featuring Caron Wheeler
15.	**Go**	Moby
16.	**Groove Is In The Heart**	Deee-Lite
17.	**Pump Up The Jam**	Technotronic
18.	**Release The Pressure**	Leftfield
19.	**The Bomb! (These Sounds Fall Into My Mind)**	The Bucketheads
20.	**Brimful Of Asha**	Cornershop

64. The Harder They Come: Orginal Soundtrack Recording

Various Artists

TRACKLISTING

Jimmy Cliff: You Can Get It If You Really Want/Scotty: Draw Your Brakes/The Melodians: Rivers Of Babylon/Jimmy Cliff: Many Rivers To Cross/The Maytals: Sweet And Dandy/Jimmy Cliff: The Harder They Come/The Slickers: Johnny Too Bad/Desmond Dekker: 007(Shanty Town)/The Maytals: Pressure Drop/Jimmy Cliff: Sitting In Limbo/Jimmy Cliff: You Can Get It If You Really Want/Jimmy Cliff: The Harder They Come

RELEASED

US: 1973 UK: July 1972

PRODUCED BY

Jimmy Cliff, Derrick Harriot, Leslie Kong, Byron Lee, Guilly Bright

Made on a shoestring budget, 1972's *The Harder They Come* was a home-grown Jamaican film, the first to find international success. That was an achievement in itself, but it wasn't the only remarkable thing about the movie. As it turned out, the movie's soundtrack was an even greater triumph, essentially introducing Jamaican music to the world.

The film, written, produced and directed by Jamaican native Perry Henzell, starred Jimmy Cliff in the lead role of anti-hero Ivan O. Martin. Cliff brought some genuine star power to the film, having already made a name for himself as a recording artist in his native Jamaica. But it was his starring role in *The Harder They Come* that would provide Cliff with what turned out to be his breakout moment. Shot on location in Kingston, the film effectively portrayed the harshness of Trenchtown ghetto life. A smash hit in Kingston, *The Harder They Come* filled theaters for months on end and remained popular with the college crowd in the US for years after its release.

It has often been said that the soundtrack became more famous than the film, and indeed its importance as a vehicle for introducing reggae to an international audience cannot be underestimated. Its songs underline the film's themes while also standing strongly on their own. With its cornucopia of styles and rhythms incorporating reggae, ska and rocksteady, *The Harder They Come* captures Jamaican music during its golden age with Cliff's songs forming the bulk of the tunes, even if a couple of them are

Jimmy Cliff posing in front of a film poster for *The Harder They Come*.

repeated. Cliff produced his own material here and it is easily among the best he ever recorded. The sweetly soulful 'You Can Get It If You Really Want' preaches perseverance in reaching for your dreams, 'Many Rivers To Cross' is an emotionally wrenching gospel ballad expressing the anguish of a man who's lost everything but the pride that keeps him going, the title track is a defiant declaration of self-dignity and the breezy 'Sitting In Limbo' conveys an attitude of determined optimism.

The non-Cliff songs are comprised of the cream of late 1960s and early 1970s reggae, chosen by Henzell. Both Desmond Dekker's '007 (Shanty Town)' and The Slickers' 'Johnny Too Bad' perfectly encapsulate the film's rude boy (Jamaican parlance for criminal rebel) theme. Other highlights include the openly spiritual declarations of The Melodians' 'Rivers Of Babylon' and the exuberant rhythms of Toots And The Maytals' 'Sweet And Dandy' and 'Pressure Drop'. The album launched both The Maytals and Cliff to international stardom.

The strength of *The Harder They Come* lies in its diverse range of pre-dub reggae styles which aside from the dance-oriented ska (borrowed from New Orleans-style R&B) encompasses the smoother 'rocksteady' style and even a bit of calypso. The sounds that Cliff and company popularized would prove to be durable and far reaching in influence. By the late '70s a generation in the UK had grown up absorbing the reggae rhythms coming out of the Jamaican immigrant community. On Britain's mainstream Radio 1, DJ John Peel played a mix of punk and reggae artists while the major UK music papers *New Musical Express* and *Sounds* regularly covered the reggae music scene.

Several UK punk acts incorporated reggae into their sound, including The Slits and The Ruts. The Clash most famously devised a punk-reggae fusion. Whether working with Bob Marley producer Lee 'Scratch' Perry on their '77 single 'Complete Control', incorporating reggae into their own songs (i.e., '(White Man) In Hammersmith Palais', 'Straight To Hell') or offering edgy reggae remakes including Junior Murvin's 'Police And Thieves' and an exemplary version of 'Pressure Drop'. The reggae influence would be felt throughout the course of The Clash's career. Frontman Joe Strummer once spoke of a certain kinship between the punks and Jamaica's dreads as similarly oppressed groups with a shared rebel spirit. Though Johnny Rotten himself acknowledged reggae as a strong influence, it was absent from his work with The Sex Pistols, but turned up in obvious form in the music of his subsequent band Public Image Ltd. The late '70s brought the more mainstream sounds of the 2-Tone ska revival movement in the UK via commercially successful bands such as The (English) Beat, The Selecter, Madness and The Specials. The Police carried their reggae-inflected pop to even greater commercial heights internationally. It should also be noted that vocal group Boney M — amazingly — scored one of the biggest selling UK singles of all time with their 1978 chart-topping version of 'Rivers Of Babylon'. The late '80s and early '90s found bands like No Doubt and The Mighty Mighty Bosstones carrying on the ska tradition, which has continued into the new century with the punk ska movement (i.e., Big D And The Kids Table, Catch 22, Suburban Legends).

As for Cliff, disillusioned with what he felt was a lack of support, he departed the Island label the same year *The Harder They Come* was released just as he appeared headed for breakout success. Island head Chris Blackwell was deeply disappointed and invested his company's promotional efforts in Bob Marley, who went on to become the international face of reggae. But it is Cliff who deserves the credit for opening the doors to the internationalization of the music on an album that, beyond its influence, still stands as one of reggae's all-time greatest albums. - Tierney Smith

65. Nuggets
Various Artists

TRACKLISTING
The Electric Prunes: I Had Too Much to Dream (Last Night)/The Standells: Dirty Water/The Strangeloves: Night Time/The Knickerbockers: Lies/The Vagrants: Respect/Mouse & the Traps: A Public Execution/The Blues Project: No Time Like the Right Time/The Shadows of Knight: Oh Yeah/The Seeds: Pushin' Too Hard/The Barbarians: Moulty/The Remains: Don't Look Back/The Magicians: An Invitation to Cry/The Castaways: Liar, Liar/The Thirteenth Floor Elevators: You're Gonna Miss Me/Count Five: Psychotic Reaction/The Leaves: Hey Joe/Michael & the Messengers: Just Like Romeo and Juliet/The Cryan Shames: Sugar and Spice/The Amboy Dukes: Baby Please Don't Go/The Blues Magoos: Tobacco Road/The Chocolate Watchband: Let's Talk About Girls/The Mojo Men: Sit Down I Think I Love You/The Third Rail: Run Run Run/Sagittarius: My World Fell Down/The Nazz: Open My Eyes/The Premiers: Farmer John/The Magic Mushrooms: It's-A-Happening

RELEASED
US: September 1972 UK: September 1972

PRODUCED BY
Lenny Kaye

When *Nuggets* was released in late 1972, only five years or so had elapsed since the end of the era in which young British Invasion-inspired US garage bands had sprouted all over the States. By 1972 standards, however, that might as well have been the dark ages. Progressive rock, heavy metal, and confessional singer-songwriters were all thriving. Mid-'60s garage rock was given little more respect than bubblegum, and regarded as a dated, embarrassingly juvenile reminder of rock's silliest, most disposable and trashiest elements as it struggled to make the leap from adolescence to adulthood. Today, compiling some of the best garage rock into a two-LP compilation seems not just sensible, but tasteful. Back when Lenny Kaye did it in the early '70s, however, it was not just out of sync with the day's critical party line, but positively courageous.

Kaye, however, recognized that garage rock had not just historic or nostalgic value, but intrinsic artistic merit as well. Sure, generally speaking it was naïve, somewhat amateurish, and not nearly as sophisticated (or good) as the major British Invasion bands – the Rolling Stones, Beatles, Yardbirds, Kinks, Animals, Them, and Zombies – that served as their obvious role models. But its very naiveté was intrinsic to its appeal, the bands thrashing about with a wildly untamed energy that came through in dollops in their over-heated fuzz guitars, high cheesy organs, and snide sub-Mick Jagger vocals. When they branched out into early psychedelia, they pulled off some *bona fide* thrilling experiments. And for all their relative rawness, the groups did come up with some dynamite pop hooks and arresting arrangements, even if they largely lacked the skills to bottle lightning with an actual classic track more than once or twice.

The Chocolate Watchband, one of the bands featured on *Nuggets*.

The 27-song lineup on *Nuggets* includes some of the core classics of the genre. The Electric Prunes' 'I Had Too Much to Dream (Last Night)' (perhaps the greatest fusion of garage rock and psychedelia), The

Standells' 'Dirty Water', The Knickerbockers' 'Lies' (the best and most accurate early Beatles imitation ever done), The Seeds' 'Pushin' Too Hard', Count Five's 'Psychotic Reaction', The Castaways' 'Liar, Liar', The Leaves' 'Hey Joe' – all were not only great singles, but actual national US hit records. Kaye also had the wherewithal to include numerous worthy items that only dented the bottom part of the Top 100, or missed it altogether, like the Thirteenth Floor Elevators' 'You're Gonna Miss Me', The Remains' 'Don't Look Back', Mouse & the Traps' 'A Public Execution' (the most accurate emulation of mid-'60s Bob Dylan), the Chocolate Watchband's 'Let's Talk About Girls', and the Magic Mushrooms' eerily over-the-top psychedelic excursion 'It's-a-Happening'. He also had the open-mindedness to include several artists, and songs, that didn't fit the stereotypical snotty garage band archetype, like The Nazz's Beatles-Who fusion 'Open My Eyes' (featuring a young Todd Rundgren), the Blues Project's 'No Time Like the Right Time', Sagittarius's *Smile*-era Beach Boys soundalike 'My World Fell Down', and the Cryan Shames' cover of The Searchers' 'Sugar and Spice'. As a consequence, *Nuggets* is far more listenable than virtually any '60s garage band comp that would follow.

That doesn't mean that Kaye's selection was either flawless, or entirely representative of the garage band sound as we've come to think of it. For The Strangeloves, Amboy Dukes, and Blues Magoos, he selected relatively obscure cuts that weren't nearly as good as those group's biggest hits ('I Want Candy', 'Journey To The Center Of The Mind', and '(We Ain't Got) Nothing Yet' respectively). (All of those omitted cuts were added to the tracklist for Rhino's 1998 expanded four-CD box set version of *Nuggets*.) Also, whether for licensing reasons or some other factor, some obvious top-drawer garage rock classics were left out, including the Music Machine's 'Talk Talk', ? & the Mysterians' '96 Tears', and the Swingin' Medallions' 'Double Shot (Of My Baby's Love)'. A few cuts were neither that garagey nor that good, like the quaintly satirical psychedelic pop of the Third Rail's 'Run Run Run' or the blue-eyed soul of Michael and the Messengers' 'Just Like Romeo And Juliet' (which was inferior to the original hit version by The Reflections in any case). But these were minor flaws in a package that not only put much of the very best garage rock into one place, but also – *very* unusually, for 1972 rock compilations of any sort – gave it detailed, loving liner notes that were scholarly without being stuffy.

It wouldn't be correct to say that *Nuggets'* influence was that wide or immediate. It didn't make the Top 200 of the album charts, and in fact was already out of print by 1976, when it was reissued on Sire. What it did do, however, was to make garage rock – and *liking* garage rock – acceptable, even hip, among both critics and emerging musicians who would lay the foundations for punk and new wave. As guitarist for the Patti Smith Group, Kaye himself was one of them, and his liner notes have even been cited as containing the first high-profile use of the term 'punk rock', though here he was using it to describe '60s bands, not their descendants. Punks of the '70s, however, would extend some of the garage ethos into their own music, putting raw, abrasive, rebellious energy back into rock 'n' roll. In those original notes, Kaye wrote that *Nuggets* was "the first volume of what is hoped will be a continuing archeological dig into the bizarre splendor of the mid-'Sixties." The *Nuggets* series, alas, never did get beyond its first volume, but it did directly spawn exactly the continuing archeological dig Kaye was envisioning, starting with the ten-volume *Pebbles* '60s garage rock series and culminating in the situation today where there are literally hundreds such various-artists and single-artist compilations, something that played its part in the whole vintage rock reissue industry. Finally, in the late 1990s, *Nuggets* itself was exhumed and expanded into the aforementioned four-CD box set, now considered a cornerstone of any thorough '60s rock collection. - Richie Unterberger

66. Talking Book
Stevie Wonder

TRACKLISTING
You Are The Sunshine Of My Life/Maybe Your Baby/You And I/Tuesday Heartbreak/You've Got It Bad Girl/Superstition/Big Brother/Blame It On The Sun/Lookin' For Another Pure Love/I Believe (When I Fall In Love It Will Be Forever)

RELEASED
US: October 1972 UK: January 1973

PRODUCED BY
Stevie Wonder

Inspired by the efforts of his Motown labelmate, Marvin Gaye, to prove to their mutual boss, Berry Gordy, that it was possible to satisfy both their own creative potential and the marketplace at the same time, Stevie Wonder spent the early part of the 1970s fighting his way out of the straitjacket in which Gordy had partially imprisoned the prodigiously talented singer, songwriter and multi-instrumentalist as a child.

Wonder, born Steveland Judkins in 1950, and blind from shortly after birth, released his first album for Motown before he was 12 years old. By the time he hit his twenties, he had written and recorded numerous hits and given Motown its first Number One album. Though many of his recordings had been very good ones, his control over what he recorded and released was non-existent. On his 21st birthday, though, everything changed: the trust fund that had been collecting Wonder's considerable royalties was turned over to his control, and his lawyers sent a letter to Gordy informing him of their client's decision to end his contract with Motown. (Gordy, who had thrown a party for Wonder's birthday the night before, at which the contract had not been mentioned, was furious.) What Wonder did next would have profound implications for the future of popular music.

Knowing he had time on his side, a string of willing suitors in the shape of other record labels, and enough cash in the bank to sit tight until he got the deal he wanted, Wonder could virtually write the terms of his next record deal himself. By the time Gordy signed on the dotted line of a new Motown contract, Wonder had got everything he wanted: complete artistic control, his own production and publishing companies, and a significant, still secret, advance. It is the sort of deal that still, more than three decades on, remains something of a holy grail to every independently minded musician.

Even as his contract

Stevie Wonder, pictured in the early 1970s.

situation had been up in the air, Wonder and his wife, Syreeta Wright, moved to New York, far away from Gordy's Detroit production line and the slightly incestuous feel of the Motown set-up, and the star had immediately begun working on new music. He block-booked lengthy sessions at Electric Lady, the studio Jimi Hendrix had built in Greenwich Village. He had decided to work with the relatively obscure duo Robert Margouleff and Malcolm Cecil. The pair had come to Wonder's attention after his bass player gave him a copy of their 1971 album *Zero Time*, released under the moniker Tonto's Expanding Head Band. Tonto wasn't a person, but the biggest Moog synthesizer the world has ever known. (To be more accurate, it was actually eight or nine different synths all hooked up together along with early sequencers and other tools.) Its name was an acronym for The Original New Timbral Orchestra, and Cecil and Margouleff had been developing the machine since the late 1960s, when they had both been engineers working with creator Robert Moog himself. Wonder, always insatiably curious about new keyboard possibilities, was hooked by the potential worlds of sound Tonto seemed to offer. And wanting to use the notoriously temperamental machine meant having to work with Cecil and Margouleff. (Anyone wishing to try to emulate the sounds Wonder, Cecil and Margouleff conjured will have to ask Devo's Mark Mothersbaugh: the electronic musician bought the complex and ever-evolving synth after it was taken out of active service in the 1980s.) The result was an album that proved the synthesizer could be turned from a lugubrious and limited instrument into a machine that could be given a tone perfectly in keeping with rock and soul's gritty traditions. From hereon in, the "No synths!" boast in a Queen liner note would come to seem increasingly Luddite as the Moog and an ever more sophisticated range of (ever smaller) synthesizers caught up with and arguably overtook the guitar as popular music's main instrument. Wonder, though, used synths more adroitly than most, seamlessly meshing Tonto with more conventional soul instrumentation on *Talking Book*.

By the time Wonder's new Motown deal was finalized, the triumvirate had over 40 songs ready. From these Wonder picked nine to comprise the first of his "emancipated" albums, and the first in an incredible stretch of five classic releases: *Music Of My Mind*. A mere seven months later, after touring the US as a little-heralded support to the Rolling Stones and an appearance at Madison Square Gardens at a John Lennon and Yoko Ono benefit concert, *Talking Book* was released. Despite what followed – the magisterial *Innervisions*; the complex but lustrous *Fulfillingness' First Finale*; and *Songs In The Key Of Life*, an album so big that even two pieces of 33rpm vinyl weren't enough to contain it, necessitating an additional free single – it remains for many the pivotal record of his career, an apogee of a period of sustained excellence few artists have ever got near achieving.

Talking Book is the record that turned Wonder from a successful Motown act into a superstar of global import: and while the technical experiments he conducted with Margouleff and Cecil are arguably what made the record so sonically influential, it is Wonder's peerless mastery of the craft of songwriting, and the record's meticulous, richly detailed production that turned *Talking Book* into a smash hit. The album opens with 'You Are The Sunshine Of My Life', a track that lays bare the contradictions the record resonates with. Although Syreeta remained not just a friend, but also a collaborator – she wrote the lyrics for 'Blame It On The Sun' and 'Lookin' For Another Pure Love' – the couple's marriage had broken down, and '...Sunshine...' (apparently in the can in time to be considered for *Music Of My Mind*, but rejected as being out of step with the earlier record's mood), a whole-hearted, gorgeous love song, was apparently written to his new muse, Gloria Barley. Who, adding another layer of emotional complexity to the song, actually appears on it: hers is the second voice heard, before Wonder sings the line about a new beginning.

From there, the record continues to sparkle with alternately effervescent, melodious pop and darkly complex mood music. 'Maybe Your Baby', a clear nod to Sly Stone, falls in the latter camp; the euphoric 'I Believe (When I Fall In Love It Will Be Forever)' in the former. 'Big Brother' broods, 'You And I' soars, and 'Superstition', the album's out-and-out funk track, embodies all those contradictions and paranoid tendencies in one infectious, irresistible blurt. - Angus Batey

67. The Dark Side Of The Moon
Pink Floyd

TRACKLISTING
Speak To Me/Breathe/On The Run/Time/The Great Gig In The Sky/ Money/Us And Them/Any Colour You Like/Brain Damage/Eclipse

RELEASED
US: March 1973 UK: March 1973

PRODUCED BY
Pink Floyd

Is *The Dark Side Of The Moon* a great album? Is it even a good album? It was undoubtedly a successful one, phenomenally so. It spent 741 consecutive weeks on the *Billboard* 200, from its 1973 release right through to 1988, and to date it has sold over 40 million copies. But sometimes now it is hard to see why this sweet, but rambling and slightly self-indulgent album had quite such a massive impact.

Part of the reason lies in the date of its release. The early 'Seventies were an unsettled period. The optimism of the 'Sixties and the effervescent psychedelia of a period of easy drugs and sex were unwinding in a post-Altamont comedown of social paranoia, economic trouble, and Vietnam nightmares. In this context the huge appeal of *The Dark Side Of The Moon* becomes more explicable. At its heart, this is a mellow, soothing album. Rather than collective political agitation, or wild ambition, it is about the ordinary pressures and pleasures of everyday life, on a simple, individual level. As such, it struck a chord with an international audience increasingly inclined to focus more on their domestic lives and less on socio-political issues that it seemed increasingly apparent were beyond their control.

In terms of Pink Floyd's history it lies halfway between their psychedelic experimentation of the 'Sixties and the more straightforward rock that history now shows they were moving towards. The album is often thought to be about Syd Barrett, the band's original singer who had descended into mental turmoil because of his excessive drug use. This was clearly one influence on the thinking of remaining members guitarist David Gilmour, drummer Nick Mason, keyboardist Richard Wright and bassist Roger Waters (who all contributed to the music, although Waters took over full responsibility for the lyrics on this album). But the wider concept behind the album was an attempt to explore the stresses placed on the individual in an increasingly incomprehensible world. Waters' lyrics show a fascination with madness, exploring the way that sane individuals come to terms with the insanity that surrounds them, through a minute attention to everyday details of our perception of time, breathing, and sensations. This is after all an album about "hanging on in quiet desperation", to quote the song 'Time'. Songs such as 'Money' and 'Breathe' examine details of modern living, while 'The Great Gig In The Sky' and 'Eclipse' are set against backdrops of the fear of death and madness. The appeal of the album lies largely in the contrast between the mundane and the spiritual that these songs encompass.

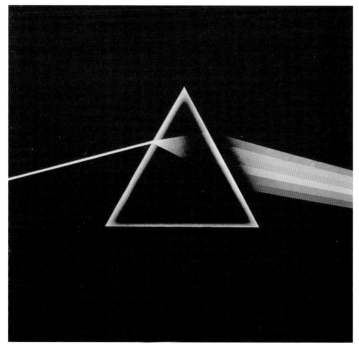

Storm Thorgerson's artwork for *The Dark Side of the Moon*.

Musically, ...*Moon* is a disparate collection of songs, given a sense of unity by the crystalline sound quality achieved by Abbey Road engineer Alan Parsons, and by a collage of concrete music, tape splices of sound effects, and snippets of people talking. The fragments of speech that periodically break through the music give the album a 'stream of consciousness' feeling. In fact they come from interviews that Waters recorded with friends and acquaintances, including studio employees, in which they answered a series of psychological questions printed on flashcards. This was just one element of Waters' elaborate preparation for the album. Where previous Pink Floyd albums had been lightly rehearsed, this album was over a year in gestation, with extensive demo taping leading on to a period of touring the work (which was then known as *Eclipse*) before the final recordings were made, themselves laborious. The result was a huge step forwards both in sound quality and songwriting. One could also argue that the huge success of this album had a deleterious effect on subsequent music as the art of music making became ever more focused on recording quality and less on warmth and spontaneous performance.

Pink Floyd were at the forefront of the idea that the primary unit of rock music was the album, and that rock was a serious artform. Like Led Zeppelin they were now intentionally recording albums without singles, with extended musical interludes and complex song structures. The simple but effective prism design of this album's cover (which like most of the Pink Floyd artwork was created by Storm Thorgerson) reinforced the idea that this was serious art rather than disposable pop music. In this respect, this was a highly influential album, though one whose influence we might regret. Music in the 'Seventies became increasingly about pomposity and bombast. However, while Pink Floyd did a great deal to establish the environment in which the dinosaurs of rock flourished, they themselves can plead not guilty to most of those dinosaurs' worst tendencies.

This album is about depth rather than pretentiousness. One could point at modern bands such as Flaming Lips, Spiritualised or Mercury Rev, and even Radiohead as artists who have taken on elements of Pink Floyd's musical complexity and who echo their lyrical concerns with the place of the individual and spirituality in the modern world. As for the purchasers of those 40 million copies, we will never know how many youths were inspired by it to sit down and try to create great rock music themselves but the law of averages dictates that it's more than a few.

The Dark Side Of The Moon may now have the smack of an album to hide at the back of the record collection but it still deserves respect, and even the occasional listen. - Hugh Barker

68. For Your Pleasure

Roxy Music

TRACKLISTING
Do The Strand/Beauty Queen/Strictly Confidential/Editions Of You/In Every Dream Home A Heartache/The Bogus Man/Grey Lagoons/For Your Pleasure

RELEASED
US: June 1973 UK: March 1973

PRODUCED BY
Chris Thomas, John Anthony, Roxy Music

Roxy Music were one of the few bands to ever successfully solve the dilemma that had plagued rock since the late '60s; how do you make music that is genuinely progressive while remaining truly popular?

In the early 'Seventies, Roxy Music would have been conscious of two things. For all that bands like King Crimson were blazing new trails through uncharted musical territory, their audience was confined to a static though devoted handful of aficionados. At the same time, pop music after an aesthetic peak in the '60s, was becoming repetitive and backward looking.

Formed in 1971 by art school graduate Bryan Ferry (vocals) and bass player Graham Simpson, Roxy Music soon recruited saxophone player Andy McKay, who also owned a VCS3 synthesizer. The VCS3 was notoriously difficult to play: it resembled a telephone exchange and required somebody with technical knowledge to make it work. McKay's friend Brian Eno could operate it and was drafted in as a technical adviser. Before long, he started to appear onstage with the band. Eno, a self confessed non-musician, brought an element of destructiveness and chaos to Roxy Music. Other bands were fairly conservative in their use of the synthesizer, using it either to imitate other instruments or employing the same unadventurous presets. Eno generated noise, 'treated' other instruments such as Phil Manzanera's guitar and McKay's sax, and allowed an element of randomness to enter into the band's performances.

Within a year Roxy Music had been greeted by some fairly hyperbolic press in the UK; they had a hit single with 'Virginia Plain' and their first, self-titled, LP became the must-have album that year. Perhaps because of the hit single, but also because of the simultaneous success of T-Rex and David Bowie, who were lumped alongside them under the catch-all banner glam rock, Roxy Music found that they were attracting a much younger audience than they had initially foreseen, even if their dress was indisputably outlandish.

When they went in to Air Studios in London to record *For Your Pleasure*, there were many in the press and the music industry who were

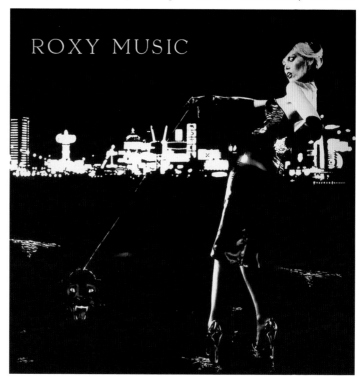

ROXY MUSIC

looking forward to seeing them fall flat on their faces. They disliked the fact that they had seemingly appeared from nowhere without paying their dues. They also disliked the glam aspects of the band. However, the release in 1973 of *For Your Pleasure* proved that Roxy were not going to go away. While the first side of the first album is arguably superior in terms of the actual songs, *For Your Pleasure* is a more consistent album. It's also much darker. The sleeve hints at this: a glamorous blonde woman – Amanda Lear, also the inspiration for Kraftwerk's 'The Model' – in fetishistic evening dress stands at a strange unnatural angle with a panther on a leash while the liveried driver of her Lincoln Continental, Ferry, looks on. It evokes the glitz of '40s Hollywood but also hints at something more disturbing. This was under-scored by persistent rumors – subsequently proven untrue – that Lear had been born a man.

Opening with the witty 'dance craze' update 'Do The Strand', the album alternates between upbeat pop tracks and strange and unsettling songs, the centerpiece being the terrifying 'In Every Dream Home A Heartache'. This is a love song to an inflatable sex doll, its lyric sitting on a trance- inducing minimalist keyboard riff. It ends with an explosion of heavy rock guitars. This song about having sex with an inanimate object is intoned by Ferry, appropriately, in a chanting monotone, the voice of a man who has done everything twice and been bored the first time (although at the end, he comes). In 'The Bogus Man', Roxy experiment with the sort of minimalist drive whose margins krautrock bands like Can and early Kraftwerk were also working within at that time. The closing title track sounds cold and brutally modern, giving the impression it was recorded under harsh neon lights.

It has been said that *For Your Pleasure* was the sound of Ferry and Eno struggling for control of the band. Yet it sounds less of a struggle than a compromise between the faintly nostalgic (the crooning, suave Ferry) and the boldly futuristic (the *avant-garde*-inclined Eno). 'Grey Lagoons' is a perfect example of this: Danny and the Juniors by way of Karlheinz Stockhausen. In any case, with Ferry's reputation as a dictator, it's hard to imagine him attaching his name to something he wasn't broadly happy with.

The images of the band on the inside sleeve were, for teenagers growing up in the '70s, as surprising and as exhilarating as the music. Back then, 'proper' musicians had long straggly hair and beards and wore faded denim shirts. Roxy Music looked like they had stepped out of a gay bar in a Buck Rogers strip. Eno particularly generated a lot of homophobic abuse. In the credits, Roxy Music even listed their hairdresser, Keith at Smile, which was possibly a statement as revolutionary for those times as any they made in their music.

For Your Pleasure was the end of that particular line-up of Roxy Music. Eno left the band shortly after and subsequent albums *Country Life* and *Siren* were massively successful, though never quite as adventurous as *For Your Pleasure*.

Nor were any of the Roxy-derived bands that followed ever really as groundbreaking in their time as Roxy Music were in theirs. For arguably the first time, Roxy Music had proven that a band could bring detachment, sophistication and cold, cold cynicism to dirty old rock 'n' roll. Ultravox, Japan, Simple Minds and even U2 all drew some inspiration from this period of Roxy Music, even if in some cases it was only to copy Brian Eno's eyeshadow techniques. Today bands like Franz Ferdinand carry the torch for Roxy Music's particular brand of British art school eccentricity.

After 35 years, *For Your Pleasure* still sounds like a futuristic album. And in another three-and-a-half decades, it probably still will.
- Tommy Udo

Yo!

Amazing to think that rap now has a history spanning a quarter of a century. Some of the most vitally important, stylistically influential and viscerally affecting **hip hop** tracks.

1.	**Rapper's Delight**	Sugarhill Gang
2.	**Adventures On The Wheels Of Steel**	Grandmaster Flash
3.	**The Message**	Grandmaster Flash & The Furious Five
4.	**Planet Rock**	Afrika Bambaataa
5.	**Radio**	LL Cool J
6.	**South Bronx**	Boogie Down Productions`
7.	**Give The Drummer Some**	Ultramagnetic MCs
8.	**Follow The Leader**	Eric B & Rakim
9.	**Plug Tunin'**	De La Soul
10.	**How I Could Just Kill A Man**	Cypress Hill
11.	**C.R.E.A.M.**	Wu-Tang Clan
12.	**Memory Lane (Sittin' In Da Park)**	Nas
13.	**Things Done Changed**	Notorious BIG
14.	**Dear Mama**	2Pac
15.	**Return Of The Crooklyn Dodgers**	Crooklyn Dodgers
16.	**Ready Or Not**	Fugees
17.	**Rosa Parks**	OutKast
18.	**Stan**	Eminem
19.	**Heart Of The City (Ain't No Love)**	Jay-Z
20.	**Crazy**	Gnarls Barkley

69. New York Dolls
New York Dolls

TRACKLISTING
Personality Crisis/Looking For A Kiss/Vietnamese Baby/Lonely Planet
Boy/Frankenstein/Trash/Bad Girl/Subway Train/Pills/Private World/Jet Boy

RELEASED
US: July 1973 UK: August 1973

PRODUCED BY
Todd Rundgren

Visually they were drag queen nightmares trafficking in the kind of freaky
high camp that even David Bowie or Marc Bolan at their most theatrical
never attempted. With a trashy get-up consisting of disheveled fright wigs,
platform heels and tight spandex pants, and lipsticked and mascaraed to
within an inch of their lives, The New York Dolls easily outflashed and
outtrashed the competition. Yet theirs was no case of style over substance.
The Dolls made just two albums before flaming out due to personal excess
and public indifference. Both albums have admirers but it was their 1973
self-titled debut that would become the definitive proto-punk album, an
exhilarating joyride delivered with a ferocious energy.

Group frontman David Johansen came across as a more
outrageous, camper version of Mick Jagger to guitarist Johnny Thunders'
even junkier Keith Richards while rhythm guitarist Sylvain Sylvain, bassist
Arthur "Killer" Kane and drummer Jerry Nolan were living proof that
technical virtuosity may be a way overrated virtue. With influences that
ranged from the anarchic noise of the MC5 to the early Stones and 1960s
girl group pop, the Dolls played with the kind of reckless abandon you'd
expect from a group running on pure inspiration. Criminally overlooked in
their time, the Dolls' Todd Rundgren-produced debut kicked up a frenzied
high energy punk sound three years before the genre had a name. Listen to
Johansen's wildly animated delivery on the certifiable classics 'Personality
Crisis' and 'Frankenstein', his roaring baritone building to a hyper frantic
climax. Johansen sings for all the world like a man possessed and the music,
surging and raging all around him, thrillingly keeps pace. The album also
encompasses the vulnerable, even tender, ballad 'Lonely Planet Boy', the
cartoonish 'Trash' and a pile-driving version of Bo Diddley's 'Pills'. As
infectious as punk music ever got, the Dolls sing of personality crises,
defiant outsiders ("Is it a crime for you to fall in love with Frankenstein?")
and jet boys flying against a Gotham backdrop. Rundgren got some flack

from critics who felt his more sophisticated pop approach was ill-suited to the Dolls' fiercely primal free-for-all spirit. In reality Rundgren took nothing away from the Dolls, as their debut's distinct lack of polish can attest.

Unfortunately the world wasn't ready for the Dolls in 1973. Their debut climbed no higher than #116 on the US chart. Its aptly titled '74 follow up *Too Much Too Soon* fared even worse, peaking at #167. Mercury Records dropped the group soon after, which led to a disastrous alliance with future Sex Pistols svengali Malcolm McLaren, who in the true spirit of anarchic rabble-rousing had the Dolls dress up in red leather and perform against a Soviet flag which only served to alienate the group from record labels who may have otherwise shown an interest in signing them. McLaren would of course go on to greater success as manager and founder of The Sex Pistols and later admitted, "I was trying to do with The Sex Pistols what I had failed with The New York Dolls." Pistols guitarist Steve Jones admitted he copied Thunders' stage moves to the point where it embarrasses him now to recall it. But then this was understandable. He has described the Dolls' performance on UK TV rock program *The Old Grey Whistle Test* as the most exciting thing he had ever seen in his life, despite compere Bob Harris' notorious snorting put-down of them as "mock rock".

Vogue photographer Toshi photographed the New York Dolls in NYC for the cover of their eponymous album.

The Dolls' do-it-yourself ethos personified on their debut served as a great influence on the '70s punk movement in general. Pretenders leader Chrissie Hynde once stated she knew all the punk bands and claimed they all owned the Dolls' albums. The Clash's Mick Jones credited the Dolls with giving him the inspiration to form a band of his own. In New York, the Dolls' popularity was such that they helped to galvanize the Gotham punk scene that saw the flourishing of strong cult followings for Blondie, Talking Heads and The Ramones. Drummer Tommy Ramone, after seeing the Dolls, vowed to get his own charismatic, quirky band together while

Richard Hell and Tom Verlaine were so impressed by the visceral impact of seeing the Dolls perform live they went on to form New Wave outfit Television.

If the Dolls' influence on US and UK punk was more musical than visual, by the 1980s the reverse was often true, with countless mediocre spandex-clad "hair bands" (i.e., Cinderella, Poison, Motley Crue) in the so-called US glam metal movement adopting the look but not the sound of the Dolls, a clear case of image overshadowing content. And let's not forget the visually outlandish Kiss, who took a less dangerous, more cartoonish approach than the Dolls but were several notches above the hair bands in terms of musical merit. If The New York Dolls were a complete commercial failure in their time, they were at least responsible for a good number of decent bands who might not have existed otherwise. The Smiths' frontman Morrissey, who once authored a book on the Dolls in his pre-Smiths days and orchestrated the brief London reunion of the band in 2004, stated in the 2005 documentary *New York Doll*, "For everybody there's an artist that captures you at just the right time. The Dolls were that for me."
- Tierney Smith

70. Grievous Angel
Gram Parsons

TRACKLISTING
Return Of The Grievous Angel/Hearts On Fire/I Can't Dance/Brass Buttons/$1000 Wedding/Medley: a. Cash On The Barrelhead b. Hickory Wind/Love Hurts/Ooh Las Vegas/In My Hour Of Darkness

RELEASED
US: January 1974 UK: January 1974

PRODUCED BY
Gram Parsons

Gram Parsons' albums never cracked the Top 100. The world wasn't ready yet for the soulful approach to country music that he pioneered in the early 1970s. Since his passing his music has however gone on to exert an enormous influence on country-rock and the roots movement.

The piercing emotional depth that informed Parson's songs came from a very real place. Former Byrds bandmate Chris Hillman once observed that Parsons' tragic family backdrop was a story straight out of Tennessee Williams. Born Cecil Ingram Connor III, Parsons was a child of privilege, his grandfather a multi-millionaire Florida citrus magnate, but Parsons' father committed suicide when Gram was 12 and his mother died of alcohol poisoning the day of his high school graduation. Parsons took refuge in music, music in which he sought from early on to infuse country with a rock 'n' roll attitude. During a brief tenure at Harvard, he founded The International Submarine Band whose sole recording, 1968's *Safe At Home*, is often described as the first country-rock album. If Parsons' work was met with public indifference he had a way of inspiring his fellow musicians with his visionary musical concepts. Invited by Byrds bassist Chris Hillman to join the band following the departure of David Crosby, Parsons steered The Byrds in a radical new direction during his three month tenure, resulting in The Byrds' country-rock sojourn, 1968's *Sweetheart Of The Rodeo*. Parsons went on to perfect his so-called Cosmic American Music (he detested the term country-rock) with The Flying Burrito Brothers, whose two landmark studio albums – 1969's *The Gilded Palace Of Sin* and 1970's *Burrito Deluxe* – sold poorly but whose influence on the country-rock movement would loom large.

The boyishly handsome Parsons, clad in a flashy Nudie suit and Rolling Stones-inspired silk scarves (he was a friend of Keith Richards), had the look, sound and attitude down pat, but his more renegade approach didn't sit too well with the country establishment. That wasn't to change once he embarked on a solo career. His ex-Byrds and Burritos colleague Chris Hillman persuaded him to check out a performance of a young unknown singer named Emmylou Harris at a small club in Washington, D.C. Impressed, Parsons asked her to join him in LA where she became his harmony/duet partner on his two solo albums, 1973's *GP* and its posthumously released follow-up *Grievous Angel*. Merle Haggard turned down the offer to produce *GP*, put off by Parsons' more maverick approach to the form, yet listening to Parsons' work in retrospect these songs sound downright traditional by today's country standards. On *Grievous Angel*, like its predecessor, Parsons was joined by three of Elvis Presley's sidemen: guitarist James Burton, pianist Glen D. Hardin and drummer Ronnie Tutt. The album was recorded just a few weeks before Parsons' death at age 26 in 1973 from a lethal mix of morphine and tequila. (Discipline, as Hillman once noted, wasn't one of Parsons' strong points).

Technically Parsons wasn't the greatest singer, but his vocal limitations lent his songs a certain cracked vulnerability. Both as a composer and interpretive singer few could match Parsons' aching sincerity on *Grievous Angel*. Parsons gives himself wholeheartedly to the material – he doesn't just sing these songs, he inhabits them. Listen to his take on the Tom Guidera/Walter Egan number 'Hearts On Fire'. The song's theme (getting dumped by a cheating girlfriend) is common enough, but there's nothing ordinary about the emotionally devastating way Parsons connects with the lyrics. *Grievous Angel* has its moments of levity - Tom T. Hall's 'I Can't Dance' and Parsons' own 'Ooh Las Vegas', but the heart of the album is the penetrating emotional depth of its ballads: the desolate '$1,000 Wedding' and the poignant 'Brass Buttons', Parsons' wistful meditation on the loss of his mother sung with heartbreaking fragility. *Grievous Angel* ends on a spiritual note with the prayerful 'In My Hour Of Darkness' (with Linda Ronstadt joining on chorus), which sounds like a religious standard but was actually written by Parsons and Harris.

Though ex-Burrito Brother and Eagle Bernie Leadon have noted that Parsons wasn't the only artist attempting to fuse rock and country, pointing to the work of The Lovin' Spoonful and Dillard And Clark, it was Parsons' pioneering efforts and the indelible impression he left with his too early passing that helped to fuel his legacy and galvanize his followers into taking his ideas to new commercial heights.

The number of artists Parsons inspired makes for a long and diverse list. Rolling Stone Keith Richards credits Parsons with influencing the country-rock excursions that thread through the Stones' *oeuvre* on *Sticky Fingers*, *Exile On Main Street* (at whose sessions Parsons was present) and beyond. You can hear Parsons' influence in the country leanings of rock artists like Elvis Costello, Tom Petty, Linda Ronstadt, The Eagles and Nick Lowe, in the work of country artists like Rodney Crowell and Dwight Yoakam, the alt-country crowd that includes The Jayhawks, Steve Earle, Wilco, Whiskeytown, The Mekons, Uncle Tupelo, Lucinda Williams on up to the still vibrant rootsy rock known as the No Depression movement. Emmylou Harris has made it her mission to champion Parsons' cause throughout the course of her long and storied career.

"And the music he had in him, so very few possess." Gram Parsons, 1946–1973.

The macabre adventure that followed Parsons' death only added to the myth surrounding him. His road manager, in an effort to abide by Parsons' wishes to be cremated in California's Joshua Tree desert, hijacked his body at LAX (where it was awaiting family burial in Louisiana) and set it ablaze. But it was Parsons' music, so brilliantly encapsulated on *Grievous Angel*, that left such an indelible impression on a legion of artists who, inspired by the honesty, heart and vulnerability of Parsons' brave pioneering spirit have kept his sound alive, carrying the torch he lit into a new millennium. - Tierney Smith

Any More For Any More?

You were wondering if we struggled to find 100 albums to fill this book? *Au contraire.* Some **top tracks** from influential albums that we had to **leave out**.

1. **Son Of A Preacher Man** — Dusty Springfield (from *Dusty In Memphis*)

2. **I Can See For Miles** — The Who (from *The Who Sell Out*)

3. **Broken Arrow** — Buffalo Springfield (from *Buffalo Springfield Again*)

4. **The Night They Drove Old Dixie Down** — The Band (from *The Band*)

5. **Little Wing** — The Jimi Hendrix Experience (from *Axis: Bold As Love*)

6. **Sympathy For The Devil** — The Rolling Stones (from *Beggars Banquet*)

7. **Everybody's Talkin'** — Fred Neil (from *Fred Neil*)

8. **Sweet Jane** — The Velvet Underground (from *Loaded*)

9. **Moondance** — Van Morrison (from *Moondance*)

10. **Won't Get Fooled Again** — The Who (from *Who's Next*)

11. **Fog On The Tyne** — Lindisfarne (from *Fog On The Tyne*)

12. **Layla** — Derek And The Dominos (from *Layla And Other Assorted Love Songs*)

13. **Sweet Gene Vincent** — Ian Dury And The Blockheads (from *New Boots And Panties!!!*)

14. **Long Hot Summer** — Tom Robinson Band (from *Power In The Darkness*)

15. **Heart Of Glass** — Blondie (from *Parallel Lines*)

16. **Wuthering Heights** — Kate Bush (from *The Kick Inside*)

17. **Billy Hunt** — The Jam (from *All Mod Cons*)

18. **It's Different For Girls** — Joe Jackson (from *I'm The Man*)

19. **Night Boat To Cairo** — Madness (from *One Step Beyond*)

20. **Sweet Child O' Mine** — Guns N' Roses (from *Appetite For Destruction*)

71. Radio City

Big Star

TRACKLISTING

O My Soul/Life Is White/Way Out West/What's Going Ahn/You Get What You Deserve/Mod Lang/Back Of A Car/Daisy Glaze/She's a Mover/September Gurls/Morpha Too/I'm in Love With a Girl

RELEASED

US: February 1974 UK: Not issued

PRODUCED BY

John Fry

By the early 'Seventies, "pop" was if not quite a dirty word amongst music fans then at least something approaching a pejorative.

White popular music was generally divided into Rock – serious if gritty, with emphasis on instrumental virtuosity – and Pop – songs, often of greater levity, based around three-minute structures and catchy choruses, with instrumental breaks kept to a minimum. Though many rock fans could of course enjoy the pop records they might hear on the radio, pop artists were considered to be inherently lightweight. This perception was partly due to the fact that most established rock bands had started out as pop groups. The fact that The Who were now making music like 'Won't Get Fooled Again' instead of, say, 'So Sad About Us' was seen as a development. The climate of the times dictated that it be so, for it was only slightly longer than a teenager's lifetime ago that rock 'n' roll – to use the original umbrella genre classification for all this – was looked down on as noisy trash by just about everybody except those who bought it. The respectability rock had acquired through the work of The Beatles, rock operas and progressive bands had been a long struggle and was not to be given up by treating pretty, melodic, concise tracks like 'So Sad About Us' as being as worthy as statement-making epics like 'Won't Get Fooled Again'.

Then a drawback to this policy began to dawn on people. The fact that musicians were now being taken seriously gave them psychological permission to produce work that was musical masturbation. As the 'Seventies wore on, the landscape of rock was increasingly blighted by guitar extemporization, drum solos and risible 'profound' lyrics. Yes, artists were given reason to believe that the people wanted to hear their bombast by the millions of units their product shifted but, again, it is not much of an exaggeration to say such sales were merely a product of the times. After all, how many of those multiple-million Emerson, Lake and

Palmer records sold in the 1970s are still listened to for pleasure? And while *Who's Next* is a stunning Who album, other work by that band in the 'Seventies like *Who By Numbers* had an intellectual gravitas but quite simply weren't any fun to listen to.

The music world was only really able to cut its losses and acknowledge the *cul-de-sac* progressivism had led rock down with the advent of punk in the late 'Seventies. Big Star, however, were quicker off the mark than that. Between 1972 and 1974 they released a pair of albums that achieved the feat that far more experienced and talented bands had seemed to conclude was impossible: the employment of three-minute, ultra melodic pop structures without the sacrificing of intelligent lyrical content or rock earthiness. It was the dawn of power pop.

Big Star's story is an unhappy one: poor distribution put paid to the hits everybody was expecting their radio-friendly music to generate. Yet their influence filtered down through subsequent generations of musicians and created an awareness that good tunes and brevity did not preclude street cred. The entire indie-pop scene is based on those principles, though frankly the formulaic wall-of-sound blurred

guitar trademark of that genre is a stark contrast to the judiciously judged instrumentation of Big Star. Meanwhile, many detect Big Star's influence on REM, Jeff Buckley, The Replacements and even Tom Petty.

Big Star hailed from Memphis and were part of a sort of family based around Ardent Records, helmed by John Fry. Fry also owned Ardent Recording Studios, where the band recorded their music. The creative nucleus was guitarists-vocalists Chris Bell and Alex Chilton. The rhythm section of Andy Hummel (bass) and Jody Stephens (drums) brought up the rear. They released a fine debut album in '72 titled *#1 Record* featuring a range of styles from pop ('The Ballad Of El Goodo'), down-and-dirty rock ('When My Baby's Beside Me'), ballads ('Thirteen' and 'Watch The Sunrise') and exotica (Hummel's 'The India Song'), all wrapped up in those tidy, concise, chart-oriented packages. However the airplay and word-of-mouth generated by the group was maddeningly prevented from translation to sales because distributor Stax failed to meet the demand by getting discs into stores.

A bitterly disappointed Bell departed and the band thereafter drifted apart despite having started a second album. Chilton continued to record at Ardent with a new band. It's significant that what got Big Star (minus Bell) back together was the rapturous reception they received from the audience at a rock writer's convention: Big Star always were the critics' darlings. The two gigs in question took place at Lafayette's Music Rooms in Memphis, arranged by Ardent's John King. Hummel later said, "That just went so well that it just seemed like a natural thing to go ahead and finish up this second record."

'What's Going Ahn', 'Mod Lang' and 'She's A Mover' actually originated at the recording sessions of Chilton's new band, but as that group had included Hummel anyway, it hardly mattered. 'Back Of A Car' is reputed, like a couple of other tracks, to have some lingering Bell influence due to a pact come to by he and Chilton to divvy up their collaborations. Essentially, however, *Radio City* marked the point at which Big Star became a Chilton vehicle, even if it's difficult to spot the difference in quality and influence of it and its predecessor.

Radio City boasts the pleasantly lugubrious 'Way Out West' and the classy soft rock tracks 'What's Going Ahn' and 'Get What You Deserve'. The album is most famous however for 'September Gurls' (sic), a glorious, chiming slab of power pop that sounded like a number one single but which once again stalled because of distribution problems. The Bangles later covered it on *Different Light*, their 1986 US chart-topping album. Chilton reputedly made no money from this, however: he is said to have previously signed away his publishing for a lump sum. If true, it is something that is symptomatic of the tragedy of the Big Star story. - Sean Egan

72. Natty Dread
Bob Marley & The Wailers

TRACKLISTING
Lively Up Yourself/No Woman, No Cry/Them Belly Full (But We Hungry)/Rebel Music(3 O'Clock Roadblock)/So Jah Seh/Natty Dread/Bend Down Low/Talkin' Blues/Revolution

RELEASED
US: 1975 UK: October 1974

PRODUCED BY
Chris Blackwell, The Wailers

Author Christopher John Farley in his 2006 book *Before The Legend: The*

Rise Of Bob Marley calls Marley "a smiling revolutionary," a uniter, not a divider. It's not so surprising then that Marley was the first reggae artist to achieve international stardom or that his influence both culturally and musically would prove to be so far-reaching.

Marley was just 16 when he auditioned for a 14-year-old talent scout named Jimmy Cliff (who would play a big role himself in the internationalization of reggae with the 1972 film soundtrack to *The Harder They Come*). Cliff introduced Marley to local music entrepreneur Leslie Kong where he recorded a few songs under the name Bobby Martell in 1962 before deciding he'd prefer the support of a group, forming The Wailers with a couple of pals from the Kingston ghetto of Trenchtown, Bunny Wailer and Peter Tosh. They recorded throughout the '60s for a variety of Jamaican labels, their rude boy ska style connecting with disenfranchised outsiders. By 1967 Marley's Rastafarian beliefs were shaping his lyrics, resulting in a growing emphasis on spiritual and social issues. Marley signed with Island Records in 1972 under the aegis of London-based Chris Blackwell, a label that would launch Marley to international success.

Soon other artists were scoring international hits with Marley's songs. Johnny Nash had a 1972 chart entry with 'Stir It Up' and Eric Clapton hit #1 on the US chart with his 1974 version of 'I Shot The Sheriff'. Following the release of *Burnin'*, Wailers Tosh and Livingston left the group to pursue solo careers, making 1974's *Natty Dread* the first album to feature Marley solidly upfront and center. More musically adventurous than its predecessor, it was the first Marley album to make a dent in the American charts (#92) and featured the debut of the I-Threes female vocal trio (wife Rita Marley, Marcia Griffiths and Judy Mowatt). With a band including The Wailers' rhythm section of Aston and Carlton Barrett on bass and drums respectively and American guitarist Al Anderson, *Natty Dread* would prove to be Marley's breakthrough album, spawning his first crossover success with the UK #22 hit 'No Woman, No Cry'.

Placing it in the context of the times, *Natty Dread* sounded truly revolutionary. It was the most overtly political album Marley had made up to that point, released as the frivolity of the disco era was dawning. Relying on a guitar-leaning rock sound, *Natty Dread* features Anderson's rock and jazz style phrasing, Aston Barrett's funky bass riffs and the spine-tingling harmonies of the I-Threes. (Song credits, however, may be suspect - Marley was given to crediting friends and family regardless of whether they actually contributed.)

Natty Dread opens with the rousing 'Lively Up Yourself', a remake of The Wailers' '71 Jamaican hit, then quickly gets more serious with Marley raising a defiant voice against all manner of social injustice. In 'Them Belly Full (But We Hungry)' he warns "a hungry mob is a angry mob".

'Revolution' calls for unified struggle as the only means of effecting political change while simultaneously affirming Rastafarian ideals: "Let righteousness cover the earth like the water cover the sea, yeah!" There's also a – in retrospect – weirdly speeded up 'No Woman, No Cry' that pales next to the vastly superior, stately version that would appear the following year on *Live!* A nostalgic look back at Marley's impoverished life in Trenchtown, the song has proven to be among his most popular, covered by everyone from Jimmy Buffett to Pearl Jam.

After many US college students discovered reggae with *The Harder They Come,* it was Marley who helped carry the influence further afield. By the time the UK punk scene had exploded in 1977, Marley had taken up residence in London. Though he was at first put off by what he viewed as the more Babylonian aspects of the scene, he came to appreciate socially conscious bands like The Clash who tackled issues of class-based oppression in their own country. Marley, who exuded rock star charisma himself, was a natural magnet for rockers who saw in him a shared rebel spirit. From their early single 'Complete Control' to their sprawling rock-reggae fusion *Sandinista!*, The Clash were but one of the numerous UK punk bands influenced by reggae rhythms. Also displaying the influence was the ska movement epitomized by The (English) Beat, Madness and The Specials and the pop reggae of The Police. Later, the militant political stance of Rage Against The Machine would show a clear debt to Marley's and reggae's example.

Just as the Jamaican community in the UK heavily influenced the punk movement, so too did the Jamaican immigrants in New York and its deejay culture provide the inspiration for hip hop. Wyclef Jean, ex-member of hip hop trio The Fugees, whose own music has been heavily influenced by Marley has stated, "There's not a hip hop artist that didn't snatch a piece of Marley." (Run-D.M.C.'s 1985 'Roots, Rap, Reggae', whose title is a paraphrasing of Marley's 'Roots, Rock, Reggae', blatantly acknowledges his influence.) Unfortunately Marley's dream of connecting with American black audiences didn't materialize and hip hop's appropriating of the rebellious street culture degenerated into something far removed from Marley's 'one world' life affirming stance. The positive aspects of Marley's art are something U2 frontman and social activist Bono understands well, calling Marley his greatest influence, the artist who inspired him to create socially aware music.

Bob Marley.

Wyclef Jean admits to consciously patterning his songs on the way Marley drew the listener in with a great groove while delivering a message in a more subtle fashion. Because Marley viewed his own music as a means of fighting oppression and defending righteousness, he spoke a universal language – in addressing inequality he was a voice of moral authority, a voice that, beyond the iconic figure Marley became in the years since his 1981 death of a brain tumor, has only grown in power and stature, resonating with and inspiring new generations of listeners. - Tierney Smith

73. Autohahn

Kraftwerk

TRACKLISTING
Autobahn/Komtenmelodie1/Komtenmelodie2/Mitternacht/
Morgenspaziergang

RELEASED
US: November 1974 UK: November 1974

PRODUCED BY
Conny Plank

In 1975, Kraftwerk (German for "Power plant") scored a most unlikely transatlantic hit with a shortened version of this album's title track. The success was a tribute to the extraordinary synthesis of gleaming modernism and pop smarts practiced by this Teutonic ensemble and – in retrospect – a remarkable glance into the future to a time when (largely thanks to them) the charts would be full of such catchy but non-organic concoctions. The age of the synth was nigh, and Kraftwerk were the standard-bearers.

This was the first great album of Kraftwerk's classic period, and the first point at which they discovered the sounds and techniques for which they are renowned. Their first three albums (and the earlier work of founder members Ralf Hutter and Florian Schneider) were essentially progressive rock (they were generally regarded as part of the Krautrock movement) but they were becoming increasingly obsessed by ambient music and with the early generation of synthesizers. On *Autobahn*, they were still using some real instruments, notably Schneider's flute, but for the first time their music became centered completely around the use of machinery. New members Wolfgang Flur and Klaus Roeder completed the line-up for this album, much of which was recorded at the band's Düsseldorf studio.

The bands fascination with using the noises of everyday life in their music and their obsession with the mechanical processes underlying synthesized music led naturally to the idea behind the title track of *Autobahn,* for which the concept was to capture in sound the sensations of a motorway journey. As so often in Kraftwerk's output, an interest in modern technology was combined with a humanistic, nostalgic look back at more old-fashioned methods. The resulting track was one of the warmest, most charming of Kraftwerk's epic pieces. 22 minutes long and originally

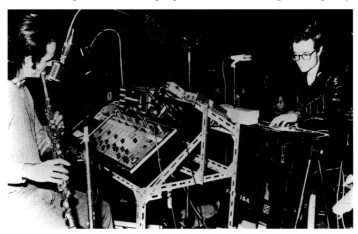

Florian Schneider
(playing the flute)
and Ralf Hutter,
performing in 1972.

taking up the whole of the first side of vinyl, it's built around the synthesized pulses that would become Kraftwerk's trademark. But much of the fascination of the track lies in the passing noise effects – the synthesized passing cars and sounds of the countryside. Despite the modern setting, this somehow gives the effect of a sunny journey in a far less crowded, more innocent age.

The repeated refrain of 'Fahren, fahren, fahren', which clearly derives from the Beach Boys' 'Fun, Fun, Fun', gives the track an unexpected link into pop history. Many songs of the 'Fifties and 'Sixties – including some by the Beach Boys – had been hymns to the motor car and had celebrated the freedom of the open road. Now Kraftwerk reprised this idea, but in a far less individualistic way – the machinery and the road are the stars of this song rather than the driver or singer. Kraftwerk's removal of the individual ego from the center of their songs was one of their most radical moves. They would take this to greater extremes in later work by blurring the boundaries between the performers and their instruments, and between man and robot. But in 'Autobahn', there is still a tangible human warmth in spite of the dislocated style and the deliberately dehumanized vocal performance. And the song also displays Kraftwerk's dry (and there-fore easily missed) sense of humor at its sharpest.

The second side of the record has moments of beauty that come close to the heights of the title track. The two 'Komtenmelodie''s follow a common Kraftwerk path of looping and reprising a basic hook through endlessly modulating variations, the first moody and intense, the second faster and consequently more catchy and cheery. 'Mitternacht' uses sound effects that are reminiscent of a scary movie soundtrack, while 'Morgenspaziergang' creates the pleasant ambience of a morning walk by combining artificial birdsong and a synthesized bubbling stream with the flute melody.

Subsequent albums including *Radioactivity* and *Trans-Europe Express* were equally inspired and influential but, as Kraftwerk's breakthrough moment, *Autobahn* has a special place in pop history. There aren't many bands who actually sound like Kraftwerk, and few who have been ego-less enough to follow their penchant for compositions that exclude autobiography and emotion. They have nonetheless had a broad influence in so many areas that it is hard to know where to start. David Bowie was an obvious early convert with his Berlin albums, adopting the spacious, instrumental approach for *Low* and much of *"Heroes"* ('V2 Schneider' was probably named for Florian). It's also difficult to imagine later synthesizer-based bands such as Depeche Mode, The Human League, and OMD sounding the way they did if it weren't for Kraftwerk. Meanwhile, late-'Seventies UK number ones 'Are "Friends" Electric?' and 'Cars' were simply Gary Numan's take on Bowie's take on Kraftwerk - the very quintessence of the domino effect of influential work that is the *raison d'etre* of this book.

Their influence wasn't only felt in the obvious electro-pop derivatives. The early proponents of hip hop and house were fascinated by Kraftwerk's technological obsessions and beats. Grandmaster Flash used Kraftwerk extensively in his early DJ-ing, as did Afrika Bambaataa, whose 'Planet Rock' was based on a loop from 'Trans-Europe Express'. The Detroit techno producers were also fascinated by the Düsseldorfers and made extensive use of various samples from their work. When bands such as Blondie and New Order started to merge elements of dance music into their rock, there were clear echoes of the pulsing beats of Kraftwerk in key tracks such as 'Heart of Glass' and 'Blue Monday'. And as dance music developed and mutated through the 'Eighties and 'Nineties, it was underpinned by techniques and song forms that had first been developed by Kraftwerk, from the ambient music of The Orb to the more elaborate structures of the Chemical Brothers. The recent Kylie Minogue hit 'Can't Get You Out My Head' could almost have been recorded as a tribute to Kraftwerk, so clear is the derivation, and many other modern songs show similar weighty roots beneath their brittle shells of modern pop glitz.

One can sit all day tracing the influence of a great record by listing tracks and artists that owe a debt to their predecessor, but the final mark of a classic album is how it stands up to the test of time. If you put *Autobahn* on today more than 30 years after it was recorded (ideally on a long car journey through a scenic landscape, but anywhere will do), it still comes across as fresh, eyebrow-raising, sleek and the sound of tomorrow - more so than the subsequent work of many of the numerous artists that were inspired by Kraftwerk and who utilize far more advanced technology. - Hugh Barker

74. Blood On The Tracks
Bob Dylan

TRACKLISTING
Tangled Up In Blue/Simple Twist Of Fate/You're A Big Girl Now/Idiot Wind/You're Gonna Make Me Lonesome When You Go/Meet Me In The Morning/Lily, Rosemary And The Jack Of Hearts/If You See Her, Say Hello/Shelter From The Storm/Buckets Of Rain

RELEASED
US: January 1975 UK: February 1975

PRODUCED BY
Bob Dylan

In his best-selling 2004 memoir *Chronicles*, Bob Dylan claims that one of his albums was inspired by a book of Anton Chekhov short stories. Dylan doesn't say what album he is referring to but that Dylan would cite Chekhov makes sense in a way. In Chekhov, considered the father of the short story, Dylan found another writer who focused on the emotional epiphany over story arc or point of view. Dylan may have learned much from Woody Guthrie about song structure, but it was to Chekhov's work that Dylan looked on this album, like Chekhov ignoring traditional structure and seeking to display internal change within his protagonists.

Blood on the Tracks is not only the most Chekhovian of Dylan's many records, it is also his most personal. Though Bob expressed surprise that any critic would consider the album autobiographical, charting Dylan's personal life against these songs shows obvious parallels. Dylan had just recently separated from his wife when he wrote these alternately angry, bittersweet, and melancholy ballads. Once asked about the popularity of *Blood on the Tracks*, Dylan replied: "It's hard for me to relate to that. People enjoying the type of pain." That he would describe the album as involving "pain" probably is as close as we'll ever get to an admission from Dylan that these songs werre autobiographical.

The pain is certainly obvious on 'Idiot Wind', which not only ranks as one of Dylan's best songs, but also one of his most honest. This is Dylan full of bitterness and rage, but his injury has given him new purpose, as if it has roused him from a slumber. He is not just angry, he is murderous, and there is the lingering sense that he can no longer control himself. The separation between songwriter and subject fades on this unnerved song, as it does on much of this album. It is this very transparency that makes this a revelatory album: artifice is forgotten, and the end result is emotional truth.

The original sleeve design for *Blood On The Tracks*.

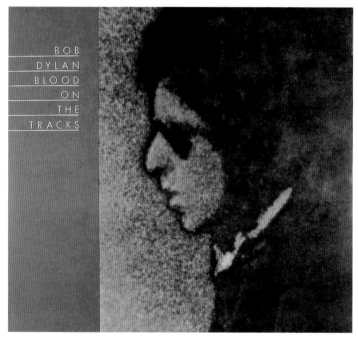

BOB
DYLAN
BLOOD
ON
THE
TRACKS

The rest of the album is equally intimate. While 'Tangled Up In Blue' and 'Shelter From The Storm' still manage a romantic heart and a longing tone, the female characters on this album are not to be trusted. On 'If You See Her, Say Hello', the singer attempts to mask his brokenness, but in the end reveals the depths of his injury: "Our separation, it pierced me to the heart." Not only does this album contain some of Dylan's best lyric writing, it is also his most sentimental. He wails on 'Shelter From the Storm' about "...old men with broken teeth stranded without love." This is an album that will forever be quoted on mash notes between lovers young and old. In a 1985 interview, Dylan said that 'Tangled Up in Blue' was his attempt to "tell a story and be a present character in it without it being some kind of fake, sappy attempted tearjerker....I wanted to defy time, so that the story took place in the present and the past at the same time."

Blood On The Tracks did not have an easy birth. In September 1974, not long after finishing his last tour with the Band, Dylan entered a New York City studio with a slew of songs, set to make an album with Phil Ramone, who was to engineer while Dylan self-produced. Dylan had a fire to him that seemed to make the sessions go even quicker than usual for this man renowned for not dilly-dallying in the studio. In just one week, he cut a number of songs and nine were selected for the final album. But on the eve of the album's release, Dylan rethought the recordings and decided he wanted another go at some of them. He retreated to Minneapolis in his native Minnesota and recut half the album with a group of uncredited area session musicians. The new takes were not that different from the original ones - both predominately acoustic sets seemed lovely - and much debate has ensued over the years about which recordings were superior. (The original, discarded cuts were widely heard because review copies cotaining them had already been sent out.)

The album was his biggest hit in years, and topped the *Billboard* charts in the U.S., while making it to Number 4 in the U.K. The album remains one of the best selling discs in Dylan's considerable catalog.

The critical weight on *Blood on the Tracks* has shifted over the years. While the initial reviews were generally positive, there were some doubters who did not recognize the album for the apogee that it was. Jon Landau wrote in *Rolling Stone* that "*Blood On The Tracks* will only sound like a great album for a while. Like most of Dylan, it is impermanent." Landau has been proven wrong on that point, as the album still tops many critic's polls, inspires countless term papers, and has influenced most every singer/songwriter to pick up a pen since. Critic Bill Wyman calls *Blood On The Tracks* Dylan's "only flawless album", praise that has been echoed by many other critics and by many musicians.

Blood On The Tracks gave Dylan new commercial life, but it played a more important role in his artistic revival. Like a match in which a former heavyweight boxer reclaims the title, the album reinvigorated Dylan's artistry and sense of language. Where most of Dylan's earlier work reflected the typical adolescent themes of rock, *Blood On The Tracks* was a mature record by a grizzled survivor. It was rock's first significant Divorce Album, a record that proved that popular music did not have to be about adolescent posturing but could encompass forgiveness and admission of failings. It thereby moved rock further on from its original image of enjoyable trash. The record served as inspiration for legions of other songwriters to tackle such dark terrain. - Charles R. Cross

21st Century Boys and Girls

An eclectic (and utterly subjective) choice of some classic **post-millennium singles**, showing that popular music is still brimming with energy, more than half a century after Elvis.

1.	Can't Get You Out Of My Head	Kylie Minogue
2.	New York City Cops	The Strokes
3.	Hey Ya!	Outkast
4.	Do You Realize??	The Flaming Lips
5.	Dead Leaves And The Dirty Ground	The White Stripes
6.	Nite and Fog	Mercury Rev
7.	Where Is The Love?	Black Eyed Peas
8.	There There	Radiohead
9.	Sound Of The Underground	Girls Aloud
10.	Cant Stand Me Now	The Libertines
11.	The Scientist	Coldplay
12.	I Hate You So Much Right Now	Kelis
13.	Take Me Out	Franz Ferdinand
14.	Dry Your Eyes	The Streets
15.	Push The Button	Sugababes
16.	American Idiot	Green Day
17.	Dirty Harry	Gorillaz
18.	I Bet You Look Good On The Dancefloor	The Arctic Monkeys
19.	Hoppípolla	Sigur Ros
20.	Crazy In Love	Beyoncé

75. Born To Run
Bruce Spingsteen

TRACKLISTING
Thunder Road/Tenth Avenue Freeze-Out/Night/Backstreets/Born To
Run/She's The One/Meeting Across The River/Jungleland

RELEASED
US: August 1975 UK October 1975

PRODUCED BY
Mike Appel, Jon Landau, Bruce Springsteen

As he entered the studio to make his third LP, New Jersey singer/songwriter
Bruce Springsteen was running out of time. Signed to Columbia by the
legendary talent scout John Hammond, who had a hand in the early careers
of Billie Holiday, Aretha Franklin and Bob Dylan, Springsteen had been
both blessed and cursed by the praise his astonishing live shows had begun
to attract. In one of the most famous concert reviews ever printed, *Rolling
Stone* critic Jon Landau exclaimed in 1974: "I have seen the future of rock
'n' roll: and its name is Bruce Springsteen."

The reviewer became manager and Springsteen, ignoring the
commercial failure of his first two LPs, began to talk up his next record as
being the greatest piece of rock 'n' roll yet devised. Quite how close he came
to blowing it is by now the stuff of legend. *Born To Run* took the better part
of two years to make, shredded the nerves of all those involved, saw off
two pivotal members of Bruce's band, and at one point was almost junked
by its creator in favor of live recordings. But the record, improbably, but
thrillingly, lived up to – and perhaps even surpassed – all the expectations
the cheerleading had encouraged.

Born To Run's eight tracks mix a screenwriterly economy of
detail with an emotional range the epic instrumentation and Spector-ish
production perfectly enhance. 'Thunder Road' opens with piano and
harmonica before adding instrumental layer upon melodic and harmonic
texture; it tantalizes, and does so knowingly – so when Bruce offers us the
chance to "waste your summers praying in vain for a savior to rise from
these streets", you know that *he* knows he's already here. 'Tenth Avenue
Freeze-Out' – the closest he gets to reprising the wordy funk-rock of the
preceding album *The Wild, The Innocent And The E-Street Shuffle* – locks into
a romantically homogenized vision of American music, its Muscle Shoals
horns framing a lyric of Dylan-like inscrutability. The low-life vignette
'Meeting Across The River' could have been a scene from *The Sopranos*, the

Jersey-set TV gangster series E-Street guitarist Steven Van Zandt would later star in; 'Backstreets' and 'Jungleland' are widescreen depictions of doomed love and casual violence, scenarios played out in the margins beside a city (New York) that seemed like the center of the world, but which remained

BRUCE
SPRINGSTEEN

BORN TO RUN

Bruce Springsteen, photographed by Eric Meola for the cover of *Born To Run*.

to the sort of New Jersey characters that people Springsteen's songs as distant, impenetrable and elusive as Shangri-La. The title track, meanwhile, was instantly iconic, with its reverberating guitar riff and "We got to get out while we're young" denunciation of the small town, working class background of its protagonists.

A massive and immediate hit, the record's legacy was complex, the combined weight of its artistic and commercial success having an almost immediate impact but with some effects not being felt for years. Meat Loaf's album *Bat Out Of Hell*, a huge seller which dominated LP charts in the US and around the world for years after its 1976 release, could not have existed without *Born To Run*'s stylistic template: not only did the hitherto unknown singer and his cohorts, writer Jim Steinman and producer Todd Rundgren, draw inspiration from Springsteen's lengthy, episodic, cinematic songs, *Bat...*'s tales of lovestruck teens heading out into tomorrow armed only with a car and a full tank are a direct result of *Born To Run*'s thematic thrust. It also re-injected blue collar values and perspectives in rock at a time when the older major stars were more concerned with drugs and tax-exiledom. Other artists have referenced the record when wanting to imbue their songs with elements of quintessentially American sincerity – compare and contrast 'Tenth Avenue Freeze-Out' and 'Angel Of Harlem', a pivotal track from U2's oft-derided *Rattle & Hum* album and movie, a road-trip project in which the Irish rock band immersed themselves in musical Americana. More surprising is its impact on less obvious followers: Badly Drawn Boy's Damon Gough, turned on to Springsteen by a BBC documentary broadcast in 1984, began collecting live Bruce bootlegs, and his patient study of how 'Thunder Road' morphed and changed over the years had a major impact on the way he wrote the songs for his Mercury Prize-winning debut album, *The Hour Of Bewilderbeast*.

But perhaps the LP's biggest effect was on Springsteen himself. The first of two commercial career peaks, *Born To Run* became both calling card and lead weight to its maker. At last he had lived up to the extravagant hype Landau's early laudation had set in train; but when he appeared simultaneously on the covers of both *Time* and *Newsweek*, the publicity machine began to work against itself. The lengthy wait for a follow-up – it would be 1978 before *Darkness On the Edge Of Town* finally emerged, by which time punk had shaken up the rock realm and other pretenders had begun eyeing Bruce's man-of-the-people throne – didn't help. Yet at times he came close to mining from the same rich seam: *Darkness...* contains the spine-chilling 'Racing In The Street', a song populated by the same kids who'd queued up to drive out of 'Born To Run''s "town full of losers", but who find that the victories they aspired to were little more than mirages; the title track of *The River* finds those young lovers after they've hurtled into an adulthood they were ill-prepared for; and the whole of the 1982 acoustic album *Nebraska* seems haunted by those same ghosts, still moving painfully along. He would not taste *Born To Run*'s commercial highs again until 1984, when *Born In The USA* – even the title nodding to a decade-old master-piece – mixed searing indictments of an America busy turning itself from the land of the free to the land of the monied with, as one British singer-songwriter might have scathingly put it, more songs about cars and girls. *Born To Run* made Springsteen's name, but it also set his *modus operandi* in cement. Certainly the record and its success provided him with some fabulous opportunities, and he never seems to have chafed at the bounds it placed on him: but those constraints remain in place. - Angus Batey

76. Horses

Patti Smith

TRACKLISTING

Gloria/Redondo Beach/Birdland/Free Money/Kimberly/Break It Up/
Land/Elegie

RELEASED

November 1975 (UK) November 1975 (US)

PRODUCED BY

John Cale

"Jesus died for somebody's sins, but not mine."

It's one of the most famous, and most-quoted, lines ever sung to open a rock album. 'Gloria', the inaugural track on Patti Smith's debut LP *Horses*, encapsulates much of what she was doing to break ground in mid-'70s rock. It blends poetry, religious irreverence, an appetite for shock, and a reverence for the best of '60s rock - which didn't keep her from turning Van Morrison's 'Gloria' upside down. In time the album came to be seen as a bellwether for the punk/new wave movement, particularly in Smith's native US.

Smith was already a respected poet in the counterculture before she began to shift her focus to musical performance. A zealously devoted rock fan, she found a kindred spirit in guitarist Lenny Kaye, who like Smith was at that time more known as a writer than a musician (see the *Nuggets* entry). At first, their collaborations were more poetry with guitar accompaniment than they were songs with poetic lyrics. The music kept developing, however, and while the poems were turning into songs, the duo became a full-blown rock quintet. They were still fairly rough-edged, however, by the time they recorded *Horses* in 1975.

While *Horses* is sometimes seen as a launching pad for a form of music that broke ties with a stuffier past, in fact it was in some respects very rooted in classic '60s rock. As innovative as Smith's marriage of poetry and rock was, some of that territory had already been laid out by Jim Morrison in The Doors, particularly in pieces that (like some of Smith's) mixed music with dramatically intoned, improvised-sounding confrontational prose. 'Gloria' itself (which, as changed by Smith, also quotes from the mid-'60s soul hit 'Land of 1000 Dances') was a classic mid-'60s British Invasion hit for Them, though the Shadows of Knights' cover was the Top Ten single in the US. Whether coincidentally or not, The Doors had also performed and improvised upon 'Gloria' onstage while inserting newly devised spoken passages, though their version did not come out until the 1980s. In addition, even after *Horses'* release, Smith often covered '60s rock classics by the likes of The Kingsmen, The Who, the Stones and the Velvet Underground.

Smith, however, was not a mere derivative keeper of the flame. While The Doors and others (such as the Velvet Underground's Lou Reed) had sometimes made detours from rock music into poetry mid-song, some of Patti's epics were just as much poetry as music. On 'Gloria', 'Birdland', and 'Land' in particular, she flits between tune and word without giving precedence to either, creating not so much long songs as stream-of-consciousness performance pieces with loose narratives. Like Reed, she didn't shy away from using gritty and at times disturbing images suggestive of abuse, unconventional sexual practices, and urban squalor. The Velvet Underground connection, in fact, was made explicit by the use of founding VU member John Cale as producer, though Smith would claim that she and the band ignored his suggestions, and that she mixed the record herself.

Observed Kaye in a 1998 interview with the author, "With Patti, certain elements of cinema, performance arts, literature, and poetry moved into our music." He recalled 'Land' as a track that Smith seemed to be seeing almost like a movie on a reel before her eyes and added, "Patti would take old songs and reconfigure them, use them in a context and as a segue, in much the same way that rock criticism sets itself up." While those qualities might have been most evident in 'Land' and 'Gloria', the shorter, more conventionally structured (and sung) tracks on *Horses* had their own striking qualities, whether the strange transmuted reggae of 'Redondo Beach', the odd offbeats and yelping vocals of 'Kimberly', which would be echoed in the work of numerous early New York new wave acts, and the achingly dramatic 'Break It Up', co-written by Smith with Tom Verlaine of

Patti Smith at the Roundhouse (Camden, London), May 1976.

Television, who had yet to release their first album.

Heard thirty years later, *Horses'* connections to punk and new wave might not seem so obvious. It's certainly not as brittle or hyper as more conventionally early punk records by, say, the Ramones, or the Sex Pistols. Yet while proto-punk-new wave records had been made since the late 1960s in the States by the likes of Jonathan Richman and the Modern Lovers, The Stooges, and the Velvet Underground, *Horses* was the first album from this crowd to make any sort of significant commercial impact. Without a hit single, and with airplay no doubt curtailed by some of the more vivid lyrics, it still made the US Top 50. It also made much of the media and hip rockdom aware of the New York new wave scene in general, in turn helping to pave the way for the modest-to-large commercial breakthroughs of Blondie, Talking Heads, and the Ramones to a national audience.

Long-term, one of *Horses'* greatest contributions was to help change the image of women rock performers in general. With the exception of Janis Joplin, few white women rock singers had come on as aggressively as Smith did. But unlike Joplin, Smith wrote most of her own material, flaunting her bohemian, tomboyish sexuality without pretension or artifice. Live, she was a mesmerizing performer, and the relatively placid, conventional rock production of *Horses* has been criticized for not capturing more of the Patti Smith Group's live raunch (though it's available on several bootlegs from the era should you want it, her January 1976 show at the Roxy in Los Angeles being not just the best music she ever recorded, but one of the best live rock recordings ever). When you hear similarly assertive alternative woman rock performers in the decades that followed, from Polly Styrene of X-Ray Spex to Courtney Love of Hole, you're hearing the ongoing echo of Patti Smith's trailblazing efforts.
- Richie Unterberger

77. Love to Love you Baby
Donna Summer

TRACKLISTING
Love To Love You Baby/Full Of Emptiness/Need-A-Man Blues/
Whispering Waves/Pandora's Box/Full Of Emptiness (Reprise)

RELEASED
US: September 1975 UK: January 1976

PRODUCED BY
Giorgio Moroder, Pete Bellotte

Disco was possibly both the most reviled and the most misunderstood music of the last fifty years.

The original wave of disco-hating culminated in the notorious Disco Demolition Night in July 1979 at Comiskey Park in Chicago, and it is perhaps only now that disco's place in pop history is being properly re-evaluated. It is now more commonly understood that disco was a truly subversive musical movement.

It was subversive for a number of reasons. Firstly because it was everything that rock wasn't. It substituted glamour for rock's grittiness, theatricality for authenticity, fun and escapism for dues-paying. Secondly it simultaneously provided a much-needed voice for ethnic minorities (in particular the black, Italian and Hispanic sectors of New York, where disco originated), and for female and gay sexuality. And finally, it once again made popular music genuinely sexual and provocative, arguably for the first time since Elvis. In all of this, *Love To Love You Baby* was an absolutely key moment, especially its outrageous 17-minute title track.

Summer grew up in Boston but moved to Europe in the late 'Sixties after landing a stage role. Eventually she settled in Munich, Germany, where she worked in the musical theatre, and started to write and record songs with producers Giorgio Moroder and Pete Bellotte. She and her collaborators had some limited success with their pop-rock but their breakthrough came when Moroder, intrigued by the growing underground disco scene in the USA, started to work on music with a stronger dance orientation. Summer wrote the basic hook and chorus for 'Love To Love You Baby'. Moroder recorded a compelling funky track that was reminiscent of early 'Seventies soul, and Summer completed the track with her vocal. The original version was three minutes long. Summer sang in a falsetto because Moroder had recorded the song in a key slightly too high for her. This lent it a certain sensuality but it was nothing compared to what the song would later become.

There are various stories as to how the song came to be extended. Neil Bogart, head of Summer's US label Casablanca, was certainly aware of the demand for extended mixes on New York dancefloors, a demand that was being met by DJs using obscure album tracks, instrumentals, and looped mixes that elongated tracks with conventional running times. Apparently Bogart tried playing 'Love To Love You Baby' on a permanent loop either at a party or while making love, and found that its hypnotic quality was enhanced by thus extending its duration. He asked Moroder to produce as long a version as possible for 12-inch single release. It was easy for Moroder to extend the track musically, but he and Summer struggled to think how to lengthen the lyrics. So instead they turned the studio lights down low (to mitigate Summer's embarrassment) and she improvised an extraordinary additional vocal, full of moans and sighs that were more orgasmic than almost anything that had ever been committed to tape before. The final result was a moist masterpiece, on a par with Jane Birkin and Serge Gainsbourg's 'Je T'Aime – Moi Non Plus'.

This was the version that became a huge international hit. This record proved that extended mixes were commercially viable, legitimized a far more raw and open sexuality within disco, and celebrated its own theatricality in a way that came to define disco in ensuing years. It made Summer a global star and kick-started Moroder and Bellotte's subsequent high-profile careers. The album *Love To Love You Baby* is inevitably centered around this track, which took up the entire first side of the original vinyl. The tracks that made up the second vinyl side are enjoyable and interesting in parts, but date less well than the classic title track.

Donna Summer, Disco Queen.

Following the success of 'Love To Love You Baby', disco moved from the underground to the mainstream. There were other massively influential and interesting disco artists including Chic, Sister Sledge and Sylvester, but Donna Summer was chiefly instrumental for opening the disco floodgates, no matter how hard she later tried to distance herself from the genre. From 1975 to 1979 disco was the culture's dominant musical style, and discos became a worldwide phenomenon. By the time that *Saturday Night Fever* – movie and soundtrack - and the Bee Gees took disco to new heights of hysteria in 1977-78, it was a genre already running out of steam, and the craze quickly turned sour. The artificiality that had been part of disco's self-identity started to grate with the mass audience that it had now reached, and its popularity quickly waned.

But even after the first wave of disco had subsided, disco and Donna Summer in particular had an enduring influence. The synth-pop of the 'Eighties, the growth of hip hop out of the ashes of disco, the new sample-based dance such as the house music of the late-'Eighties and

'Nineties, and most of the output of Madonna and her imitators derived directly from the celebratory, metronomic escapism of early disco. A huge proportion of successful contemporary pop music still draws on the disco template. Donna Summer's heavy breathing in 'Love To Love You Baby' has had far raunchier descendants, but remains a pivotal moment in the history of pop music.

Unlike many 'disco divas', Summer was a singer who contributed a considerable amount to the writing of her own hits. Those hits helped to define and break a significant musical movement. Not only is disco an underrated genre but Donna Summer is unfortunate to be one of the most underrated stars of her time. - Hugh Barker

78. Frampton Comes Alive!
Peter Frampton

TRACKLISTING
Something's Happening/Doobie Wah/Show Me The Way/It's A Plain Shame/All I Want To Be (Is By Your Side)/Wind Of Change/Baby, I Love Your Way/I Wanna Go To The Sun/Penny For Your Thoughts/(I'll Give You) Money/Shine On/Jumpin' Jack Flash/Lines On My Face/Do You Feel Like We Do?

RELEASED
US: January 1976 UK: March 1976

PRODUCED BY
Peter Frampton

In the film *Wayne's World 2*, Wayne's wannabe rock-star girlfriend buys some vinyl albums at a garage sale. She holds one up and asks if he's seen it before. "Exqueese me?" Wayne replies. "Have I seen this one before? *Frampton Comes Alive!*? Everybody in the world has *Frampton Comes Alive!* If you lived in the suburbs you were issued it. It came in the mail with samples of Tide."

It certainly was a ubiquitous record and for anyone who came of age in the pre-punk mid-'70s, it was inescapable. It's not an album that is fondly remembered, though, particularly not by the know-alls who usually end up as rock critics and rock historians: it's an album that is often invoked as an example of how bad things were back in the day. The record stayed at number one in the States for 17 weeks and ultimately sold over 17 million copies worldwide. Though its status as top-selling live album of all time was recently overtaken by Garth Brooks' *Double Live*, there is some controversy over the fact that the two discs of the Brooks album were counted as separate releases: Frampton, at the time of writing, is trying to reclaim his place at the top by having *Frampton Comes Alive!* reclassified as two discs.

Its success was spurred on by the hit singles 'Show Me The Way', 'Baby, I Love Your Way' and the extended jam 'Do You Feel Like We Do?', which all became FM radio staples. Frampton's use of the vocal-distorting voicebox was a novel enough innovation to guarantee him some interest in the fickle pop market. And his well-crafted if very conventional soft-rock songs struck a chord with the sort of kids who wanted a fairly unchallenging feelgood soundtrack to such late teen pursuits as heavy petting, cruising through the streets of their small town in dad's pick-up and maybe smoking the odd jay or sharing a bottle of ripple wine with their buddies. Frampton also had the look that caught the times: the bubble hair, the wholesome good complexion and sparkling puppy dog eyes. He appealed to girls who had grown out of David Cassidy and Donny Osmond yet who found Led Zeppelin a bit threatening.

Every artist or band records a live album sometime in their career. A few of these live albums, like The Grateful Dead's *Live/Dead* and James Brown's *Live At The Apollo* are superior to anything that the artist ever recorded in a studio but for most they are merely a convenient way to hasten the end of a contract with a label or simply to make money with little effort. *Frampton Comes Alive!* is as good as it ever got for Peter Frampton. Not only more definitive an artistic statement than any of his studio affairs, it was also the album that 'broke' him. It also 'broke' a format. Such was its phenomenal success that it virtually created an industry, or at the very least validated its commercial appeal: the double vinyl live album.

Frampton Comes Alive! is an anomaly in that it was a double live album from an artist who was not particularly successful at the time. Frampton wasn't then a big concert draw - he was widely perceived as being an eternal support act - and his previous four albums *Wind of Change* (1972), *Frampton's Camel* (1973), *Somethin's Happening* (1974) and *Frampton* (1975) had had mediocre sales. Frampton had already been a teeny pop idol in Britain with The Herd in the '60s and had played in ex-Small Faces frontman Steve Marriott's hard rock band Humble Pie. It seemed, in 1975, that he had already had more than one bite at the cherry.

Releasing a double live album, then, seemed like an odd move. In fact, it was planned as a single disc until A&M co-founder Jerry Moss heard it and asked: "Where's the rest?" It was mainly the brainchild of manager Dee Anthony who had previously used live albums to boost the careers of his charges Joe Cocker (*Mad Dogs and Englishmen*), The J Geils Band (*Live Full House*) and Humble Pie (*Performance: Rockin' The Fillmore*). Most of the tracks were recorded on 24-track at the 5400 capacity San Francisco Winterland Ballroom on the first occasion that Frampton and his band had played a headline show there, but other songs and parts were recorded on 16-track at smaller venues such as Marin Civic Center, San Rafael, the Island Music Center, Long Island, and the University Of New York. Audience noises and effects were dubbed on to make it sound consistent, as though it was all recorded in a larger venue.

It was always common practice to beef-up live recordings in the studio. Notoriously, *James Brown Live At The Apollo* seems to have been a studio recording with audience sounds added later. *Frampton Comes Alive!* isn't a complete concert performance and there have always been rumors that it was heavily overdubbed in the studio. Even at the time of its release there were questions asked about the unlikely clarity of the vocals. But that's not to take anything away from *Frampton Comes Alive!*: if it's a fake then it's such a good one that it hardly matters. Frampton and his touring band - keyboardist Bob Mayo, bassist Stanley Sheldon and drummer John Siomos - had crossed the US many times, honing their sound before audiences both welcoming, indifferent and hostile. Whatever else you say about him, you can't take away the fact that Frampton was a skilled and exciting live performer. Compare the songs here with the studio album versions: the non-live versions sound flat. You could never imagine them being hit singles.

The original cover for *Frampton Comes Alive!*

There was perhaps something ironic in the fact that when Frampton toured incessantly following the album's success, it was in effect his undoing. The follow up *I'm In You* sold over a million but he hadn't had enough time to write and as a result it was generally perceived as artistically substandard.

Frampton Comes Alive! however changed the way that live albums were perceived by artists, labels and consumers. - Tommy Udo

"Coupled With"

In the age of the single-sided CD and downloaded tracks, the flips of 7-inch vinyl records are now only a footnote of history. Usually occupied by filler, they occasionally contained gems. Some great **B-sides**…

1. **Grow Your Own** — Small Faces (Flip of 'Sha La La La La Lee')
2. **This Boy** — The Beatles (Flip of 'I Want To Hold Your Hand')
3. **(I'll Feel) A Whole Lot Better** — The Byrds (Flip of 'All I Really Want To Do')
4. **Rain** — The Beatles (Flip of 'Paperback Writer')
5. **I'm Not Like Everybody Else** — The Kinks (Flip of 'Sunny Afternoon')
6. **Don't Let Me Down** — The Beatles (Flip of 'Get Back')
7. **Ruby Tuesday** — The Rolling Stones (Flip of 'Let's Spend The Night Together')
8. **Revolution** — The Beatles (Flip of 'Hey Jude')
9. **Acquiesce** — Oasis (Flip of 'Some Might Say')
10. **Coloured Rain** — Traffic (Flip of 'Here We Go Round The Mulberry Bush')
11. **Stone Free** — The Jimi Hendrix Experience (Flip of 'Hey Joe')
12. **Not Fade Away** — The Crickets (Flip of 'Oh Boy!')
13. **The Prisoner** — The Clash (Flip of '(White Man) In Hammersmith Palais')
14. **Why?** — The Byrds (Flip of 'Eight Miles High')
15. **Armagideon Time** — The Clash (Flip of 'London Calling')
16. **Spooky** — Dusty Springfield (Flip of 'How Can I Be Sure')
17. **Don't Worry Baby** — The Beach Boys (Flip of 'I Get Around')
18. **Just Like Tom Thumb's Blues (Live)** — Bob Dylan (Flip of 'I Want You')
19. **Yes It Is** — The Beatles (Flip of 'Ticket To Ride')
20. **Almost Grown** — Small Faces (Flip of 'Hey Girl')

79. Ramones

Ramones

TRACKLISTING
Blitzkrieg Bop/Beat On The Brat/Judy Is A Punk/I Wanna Be Your
Boyfriend/Chain Saw/Now I Wanna Sniff Some Glue/I Don't Wanna Go
Down To The Basement/Loudmouth/Havana Affair/Listen To My Heart/
53rd & 3rd/Let's Dance/I Don't Wanna Walk Around With You/Today Your
Love, Tomorrow The World

RELEASED
US: May 1976 UK: July 1976

PRODUCED By
Craig Leon, Tommy Ramone

Their lyrics were wilfully, cartoonishly stupid. Their music displayed only the most rudimentary of musical skills. Clad in black leather jackets and sporting their trademark bad bowl haircuts they boasted little in the way of conventional sex appeal. And while they were punks – yes, perhaps the very first – they lacked the snarl. Yet The Ramones started a music revolution with the release of their self-titled 1976 debut.

Taking their surname from the assumed name Paul McCartney would use when he checked into hotels (Paul Ramon), singer Joey, guitarist Johnny, bassist Dee Dee and drummer Tommy were all Queens natives who met as teenagers and shared a love of 1960s girl groups, garage rock, the MC5 and The Stooges. Recorded in 17 days on a shoestring budget of $6,200, *Ramones* featured a cover shot of the band slouched against the back wall of CBGB's, the famous club on Manhattan's Lower East Side where they had presided over a vibrant cult scene that included a fledgling Blondie and Talking Heads. A reaction against the technical virtuosity of progressive rock and what they saw as the numbing vacuity of disco (even The Ramones at their most simplistic were saying *something*), *Ramones* was an album absolutely right for its times.

Though it proved to be too offbeat for radio, peaking at #111 on the US chart, it was one of the first albums to present a radical alternative to the bloated self-indulgence of mainstream mid-1970s rock. The Ramones brought back the primal energy of early rock with fast and furious songs that clocked in at, on average, two minutes. Within their rudimentary three chord buzzsaw sound are echoes of girl group melodicism with a singalong quality as catchy as the best bubblegum (Joey Ramone was said to have been inspired by The Bay City Rollers' 'Saturday

Night') and as simplistic as nursery rhymes, albeit sometimes rather twisted ones (the titles – 'I Wanna Be Your Boyfriend', 'Judy Is A Punk', 'Now I Wanna Sniff Some Glue', 'I Don't Wanna Go Down To The Basement', 'Beat On The Brat' – pretty much said it all). The album lasts a mere 29 minutes, which was the maximum length of the band's live shows.

Its opening salvo 'Blitzkrieg Bop' is a breakneck punk call to arms that sets the pace for all the songs that follow. *Ramones* is a study in inspired amateurism. Never have a band done so much with so little, whether indulging in their love of 1960s pop in their inspired

remake of the old Chris Montez hit 'Let's Dance' or indulging in punk's earliest manifestation of mock-Nazi themes in 'Today Your Love, Tomorrow The World' ("I'm a shock trooper in a stupor, yes I am").

If American audiences with their traditionally more conservative tastes weren't ready for The Ramones, Britain fortunately, would prove to be far more receptive. The Ramones' well-received UK concerts in July 1976 which took place over two months after the release of their debut and preceded the first gigs of The Clash and The Buzzcocks would prove to be a direct inspiration to the first wave of English punk bands. In the case of The Clash, ultimately the UK's biggest punk export, The Ramones' influence was

The Ramones, pictured in London, 1977.

unmistakable. Listen to the furious one-two punch of The Clash's early single 'White Riot' or much of their 1977 self-titled long playing debut, especially 'Janie Jones', with its blurred rhythm guitar. For Clash singer Joe Strummer, The Ramones' just-the-raw-essentials approach held enormous appeal. "That's one thing I learned from The Ramones," he once stated. "Slam! There's that number...where's the next one? Because people are watching, people have got things to do! It's a busy world out there. Give it to them!"

The Ramones would go on to record for another 20 years, staying mostly true to their less-is-more ethic but remained largely outside of the mainstream. They called it quits in 1996 following their appearance at the Lollapalooza festival. The Ramones left their raw, stripped down mark on the L.A. punk scene (X, Dead Kennedys), the Riot Grrrl movement of the 1990s, the US hardcore punk movement of the 1980s and 1990s, the sound of early '90s grunge, alternative and modern guitar rock, from Husker Du (who Joey viewed ungenerously as a Ramones rip-off) to The Red Hot Chili Peppers and Green Day. Even U2's Bono was a convert, crediting The Ramones with inspiring a fledgling U2 in the way they "stood for the idea of making your limitations work for you." Time, it turns out, has been good to the concept of The Ramones: in the years since their breakup their stature has only grown. It has not been so good to them as individuals. Three of the original four are gone now. By the early part of the century, Johnny and Joey had succumbed to cancer and Dee Dee to a heroin overdose. But it seems somehow fitting that we'll remember them forever young. After all, they maintained a defiantly adolescent vibe throughout the course of their career. - Tierney Smith

80. Arrival

ABBA

TRACKLISTING
When I Kissed the Teacher/Dancing Queen/My Love, My Life/Dum Dum Diddle/Knowing Me, Knowing You/Money, Money, Money/That's Me/Why Did It Have to Be Me/Tiger/Arrival

RELEASED
US: January 1977 UK: November 1976

PRODUCED BY
Benny Andersson, Bjorn Alvaeus

Contrary to what has become received wisdom, the world was not oblivious to the charms of ABBA until the passage of time had eased people's worries about being perceived as uncool for professing a penchant for their product (i.e., some time in the mid-1980s).

Though one might be able to dismiss the millions upon millions of people who bought their records when they were extant on the grounds that the fact that Barbara Cartland was the world's best-selling novelist hardly proves anything, it's a bit more difficult to ignore this quote from no less than *uber*-punk Joe Strummer from 1981 when told by a journalist that The Clash sounded like ABBA on an Ellen Foley record on which they played: "That's a compliment!.. They hardly ever lay a turkey on you."

While ABBA would arguably make better albums than this – the succeeding *The Album* and *Voulez-Vous* each have strong claims to be the *magnum opus* – *Arrival* was the album which crystallized the group's sound following a rather uncertain couple of years in which they seemed unable to properly capitalize, either artistically or commercially, on their triumph in the 1974 Eurovision Song Contest with the rip-roaring classic 'Waterloo'.

It was in fact that very triumph in a contest known for inane glorified jingles – albeit catchy ones – that created such a resistance in so many quarters for such a long time to recognizing ABBA as genuine artistic heavyweights, although their unashamedly ostentatious outfits and un-rock 'n' roll domesticity (the act was comprised of two married couples) didn't help matters. Neither did the fact that they broke really big in 1977, a year characterized by the three-chord anomie of angry young punks. However, even the tone deaf should surely have been able to perceive that, as this was a band who wrote their own material, there was talent at work here.

Those songwriters were guitarist Bjorn Alvaeus and keyboardist Benny Andersson. The former's main department was lyrics, something in which he was assisted at this stage of ABBA's career by band manager Stig Anderson. Agnetha Fältskog and Anni-Frid Lyngstad provided sumptuous vocals. Because ABBA were never a self-contained group, they were always obliged to hire bassists and drummers, although the fact that Sweden had a little-known repository of highly skilled sessioners meant that they were not penalized by this: many is the non-Swedish musician who will extol the virtues of ABBA's long-term bassist Rutger Gunnarsson and drummer Ola Brunkert.

After a couple of clunky follow-ups to 'Waterloo', ABBA began to find their feet with the sensual 'S.O.S.', well over a year after the Eurovision success. 'Mamma Mia', a single with an extraordinarily snaking melody, followed. The even more extraordinary 'Fernando' – a song about Latin American revolutionaries – followed it to the top of the UK chart. Recorded at the same time as the other tracks on *Arrival*, 'Fernando''s inclusion would have been welcome here, considering the rather parsimonious running time of barely over half-an-hour.

There again, its inclusion might have seemed a bit of a cheek considering the fact that the album was already choc-ful of hits. 'Money, Money, Money', 'Knowing Me, Knowing You' and 'Dancing Queen' were not only chart smashes, they also constitute three of the most iconic ABBA songs ever released. 'Money, Money, Money' was a show-tune-esque creation displaying the act's knack for a catchy chorus and powerhouse production techniques. Though it actually predated any romantic splits in the band, 'Knowing Me, Knowing You' feels perfectly in tune with the anguished lyrics about separation that Alvaeus began to pen for ABBA when his divorce with Faltskog was going through. As for 'Dancing Queen', its opening piano glissando itself is iconic, let alone its zigzagging strings and teen-friendly lyric that panders to every kid's fantasy about being the prettiest person and niftiest mover on the dance floor. Bizarrely, on this track the musicians achieved their aim of a 'dance' feel (before the spread of disco provided everybody with a template for that) by creating a mixture of George McCrae's 'Rock Your Baby' and a Dr John album. Though the record is redolent of neither – nor indeed does it sound like a dance song as the term was understood then – its opening notes continue to instantly fill dance floors worldwide.

Björn, Agnetha, Anni-Frid, Benny, in classic mid-1970s ABBA-wear.

    'Dancing Queen' was actually amongst the first *Arrival* tracks on which work was done, but there was a long gap between the album's inaugural sessions in August 1975 and the resumption of recording. Not only was work being done on a solo album by Anni-Frid but the group were still having to travel the world promoting their previous album and singles, including a visit to Australia, in which country they ultimately reached a status approaching royalty. It was only in March '76 that they could give *Arrival* their full attention, recording at Metronome and Glen Studios in Stockholm.

    The formula of ultra-modern, slick pop – almost rigid instrumentation, occasional washes of synth, clinically arranged vocal harmonizing – is maintained throughout except on the old-timey feeling, Alvaeus-sung 'Why Did It Have To Be Me' (easily a number one had they chosen to issue it on 45) and the title track, a bizarre bagpipe instrumental finale.

ABBA arrived at a time when it was not quite acceptable for serous musicians to be pop-oriented, the shadow of progressivism still looming large, but they showed by sheer example that pop did not rule out substance. An additional, unintended influence provided by ABBA is their contribution to breaking down barriers in music. Come that mid-1980s re-evaluation of the group - partly caused by the phenomenal success of the first ABBA compilation designed for the CD age, *ABBA Gold* (1992) – a certain watershed was reached and a discernible relaxation of standpoint was effected. Guilty pleasures are now less common because people have been given permission to like what they want on the grounds that, to use a current phrase, "It's all good". In ABBA'S case, it was better than most.
- Sean Egan

81. Damned Damned Damned
The Damned

TRACKLISTING
Neat, Neat, Neat/Fan Club/I Fall/Born To Kill/Stab Your Back/Feel the Pain/New Rose/Fish/See Her Tonight/1 of the 2/So Messed Up/I Feel Alright

RELEASED
US: April 1977 UK: February 1977

PRODUCED BY
Nick Lowe

The history books have not been too kind to The Damned. The band are considered toytown punks compared to giants like the Sex Pistols and The Clash.

This is partly because they committed the quasi-sin of being the only major UK punk band of the late 1970s to spurn politics and partly because a large part of their credibility was perceived to be destroyed when they were kicked off the Sex Pistols-headlined 'Anarchy In The UK' 1976 UK tour for allegedly being prepared to perform a show for local councillors who wanted to satisfy themselves that punks were not filthy and depraved.

However, The Damned's punk credentials are absolutely unquestionable. They had a knack for pipping everyone to the post: their

'New Rose' was the first UK punk single and *Damned Damned Damned* the first punk album. Additionally, Damned drummer Rat Scabies (aka Chris Miller) has the quintessential designedly obnoxious UK punk name.

Like many of their contemporaries, The Damned were absolutely weary with the somnambulant mid-'Seventies music scene. By '75 (at least), the ex-Beatles, the Stones, Dylan, Clapton, The Who, Led Zeppelin etc etc had all lost their sense of urgency, both in their music

The Damned in Copenhagen, 1977.

(which usually sounded tired and middle-aged or else bloated by self-indulgent extemporisation) and their rate of productivity (which had dwindled to an album every couple of years – and no stand-alone singles – due to the fact that that they no longer *needed* to work). The Damned's generation wanted music of a far greater vitality and found they had to make it themselves. Speed was the drug of choice of the UK punk bands and speed the abiding principle of their music.

In fact nobody was faster than The Damned. Those who assume that they took their cue, tempo-wise, from the also super-fast Ramones, however, are mistaken: Scabies has said that the only time they heard of their kindred spirits in the scene across the Atlantic like The Ramones and Richard Hell was leafing through *Punk* magazine in a London record store near where they would sign on the dole (welfare). Instead, and despite punk's supposed year zero approach, it was to an older generation – albeit its edgy fringes – to whom the Damned looked for inspiration: The Stooges, the MC5, and the Velvet Underground, although the more recent New York Dolls also commanded some respect.

The original Damned consisted of Scabies, bassist Captain Sensible (Ray Burns), Brian James on guitar and vocalist David Letts, who styled himself Dave Vanian and dressed like Count Dracula. It was James who wrote the band's fast but melodic songs.

Despite the hostility they engendered from some for their apolitical stance and (at least in those days) macho posturing, it should be noted that unlike the Sex Pistols and the early Clash, The Damned had sufficient humanity not to spurn the emotion of love. Their debut single 'New Rose' might have had the velocity of a Concorde and a brutal drum motif but it celebrated the giddy feeling of the beginnings of a romance quite movingly. The single, like the subsequent album, was produced by Nick Lowe, another Stiff artist. Not that production mattered too much in 1976/1977: the album contained very few overdubs but sought instead to capture the simplicity and excitement of the band's stage act. Nonetheless, Lowe did ensure both a bright, clean finish and that James' memorable guitar riffs had an absolutely menacing razor-like sharpness to them. It has long been rumoured that Lowe was responsible for providing an additional production boon, namely varispeeding the tapes to achieve that blurred effect. Both Sensible and Scabies have denied it, Scabies pointing out that the record's tracks are all in normal tuning and Sensible commenting that the band actually played faster than that live, necessitating them starting their set from the beginning when they would finish before their allotted stage time was over.

Damned Damned Damned was recorded in a mere ten days in Pathway, a North London studio so small that musicians had to lean forward because of the inclines caused by stairs overhead. The album boasted twelve blasts of acetylene-torch rock, few of which maintained the generosity of spirit found on the 'New Rose' single (also included) but all of which matched, and sometimes topped, that record's intensity. Particularly impressive are the opening, breathless 'Neat, Neat, Neat', the stomping '1 Of The 2', and 'Fish', the latter featuring some remarkable quicksilver and liquid fretwork from James. Though relatively sedate, the groupie anthem 'Fan Club' was also very easy on the ear. The band's roots were showing in the closer, a cover of the Stooges' 'I Feel Alright' (aka '1970').

The album's unforgettable sleeve lived down to the general public's perception of punk: the band were shown licking what looked like vomit (supposedly a staple of punk life) off each other. In fact it was a cream pie, but the band were probably pleased by the misapprehension.

Though the first punks, by 1977 the Sex Pistols weren't in a position to influence many beyond the small number of people who had already seen them live: barred from playing gigs and releasing singles only at long intervals due to being sacked by successive record companies, they were essentially absent. The Damned therefore defined a genre almost by default. It will never be known how many punk bands and records they inspired but the high speed of their music and celebration of mayhem of their lyrics was certainly the prominent flavour of the season as record company executives neglected the prog rockers on their roster to cosy up to snotty young two-chord nobodies.

It wasn't just the kids who were impressed though. No less than Jimmy Page was a fan, attending Damned gigs at the capital's Roxy Club. It's certainly the case that at this juncture Led Zeppelin decided to rid from their music what they acknowledged had been a tendency to bloated self-indulgence (at least live) in recent years. The fantasy had come true: the punks who had been partly motivated by disillusion with their musical elders now really had taught the old dogs some new tricks. - Sean Egan

82. Rumours

Fleetwood Mac

TRACKLISTING
Second Hand News/Dreams/Never Going Back Again/Don't Stop/Go Your Own Way/Songbird/The Chain/You Make Loving Fun/I Don't Want To Know/Oh Daddy/Gold Dust Woman

RELEASED
US: February 1977 UK: February 1977

PRODUCED BY
Fleetwood Mac, Ken Caillat, Richard Dashut

Following the departure of guitarist Bob Welch from Fleetwood Mac in 1974, many must have questioned the wisdom of the band embarking on another leg of their career as they moved ever further away from the original acclaimed outfit led by the long-departed guitar and writing giant Peter Green.

It was drummer Mick Fleetwood's move to hire the little known singer-songwriter Lindsey Buckingham. At Buckingham's insistence, Stevie Nicks, his girlfriend and professional partner in duo Buckingham

Nicks, also came on board. The two were joining the powerhouse rhythm section of mainstays Fleetwood and bassist John McVie and McVie's wife, British singer-songwriter/keyboardist Christine McVie. (Fleetwood had heard a few tracks from Buckingham Nicks when sound engineer Keith Olson had used their songs to demonstrate the sound quality at a Van Nuys recording studio Fleetwood was checking out at the time.)

Thus re-aligned and rejuvenated, the group's radical shift in direction set the stage for a dizzying change of fortune for the band. With no less than three talented singer-song-writers on board and with them debuting a punchier, more accessible sound, the new Mac found huge favor with the record buying public. The self-titled 1975 debut of the

The *Rumours* line-up of Fleetwod Mac in 1976.

reconfigured lineup began a slow but steady climb up the US charts, ascending to the top one year and two months after its release. A five-million seller, it spawned three hit singles ('Over My Head', 'Rhiannon', 'Say You Love Me') and set the stage for even greater success to come. The distinct personalities and immense visual appeal of the group's members was a definite plus as well: Stevie Nicks was an ethereal husky-voiced enchantress, Christine McVie an elegant songstress, Buckingham a kinetic sonic explorer, John McVie the steady workmanlike bassist and Mick Fleetwood a man whose drumming was a singular as his gangly wild-eyed appearance.

After a lengthy gestation (delayed in part by Buckingham's perfectionist tendencies), *Rumours* was released in 1977. It proceeded to spend an incredible 31 weeks at #1 in the US, selling over 17 million copies there alone. In the UK, *Rumours* spent 443 weeks on the album chart. Catapulting the band into the rock superstar stratosphere, its songs became an omnipresent presence on the radio. The personal tumult surrounding the band only added to the legend surrounding *Rumours*. During the making of the album, Nicks and Buckingham split, the McVies were divorcing and Fleetwood separated from his wife Jenny Boyd. Add to that the escalating drug abuse and you have all the makings of tabloid heaven. Their songs traced these imploding relationships, reading like a diary open for all the world to see. The end results prove if nothing else that pain can be a powerful catalyst for inspiration. *Rumours* showcased a band at the height of their creative powers, channeling their not-so-private turmoil into song from three different perspectives. The opening line of the album's first track, Buckingham's 'Second Hand News' ("I know there's nothing to say, someone has taken my place") sets the stage for the greater drama to come. In the galvanizing thrust of 'Go Your Own Way', Buckingham is downright bitter ("Packing up, shacking up is all you wanna do"). Nicks' songs look outward, addressing her ex's pain – his loneliness and loss in the beguiling 'Dreams' (subtle mockery perhaps?) and the bewitching 'Gold Dust Woman' ("Did she make you cry, make you break down, shatter your illusions of love?"). McVie's songs are more upbeat, whether celebrating a new relationship ('You Make Loving Fun'), sending good wishes to her ex in the exuberant shuffle 'Don't Stop' or offering emotional solace to Fleetwood in 'Oh Daddy'.

Far beyond its voyeuristic appeal, *Rumours*' success was also due to the simple fact that it was comprised of a terrific batch of songs with fine melodies, lush harmonies and killer hooks. It's sparkling, polished songcraft at its best, each song uniquely stamped with its author' personality, yet taken together forming a thrillingly cohesive work. Sheryl Crow, an admirer of the album's unedited display of truth-telling, rightly noted, "You have five really distinct personalities...and none of them are invisible." Moreover, the prominence of Nicks and McVie helped open the doors to the acceptance of women in rock. Witness the popularity of female performers in the New Wave era.

Rumours' greatest legacy, though, is in the way it illustrated how compatible heart-wracking confessionalism and a high gloss approach can be. With *Rumours*, Fleetwood Mac essentially showed the world how it was done. You can hear their influence in the simultaneously bright and in-your-face stylings of artists like Sheryl Crow, 10,000 Maniacs, Michelle Branch and Jewel. Courtney Love, who has made no secret of her admiration for Fleetwood Mac, released an *homage* of sorts to *Rumours* and the whole debauched LA high life on her band Hole's 1998 album *Celebrity Skin*. (Interestingly, Love once remarked that "there's never been a period in rock as debauched as the period after *Rumours*.") A timeless musical document that stands as one of the best-selling albums of all time, *Rumours* is a case of musical accessibility and almost forbiddingly personal songcraft colliding to brilliant effect. - Tierney Smith

Just The One

Where would the charts be without **one-hit wonders?**
In fairness, some here did hit the charts again but remain
stubbornly known for just one song.

1.	**In The Year 2525**	Zager & Evans
2.	**Something In The Air**	Thunderclap Newman
3.	**Wipe Out**	The Surfaris
4.	**Up Town Top Ranking**	Althia And Donna
5.	**MacArthur Park**	Richard Harris
6.	**Fire**	The Crazy World Of Arthur Brown
7.	**Theme From M★A★S★H**	MASH
8.	**Spirit In The Sky**	Norman Greeenbaum
9.	**Venus**	Shocking Blue
10.	**Yellow River**	Christie
11.	**Resurrection Shuffle**	Ashton, Gardner & Dyke
12.	**Hocus Pocus**	Focus
13.	**How Long**	Ace
14.	**Black Betty**	Ram Jam
15.	**Pop Muzik**	M
16.	**Turning Japanese**	The Vapors
17.	**In The Summertime**	Mungo Jerry
18.	**99 Red Balloons**	Nena
19.	**Perfect**	Fairground Attraction
20.	**Louie Louie**	The Kingsmen

83. The Clash
The Clash

TRACKLISTING
US:Clash City Rockers/I'm So Bored with the U.S.A./Remote Control/
Complete Control/White Riot/(White Man) In Hammersmith Palais/
London's Burning/I Fought the Law/Janie Jones/Career Opportunities/
What's My Name/Hate & War/Police & Thieves/Jail Guitar Doors/
Garageland

UK: Janie Jones/Remote Control/I'm So Bored With the U.S.A./White
Riot/Hate & War/What's My Name/Deny/London's Burning/Career
Opportunities/Cheat/Protex Blue/Police & Thieves/48 Hours/Garageland

RELEASED
US: July 1979 UK: April 1977

PRODUCED BY
UK: Mickey Foote
US: Mickey Foote, Lee Perry, The Clash

Though the Sex Pistols had essentially kicked off the whole UK punk scene they were beaten to the punch in the album stakes by former disciples The Clash. However, the reason that The Clash's long playing debut turned from their own manifesto into a manifesto for punk *per se* is not through a process of default but both because it was musically brilliant and because the issues it addressed and the way it addressed them spoke to an entire generation in a Britain that seemed to be splitting at the seams and who found that those issues were not being tackled by older rock acts who were both geographically (through tax exiledom) and materially distant from their lives and problems.

    Clash rhythm guitarist and main singer Joe Strummer co-wrote Clash songs with lead guitarist and fellow vocalist Mick Jones. Bassist Paul Simonon was not in a position at this time to contribute writing-wise: he was still trying to master his instrument via playing parrot-style lines taught him by Jones. This was the true You-Can-Do-It-Too spirit of punk, whose adherents had realized that the supposedly dazzling extemporization of the likes of Emerson, Lake and Palmer and Led Zeppelin was often unlistenable self-indulgence that was in danger of killing rock. Drumming duties at this point were handled by the excellent and underrated Terry Chimes.

    The Clash was recorded in three four-day sessions in February 1977 at CBS Studio 3, London. There was no attempt to interfere with the

recording process by record company bosses who didn't even pretend to
understand the punk movement they were (with pinched nostrils) allowing
through the door. The band's live sound man Mickey Foote was nominally
the producer and his inexperience contributed to the album's murky mix –
which inadvertently contributes to an enjoyable air of dimly-lit menace.

Though lauded abroad, *The Clash* had a particular resonance in
the UK. This was a British rock album through and through in a day and
age when there was - the odd Kinks LP aside – no such thing. It was also
that (then) rare beast: a political album. Nothing has ever conveyed better
the gray, dreary nature of Britain for those at the bottom of the country's
pile than this record. For many thousands of young people this album
described their lifestyle and their mindset: anthems of disaffection with
dull environments, low wages, petty, power drunk authority figures,
pompous politicians and soul destroying employment prospects. Yet the
album is exhilarating more often than it's depressing. This is mostly due
to its breakneck pace. Except for 'Police And Thieves' and 'Garageland',
everything here is fast and short: in another display of their contempt for

the rock aristocracy's showboating virtuosity, the band are almost fanatical in their determination to make their point and depart the stage.

Apart from 'Remote Control' – a litany of musical and socio-political clichés – there's nary a bad track on *The Clash*. Frantic opener 'Janie Jones' sees Strummer sing in the third person about an office worker who takes refuge from the routine of the shift rota and the photocopy room via rock 'n' roll, famous brothel madam Janie Jones and getting stoned, in that order. 'I'm So Bored With The USA' straps an ear-splitting, acetylene torch guitar riff – one of the most intense ever – to a lyric that addresses the resentment felt by many Britons at the dominance of their culture by American product. 'White Riot' has The Clash calling on their Caucasian contemporaries to violently demonstrate their fury with their lot the way that black youths had done at the 1976 Notting Hill carnival. This album version of 'White Riot' – profoundly different to the prior, more sedate single version – is simply one of the most exciting rock recordings of all time. The anti-work ethic 'Career Opportunities' is another display of the band's apparently effortless ability to compose anthems for their disaffected constituency and 'London's Burning' another powerful blast of invective against sepia-toned inner-city proletarian life married to a fine, strident riff and a defiant chorus. The six-minute cover of reggae number 'Police And Thieves' is incongruous but works perfectly, artistically stunning in its hypnotic, languid beat. The album closes with a track that, like 'Police and Thieves', shows that the band's musical abilities were greater than their short 'n' sharp proclivities might indicate. The thoughtful, melancholy and highly melodic 'Garageland' is a farewell to a punk scene that – reliant as it was on an outsider status that ceased to exist when the punk acts were welcomed in by the music establishment – was dying even as its lyric was written.

The American version of *The Clash* differs massively to the original UK release. Initially refusing an American release because of its poor sound quality, the US record company finally relented after the album sold 100,000 import copies but insisted on making it more attractive by throwing on singles, performing tweaks with the running order for fatuous 'conceptual' effect ('White Riot' followed by '(White Man) In Hammersmith Palais', 'Remote Control' followed by 'Complete Control', etc.) and throwing in a free 45. The result was a ludicrous hodgepodge of three different eras of the fast developing band but, if truth be told, a supremely listenable collection.

The musical styles and spiritual philosophies of acts like Stiff Little Fingers, U2, Nirvana, Pearl Jam, the Manic Street Preachers and Green Day were directly inspired by this album. After *The Clash*, rock would never be quite so complacent – artistically or politically – again. - Sean Egan

84. Bat Out of Hell
Meat Loaf

TRACKLISTING
Bat Out Of Hell/You Took the Words Right Out Of My Mouth (Hot Summer Night)/Heaven Can Wait/All Revved Up With No Place To Go/Two Out Of Three Ain't Bad/Paradise By The Dashboard Light/For Crying Out Loud

RELEASED
US: October 1977 UK: March 1978

PRODUCED BY
Todd Rundgren

In the UK, it has remained within the Top 200 bestselling albums for nearly 30 years, never dropping out of the chart since its first entry, only one of two albums ever to do so. It is also one of the few American albums whose sales abroad were phenomenal while at home it initially sold slowly and poorly. In subsequent interviews, the album's creators Meat Loaf and Jim Steinman recalled arriving in Melbourne, Australia to be greeted by 10,000 fans and a convoy of Hell's Angels who escorted them from the airport to the hotel, while the following week back in the States they played a tiny club in Dayton, Ohio where urine from an overflowing toilet upstairs dripped on the stage.

Although it is credited solely to Meat Loaf, *Bat Out Of Hell* is a collaboration between that heavyweight actor/singer (real name Marvin Lee Aday) and songwriter Jim Steinman. The two met when Meat Loaf auditioned for a role in Steinman's Vietnam War-themed musical *More Than You Deserve*. Meat Loaf sang a song from his first album *Meatloaf* [sic] *& Stoney*, released by Motown subsidiary Rare Earth in 1971. The album was a flop but Steinman was impressed by the Loaf's huge vocal presence and eventually they talked about the song cycle that would eventually become *Bat Out Of Hell*.

Steinman had already written some of the songs as part of a musical project called *Neverland*, basically the story of Peter Pan reimagined as a dark *Warriors*-style musical about gang warfare. It was the traditional subject matter of rock 'n' roll pumped up to the level of grand opera. 'Bat Out Of Hell' is a classic teenage death song like 'Leader Of The Pack'. 'Paradise By The Dashboard Light' is a story about kids transformed into Tristan & Isolde by having sex in cars. They were funny but also had a serious emotional edge and required the huge voice of Meat Loaf and an epic Wall Of Sound production to make them work.

Jim Steinman always said that his influences were Wagner, Phil Spector and the films of Alfred Hitchcock and that he conceived *Bat Out Of Hell* as a movie in his head. Like a movie, the album was a huge collaborative effort of many individual talents. The album's massive heavy metal/E Street Band sound was mainly due to the *pro bono* production work

The cover artwork for *Bat Out of Hell*, with illustration by comic book artist Richard Corben.

undertaken by Todd Rundgren, who loved the songs and wanted to make the album even though 17 other producers and 30 labels had turned it down. Rundgren played guitar on the record, including the sound of the motorcycle, which Steinman had nagged him about all the way through the sessions: Rundgren, at the last moment, scraped the strings of a guitar to uncannily replicate the sound of an engine revving. He also drafted in Kasim Sulton and Roger Powell from his prog band Utopia as well as Roy Bittan and Max Weinberg from Bruce Springsteen's E Street Band. That's not to take anything away from Meat Loaf; he is more than just a hired voice – he is Steinman's muse – but on *Bat Out Of Hell*, he remains merely one actor playing a role.

There was nothing subtle or tasteful about *Bat Out Of Hell*. It went against the grain of the restrained West Coast albums like Fleetwood Mac's *Rumours* and The Eagles' *Hotel California* that dominated the mainstream charts at the time. It also had little to do with the emerging punk and new wave scenes in New York and England. And despite the imagery – the metallic gothic logo and the barbarian/biker fleeing the giant bat on the cover – it wasn't a heavy metal album, though its influence on the emerging power-metal scene in the '80s was to be pronounced.

Bat Out Of Hell marked a realization on the part of some observers that after years of taking itself incredibly seriously, rock 'n' roll was still, at heart, a branch of showbiz. The observant saw right away that *Bat Out Of Hell* had to be understood in terms of musicals like *The Rocky Horror Show* and *Grease*. The songs are only a part of the package: the live performances that Meat Loaf gave (where he acted out the songs, trading lines in rock operettas with proto-goth singer Karla DeVito, though on the record the vocals were actually by Ellen Foley) and even the cover image by comics artist Richard Corben were all hugely important to the album's phenomenal sales. In a stroke of marketing genius, manager David Sonnenberg persuaded Epic records (the unenthusiastic parent company of Cleveland International, who eventually released *Bat Out Of Hell*) to pay for four promotional clips to be shot, despite videos still being an expensive and unusual promotional tool. Beneficially, the clip for 'Paradise By The Dashboard Light' started to play in cinemas as a short and when the clip for the title song aired on the UK's token rock show *The Old Grey Whistle Test*, the viewer response was so overwhelming that the BBC took the unprecedented step of showing it again the following week.

The album was released in 1977 to poor US sales but a combination of incessant touring – touring that would exhaust Meat Loaf himself, driving him to despair and almost ruin his voice – and a few lucky breaks – such as the acclaimed March 1978 appearance on *Saturday Night Live* – the album gradually built up a momentum. Six months after it was first released, sales took off at a phenomenal rate. Meat Loaf became the undisputed star of the show, something that one could understand grating on Steinman's nerves, although he did write the songs for Meat Loaf's *Bat Out Of Hell II* (1993).

Bat Out Of Hell, like *Star Wars*, which hit the cinemas in the same period, was proof that there would always be a massive demand for classic themes recast in an epic setting. - Tommy Udo

85. Never Mind The Bollocks Here's The Sex Pistol's
The Sex Pistols

TRACKLISTING
Holidays In The Sun/Bodies/No Feelings/Liar/God Save The Queen/Problems/Seventeen/Anarchy In The U.K./Submission/Pretty Vacant/New York/EMI (Unlimited Edition)
* Note: American edition transposed God Save The Queen and Problems

RELEASED
US: October 1977 UK: October 1977

PRODUCED BY
Chris Thomas

Some would question the inclusion of this album in this book. By the time it appeared, the Sex Pistols had already released the four singles that summed up their menacing musical and sociological significance.

Though all those four singles appeared on *Bollocks*, the album itself is viewed in some quarters as a coda to the glorious period of just under a year across which those 45s were released and in which the Pistols succeeded the Rolling Stones as society's outlaws. This view is partly for aesthetic reasons – rarely do the album tracks match the excellence of their single releases – and partly because the band themselves were only in existence in any meaningful way (i.e. with Johnny Rotten in their ranks) for four months after its release. *Bollocks* has the air of a tail-end.

However, the assumption that it was their singles alone – or even in large part - that defined the Sex Pistols' profound influence is erroneous. For the fact is that when those singles came out, the public were often unable to hear them. Such was the censorious nature of the times – one of the very things, of course, that the Pistols were protesting about – they were often banned from the airwaves. Following their infamous four-letter outburst on British tea-time TV in December 1976, their debut single 'Anarchy In The U.K.' was not only experiencing non-existent airplay but was banned by many stores. Meanwhile, there was no question of their follow-up – the murderously anti-royalist 'God Save The Queen' – getting on the airwaves, a ban far easier to arrange at a time when there was only one national radio station in Britain. Only with the release of their third single 'Pretty Vacant' could the media no longer find an excuse not to allow the public to hear for themselves the product of a band who they, the public, had been informed were talentless. Many were the jaws dropped by members of said public in surprise in July 1977 when the evidence presented to them by 'Pretty Vacant' coming into their living rooms indicated that the Sex Pistols were in fact a highly efficient rock band, albeit one whose music had a slightly demented undertow.

The Sex Pistols started out as a loose group of teenagers whose rock 'n' roll dreams were nurtured by Malcolm McLaren, owner of the King's Road, London fashion shop in which they congregated. Both McLaren and his protégés were painfully aware of a vacuum in music, with glam and pub rock (a UK R&B revival) having failed to fill the void left by the complacency of the 'Sixties superstars who had grown distant and unproductive. McLaren's shop was close to Kings Road stores patronized by old guard figures like the Rolling Stones, Roxy Music and Marc Bolan. Pistols bassist Glen Matlock has said, "That had already been and gone. There's Malcolm, who didn't have a lot of money, looking down on all these people, so we looked down on them as well." When the Pistols started articulating these anti-old-guard thoughts in their interviews, it was breathtaking insolence. Nobody had ever dismissed the Rolling Stones – the epitome of rock 'n' roll rebellion – as establishment before, not least unsigned kids. This disrespect – though not necessarily articulated explicitly in their music – is part and parcel of the Pistols phenomenon, the impetus for dozens of other wannabes to not be overawed by the considerable technique it seemed was required to be in a band and to have a go themselves. Though the often-spouted cliché that few saw the Pistols live but all those who did formed a group is obviously exaggeration, it does hold a grain of truth: just ask Adam Ant, Billy Idol, Pete Shelley, Siouxsie Sioux, Joe Strummer and myriad other soon-to-be new wave stars.

The period Matlock recalls actually predated the arrival of John Lydon, restyled Johnny Rotten when he took the post of Pistols vocalist, joining Matlock, guitarist Steve Jones and drummer Paul Cook. Chosen for his unnerving staring eyes and wheezing voice, he miraculously turned out to also have a unique lyric-writing ability, his demented, self-loathing rhyming schemes the main quality that set the band apart from everything else on the music scene.

There were several attempts to record the band's debut single, producers Chris Spedding and Dave Goodman unsuccessfully trying to capture both the live power that had seen them gaining music press raves and the danger that had gained them music press disdain (violence frequently attended their gigs, with the band members sometimes joining in) before work with Chris Thomas yielded the record with which they would introduce themselves to the wider world. (Mike Thorne would also supervise one session.) 'Anarchy In The UK' was a magnificent, roaring manifesto, Rotten's voice catching as he declared his hatred of all authority while Jones' searing, fluid guitar work (including two solos) demolished the rumors fostered by McLaren (who believed in the virtue of incompetence) that the group couldn't play.

It was the first and last recording by the line-up that had already made the Pistols a semi-legend. Following internal disputes, Matlock left three months after 'Anarchy..'s release. He was replaced by Sid Vicious, who couldn't play but looked the punk part. His musical incompetence didn't matter too much – Jones would play bass on the Pistols' remaining recordings – but the fact that Matlock wrote the Pistols' melodies seemed to: ten of the twelve songs on *Bollocks* date from the Matlock era. The band's reputation as rebels was sealed by the 'God Save The Queen' single (May 1977) , a snarling diatribe against the monarchy released at the very time – the celebrations of the Queen's Silver Jubilee – when it was most taboo. The band's members were

Sid Vicious and Johnny Rotten on stage together, 1977.

physically attacked on the streets and the record was banned form the airwaves. Somebody seemed to agree with the sentiment though: it sold by the bucketload. The only reason it didn't reach the top in the 'official' UK chart was because the compilers were instructed by the British Phonographic Institute not to count the sales of the records in Virgin retail outlets that week. (Virgin was by now the Pistols' label after they had been dumped as too hot to handle by first EMI, then A&M.) 'Pretty Vacant' was a fabulous anthem of apathy (written by Matlock alone) that became a UK top ten. 'Holidays In The Sun' (October '77) was a frightening if inchoate diatribe with a jackboot opening that indicated they could still write good stuff without Matlock, even if the fact that the riff was stolen from 'In The City' by punk Johnny-come-latelys The Jam was a bad portent.

The momentum of those first four records simply could not be maintained: there was only so much with which to outrage the public. *Never Mind The Bollocks* was the final shot, from the title ("Bollocks" being a slang word for testicles that is at least as offensive as the word "shit" to British ears) down. The inclusion of all four singles, for many, contradicted punk's value for money ethos – but who can really complain about the presence of epoch-marking greatness? Of somewhat more concern is that that other punk ethic – sprightliness – seemed to have been lost sight of in a stodgy barrage of guitar overdubs. Many in fact preferred the bootleg *Spunk*, which was essentially the same album with versions of the songs less burdened by sludgy superimpositions. (They can now be compared by purchasing the CD *This Is Crap*, which contains both.) However, if one takes away 'No Feelings', 'Liar' and 'Problems' – a triumvirate of boorishness – there is some great music present in addition to those remarkable 45s: the disturbing anti-abortion song 'Bodies', the deliciously moronic 'Seventeen', the atmospheric 'Sub-Mission', the scathing David Johansen put-down 'New York' and the glorious finale 'EMI', in which the band tear into the corporation that lost their nerve over their notoriety.

Of course, it would be absurd to suggest that the Sex Pistols and punk changed everything. The rock aristocracy continued to shift truckloads of product regardless of the new wave that had supposedly washed them away and the political establishment remained untouched – largely unaware, actually – of punks' dissatisfaction with them. The complaint "Like punk never happened" – a phrase that expresses dismay at the way that what had seemed punk's seismic effects had so quickly dissipated - was in common circulation well before Dave Rimmer used it for a book title in 1985. Nonetheless, the spirit of punk lives on in many quarters: whether it be via the refusal of the public to blindly accept any more ELP-type bombast or the questioning spirit of events like Live Aid and Live 8. Many, many significant bands would not have existed – or not in the form they did – without the Pistols' example, among them The Clash, Stiff Little Fingers, U2, Ash, Green Day, Nirvana, Pearl Jam and Oasis.

Of course it could also be suggested that the vulgarity and spite of much of modern popular culture (especially in Britain) would not have come about without the Pistols' example, nor a self-assertiveness amongst people that too frequently brims over into obnoxiousness and callousness. There again, it is a society where probably never again will a non-obscene record be artificially kept off the top of the charts and banned from wide public consumption because people in power don't like it. - Sean Egan

We Can Do It Too!

They're not rubbish but somehow they've never acquired the knack of sustaining high quality across the entire length of an album. **Great tracks** by people who **don't usually make classic albums**.

1.	**Do You Believe In Magic**	The Lovin' Spoonful
2.	**Catch The Wind**	Donovan
3.	**California Dreamin'**	The Mamas And The Papas
4.	**Crocodile Rock**	Elton John
5.	**American Pie**	Don McLean
6.	**Song Sung Blue**	Neil Diamond
7.	**Bohemian Rhapsody**	Queen
8.	**Every 1's A Winner**	Hot Chocolate
9.	**American Girl**	Tom Petty And The Heartbreakers
10.	**Can't Stand Losing You**	The Police
11.	**Baker Street**	Gerry Rafferty
12.	**Dreadlock Holiday**	10cc
13.	**Making Plans For Nigel**	XTC
14.	**Walking On The Moon**	The Police
15.	**Scenes From An Italian Restaurant**	Billy Joel
16.	**Horse With No Name**	America
17.	**Save Me**	Queen
18.	**Food For Thought**	UB40
19.	**Centerfold**	J Geils Band
20.	**That's All**	Genesis

86. Dub Housing

Pere Ubu

TRACKLISTING

Navvy/On The Surface/Dub Housing/Caligari's Mirror/Thriller!/I Will Wait/Drinking Wine Spodyody/Ubu Dance Party/Blow Daddy-O/Codex

RELEASED

US: April 1979 UK: November 1978

PRODUCED BY

Ken Hamann, Pere Ubu

Nothing was predictable in the world of Pere Ubu. Lurching from anarchic chaos to hysterical pop throughout their career, the band were regarded as new wave pioneers even though they rarely sounded remotely 'punk'. In fact singer and lyricist David Thomas once complained that the new wave movement "wiped out a generation of musicians" by giving those musicians a template to copy. For Pere Ubu, it was more important to be eclectic and to refuse labels than to become part of the in-crowd.

Following extraordinary early singles such as '30 Seconds Over Tokyo' and the breakthrough album *The Modern Dance,* Thomas's reaction to the homogenization he already perceived in new wave was to lead his Cleveland-based band into another leap in the dark with follow-up album *Dub Housing.* The industrial whines and clatters of *The Modern Dance* were still present, and an approach built around distorted pop-rock hooks survived. But *Dub Housing* went further than its predecessor and deconstructed even the most basic musical forms. The band (Thomas, guitarist Tom Herman, bassist Tony Maimone, keyboardist Allen Ravenstine, drummer Scott Krauss) were all highly talented and there are recognizable elements of free-form jazz, funk rhythms and musique concrete. The use of background noise (both cinematic and urban) and voices in tracks such as 'Caligari's Mirror' demonstrates one of the most successful attempts to introduce concepts of cut-up and randomness to pop music, well before the age of sampling. Together with Thomas' strange wailing voice, and fragmented lyrics that merge the *avant-garde* with the everyday, the result is a weird but entrancing record.

In their time, Pere Ubu were less well-known than Talking Heads or Devo, both of whom had a degree of chart success using similar techniques and ideas. (Thomas regarded both bands with respect, perceiving them as bands that had grown in isolation, prior to the simplifications of later punk.) But Pere Ubu have had a lasting influence.

There is a clear line of descent from *Dub Housing* to Husker Du and also to a singer with a similarly rotund form and eccentric persona, The Pixies' Black Francis (aka Frank Black). The Pixies added their quiet/loud rock dynamics to songwriting that was frequently *avant-garde*, ribald and comical. In the process they accidentally created the template for the grunge music that would follow, although most grunge was far more humorless and dour than anything laid down by either Pere Ubu or The Pixies. Some of the most eclectic and cacophonous sounds of the 1980s were also influenced by this album, including bands as disparate as The Pop Group, The Birthday Party, The Fall, Gang of Four, and even The Cure (at least in the form of Robert Smith's curiously romantic caterwauling). Later on, one can hear echoes of Pere Ubu's art-rock noise assault in bands such as Sonic Youth (via the no-wave movement), Nine Inch Nails, and Radiohead. There was also a parallel between *Dub Housing's* dark, oppressive atmosphere and the contemporary recordings of Joy Division. Both bands stood slightly apart from the more

extrovert, aggressive elements of punk/ new wave, and both pointed forward to some of the more interesting aspects of the following decade of music. It has been suggested that Martin Hannett's Eraserhead-style production on *Unknown Pleasures* owed a big debt to the early Ubu recordings. It's certainly true that both utilized machine noise and loops to hypnotic effect, and that both helped to create the moods and rhythms of 1980s post-punk.

The original artwork for *Dub Housing*.

Recently, post-punk has come back into fashion. Bands such as Franz Ferdinand, Bloc Party, The Beatings and The Kaiser Chiefs have become internationally successful recycling the arty deconstructions of the early 'Eighties. As with all revivals, there is more imitation than innovation here, but occasionally a fragment shines through of something more risky, more extraordinary, more downright weird. When it does, one can often sense a faint, distant but unmistakable echo of Pere Ubu. - Hugh Barker

87. Setting Sons
The Jam

TRACKLISTING
Girl On The Phone/Thick As Thieves/Private Hell/Little Boy Soldiers/
Wasteland/Burning Sky/Smithers-Jones/Saturday's Kids/The Eton Rifles/
Heat Wave

RELEASED
US: November 1979 UK: November 1979

PRODUCED BY
Vic Coppersmith-Heaven, The Jam

The nature of the popularity of The Jam in Britain in the early 1980s is extraordinary for more than one reason.

Firstly because of the way that they outstripped The Clash and the Sex Pistols, bands of whom they had once been seen as the poor relations: it had never occurred to Jam frontman and guitarist Paul Weller to write songs about the tribulations of his working class background until he saw the Pistols in action.

The second reason is that, for all the objectives of punks of bringing social relevance to popular music, none of them really envisaged achieving the feat The Jam could ultimately claim: securing a string of big hits − several of them number one records − with what were protest songs by any other name. Additionally, they were songs sung in their own English accents instead of the Americanisms then considered *de rigueur*. Admittedly, The Clash cut themselves off from the possibility of achieving a similar string of hits the instant they made a permanent decision not to appear on TV program *Top Of The Pops*, the main method of selling a record to the masses of the era in Britain, but even if The Clash hadn't decided that lip-synching was un-punk, its doubtful that − notwithstanding their fine music − they would have notched up quite as many chart entries. For The Jam had both a commercial touch and an Everyman aura, a knack for sheened, highly melodic, anthemic hard rock and Weller for frequently superb lyrics that encapsulated the experiences and mindsets of his social caste.

Though they would have greater success with other albums, *Setting Sons* is The Jam's masterpiece and probably their only classic album, although many speak highly of the previous *All Mod Cons*. That latter album had been something of a comeback for The Jam following the disastrous reception to their second album *The Modern World,* recorded in undue haste after their excellent debut *In The City*. *All Mod Cons* had seen The Jam move their songs in more of a pop direction – or at least as pop as a band could get when its subject matter was so gritty and when its personnel boasted in drummer Rick Buckler and bassist Bruce Foxton one of the most fearsome rhythm sections ever heard. However, the multi-layering that would fatten and expand the sound of the trio, enabling a proper aural depiction of Weller's increasingly ambitious visions, would not happen until *Setting Sons*, which album pointedly gives joint arrangement credit to The Jam and co-producer Vic Coppersmith-Heaven.

The sleeve design for *Setting Sons*.

Originally, *Setting Sons* was to have been a concept album based on a short story by Weller's friend Dave Waller, a former member of The Jam. Weller's idea was to depict three friends who meet up after a civil war, one having become a leftist, one a right-winger and the third politically neutral. Though such ideas may sound quaint now, at a time when the country was about to be torn apart by Thatcherism – which saw the growing prosperity of some counterpointed by the increasing impoverishment of others – it didn't seem too far-fetched a plot. In the end, the idea was abandoned, although conflicting accounts have been given as to why. Some sources have suggested that Weller simply ran out of time before the album's delivery deadline, something not helped by the more meticulous production work. Weller himself said not long afterwards that he had been put off the idea by fans who had read about the idea and who wrote to him complaining that this kind of concept album was a throwback.

Whatever the reason, only four songs materialized from that concept idea. Interestingly, all are superb: 'Thick As Thieves', a song lamenting lost boyhood friendships that is no less poignant for it being so rousing, 'Burning Sky', which tackles the same theme from both a more adult and a more conservative perspective ("There's no time for dreams when commerce calls") to a vaguely oriental backdrop, the anti-war anthem 'Little Boy Soldiers' (with its unforgettable kiss off-line where the protagonist imagines his mother receiving his coffin with an attached letter saying "Please find enclosed one son, one medal and a note to say he won") and, best of the lot, 'The Eton Rifles', a song about class warfare with a lyric that approaches comedy – albeit bitter in nature – but whose music is thunderous and smoldering. Released as a single (in slightly less developed form), the latter became The Jam's first top ten UK hit, climbing to number three.

Though that quartet indicated that *Setting Sons* could have been an even better album if the concept had been pursued, there was still great music amongst the rest of the tracks. 'Private Hell' is a depiction of an empty-nester housewife that is brilliantly, if cruelly, observed and has appropriately relentless instrumentation. 'Wasteland' and 'Saturday's Kids' examine the dreariness of proletarian existence, the first melancholically, the second if not joyously then anthemically. 'Smithers-Jones', Foxton's sole writing contribution, is emblematic of the group's maturation: a re-recording of a song previously released on a B-side, it is transformed via a twenty piece orchestra. While Motown cover 'Heatwave' is a lazy choice for a closer – some of their stand-alone self-written singles and B-sides of the period would have been a more welcome presence – it's an undeniably powerful rendition. 'Girl On The Phone' – the opening glorified jingle – is the album's only dud.

The Jam no longer enjoy anything like the same status they did – the once supposedly discredited Clash have been posthumously rehabilitated by the critics who scorned them when extant and have over-hauled them in their affections – but the way they consistently triumphed in the British music weeklies' annual polls confirms that their standing and influence at the time was huge. If they weren't the proverbial voice of a generation – nobody can be, due to class and national differences – they certainly spoke for their young, working class and lower middle class audience magnificently well. They also triumphantly proved true the fundamental tenet of punk: that neither social commentary nor taking pride in one's indigenous culture rule out commercial success. - Sean Egan

88. London Calling
The Clash

TRACKLISTING
London Calling/Brand New Cadillac/Jimmy Jazz/Hateful/Rudie Can't Fail/Spanish Bombs/The Right Profile/Lost In The Supermarket/ Clampdown/The Guns of Brixton/Wrong 'Em Boyo/Death or Glory/ Koka Kola/The Card Cheat/Lover's Rock/Four Horsemen/I'm Not Down/Revolution Rock/Train in Vain

RELEASED
US: January 1980 UK: December 1979

PRODUCED BY
Guy Stevens

While the status of *London Calling* is now assured, it was in no way universally greeted as a classic upon its release. An example, if an extreme one, of the vitriol that was aimed at it from some quarters is provided by the comments of *New Musical Express* writer Barney Hoskyns who in a live review stated that "the only track of real merit" on the double-set was the cover job 'Brand New Cadillac'.

From today's perspective such comments about an album that is plainly quite magnificent seem absurd. But the fact of musical excellence was not the issue in those extraordinary, posturing times, nor that The Clash had produced a double album but successfully insisted on it being made available to their fans for the price of a single record. A significant number of critics decided to perceive *London Calling* as an atrocious betrayal of punk principles. Why? The Clash had gone *American*.

The shadow of the band's debut album's 'I'm So Bored With The USA' loomed large, as did the fact that they and their punk contemporaries had made a virtue out of how British they were. So much so that the fact that they continued to sing in their own English accents and that the album had a considerable reggae element (a form of music that then had made almost no inroads in the States) were deemed irrelevant in the face of the sacrilege of The Clash now frequently employing slick production methods and sounding not unlike the early '70s Rolling Stones. The exuberant tone of the album also rankled with some. How could a punk band sound happy?

And for that matter, how could they use keyboards and horns? Minimalism and miserablism had initially defined punk – the you - can - do - it - too philosophy and the insistence of social realism made them do so by default – but they were a straitjacket the band were throwing off. Though their music continued to acknowledge and discuss the harsh realities of the lives of their fans, it had also become glossy, melodic, generous and warm.

In one sense, slickness was something The Clash could hardly help: while they were never musically maladroit in the first instance, with practice inevitably comes greater competence. The band that recorded *London Calling* (now with Topper Headon on drums) were a dozen times more proficient than the group who had made *The Clash*.

And evidentially a dozen times wiser. They had realized that social commentary wasn't merely a matter of creating anthems that railed against their alleged oppressors. It could also involve thoughtfulness and acknowledgement of shades of gray.

The band began rehearsing what would be the follow-up to their second, hard rock-oriented, album *Give 'Em Enough Rope* at a quiet rehearsal space in Pimlico, London. Recording proper began

Mick Jones and Joe Strummer on stage.

at Wessex Studios in late August '79 and the album was finished – bar the mixing – a month later. Ex-Mott The Hoople manager Guy Stevens officially helmed the controls but eyewitnesses claim that it was really a Mick Jones/Bill Price production job. Certainly the resulting album bears Price's trademark sound: the same widescreen, larger-than-life attributes as late Mott The Hoople albums, on which Price also engineered. *London Calling* is in fact one of the best produced albums of all time, quite amazingly rich and layered and sublimely mixed. The combination of this and its joyous music makes it easily the most accessible thing The Clash released in their career.

Great tracks abound but a few deserve special mention. The title track – a hit single – is a haunting and breathless recounting of a nuclear catastrophe. 'Brand New Cadillac' is greasy, dirty rock 'n' roll with a fantastic over-the-top Simonon bass riff. 'Jimmy Jazz' explores tensions between ethnic minorities and the police in a horn-augmented quasi-swing number with a blissful strutting instrumental break. Simonon's debut song-writing effort 'The Guns Of Brixton' tackles a similar theme to a menacing reggae arrangement. 'Rudie Can't Fail' comes across like a smorgasbord of different musical styles: reggae, rock, jazz and even a tinge of calypso. 'Spanish Bombs' explores the issue of terrorism. One album before, The Clash would have devised a thunderous accompaniment for the latter song. Now, they come up with a track employing the smooth-rolling, tasteful attributes of soft rock, as they also do on 'Lost In The Supermarket'. 'Lover's Rock' is a track with a gorgeous summery air and saucy songwords.

The two biggest indicators of how The Clash had changed as both musicians and people are 'Death Or Glory', whose lyric exposes the way youthful idealism and No Compromise stances are eroded by the realities of life, and 'The Card Cheat', the heart-rending tale of a man who tries to find fortune through devious means but − fatally − doesn't realize he is out of his depth. The backing for the latter track? Spector-like pomp.

The album closes with an emotionally and musically devastating triumvirate. Jones' confessional 'I'm Not Down' is a stupendously powerful and moving affirmation of life in the face of adversity. The re-write of the Jackie Edwards reggae 'Revolution Rock' sees Strummer castigate the rock-hearted Kingston gangsters who make the lot of the poor unbearable. When he describes people dying of malnutrition while "cargo food goes rolling by", his voice cracks with emotion. After leaving us emotionally exhausted with those two numbers, the mellow ambience of soul ballad 'Train In Vain' acts like a soothing balm on our exhausted, wracked emotions.

A quarter of a century removed from the rather earnest times that were the afterglow of punk, then-burning issues now seem quaint. What continues to matter is the music. *London Calling* can now be recognized not as the album on which The Clash spat in the fact of punk but on which they reinvented it, proving that it was about a social and artistic conscience − not about three chords and a studied gloom. The album also in a sense redefined rock music, whose template was previously the copyright of the Rolling Stones. Though both bands were true believers in the validity of rock 'n' roll grit and rebellion, where the Stones were usually contemptuous, The Clash were usually tender-hearted and where the Stones were haughty, The Clash were streetwise. In short, The Clash had become what the Rolling Stones would have been if the Stones had come after punk rather than caused it. - Sean Egan

89. Closer
Joy Division

TRACKLISTING
Atrocity Exhibition/Isolation/Passover/Colony/A Means To And End/ Heart And Soul/Twenty Four Hours/The Eternal/Decades

RELEASED
US: December 1980 UK: July 1980

PRODUCED BY
Martin Hannett

They made some of the most depressing music ever created with a lead singer who sounded as though he were barely able to raise his voice amid the weight of all his sorrows. Frontman Ian Curtis's gloomy persona was, it turns out, no mere affectation: he hanged himself in May of 1980 two months before this album's release, which only raises the chill factor. In *Closer* (a title that can, interestingly, be taken two ways: as in proximity to something or in the final act of somebody or something) Joy Division fuse the emotional intensity of punk with a raw, desolate lyrical style.

Though viewed as a post-punk new wave band, Smashing Pumpkins' frontman Billy Corgan once made the claim that Joy Division was, of all things, a heavy metal band: "Peter Hook [bassist] told me they were basically trying to make a primitive version of Black Sabbath and Led Zeppelin, whereas today's bands just want to sound exactly like Joy Division without understanding the heaviness of them."

Recording for the indie label Factory Records, the Manchester-based quartet – comprised of Curtis, Hook, guitarist-keyboardist Bernard Sumner and drummer Stephen Morris – started out as an edgier punk outfit named Warsaw before changing their name to Joy Division, a creepy moniker derived from the name given to the prostitution units reserved for Jewish sex slaves in Nazi concentration camps. Joy Division's first album, 1979's haunting *Unknown Pleasures*, draws on chilly European synth soundscapes *a la* Kraftwerk but with an added emotional angst. But it is *Closer*, Joy Division's second album, that best encapsulates the band's grimly somber approach. Slower and even bleaker than its predecessor, *Closer* does not make for an easy listen, though the catchy guitar/synth pop has its moments of driving urgency. Blanketed in existential dread and with its icy synthesizers creating a stark air, the album is unrelentingly grim. You could say that *Closer* was Curtis' dark night of the soul. He sings in a ghostly baritone that sounds strangely distant, as though he were disembodied, barely tethered to the earth, and in some ways that is true. *Closer* is the sound of a man letting go. It's there in the suicidal despair of 'Passover', the funereal anxiety of 'The Eternal', the chilling ambience of 'Decades' ("We knocked on the doors of Hell's darker chambers," goes one line). *Closer* is an album utterly lacking in the comic element one finds in even Morrissey's most self-pitying laments. The album's opener 'Atrocity Exhibition' in which Curtis creepily intones, "This is the way, step inside," says it all. Though some who knew him insist Curtis wasn't such a gloomy guy in real life, he was clearly a troubled soul. Consider the deep despondency expressed in 'Twenty Four Hours' ("Now the reason's ceased for life").

It is worth noting that nothing on *Closer* approaches the brilliance of the eerily prophetic Joy Division single 'Love Will Tear Us Apart' that preceded *Closer's* release. Like 'Twenty Four Hours', it reads like a suicide note, so would have been a perfect fit for this album. By the time he made *Closer*, Curtis's problems had clearly begun to overwhelm him. Prone to epileptic fits that required medication that only worsened his mood swings, his affair with a Belgian girlfriend had broken his marriage apart. With the added stress of a looming American tour on his mind, Curtis hanged himself in the kitchen of his home, aged 23. Joy Division called it quits a few months later. Their remaining members went on to greater success in the rock/synthesizer outfit New Order.

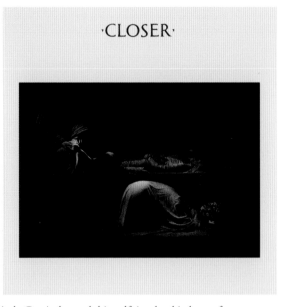

Peter Saville's funereal cover design for *Closer*.

The early death of Curtis only increased Joy Division's mystique, making them all the more attractive to their similarly angst-ridden followers and setting the template for the moody merchants of gloom that followed in their wake. The pronounced melancholy as epitomized on *Closer* inspired groups with a gloomy self-absorbed bent (think goth rockers – never mind that visually Joy Division didn't dress the part). Bono has cited them as an inspiration and once humbly proclaimed he wasn't in Curtis's league. *Closer's* influence can be felt in the moody, atmospheric soundscapes of U2's *Boy* and *The Joshua Tree*, the works of Echo And The Bunnymen, The Psychedelic Furs and The Cure. Even Paul Weller once admitted that the intensity of The Jam's driving 'Private Hell' was his attempt at creating a Joy Division song. The band's influence has continued to be felt in the 1990s in the work of Nine Inch Nails (who covered 'Dead Souls' for the soundtrack of the 1994 movie *The Crow* based on the graphic novel by James O'Barr who, incidentally, took Curtis and the music of Joy Division as his inspiration) as well as Moby, Smashing Pumpkins and Radiohead, whose frontman Thom Yorke's spasmodic stage moves and haunting stare are reminiscent of Ian Curtis.

No band has ever come close to plumbing the depths of despair quite like Joy Division did, though. In that department, they were in a league of their own. - Tierney Smith

90. Dare!

The Human League

TRACKLISTING
The Things That Dreams Are Made Of/Open Your Heart/The Sound Of The Crowd/Darkness/Do Or Die/Get Carter/I Am The Law/Seconds/Love Action (I Believe In Love)/Don't You Want Me

RELEASED
US: February 1982 UK: October 1981

PRODUCED BY
Martin Rushent, The Human League

A year before the recording of *Dare!*, things were looking bleak for the Human League. Since their 1977 formation, the group had been moderately successful, producing electronic music that was heavily influenced by Kraftwerk, with a rather pretentious lyrical approach. However, founder members Martin Ware and Ian Marsh had just left to form the group that would become Heaven 17. Having recently signed to Virgin, singer Phil Oakey and 'Director Of Visuals' Philip Adrian Wright found that they were the only personnel left to fulfill a European tour the League were committed to. Oakey's solution was to recruit bassist Ian Burden and, famously, two schoolgirls he had met in a Sheffield nightclub, Susanne Sulley and Joanne Catherall, to sing back-up vocals. Guitarist Jo Callis later completed the new line-up. A last-ditch gamble by Oakey, the somewhat unexpected result of the band's reshuffle was world domination.

Electronic music at this stage was mostly a rather dour affair, reflecting the theoretical and anti-emotional approach of Kraftwerk and David Bowie's Berlin period. By 1980, disco was rapidly becoming unfashionable and the flamboyant and theatrical approach to electronic music that had been created by Giorgio Moroder in his recordings with Donna Summer was not favored by underground creators of synth music such as the original line-up of the Human League. The band's early material had adopted the Kraftwerk approach to words – celebrating the machine rather than the human, and focusing on weird or science-fiction ideas. But while Kraftwerk's avoidance of introspection and a utobiographical subjects seemed to mesh perfectly with their *avant-garde* electronic approach, it was also a limiting factor in what electronic music could achieve. Without the personal, emotional aspect of pop music, electronic music was unable to make deep connections to listeners. However, working with producer Martin Rushent, the new Human League started to create electronic music that was far more open and emotional, more personal and joyful, than its precedents. This was classic melodic,

hook-heavy pop but rendered with synthesizers. At the time the band were identified as part of the New Romantic movement, but their enduring influence was to be prime movers in shaping the genre of electro-pop.

The *Dare!* line-up of The Human League.

Oakey's lyrics were still clumsy at times on the songs recorded for *Dare!*, and some of the music was still intense and moody ('I Am The Law', 'Seconds'). In truth, part of the change in the band was simply a presentational one. Having female backing singers made them look more like an old style soul or pop ensemble and this in itself changed the audience's perceptions. But *Dare!* did contain huge pop songs the League would never before have countenanced. 'Sound Of The Crowd' and 'Love Action' are perfect dancefloor numbers that cleverly use electronic sounds to create a disco-influenced stomp. 'Open Your Heart' was also a hit, and again showed a lyrical progression. The early Human League simply couldn't have recorded a romantic song like 'Open Your Heart'.

Of course, the major international breakthrough hit was 'Don't You Want Me'. A throw-away recording, with the lyrics based on a photo love-story Oakey had read in a comic book, the band didn't want it released as *Dare!*'s fourth single, but thankfully the record company got their way. Its cheesy story, classic synth riffs, and insanely catchy chorus would probably have been enough to make it a hit even without the attendant faintly ludicrous but oddly moving video which saw the girls emoting, strutting and posing their way through the song's narrative while Oakey glowered through his peculiar lop-sided fringe. The video seemed tailor-made for the still new MTV, which played it on heavy rotation. To this day the song sounds brilliant, anthemic and iconic. *Dare!* was already a success, but it was 'Don't You Want Me' that took the band to number one in both the UK and the US.

Looking back, the Human League can seem a bit ridiculous, in spite of the enduring appeal of some of their best songs. But they were a breakthrough act for electronic music, with pop-oriented synth bands such as Depeche Mode, Erasure, Visage, Blancmange, and The Pet Shop Boys achieving success in their wake. By bringing a chart sensibility to electro, they also paved the way for the pop crossover of the New Romantic movement, with bands like Duran Duran and Spandau Ballet. Along with their contemporaries Soft Cell, they brought a human, romantic angle to music created using supposedly charmless synthesized sounds. Twenty years later, one could still hear their influence in another band from Sheffield that utilized two-finger keyboard lines to great effect: Pulp's bedsit romanticism owes a significant debt to the Human League. As do a few of the latest crop of post-punk revivalists.

'Blue Monday' by New Order is often cited as the key record that merged the sounds of disco with the more credible post-punk tradition, and by doing so laid the foundations of the dance music of the late 'Eighties and early 'Nineties. But the Human League were there first. Starting from music that was intellectual and serious and support slots with gloom-mongers like Siouxsie And The Banshees, the band moved within a few short years to embracing the best parts of the disco movement and to making electronic music that was fun and sensuous. Theirs were clever records, brilliantly conceived and recorded. But they were also dancefloor hits and unashamed singalongs that helped to establish electro-pop as a viable, hugely commercial genre. - Hugh Barker

91. Thriller
Michael Jackson

TRACKLISTING
Wanna Be Startin' Somethin'/Baby Be Mine/The Girl Is Mine/Thriller/ Beat It/Billie Jean/Human Nature/P.Y.T. (Pretty Young Thing)/The Lady In My Life

RELEASED
US: December 1982 UK: December 1982

PRODUCED BY
Brian Banks, Michael Jackson, Quincy Jones

Thriller turned Michael Jackson's life upside down.

Already one of the most famous figures in pop music, after a childhood either enriched or destroyed (depending on your perspective) by years spent in the public eye with his four brothers as the Jackson 5, his second collaboration with producer Quincy Jones took him to a level of superstardom that remains unequalled in the history of popular music. Reliable figures are impossible to obtain, but by most reckonings, *Thriller* is the biggest-selling album of all time, *Guinness World Records* guesstimating its current sales at in excess of 51 million, very likely a conservative number. (It's worth bearing in mind that even at the height of his huckster powers, Colonel Tom Parker could only dream of "50,000,000 Elvis fans".) In the US it was, as of April 2005, certified a staggering 27 times platinum; it stayed in the *Billboard* top 10 for an entire year; seven tracks – there are only nine on the album – were released as singles, and all made the *Billboard* top 10. The word "Godlike" is bandied around in pop writing almost as lazily as "genius", but *Thriller* gave Jackson the sort of numbers even some major religions don't have. The impact it had on music, music-making and, perhaps even more pivotally, on the marketing of music (the videos from *Thriller* shattered MTV's unofficial color bar once and for all) is considerable and fundamental. It smashed boundaries and disproved most preconceived notions of music-buying demographics, proving that pop could transcend race and genre.

Recording began in April 1982, but the genesis of the record went back way earlier, to the first time Jones and Jackson worked together on *The Wiz* soundtrack album. The pair got along famously, in no small part because the experienced and gifted Jones, who had worked with everyone from Frank Sinatra to Aretha Franklin, was able to respond to the growing former child star – whose need to find self-expression was constrained by his uncertainty about speaking out – as both equal and mentor. Jackson had to demand that his label, Epic, sanction Jones as producer for his 1979 album, *Off The Wall*: the suits were concerned that the veteran, with his background in jazz only recently augmented by producing platinum albums for the Brothers Johnson, would give Jackson a sound out of step with the disco era. Instead, Jones and the team he dubbed "the Killer Q Posse" – the songwriter and former Heatwave member Rod Temperton, engineer Bruce Swedien, keyboard virtuoso Greg Phillinganes, trumpet player and arranger Jerry Hey, Brothers Johnson bassist Louis Johnson, drummer John Robinson

Michael Jackson, pictured on the cover of *Thriller*.

and percussionist Paolinho Da Costa – fashioned a discofied masterpiece, one that is probably *Thriller*'s superior in terms of overall quality, a record that sold ten million copies in quick time and became the biggest-selling album by a black artist.

In the middle of the sessions for *Thriller*, Jackson and Jones found themselves diverted by an offer from Stephen Spielberg to write and record a song for an album to tie in to his film *E. T.* Clearance for the manager-less Jackson to appear on the record had not been obtained, causing legal chaos, and by the time the logjam was eventually broken, Jones and Spielberg were not speaking. The drama had also shaved all but two months off the time frame for making the already pressured follow-up to *Off The Wall*.

Temperton and Jones went through an astounding number of songs to find suitable material – Jones maintains the number of ideas considered was in excess of 600 – and Jackson was writing too. The deadline imminent, and in response to Jones' urging him to try his hand at a pop-rock song in the vein of The Knack's 'My Sharona', Jackson reluctantly played Jones a demo. The song, 'Beat It', not only made the album, it almost caused a conflagration in the studio, Swedien noticing flames coming out of a studio speaker during one of Michael's vocal takes. Eddie Van Halen supplied a guitar solo, during hectic sessions where three studios were working simultaneously.

The desperation had been ratcheted up several notches by the release of the album's first single, 'The Girl Is Mine', ahead of *Thriller*'s completion, and the Killer Qs did not put the album to bed until 9am on deadline day. Three hours later they were distraught to discover that the mastered record sounded, in Jones's estimation, like "24-karat sonic doo-doo". They had over-filled the vinyl on the album's two sides, and had to hastily edit several tracks – excising chunks from 'Billie Jean'"s intro, and an entire verse from 'The Lady In My Life'.

The story of the album's recording and its sales figures are indeed remarkable, but nobody would remember *Thriller* had the music not been of the strength it is. This is a record with something for everyone – from the taut, confrontational funk of the opener, 'Wanna Be Startin' Somethin'', through 'Beat It'"s rock dalliances, the pure pop of the Paul McCartney duet 'The Girl Is Mine'; the lengthy title track, written by Temperton to his 'Boogie Nights' template, and featuring a rap by Vincent Price; and, perhaps best of all, 'Billie Jean'. According to Jones' autobiography, Jackson claimed that the inspiration for 'Billie Jean'"s lyric came after a female fan had broken in to his garden and subsequently tried to sue him for maintenance payments for a child. Jones reputedly thought the title should be altered – because people might think the song was about tennis player Billie Jean King. None of which bothered the record buying public, or altered this record's triumphant place in pop history. - Angus Batey

92. Run-D.M.C.
Run-D.M.C.

TRACKLISTING
Hard Times/Rock Box/Jam-Master Jay/Hollis Crew (Krush-Groove 2)/Sucker M.C.'s (Krush-Groove 1)/It's Like That/Wake Up/30 Days/Jay's Game

RELEASED
US: June 1984 UK: May 1985

PRODUCED BY
Russell Simmons, Larry Smith

While Public Enemy's Chuck D is fond of describing his band as hip hop's Rolling Stones, he has also been known to suggest that Run-D.M.C. are the genre's Beatles. Such comparisons are always at least a little suspect but this one does at least offer a glimpse, for the outsider, of the Queens, New York, trio's pivotal importance.

In the emerging realm of rap historiography, the release of Run-D.M.C.'s third LP, *Raising Hell*, is increasingly seen as the starting point for what has become known as the music's golden age. That 1986 record turned the Homburg-hatted band into global pop stars, courtesy of a string of strong songs, simplistic but inspired sampling and an unforgettable collaboration on wax and video with the then faded rock stars Aerosmith. It also showed that hip hop albums could sell as well as rock records, and could be made and marketed with a run of singles in just the same way. Creatively, it proved that sampling, if used imaginatively and with some intelligence as well as musical savvy, could be a liberating compositional tool, and turned hip hop into the most democratizing force in music-making since punk's decrying of old-fashioned virtues of practice and technique. The album galvanized New York in particular, turning rap fans on to the possibilities of becoming artists, and making extant acts step their games up to a higher level of creative proficiency. It was, all in all, a benchmark release, and the group, who made a further four albums before being formally disbanded by lead rapper Joseph "Run" Simmons in the wake of the still unsolved murder of band member DJ Jason "Jam Master Jay" Mizell in 2002, would never better it.

But while it was their finest hour, *Raising Hell* was not Run-D.M.C.'s most influential record. That accolade goes to their first, self-titled, album, one begun when the group were still officially a duo, with a regular guest DJ, before they conspired with Rick Rubin to

meld rock and rap in a homogenous, sample-based setting, even before they named themselves "Kings Of Rock" and shot a video where they stomped through a fictitious pop museum, deriding the stars whose careers they'd come to trample all over. Rather than form one bookend to an arbitrary period in rap history, this album marked a decisive, seismic change in the music's foundations. *Run-D.M.C.* is now looked on as the release that separates rap's old school from everything that followed. The distinction, to all but rap devotees, might seem arbitrary, confusing, even pointless but to anyone with more than a passing interest, this is hip hop's most crucial dividing line – as fundamental a point in the music's timeline as the birth of Christ is to the western calendar. Its release changed everything, though this was not necessarily recognized at the time.

     Friends from school days, Joe Simmons and Darryl McDaniels – soon to abandon the nickname Grandmaster Get High in favor of an

Run D.M.C. pictured on the cover of their eponymous debut album.

acronym based on his initials: D.M.C. – began listening to rap music at block parties in the area they grew up in, the Hollis district of the New York borough of Queens. Joe – who went by the name Run – had an in into the nascent rap business: his brother, Russell, hosted parties, and managed Kurtis Blow, the first rapper to sign a deal with a major label. Run had DJ-ed for Blow and understood the rudiments of the rapper's craft. McDaniels, meanwhile, had begun to write rhymes, and the pair would practice in his basement, honing songs, rapping to beats cut back and forth on a pair of turntables. After months of pestering, Russell eventually decided to let his brother try to make a record. Using a beat created by bass player Larry Smith, an experienced musician with a home studio, and a group called Orange Krush, who had been working on tracks for Kurtis Blow, Simmons took lyrics McDaniels had written and doled them out between the two aspirant rappers, two lines at a time. After a little work, they had even fashioned a chorus, giving this absolutely stark, almost mechanical slice of pared-down hip hop some serious potential. The track, 'It's Like That', became the duo's first single, paired with another, even more rudimentary cut, 'Sucker M.C.'s (Krush-Groove 1)', on what became one of the most important and influential rap singles ever released.

In truth, there's not much more to *Run-D.M.C.* than that: two guys shouting rhyming couplets over hard drums and minimal sound effects. 'Jam-Master Jay', recorded after the first single, when Jay was becoming a fully-fledged member of the group, adds some limited sampling and Jay's brutal, heavy scratch work, showing how the turntable – hip hop's quintessential musical instrument – could be used to apply both melody and percussion to the musical mix. But by reducing the music to its elements, and being true to the aesthetic of those early park jams from which rap first emerged, Run-D.M.C. revolutionized the form. Before them, rap records had tended to use live bands to replay the records DJs used in the park jams: 'It's Like That', 'Sucker M.C.'s' and this debut album – an unexpected commercial success at a time when rap was viewed very much as a singles-only music – showed that the art form could be both creatively successful and commercially viable, so long as its makers remembered to stay true to the music's sonic and cultural values. They would innovate in other areas – as vocalists, as lyricists, even as sartorial ambassadors for an emerging street culture – but it is here that Run-D.M.C. made their biggest impact. Everything that came after in the rap world had to choose whether to respond or react to their template. - Angus Batey

If Loving You Is Wrong, I Don't Want To Be Right

There are some songs that one is embarrassed to be caught singing, songs that will never be cool but which - in your heart of hearts - you know you love. Twenty **guilty pleasures**...

1.	**The Most Beautiful Girl**	Charlie Rich
2.	**The Young Ones**	Cliff Richard
3.	**Downtown**	Petula Clark
4.	**I Got You Babe**	Sonny & Cher
5.	**Yummy Yummy Yummy**	Ohio Express
6.	**Seasons In The Sun**	Terry Jacks
7.	**Stand By Your Man**	Tammy Wynette
8.	**Close To You**	The Carpenters
9.	**Crazy Horses**	The Osmonds
10.	**Angelo**	Brotherhood Of Man
11.	**Copacabana (At The Copa)**	Barry Manilow
12.	**Sweet Sweet Heart**	The Vibrators
13.	**Evil Woman**	Electric Light Orchestra
14.	**Easy**	The Commodores
15.	**Video Killed The Radio Star**	Buggles
16.	**Kings Of The Wild Frontier**	Adam And The Ants
17.	**Jack And Diane**	John Cougar
18.	**Wild Boys**	Duran Duran
19.	**China In Your Hand**	T'pau
20.	**I'm Too Sexy**	Right Said Fred

93. Like A Virgin
Madonna

TRACKLISTING

Material Girl/Angel/Like A Virgin/Over And Over/Love Don't Live Here
Anymore/Dress You Up/Shoo-Bee-Doo/Pretender/Stay★
[★ The single 'Into The Groove' was added to some later editions.]

RELEASED

US: November 1984 UK: November 1984

PRODUCED BY

Madonna, Stephen Bray, Nile Rodgers

Like A Virgin was the second album by singer Madonna Ciccone and
her first certified smash. It introduced two of her biggest hits, the title song
and 'Material Girl,' but more importantly it introduced the persona of
Madonna, which ultimately was larger than the album.

Prior to *Like a Virgin*, Madonna had been considered a disco act
with only minor potential, but the huge success of this album proved
that she was a pop star. Additionally, that her stardom was assisted by a
series of memorable videos accompanying its singles, proved that she
was a very modern pop star, a true MTV generation icon. Madonna
dedicated the album to "all the virgins of the world", but that line was
a typically calculated move on the part of someone who then had a 'tarty'
public persona to create headlines. Still, *Like a Virgin* is Madonna's best
overall album.

The reason this album works, where others by her don't, is that
she has chosen material in her vocal range – mostly dance numbers that
don't require Celine Dion histrionics. One critic once described her voice
as sounding like "Minnie Mouse on helium", but that can't be said about
this album. *Like A Virgin* proves that 'Madge', as the tabloids called her,
can sing. Unfortunately, as Madonna's persona took over her music later
in her career, her skill has been overshadowed by her celebrity.

Madonna switches producers the way Cher switches outfits, and
on *Like A Virgin* she uses both Stephen Bray and Nile Rodgers. Rodgers,
known for his work with Chic, David Bowie, and Diana Ross, knows
exactly how to pump up the diva-ness here without going over the top.
And Rodgers – who was responsible for many of the best dance hits of
the 'Seventies – adds just enough of the disco flavor to entice dancing, yet
he doesn't outshine Madonna to become the star of this record himself.

Many artists have a second album slump, finding it hard to

develop material quickly after a successful debut. *Like A Virgin*, however, is the best collection of songs Madonna ever put on one album - though obviously the fact that she had a good team of writers, including Stephen Bray, Peter Brown, Tom Kelly, Robert Rans and Billy Steinberg, helped somewhat. The title track is magnificent, with the coy sexuality never played too far. 'Material Girl' is a hard-faced hymn to money and dismissal of romance utterly in tune with the spirit of the 'Eighties, even if it is sonically more like Cyndi Lauper than Madonna. 'Angel' and 'Over And Over' joined those two tracks on the hit parade. Though there are a couple of thro aways on the album, that's a better percentage than Madonna's latest albums, whichboast one hit and eleven duds.

Madonna Louise
Veronica Ciccone.

The best song on *Like A Virgin* didn't appear on all pressings. The initial US album did not include 'Into The Groove,' which was found on the soundtrack to *Desperately Seeking Susan* (Madonna's best film, though that praise is obviously not saying much). 'Into The Groove' is, without question, Madonna's single best song, a track that combines her talent for rhythm with a plaintive vocal that shows a softer side to the diva. Like some of the other songs on *Like a Virgin*, it displays a more vulnerable side of the artist. You can actually believe here that she cares whether the man she seeks loves her or not; her yearning seems for once real and unaffected.

Like a Virgin was a hit the moment it was released, with the title track becoming Madonna's first number one single. It went on to become one of the best-selling albums of the year, though the record, and the music contained herein, was quickly overshadowed by Madonna's star turn as a paparazzi target. A month after *Like A Virgin* was released, she was more famous for her outrageous clothes and boyfriends than she was for her singing. She debuted the song 'Like A Virgin' at the first MTV Video Music Awards show. As might be expected, her outfit and movements that night drew more attention than her singing performance. She wore a white wedding dress and as she writhed around on the floor her panties and garter belt were exposed. She was also wearing a belt that read "Boy Toy", as she was on the cover to *Like A Virgin*. It was brilliant marketing but it served to eclipse the music. At the awards show that year, Madonna lost all the awards

295

she was nominated for. That hardly mattered: once Madge had been launched, she was unstoppable.

Madonna's music has been influential, but only insofar as that of any massively successful star becomes by a process of osmosis: she was not the first at anything but certainly popularized and made more viable the mediums she operated in. Her main influence has been on the way women in music are viewed by the public, the media and – perhaps most importantly, for the way she has widened boundaries for female artists – the industry. Rarely will one find an article on Madonna that doesn't include words and phrases like "feisty", "tough cookie", "no-nonsense" and "confident". If she wasn't the first woman to be completely in charge of her career and her image, she may as well have been because – for people too young to remember her antecedents – she is perceived that way. This perception itself comes partly from being arguably the most successful female artist of all time. Many have a problem with her being seen as either a heavyweight artist (she is dependent on others for songs, although does often write good lyrics) or a feminist (she must be the most saucily clad women's liberationist in history) but, there again, that sort of controversy has itself always been a part of what Madonna is about. - Charles R. Cross

94. Graceland
Paul Simon

TRACKLISTING
The Boy In The Bubble/Graceland/I Know What I Know/Gumboots/Diamonds On The Soles Of Her Shoes/You Can Call Me Al/Under African Skies/Homeless/Crazy Love, Vol. II/That Was Your Mother/All Around The World or The Myth Of Fingerprints

RELEASED
US: September 1986 UK: September 1986

PRODUCED BY
Paul Simon

The late Rolling Stones guitarist Brian Jones promoted traditional Moroccan music in the form of 1971's posthumous album *Brian Jones Presents The Pan Pipes Of Joujouka*, the earliest example of a Western pop musician promoting a 'world' music sound. In the early 1980s UK artists like Bow Wow Wow and Adam Ant anchored their songs with a Burundi beat, while Talking Heads' 1980 album *Remain In Light* boasted a strong world music dynamic. However, it took Paul Simon's *Graceland* to show the world how commercially viable such an artistic enterprise could be.

Paul Simon was already incorporating world elements into his music long before his all-out embrace of it on *Graceland*. In fact, he had been making forays into a variety of eclectic rhythms for pretty much the better part of his career. 1970's *Bridge Over Troubled Water*, his last studio record with Art Garfunkel prior to the duo's breakup, contained his arrangement of an 18th century Peruvian folk melody 'El Condor Pasa (If I Could)', which Simon recorded with Peruvian folk instrumentalists Los Incas. They would rejoin him on 'Duncan', a standout track from his eponymous 1972 debut

The original cover design for *Graceland*.

PAUL · SIMON
GRACELAND

(an album that contained further musical exotica in the reggae-flavored 'Mother And Child Reunion').

The catalyst for what would turn out to be Simon's musical *tour de force* was a tape of South African music given to him by a friend which reminded Simon of the exuberant spirit of 1950s rock 'n' roll. Suitably impressed, Simon set about traveling to South Africa where he met Joseph Shabalala, leader of the 10-man *a cappella* vocal troupe Ladysmith Black Mambazo. The group had recorded a number of albums in the 1970s and 1980s in their harmony rich Soweto-based form of traditional South African street music known as Mbaqanga, but it was their association with Simon that would win them some long overdue recognition from the rest of the world. Simon said at the time that *Graceland* was aimed at promoting both the rich musical culture of South Africa and its people. He was aiming high in his stated desire to get his generation to take notice, given that he felt literature and movies had supplanted music as an illuminating force. "If I don't make this really interesting," Simon said at the time, "then, well, maybe it will sell a half a million albums, but I won't have any effect on the thinking." In fact, he succeeded – while also revealing how, given the right collaborating partners, an already inspired artist could be pushed to new heights of creativity.

Simon's trip to South Africa was a move that would engender a good deal of controversy, with him coming under fire for defying the U.N. cultural boycott imposed against the then prevailing apartheid regime by recording in Johannesburg. (Given that Simon was merely showcasing the talents of South African musicians, the United Nations' anti-apartheid committee refused to condemn him.)

Recorded at various studios in the US, UK and South Africa, *Graceland* blends African rhythms with conventional pop formats that serve to make them more accessible to Western ears. The album's melodious guitar lines, tribal drums, bouncy accordion riffs and breathtaking harmonies make for an intoxicating brew. Always a literate writer, Simon's lyrics take on an allegorical, non-linear approach here. On 'I Know What I Know' (featuring punchy female harmonies from The Gaza Sisters), he's the pithy observer, while 'Crazy Love Vol. II' and 'Gumboots' (the latter benefiting from the smooth vocal sounds of Soweto jive group The Boyoyo Boys) constitute pure comedy. Elsewhere we find the sheer poetry of 'Diamonds On The Soles Of Her Shoes', and a work of haunting, heartbreaking beauty in the form of the plaintive *a cappella* 'Homeless', which Simon co-wrote with Joseph Shabalala and which features stunning vocal work from Ladysmith Black Mambazo. Simon ends the album with exotica of a different stripe, the rousing Cajun zydeco 'That Was Your Mother' (backed by Good Rockin' Dopsie And The Twisters) and the conjunto sounds of 'All Around The World Or The Myth Of Fingerprints', for which he is partnered by East LA band Los Lobos.

Graceland topped the UK charts and climbed to #3 in the US. It was a 14 million-seller and spawned three hit singles ('Graceland', 'The Boy In The Bubble' and 'You Can Call Me Al'). For a while, it was perceived as an archetypal CD album, one of the releases indelibly associated with the compact disc via its status as one of that medium's first mega-sellers. Having placed world music on the map and in the consciousness of the mainstream record buying public like no other album before it, *Graceland*'s acceptance opened the doors for other artists to boldly promote their own world music projects. Talking Heads frontman David Byrne launched his Luaka Bop label in 1989 which specialized in a variety of Latin sounds. Peter Gabriel founded his Real World label that same year, which featured a variety of world artists. In 1992 Ry Cooder had a best-selling world album (*A Meeting By The River*) in collaboration with Indian musician V.M. Bhatt. *Billboard* magazine would go on to establish a world music chart and the Grammys (which awarded *Graceland* Album of the Year in 1987) instituted a world music section. Simon's role in raising the profile of world music facilitated its marketing and availability, with more broadcasting outlets including public radio and webcasting as well as radio programs devoted to the form, all of which has led to a growing interest in and support of non-Western music. In addition, artists as diverse as Dave Matthews, Shakira and Tool have incorporated world elements into their music.

Much heralded in its time, *Graceland*'s astonishingly effective fusion of pop songcraft and African rhythms remains one of the singular, most influential albums of the rock era. "These are the days of miracle and wonder," Simon sings in the hypnotic opening track 'The Boy In The Bubble'. From a musical standpoint, indeed it was. - Tierney Smith

95. It Takes A Nation of Millions To Hold Us Back
Public Enemy

TRACKLISTING
Countdown To Armageddon/Bring The Noise/Don't Believe The Hype/Cold Lampin' With Flavor/Terminator X To The Edge Of Panic/Mind Terrorist/Louder Than A Bomb/Caught, Can We Get A Witness?/Show 'Em Whatcha Got/She Watch Channel Zero?!/Night Of The Living Baseheads/Black Steel In The Hour Of Chaos/Security Of The First World/Rebel Without A Pause/Prophets Of Rage/Party For Your Right To Fight

RELEASED
US: April 1988 UK: April 1988

PRODUCED BY
Hank Shocklee, Carl Ryder, Eric (Vietnam) Sadler

With their blend of musical ingenuity, lyrical power, perfectly conceptualized image and contrasting personnel, Public Enemy may have been the greatest group of all time – rock, rap, all-comers.

Formed in the mid-1980s by denizens of a Long Island college radio station-cum-sound system, Spectrum City, the band solidified into two separate entities. There was the studio team, led by producer Hank "Shocklee" Boxley, and including Eric Sadler and Bill Stephney, who constructed the noisescapes Shocklee later memorably called "music's worst nightmare"; then there was PE's live manifestation, with the DJ, Norman "Terminator X" Rogers, holding court at the back of the stage, with vocalist William "Flavor Flav" Drayton flanked by the group's Minister Of Information, Richard "Professor Griff" Griffin, and his posse of militarily-garbed dancers, The Security Of The First World. The common thread linking both entities was Carlton "Chuck D" Ridenhour, the group's front man, conceptual lynchpin and lead rapper, who also, under the alias Carl Ryder, helped make the music. Graphic designer Chuck even designed the band's logo: in many respects he *was* – and still is – Public Enemy.

The two entities united on this second album in a way they didn't manage before and haven't since. The group, who had initially resisted entreaties to sign to a label, eventually gave in to extensive cajoling from Def Jam Records founder Rick Rubin, who overruled his partner, Russell Simmons, to offer the group a deal. Convinced that rap could take Chuck's message – a convoluted, often contrary and sometimes confusing amalgamation of black power-era sentiment with an increasingly militant black nationalism – to the people, PE relented, opting to attempt to subvert the music industry from within. Their first LP, Yo! *Bum Rush The Show*, was an attempt at insinuating the group into the then burgeoning hip hop universe, but by the time it was released in 1987 it had been sitting on the shelf for months, following Def Jam striking a deal with the major label Columbia, which though it gave the former indie wide distribution also meant their records had to take their place in the queue between the parent company's cash cows.

Frustrated as late 1980s New York rap moved on without them, Chuck and Hank took matters into their own hands. Inspired by the need to out-do Eric B & Rakim's 'I Know You Got Soul', which Chuck then felt was "the best fuckin' record I had ever heard in my fuckin' life", they upped their own ante by looping a sample from the opening of 'The Grunt', a single by James Brown's backing band, The JB's (locking himself away at home writing lyrics to an endless tape of the replaying sample, Chuck was interrupted by his mother, who thought he had left a kettle on the boil), applying it to a drum beat based around another Brown beat ('Funky Drummer'), and created their first signature song, 'Rebel Without A Pause'. The track was hot, but it had to be released straight away: needing permission from Simmons to add the track to the B-side of the *Yo!* single, 'You're Gonna Get Yours', the band discovered he was on his way to Europe with Run-D.M.C. Chuck drove to the airport and tried to speak to

Public Enemy at the 1988 Montreux Rock Festival.

Simmons, but could only get to Run, Russell's brother, but Run told them to just do it regardless. Released six weeks later, the record was an instant sensation, catapulting PE to the forefront of the New York rap revolution. Russell was livid... at first.

That ...*Nation*... sounds very much like a live album is no accident. 'Bring The Noise', written deliberately so that the band had something of a more uptempo, rock-ish number to play live, gave the record an early impetus, as did 'Rebel...', which begins with a sample of Jesse Jackson speaking to the crowd at the Wattstax festival held in Los Angeles in 1972. The opening track, 'Countdown To Armageddon', is simply the introduction to the band's first ever London gig, supporting LL Cool J and Eric B & Rakim at the then Hammersmith Apollo in 1987.

Routinely accorded the title of greatest rap album of all time, ...*Nation*... isn't necessarily even the best PE album. Conventional wisdom isn't always right - and it is worth noting that the record was not as shocking to existing fans as it was to the rest of the music-buying world. Several of the songs had already been released – 'Bring The Noise' and 'Rebel...' had both made the journey from B-side to hit single, and 'Don't Believe The Hype', which preceded ...*Nation*... to the shops, had been played on radio weeks ahead of time, as had the flipside, 'Prophets Of Rage'. Several of the remainder – 'Countdown To Armageddon', 'Mind Terrorist', 'Show 'Em Whatcha Got', 'Security Of The First World' – are just interludes, while 'Cold Lampin' With Flavor' and 'Terminator X To The Edge Of Panic' are solo showcases for Flav and X respectively. This leaves only six *bona fide* brand new songs, though among them are two undeniable masterpieces – the anti-crack anthem 'Night Of The Living Bassheads', which samples from a different part of 'The Grunt', and 'Black Steel In The Hour Of Chaos', a hymn to nonconformity fashioned around a loop taken from Isaac Hayes' 'Hyperbolicsylabicsesquedalymistic'.

But regardless of any question over its immediate appeal, the record's enduring impact is impossible to overstate. It became the bridge between rock and rap – not just through 'She Watch Channel Zero?!''s Slayer samples, but in its entire attitude and ethos. It took PE to a different stratosphere of critical and commercial acceptance, and as a result elevated hip hop from a genre widely dismissed as "not music" to the respect level of *avant-garde* jazz. The group's militancy and socio-political themes ('Rebel...' namechecked black Muslim leader Louis Farrakhan; 'Prophets Of Rage' excoriated British Prime Minister Margaret Thatcher; Griff's collection of speeches by black leaders such as Malcolm X were used extensively) saw them inherit the mantle of the world's premier rebel-rock group from The Clash. And, for a while, their way of doing things was the only one that mattered. Rap's focus shifted in the early 1990s, and a more easily saleable hybrid – gangsta – took over. But ...*Nation*... signified the point where rap began to live up to its billing as the most revolutionary and forward-looking music around: and there are still numerous artists and fans who take inspiration from that heady era. - Angus Batey

Wheat From Chaff

Many is the boring album on which can be found a single example of the artist remembering for the space of one track precisely the sort of technique that made him celebrated in the first place. Some **great songs** from **albums** otherwise ranging from **mediocre** to **awful** in quality.

1.	**People Are Strange**	The Doors (from *Strange Days*)
2.	**Hey Bulldog**	The Beatles (from *Yellow Submarine*)
3.	**Days Of 49**	Bob Dylan (from *Self Portrait*)
4.	**Dapple Rose**	Slade (from *Play It Loud*)
5.	**Mind Games**	John Lennon (from *Mind Games*)
6.	**Rebel Rebel**	David Bowie (from *Diamond Dogs*)
7.	**Nice 'n' Sleazy**	The Stranglers (from *Black And White*)
8.	**Who Are You**	The Who (from *Who Are You*)
9.	**You're In My Heart (The Final Acclaim)**	Rod Stewart (from *Foot Loose And Fancy Free*)
10.	**(I Don't Want To Go To) Chelsea**	Elvis Costello And The Attractions (from *This Year's Model*)
11.	**Public Image**	Public Image Ltd (from *Public Image*)
12.	**Banana Republic**	The Boomtown Rats (from *Mondo Bongo*)
13.	**All My Love**	Led Zeppelin (from *In Through The Out Door*)
14.	**Down In The Hole**	The Rolling Stones (from *Emotional Rescue*)
15.	**Silly Thing**	The Sex Pistols (from *The Great Rock 'N' Roll Swindle*)
16.	**Romeo And Juliet**	Dire Straits (from *Making Movies*)
17.	**Silver Lining**	Stiff Little Fingers (from *Go For It*)
18.	**This Is England**	The Clash (*Cut The Crap*)
19.	**E=MC2**	Big Audio Dynamite (from *This Is Big Audio Dynamite*)
20.	**Red Headed Woman**	Bruce Springsteen (from *MTV Plugged*)

96. Straight Outta Compton
N.W.A.

TRACKLISTING
Straight Outta Compton/F—- Tha Police/Gangsta Gangsta/If It Ain't
Ruff/Parental Discretion Iz Advised/Express Yourself/Compton's In The
House/I Ain't Tha 1/Dopeman (remix)/Quiet On Tha Set

RELEASED
US: August 1989 UK: September 1989

PRODUCED BY
Dr Dre, Yella

Created by a semi-reformed drug dealer, Eric "Eazy-E" Wright, NWA –
Niggaz With Attitude – set out to expose and explain the largely unknown
civil war that was raging between black and Hispanic gang members in the
impoverished districts of south central Los Angeles. The notion that young
men were killing each other in petty turf wars barely half an hour's drive
from Hollywood and Beverley Hills was shocking. So, too, was the
way NWA talked about it – their shtick married cocksure bravado, a
seeming relish for the battle and a chilling abdication of any sense of
responsibility with an attitude to casual sex, and women in general, that was
unreconstructed to a prehistoric extent.

Yet *Straight Outta Compton*, as repulsive and abhorrent as it was,
remained irresistible. The lyrics, written mainly by the 17-year-old Ice
Cube, were Shakespearean in their tone and timbre, the young man's voice
making his lip-curled disdain audible. They were set to beats concocted by
Andre "Dr Dre" Young, in charge of the first of what remains an unbroken
run of sonically near-perfect hip hop albums that includes many of the
genre's biggest selling titles. From the title track's self-explanatory address, to
'F—- Tha Police''s reportage and the determinedly amoral 'Parental
Discretion...', this is a record that revels in its own base instincts, and which
connected with a massive audience as a result.

As is the case with several albums in this book, the main
influence *Straight Outta Compton* has had is not necessarily a good one. The
endless stream of profanities NWA used provoked outraged uproar among
people the album was never likely to interest. Media outlets empirically
analyzed NWA, listing the number of "fuck"s on the record, the act of
counting implying there was an acceptable level the group had knowingly
and wilfully breached. Though the debate raged around the peripheral issues
of style rather than the substantive ones of content, the effect was to raise

curiosity, and sales – ensuring that any "reality rap" release that followed it had to outdo *Straight Outta Compton* in the swearing, sexist, fuck-you-too stakes. Forget critiques of racist cops or shedding light on LA's gang war: cramming in the maximum number of profanities became rap's new gold standard.

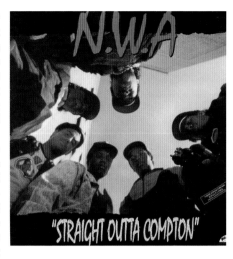

These gangsta rap pioneers never recovered from the departure of Cube, who quit the band in a row over royalties. The follow-up, *Efil4Zaggin*, sold well, but found the group trapped in a creative cul-de-sac. Dre's departure, released from his contract, according to Eazy's later law suit, only by threats of physical violence, marked the end. Ren and Yella never made the solo albums they had threatened; Eazy fared better, his solo career augmented by his discovery and nurturing of the mid-1990s stars Bone, Thugz & Harmony, but he died in 1995 of AIDS-related illness. Making peace with Dre, he issued a statement from his death bed as life ebbed away, calling on young people to look to his sorry demise as an example, and to act responsibly in their sex lives. The sexual predator turned relationship counselor? The contradiction perfectly encapsulated the group's conflicted legacy. - Angus Batey

97. Metallica

Metallica

TRACKLISTING
Enter Sandman/Sad But True/Holier Than Thou/The Unforgiven/ Wherever I May Roam/Don't Tread on Me/Through the Never/Nothing Else Matters/Of Wolf and Man/The God that Failed/My Friend of Misery/The Struggle Within

RELEASED
US August 1991 UK August 1991

PRODUCED BY
Bob Rock, James Hetfield, Lars Ulrich

It is usually referred to as "the black album" because of the black sleeve and for some of Metallica's old school fans that name has an extra resonance. It is, they say, the album where Metallica "sold out" and abandoned thrash metal to simper ballads like 'Nothing Else Matters' on MTV. Earlier Metallica albums, like their masterpiece *Master Of Puppets*, were dense and highly technical, full of complex guitar solos and very long songs broken into different parts. But Metallica's journey towards the mainstream had arguably started with 1988's *...And Justice For All*, particularly on the radio-friendly – if still undeniably very heavy – single 'One'. And in any case, by 1991 the 'mainstream' had actually started to move towards Metallica: there was an appetite for much heavier music and the perceived divisions between punk, metal and alternative or indie rock that had seen some bitter turf wars in the '80s seemed to be over. Or at least there was a realignment: metal fans, into the harder end of the genre, found that the music they liked had more common ground with hardcore and industrial than with the more lightweight hair metal bands such as Bon Jovi and Poison. That worked the other way too: people who had previously dismissed heavy metal started to come around to bands like Faith No More, Slayer and Anthrax. The boundaries between metal and other forms of music were starting to blur. It was fertile ground for Metallica.

The band had been together for almost a decade and in that time had helped to completely reinvent heavy metal. Thrash was a hybrid of the sort of heavy metal produced by so-called New Wave Of British Heavy Metal bands like Iron Maiden, Samson and Venom, defined by aggressive punk/hardcore drumming and vocals. They had a vision of what heavy metal could be and while they never intended to "sell out" they wanted their music heard beyond the confines of any fan-imposed ghetto.

Metallica had always suffered from poor production. The beefy and powerful sound that they got live never seemed to be adequately captured in the studio. After *...And Justice For All*, they decided that if they were going to move forward they were going to have to improve the sound of their records.

Producer Bob Rock, who they finally chose to work on their fifth album, had worked with The Cult, Bon Jovi, and Mötley Crüe, populist bands that seemed to be the antithesis of everything Metallica stood for. Yet he had a knack of getting an extremely loud final mix and of polishing a band's sound enough to make them commercially viable while never castrating them, in the way that many corporate producers did. The sessions for the album were arduous: the band and producer fought over everything and the band – whose major faultline was the clash of egos between singer James Hetfield and drummer Lars Ulrich – squabbled among themselves. The budget was exceeded – some estimates say that the album cost US$1 million to make, something of a record at the time, though less unusual today – and the recording dragged on for almost a year.

It was a stripped-down Metallica that emerged: the songs were shorter and punchier. They were also among the best that they had ever written. The album opened with 'Enter Sandman', probably Metallica's best-known song. Originally about cot death syndrome, the lyrics were rewritten to make them about nightmares as it was feared that a song about dead babies would never get played on radio or MTV. It has become a staple piece of "entrance music" in the US for wrestlers and boxers, the implication being that they are going to knock out their opponents and put them to sleep. The ballad 'Nothing Else Matters' – supposedly written by Hetfield while talking on the telephone to a girlfriend – was a departure for the band. While the song 'One' had elements of a ballad, it was not as downright mellow as this track. 'Nothing Else Matters' became a live favorite and has almost replaced 'Stairway To Heaven' as the aspiring guitarist's riff of choice when they're trying out new guitars in the music store. The almost country tinged 'Don't Tread On Me', with its snatch of Leonard Bernstein's 'America' from *West Side Story*, relates to the cover

Metallica onstage in 1984.

theme: a faintly visible coiled rattlesnake taken from the Gadsden flag, the defiant symbol of American resistance from the early days of the American revolution which bore the words "Don't Tread On Me". It is both a patriotic song and an anti-patriotic one at the same time, looking at the idealism that had once motivated America now turned, at the time of the first Gulf War, into power-mongering and bullying.

The album and the first single, 'Enter Sandman', were played heavily on radio and MTV. The subsequent tour saw Metallica break through into true superpower status, playing stadiums, often without support acts, showing only some clips from their documentary on the making of the album before they came onstage. They won their third Grammy for *Metallica*

More importantly, they took metal out of the confines of the underground and while few of their contemporaries would follow them – metal remains and probably always will remain 'cult' music – they did blaze a trail for a new, more modern variant of metal in the '90s, manifested in acts like Korn, System Of A Down and even Marilyn Manson, who went way beyond the limited definitions of the self-appointed purist metal fans.

Metallica themselves have never been able to match the album. Despite being one of the biggest bands in the world, their subsequent Bob Rock-produced albums *Load, Reload* and *St Anger* have all been perceived as artistic flops, and they continue to this day to coast on the momentum that they created in 1991. - Tommy Udo

98. Nevermind

Nirvana

TRACKLISTING
Smells Like Teen Spirit/In Bloom/Come As You Are/Breed/Lithium/
Polly/Territorial Pissings/Drain You/Lounge Act/Stay Away/On A Plain/
Something in the Way/Endless Nameless

RELEASED
US: September 1991 UK: September 1991

PRODUCED BY
Butch Vig, Nirvana

When Nirvana vocalist, guitarist and figurehead Kurt Cobain first sat down to pen the songs that would eventually end up on *Nevermind*, he had no idea he was about to start a revolution. Nonetheless, in an early draft of 'Smells Like Teen Spirit', he posed the question, "Who will be the king and queen of the outcasted teens?" The answer, of course, was that after *Nevermind* was released, Cobain himself became the king of outcasted teens. When he married fellow musician Courtney Love in 1992, she became queen. And though their rule was short – ending with Cobain's 1994 suicide – it was a reign that is still the subject of much talk and analysis.

Nevermind is to rock albums what Converse trainers are to footwear: something that will never go out of style and which will forever carry a *cachet* of coolness. The record was so successful, both with critics and fans, that it has achieved a status above analysis. Most critics argue that the subsequent *In Utero* was actually a better Nirvana album – an argument Cobain himself made – but how can one de-rank a record that changed music? *Nevermind* ranks as one of the few records that are important enough to stand as a time mark in the progression of rock. Just like *Sgt. Pepper's...*, *Nevermind* is a constant pop culture reference point. The album launched the very idea of alternative rock as a legitimate genre. It also, by dint of topping the charts, destroyed the concept of alternative rock: once notorious for their conservatism, the American charts were now – like their British counterparts had always been – open to anything. That Cobain and Co. found massive mainstream success singing about anger changed the rules for what song-writers were allowed to emote over. And Cobain's own iconoclasm once again gave power back to musicians rather than record companies.

As for the album itself, it has been memorialized and reviewed to the point where many might forget what is actually on the disc. Despite Cobain's dismissal of it as "candy-ass", much of the credit for the record's

Kurt Cobain in Holland, 25 November 1991.

success is due to the production of Butch Vig. Vig made *Nevermind* a showcase for his own expansive production style. As a drummer himself, he figured out how to make Dave Grohl's drums sound so loud on these recordings that the effect is jarring (Vig used a drum tunnel to achieve this). And if Nirvana's greatest sonic trick was quiet – contrasted – with – loud, Vig magnificently exploited this, and turned 'Smells Like Teen Spirit' into an anthem. While some of that credit must go to the band – Grohl played like a monster during this session, as did bassist Krist Novoselic – the earlier 'boom box' demos recently released prove that 'Teen Spirit' owes much to Vig and his ability to popify Nirvana's punk leanings. Still, 'Teen Spirit' is a classic rock song even before the drums and bass come in. The opening riff – which is Cobain's alone – is one of the single most memorable guitar runs in rock history, and with a few notes it is able to suggest a bevy of emotions. While 'Teen Spirit' – which became a transatlantic top ten single – was the kind of juggernaut that couldn't be avoided, there are a half dozen songs on *Nevermind* that belong in any ultimate rock playlist. 'Come As You Are', one of Cobain's many anthems to his own drug addiction, is the kind of pop fusion that made Nirvana famous. 'In Bloom', 'Breed', and 'Lithium' are all upbeat rockers that The Pixies would have died to have crafted. And 'Polly', written from the perspective of a sex maniac and torture artist, is a chilling song that is brilliantly executed. Add in the ending epithet of 'Something In The Way', which sounds like a funeral dirge, and the result is the kind of great record that tops polls. For the span of several months, it also topped the charts. 'Endless Nameless' is the hidden track, a juvenile idea at best, but one undertaken before the idea of hidden tracks was commonplace.

Cobain originally conceived *Nevermind* as a vinyl record, and he planned to have a 'boy' side and a 'girl' side. On the boy side, he'd include his screw-around songs about his friends ('Lounge Act', 'In Bloom'), while the girl side would contain all his angry unrequited love songs. It was bitterness that fuelled most of the songs on *Nevermind*, and that anger is most obvious when Cobain snarls that chorus to 'Teen Spirit'. Still, few ever thought a songwriter could come up with lines like "I could eat your cancer", a sentiment that won't show up on a greeting card soon. Cobain had been writing this kind of sick stuff for several years before *Nevermind*, but on this album he brought that skewed vision to the world, and the world, surprisingly, embraced it.

Novoselic once cited the reason *Nevermind* was so huge as Cobain's knack for understanding the mainstream even while he tried to corrupt it with a punk counterculture. "Kurt's knack for melody and that whole sensibility is something that humans really responded to on a big level", Novoselic said. The album was such an immediate hit that there were temporary shortages of product. 'Teen Spirit' launched an onslaught of media attention on Seattle, and on the musical phenomenon of 'grunge,' which more accurately described bands like Mudhoney and Tad than Nirvana.

Success became an immediate curse for Cobain. Eventually, he decided to stop touring and retreat into his heroin addiction. That solution, in his crazy twisted thinking, seemed easier than facing the level of fame that *Nevermind* created. After *Nevermind*, Cobain used his now huge royalties to further fuel his drug addiction. Once he had money and power, he listened to no one. Less than two-and-a-half years after the release of *Nevermind*, Cobain was dead, apparently having shot himself in the head. *Nevermind* made Kurt Cobain, yet it was also a record that destroyed him.
- Charles R. Cross

99. The Chronic
Dr Dre

TRACKLISTING
The Chronic (Intro)/F—- Wit Dre Day (And Everybody's Celebratin')/Let Me Ride/The Day The Niggaz Took Over/Nuthin' But A "G" Thang/Deeez Nuuuts/Lil' Ghetto Boy/A Nigga Witta Gun/Rat-A-Tat-Tat/The $20 Sack Pyramid/Lyrical Gangbang/High Powered/The Doctor's Office/Stranded On Death Row/The Roach/Bitches Ain't Shit

RELEASED
US: December 1992 UK: February 1993

PRODUCED BY
Dr Dre

In the early 1990s, *The Chronic* did for gangsta rap what *Nevermind* did for alternative rock.

Both introduced not just artists but entire genres of music to new audiences; both were surprise hits; and both album's lead singles – 'Nothin' But A "G" Thang' and 'Smells Like Teen Spirit' – became anthems for different but analogous sections of directionless, frustrated and effectively disenfranchised American youth. While Kurt Cobain's group encapsulated and articulated the hopeless, focusless anger of provincial white trash, Dr Dre and his new-found rapping sidekick, Snoop Doggy Dogg, catalogued the drinking, partying, screwing aimlessness of the gang affiliates of the troubled districts around south central Los Angeles. Neither record even dreams about offering any solutions: neither artist is attempting to change anything. Both, in their own way, offer desultory resignation at the status quo rather than indulge in the supposed rock 'n' roll tradition of active rebellion. The vacuity is shocking, but far from accidental.

The Chronic represented a sense of resignation that had become dominant in the face of frankly overwhelming odds. Even the rioting that followed the acquittal of four police officers videotaped beating the black motorist Rodney King in Los Angeles in 1991 served to prove just how voiceless the city's non-white, non-monied population actually were and how little they were listened to even when their screams were broadcast worldwide. Dre's former NWA bandmate, Ice Cube, howled with rage at the verdict and reveled in the destruction in its aftermath on his finest album, The Predator, and took his bile-flecked message of revenge and resistance to the top of the Billboard charts, but it was to be rebel rap's last hurrah. Within months, The Chronic's arrival changed the sound, the pace and the tone of hip hop: and it altered – certainly substantially, possibly irrevocably – the music's sense of purpose.

Though credited to Dr Dre (aka Andre Young), the record was a collaborative affair, the work of a team Young had quietly put into place after his acrimonious departure from NWA. He hired a former professional footballer, Marion "Suge" Knight, as his new manager, a terrifying man-mountain who did little to discourage a legend that quickly built up around him as someone not to cross. The label Knight established – Death Row Records – would become the most infamous imprint of gangsta rap, a new variant of hip hop which reveled in gritty streetwise imagery and often glorifications of violence to multi-million-dollar success. Later, Death Row became synonymous with actual crime, rather than just records about it.

Dre still built his tracks around samples, but he had altered his aural palette. Gone were the snapping, snarling drums and the Public Enemy-style sirens and noise of NWA's early work, in their place an aesthetic derived largely from the laid-back, psychedelic funk of George Clinton's Parliament-Funkadelic axis. To anyone weaned on New York hip hop, the effect was disorienting, and rightly so: this music was made in a different environment, for a different listenership. Forget the boom boxes on the basketball courts, or Walkmans on the subway: this was a sound built for LA's car-centric culture, a music perfect for pumping from the system of your customized Cadillac as you cruised, top down, through southern California's permanent summertime.

What Dre needed to complement his new sound was a new style of rapper, and he found that in a sleepy-eyed teenager from the LA suburb of Long Beach. By the time Dre discovered Calvin Broadus, the young man with the southern background calling himself Snoop Doggy Dogg had developed a languid style halfway between singing and rapping. His gangly frame and easygoing nature gave him an air of engaging amiability but Snoop had grown up with LA's gang culture as an everyday part of his life and knew how and when to switch his charm to a chilling malevolence. He was the perfect gangsta rapper, but his impact went far beyond the sound and the style. His true-life travails – he was charged with being an accessory to murder between the release of *The Chronic* and his own solo debut, *Doggystyle*, in 1993, then acquitted – would help cement the necessity of a true-crime backstory for a new generation of rap stars.

Andre Young, better known as Dr Dre.

With Snoop on board as front man and number one lyricist, and a gaggle of eager new-comers ready to stake their claim (Kurrupt, Daz, The Lady Of Rage, RBX), Dre assembled a sonically staggering but ultimately patchy album around a clutch of superb songs. '... "G" Thang' is a slice of synth-draped aural sunshine with a heart of repressed menace, like being at a party where the drink has just started to turn a couple of hotheads aggressive. 'Let Me Ride', based around a beautiful Parliament sample, hymns the cars, the girls and the lifestyle of a self-financed street legend. 'Lil' Ghetto Boy', the one song where introspection is tolerated, perhaps even encouraged, is as fine a piece of writing by Snoop as he ever turned in during a career that now spans almost a dozen solo albums. '...Dre Day' is a bombastic series of aggressive responses to anyone Dre felt had wronged him (NWA's Eazy-E; east coast rapper Tim Dog, who had taunted the west on his comedic dis 'Fuck Compton'; Miami rapper Luther Campbell). 'Lyrical Gangbang' showcases the Death Row rappers riding a beat blatantly filched from that hoariest of hip hop staples, even then: John Bonham's drum introduction to Led Zeppelin's 'When The Levee Breaks'.

Never mind (ahem) that *The Chronic* was groundbreaking, occasionally intelligent, always musically lucid and created by people with musical chops and stories worth telling: its success merely proved to the record industry's cheapskate hucksters that having someone lazily drawl tales of misogyny, gang crime and getting high over beats filched from old

313

P-Funk records would be sufficient to rake in the dollars. They turned gangsta rap into the pop music equivalent of crack cocaine: easy and cheap to make, fiendishly addictive, creating and pandering to an enslaved and ever-growing audience. The rot set in. That such blatant cynicism both flew in the face of what *The Chronic* – unpleasant in parts, but frequently inspired – had been about and yet, at the same time, endorsed its celebration of alienated, shoulders-shrugged resignation so utterly, is just part of the cloak of ironies that surrounds this most frustrating of musical touchstones.
- Angus Batey

100. Spice
The Spice Girls

TRACKLISTING
Wannabe/Say You'll Be There/2 Become 1/Love Thing/Last Time Lover/Mama/Who Do You Think You Are/Something Kinda Funny/Naked/If U Can't Dance

RELEASED
US: February 1997 UK: November 1996

PRODUCED BY
Richard Stannard, Matt Rowe, Absolute

It's easy to ridicule the Spice Girls in the modern context of endless 'failed' solo Spice Girl projects. However, the fact that the subsequent careers of the five individual ex-members always seem like flops no matter how relatively successful they are only underlies the globe-straddling phenomenon the Spice Girls constituted in the mid-1990s.

In fact, only one of their ten singles didn't reach the top in their native UK, 'Stop' falling disgracefully short at number two. (They had five US top tens). They were not merely a phenomenon in the sense of selling CDs – although they did indeed shift staggering quantities of 'units' – but also in terms of their social presence. They were *everywhere*, their visages beaming out not just from record racks but sweet counters, advertising hoardings, DVD and video racks, TV commercials and computer game displays, selling either their own product or attaching their beneficial endorsement to those of others. It's impossible to disentangle the social effect of the Spice Girls' records from that of their image (and by the time of the lead-off single from their second album, 'Spice Up Your Life', this cross-fertilization was reflected in a perfectly justified self-referentialism) but there seems little reason to doubt that their effect was profound.

"Girl Power" was their motto (although in fact they had nicked it off a short-lived 'Nineties female duo called Shampoo). Some might laugh at the suggestion that these often scantily clad women had anything to do with the feminism implicit in that phrase. Though Geri Halliwell (Ginger Spice) bursting out of a dress made of a Union Jack dishcloth is one of the iconic images of the era, writer Julie Burchill has caustically observed that dressing in such a manner is a form of 'liberation' men have never tried to deny women. However, for girls and young women turned off by the idea that they couldn't be liberated if they wore make-up, dressed up or enjoyed the company of boys and men, it was an intoxicating creed.

Partly because of the total intertwining of the Spice Girls as artists and the Spice Girls as public personas, the fact they were essentially either talentless or almost talentless was an irrelevance. None of them played instruments or wrote much original melody and only one of them – the soul-diva-esque Melanie Chisholm – was a more than above-average vocalist. However, it wasn't just that fact that made the group's slender abilities a non-issue. The other was that they were then the latest in the tradition of bubblegum pop started by the creators of The Monkees way back in 1967. With top songwriters at their disposal to mould their inchoate lyrical ideas into something anthemic and punchy and put melodies behind those lyrics, and with top session musicians (and – these days – sequencers) to complement those ideas, the results were always going to be as instantly loveable as all those Monkees, Ohio Express and 1910 Fruitgum Co records back in the day.

The first – and destined to be forever the most well-loved and famous – of those songs was 'Wannabe', the manifesto with which the Spice Girls declared themselves to the world in July 1996.

Richard Stannard and Matt Rowe – who had composed three hits for the highly successful boyband East 17 – were the writing duo with whom the girls collaborated on this hymn to not sacrificing your female mates for your boyfriend ("If you wanna be my lover, you gotta get

with my friends") and sex ("Zig-a-zig-ahh", apparently). Just as the line-up of the Spice Girls was designed to appeal to all shades of the rainbow (a tomboy, a vamp, a silly, giggly one, etc) so 'Wannabe', intentionally or otherwise, contained music elements that would make it feel familiar to all sections of a disparate audience: the rapid-fire verbal delivery of the verses was redolent of rap, the intermittent guitar riffs were hard rock and the drum loops had a rhythm within the comfort zone of the jungle/drum 'n' bass generation. Backed by a video that announced the Girls' arrival in a flurry of flounces, yelps and back-flips the song soared to number one in their home country. It also, eventually, achieved the same feat in America.

For one slightly alarming moment, it seemed the Spice Girls' story might be beginning to stall immediately afterwards. Follow-up 'Say You'll Be There' – provided by Eliot Kennedy and Jon Buck – was enjoyable but relatively conventional and boasted an incongruous harmonica part by Judd Lander that seemed inordinately influenced by Stevie Wonder. Not that this stopped it also topping the UK chart. But then came Stannard & Rowe's '2 Become 1', a creamy piece of pop perfection and furthermore a love ballad which reassured males that however feisty they were, the girls still needed them in their lives. Surprisingly, the fact that this, '2 Become 1's parent album, had been released by the time it came out didn't stop the single scaling the charts. Ditto the funky, brass-propelled 'Who Do You Think You Are'. Said album was divided up between tracks composed by three different writing teams – the two previously mentioned plus one collaboration between Kennedy & Bayliss and four from Andy Watkins & Kim Wilson.

The song 'Mama' was a minor masterstroke: though anthems to loving your mum might not exude much cool, they certainly addressed a big facet of the lives of teenage girls that pop normally doesn't. Meanwhile, that *Spice* included a song called 'Naked' in which these five beautiful young women enunciated lines like, "Don't be afraid to stare, she is only naked" provided a dry-lipped *frisson* for the males in their ever-growing audience. Whether any part of that audience saw any contradiction between that and 'Love Thing' – in which the narrator communicates to her boyfriend that he is secondary to her female friends through lines like "You're not the only thing I've got on my mind" – is debatable.

But then so is the subject of the whole Spice Girls phenomenon, apart from the fact that – love them or hate them – they molded the minds of millions of their then young, now adult fans. - Sean Egan

And Lest We Forget...

And still there are more great artists not represented
via either the albums selections or any of the other lists.
Twenty great songs by **worthies not** otherwise
featured in this book.

1.	**Saturday Gigs**	Mott The Hoople
2.	**Mandolin Wind**	Rod Stewart
3.	**Proud Mary**	Creedence Clearwater Revival
4.	**Dexys Midnight Runners**	Come On Eileen
5.	**Low Rider**	War
6.	**Hotel California**	The Eagles
7.	**Oh! Pretty Woman**	Roy Orbison
8.	**Jolene**	Dolly Parton
9.	**Under The Bridge**	Red Hot Chili Peppers
10.	**Angels**	Robbie Williams
11.	**Perfect Day**	Lou Reed
12.	**Roadrunner**	Jonathan Richman And The Modern Lovers
13.	**Crash**	The Primitives
14.	**Groovin'**	The Rascals
15.	**Sky Pilot**	Eric Burdon & The Animals
16.	**Ghost Town**	The Specials
17.	**Moon Tears**	Grin
18.	**Labelled With Love**	Squeeze
19.	**Sunshine On Leith**	Proclaimers
20.	**Solsbury Hill**	Peter Gabriel

Contributors

Hugh Barker is the co-author (with Yuval Taylor) of *Faking It: The Quest For Authenticity In Popular Music* (published by Norton/Faber 2007). He spent many years in the music business as a songwriter and performer in the band Animals That Swim and as a club promoter. Now working as a writer and publisher, he lives in North London with his wife and daughter.

Angus Batey has been writing about music since the 1980s. His work has appeared in titles ranging from *NME, Q* and *CMJ* to *The Times, The Daily Telegraph* and *The Guardian*. He is a regular contributor to *Mojo* and is Writer-at-Large for *Hip Hop Connection*, for whom he has written since 1990. Outside music writing, he reviews books, previews satellite TV shows and reports on English county cricket matches for *The Times. Rhyming & Stealing,* his biography of the Beastie Boys, was published in 1998, and he contributed to the third edition of *The Mojo Collection* (2000).

Charles R. Cross was Editor of *The Rocket,* the American Northwest music magazine, from 1986 through 2000. Cross is the author of five books including *Heavier Than Heaven: The Biography of Kurt Cobain*, which won the ASCAP Timothy White Award for Outstanding biography. His biography of Jimi Hendrix, *Room Full of Mirrors*, came out in 2005 and was a national bestseller. Cross' writing has appeared in numerous magazines including *Rolling Stone, Esquire, Playboy, Spin, Spy, Guitar World, No Depression* and many others. He has written for many newspapers and alternative weeklies including the *London Times*, the *Seattle Times*, the *Seattle Post-Intelligencer*, and *Seattle Weekly*. He lives with his family near Seattle.

Sean Egan has written for, amongst other outlets, *Billboard, Billboard.com, Classic Rock, Discoveries, Goldmine, Guitar, Record Collector, RollingStone.com, Serve And Volley, Sky Sports, Tennis World, Uncut* and *Vox*. He also writes CD liner notes. He is the author of books on The Verve, The Animals, Jimi Hendrix, The Creation, songwriters and two on the Rolling Stones. One of his books – *The Making Of 'Are You Experienced'* – was nominated for an Award for Excellence in Historical Recorded Sound Research by the Association for Recorded Sound Collections. He is also the author of the critically acclaimed rock 'n' roll novel *Sick Of Being Me*.

Tierney Smith is a music journalist born in Erie, Pennsylvania who has written for *Relix, Cleveland's Scene*, and is a regular contributor to *Goldmine* and *Discoveries*. She firmly believes there's nothing quite like the transcendent power of a great song and that owning a fantastic, diverse record collection is indispensable. Though she believes that in music, variety is the spice of life, she has a special predilection for rock music in all its diversity. A health food junkie living in a fast food town, she makes her home in Warren, Ohio which, incidentally, is some 50 miles from the Rock And Roll Hall Of Fame.

Tommy Udo has worked for music weeklies *Sounds* and *NME*, magazine *Uncut* and radio station Xfm as well as several thousand magazines that have subsequently folded, died or otherwise disappeared from the face of the earth. He has also written books on industrial music, nu metal, Charles Manson and Trent Reznor. He currently edits the extreme section in *Metal Hammer UK* and lives in London with his family and a 300 GB hard disc loaded with tens of thousands of obscure progressive, psychedelic, jazz-rock and funk albums that you have never heard of and probably never will.

Richie Unterberger is the author of several rock history books, including *Unknown Legends of Rock 'n' Roll*, the two-volume 1960s folk-rock history *Turn! Turn! Turn!: The '60s Folk-Rock Revolution / Eight Miles High: Folk-Rock's Flight from Haight-Ashbury To Woodstock, Urban Spacemen & Wayfaring Strangers: Overlooked Innovators & Eccentric Visionaries of '60s Rock; The Rough Guide To Music USA* and the upcoming *The Unreleased Beatles: Music and Film*. He is a frequent contributor to the *All Music Guide, MOJO,* and *Record Collector,* and has written nearly 200 liner notes for CD reissues on various labels. He lives in Oakland, California.